Paul Ber

ALSO BY E.J. FLEMING
AND FROM MCFARLAND

Wallace Reid: The Life and Death of a Hollywood Idol (2007)

Carole Landis: A Tragic Life in Hollywood (2005)

*The Fixers: Eddie Mannix, Howard Strickling
and the MGM Publicity Machine* (2005)

*The Movieland Directory: Nearly 30,000 Addresses
of Celebrity Homes, Film Locations and Historical Sites
in the Los Angeles Area, 1900–Present* (2004; paperback 2009)

*Hollywood Death and Scandal Sites: Sixteen Driving
Tours with Directions and the Full Story,
from Tallulah Bankhead to River Phoenix* (2000)

Paul Bern

*The Life and Famous Death
of the MGM Director and
Husband of Harlow*

E. J. FLEMING

McFarland & Company, Inc., Publishers
Jefferson, North Carolina, and London

LIBRARY OF CONGRESS CATALOGUING-IN-PUBLICATION DATA

Fleming, E.J., 1954–
    Paul Bern : the life and famous death of the MGM director
and husband of Harlow / E.J. Fleming.
       p.   cm.
    Includes bibliographical references and index.

    ISBN 978-0-7864-3963-8
    softcover : 50# alkaline paper ∞

    1. Bern, Paul, 1889–1932.   2. Motion picture producers and
directors — United States — Biography.   I. Title.
PN1998.3.B47655F54   2009
791.4302' 33092 — dc22 [B]   2008050551

British Library cataloguing data are available

On the cover: detail of a Paul Bern studio portrait, 1927

Manufactured in the United States of America

*McFarland & Company, Inc., Publishers
  Box 611, Jefferson, North Carolina 28640
  www.mcfarlandpub.com*

For Barb
My proofreader and best friend.

Table of Contents

Acknowledgments

Telling a story about people who lived and died almost a century ago is a difficult and often frustrating process. The story, as they say, is in the details, and biographers search for that one tiny detail that will answer a question, fill in a gap, or help bring a person to life. Without these people I would not have found the details that brought Paul Bern into view. I want to sincerely thank all of them and apologize to those whom I may have forgotten.

A special thank you to my good friend Darrell Rooney for sharing his knowledge, his extensive photographs collection, his Jean Harlow research materials, and his passion for the story of Jean and Paul. The book would not have been possible without him. He also introduced me to Mark Walsh and Nancy Nadel, who invited me to Jean's 1930s Palm Drive house for a party celebrating her life and death. And thanks to Charlie Chandler, who graciously invited us into Jean's Club View house for an impromptu tour and visit, and to acclaimed photographer Mark Viera. Thank you Mark for your wonderful photograph of me with Jean's Packard in front of Club View, using the Hurrell camera used for the same shot of Jean in 1933.

I'm especially thankful to Ron and Maggie Hale for graciously inviting me and my trusty assistant Darrell into their beautiful Easton Drive estate that was so important to the story. Their stories and information about the original property were an invaluable help to tell the story of Paul's death and I am truly grateful for the opportunity.

Betsy and Raymond Bern shared remembrances of Raymond's father, Paul's beloved brother and best friend Henry, that helped put a personal face on both men. Betsy and Raymond's son Paul Henry Bern shared stories and long-lost photographs with me. I'm glad to have been able to tell Paul's story for them.

Tammy Matz shared her memories of her great-aunt Jeanette Loff and Donald Gallery shared recollections of his mother Barbara La Marr and the man he always knew as his father, something I'd believed for 20 years. Cecelia Rasmussen of the *Los Angeles Times* arranged my introduction to Donald.

My friends and fellow writers Lisa Burks, Michelle Vogel and Liz Nocera continue to offer friendship, support, and introductions. Lisa sent me a Cecilia Rasmussen story that led me on the search for Paul's long-lost son and she introduced me to Bill Lewis, who shared his wonderful mural materials, personal photos and memories of growing up with Paul's mural hanging in his dining room. She also hooked me up with Mark Mazek, who shared his amazing collection of gravesite photos. I'm looking forward to Lisa's upcoming book about long-ignored Franchot Tone. Liz introduced me to Linda Frank, who shared some of her Paul Bern research materials with me.

At the Herrick Library at the Academy of Motion Picture Arts and Sciences, Barbara Hall and the staff of the Special Collections section are always helpful and knowledgeable. They make it easy to navigate reams of dusty history and offer excellent advice to novice historians like me. This time it was Jenny who offered wonderful research direction and suggestions during my visits.

Betty Lawson, archivist and historian at the American Academy of Dramatic Arts, spent days digging up information about Paul and Dorothy and the Class of 1911 and answered my endless "one more question" emails.

Gary Hamann did his usual masterful research, some of which can be found at his "Old Movie Section" at www.gdhamann.blogspot.com. He also introduced me to James Robert Parish, who offered helpful advice. Lisa Straub provided some wonderful pictures of Paul and Jean.

Susan Swiggum at the website TheShipsList.com dug up information about the ship that brought Paul Bern to America in 1898 and she introduced me to Don Hazeldine, who managed to find original photos of an obscure 1800s German freighter in his incredible archive of maritime history.

Ron Tardanico of Prudential-Douglas Elliman Real Estate in Manhattan helped me decipher what happened to the Levy family's Manhattan neighborhood. Nuanna at the Marion (Indiana) County Clerk's office helped me find 125-year-old marriage records and Jordan VanDeventer and Marilyn McCoy at the Monroe (Indiana) County Clerk's office helped research the Roddy family in the 1800s. Carrie at the Franklin County (Ohio) Probate Records office spent hours looking for Dorothy's birth and family records.

Bill Nelson provided excellent detail about the Annie Russell Old English Comedy Company and wonderful photos of Annie Russell. Kathy Jolowicz, the resident historian of New York's Yorkville neighborhood, read over my Yorkville text and offered valuable insights into the area during Paul's time at the Yorkville Theater, as well as clarifications regarding the *General Slocum* disaster and the status of the Yorkville Theater.

George Fogelson continued his excellent research work for me in L.A., fighting his way through directories, probate offices and archives. Bob Spearing did excellent research in New York City, Toronto, and Los Angeles confirming where Paul lived, filling in some big blanks in the story. And Steven Shubert and Teresa Stangl-Walker at the Toronto Reference Library hunted down materials about Paul's time there in 1914 and the elusive Conness-Till Film Company.

Everyone added something that helped me tell Paul Bern's story and for that I am sincerely thankful. None of this would work at all without the support and encouragement of my family, my wife Barb and our children Abby, Ted, and Colin, and my friends Tom and Mary Dormin and Bill and Linda Campbell, whom I keep forgetting to mention.

Barrington, Illinois
January, 2008

Preface

The October, 1932, issue of *Motion Picture* magazine described the man that movie star Jean Harlow had just wed: "For Paul Bern, there is no Right and there is no Wrong. There is no Black and no White. There is no Good and no Bad. There are only human beings... Just *people* caught between the cradle and the grave, doing the best they know how in, sometimes, the worst of all possible ways, needing belief more than bread, a brother more than a judge. This is the man Jean Harlow has married."[1]

Just a few months earlier, the movie colony started buzzing about the stunning engagement of sexy, beautiful, 21-year-old "Platinum Blonde" Jean Harlow to the unassuming, balding 42-year-old producer-director.

Bern was known as "Hollywood's Father Confessor." He had been in Hollywood since the early 1920s and rose to the position of one of MGM's most respected directors and studio wunderkind Irving Thalberg's closest advisor and friend. He was among the most creative men in the movies during "The Golden Age of Hollywood," along the way earning a reputation for abounding compassion, for being a loyal and supportive friend, and for offering assistance whenever it was requested of him.

Bern helped *anyone* who asked. *Picture Play* offered, "Tell it to Paul Bern," subtitled "The kindest man in Hollywood has helped all who need it...."[2] Writer Jane Ardmore described him as a "handsome, slender, brilliant intellectual, distinguished by his profound interest in other human beings and his profound sympathy for their troubles."[3] *Photoplay* described the upcoming wedding and Jean's "carrying off ... the town's most eligible bachelor."[4] Even acerbic gossip writer Hedda Hopper said of him that "if Jean Harlow doesn't make Paul happy, there are a thousand women in Hollywood who will cut her throat for her."[5]

Quite simply, it was impossible to find *anyone* who ever said *anything* negative about Paul Bern. Everyone loved Paul Bern. But then something interesting happened. He died. And almost overnight his legacy was rewritten. He would somehow soon embody everything evil in men.

On a sultry Labor Day Monday morning, Paul was found dead in the secluded canyon home he had shared with his new bride for barely two months. He had been shot once in the head, murdered. But nobody would know that he was murdered. People would be told that he killed himself, that Paul Bern was a vile, despicable, depressed, impotent, morose wife-beater so tortured by his failings that he had no choice but to kill himself. He would be accused of trying to rape Jean Harlow with a sexual device and of beating her bloody with a cane on their wedding night.

But not a soul in Hollywood came to Paul's defense. The silence was deafening. Just the day before his death, *Motion Picture* magazine described him as the "small, dark man with the ivory skin, the luminous eyes, the tender, listening smile, [who] pays the bills for lean purses, teaches the dying to meet death with a smile and the living to meet Life with a *beau geste* ... guides back footsteps that have strayed, fights for those who have fallen ... gives time and sympathy to those who are in difficulty ... [and] the first to help in adversity."[6] But not one of his countless movie star friends uttered a word of support or denied the vile stories filling newspapers. The vilification of Paul Bern was accepted without question.

How does universal adoration and respect become collective condemnation in death? How does a legacy become so tarnished that a lifetime of good deeds and good grace is ignored and forgotten? That is the tragedy of Paul Bern.

☙ ONE ❧

Paul and Dorothy

Paul Bern was born Paul Levy on December 3, 1889, about as far away from Hollywood and the movies as one could be, in Wandsbek, northwest of the port city of Hamburg in northern Germany near the North Sea. The city dates to the mid–12th century, named from an old German word for "border river"; the River Wandse formed a natural border flowing through Lake Alster and downtown Hamburg.[1]

Since the eleventh century, Hamburg's harbor — strategically located near the sea alongside the fast-flowing Elbe River — has been Central Europe's main seaport. During the 1800s, Atlantic trade expansion made the harbor Europe's third-largest port and Germany's principal trade port, a hub for trans–Atlantic passenger travel and Europe's "Gateway to the World."

The city is made up of seven boroughs, each with its own government. Wandsbek is the capital of the largest of the seven, Stormarn. Wandsbek village was just outside of Hamburg near Lake Alster and had a crowded inner city surrounded by farmland. Three neighborhoods (Eilbek, Wandsbek and Marienthal) are urban and part of Hamburg but the northern districts (Wohldorf-Ohlstedt, Volksdorf and Duvenstedt) are rural, farming lands.[2] Wandsbek was known for beer- and wine-making, leather tanneries and chocolate, and was connected to Hamburg by a sophisticated tram system.

In the 1880s the cobblestone streets and neighborhoods were crowded with 30,000 people. In the industrial area near the port were the Malton-Weinkellerie winery and the massive Reichardt Cocoa Works, the largest chocolate-maker in Europe. Some of Reichardt's buildings were a mile long and 2,500 workers had access to heated indoor swimming pools and gyms, dining rooms seating 1,250 and hundreds of worker apartments. Clouds of cocoa powder hung over Wandsbek like a fog.

The inner city was a maze of streets with block after block of handsome, three- to five-story stone and brick buildings adorned by colorful awnings. Ground-floor businesses served companies at the port, and there were cafes,

3

Downtown Wandsbek, center of a busy city offering culture and beautiful archi-tecture.

restaurants, and retail stores. The upper floors of each building were for apart-ments. The spires of Christ Church and the Church of the Cross soared 300 feet above the Wandsbek skyline, and there were museums, ornate opera houses like the Neumann and Stadtisches Lyceums, and lavish downtown hotels like the Reisner with its opulent balconied four-story banquet hall seat-ing 2,000. The city was cosmopolitan and lovely.

Lined with trees and beautiful homes, the wide boulevards like Rennbahnstrasse, Juthornstrasse, Hamburgerstrasse, or Lubeckerstrasse[3] snaked out from the city with tram tracks down their centers. Dozens of parks dotted with pristine lakes and streams were scattered about, like the densely forested Wandsbek Grove with its miles of gravel footpaths filled with people. It was a short tram ride to the parks or the public facilities at Lake Alter where large outdoor baths, cabana and locker facilities and a long board-walk overlooked beaches. It was a short ride to the mountains too.

Julius Levy was born in Wandsbek in 1840 to a working class family and in 1869 he married Henriette Hirsch, the daughter of a neighbor and nine years his junior. Julius and Henriette lived at No. 13 Hamburgerstrasse,[4] a main street leading to Hamburg dissecting the west side near the river. It's possible Julius worked in the same building since the street's three- and four-story stucco and brick buildings all had businesses on the ground floor. It was a short distance to Henriette's home at No. 8 Rennbahnstrasse in a more res-idential area.[5]

In the 1877 City Directory, Julius listed his occupation as "Kontorist"

Hamburg   Alter Hamburger Hof zwischen Mühlenstr. u. Steinweg.

The Levy family lived on Hamburgerstrasse, a downtown street of apartments and businesses serving the nearby port.

Wandsbek   Schlossstrasse.

Verlag u. Lichtdruck v. Knackstedt & Näther Hamburg. 661.

They family moved to a Wandsbek neighborhood before leaving for the U.S.

(clerk) for a shipping company. Henriette was listed as "Status — Witwe" (wife). In the late 1870s Julius opened a small candy store and in the mid–1880s the family moved to a large house on Lubeckerstrasse, a street lined with stately stone and brick houses. Their son Paul was born there in 1889.

The size of the Levy family can't be confirmed. It was later suggested that Paul was one of 16 or 18 children and that nine died in infancy but no death records remain to confirm the accounts. There is evidence of only six or seven: daughters Friederike (born December, 1870), Selda (April, 1878), and Erna (August, 1884) and sons John (March, 1879), Paul (December, 1889) and Henry (January, 1891).[6]

Surviving family members recalled another son, James, coming to the U.S. with the family and also believe Henriette was married once before, though she was only 20 when she married Julius. Raymond Bern also recalls Henry speaking in German to other siblings — he spoke English like "Winston Churchill" — in Germany before World War I, so there were probably other children.[7]

No records exist but worth noting are several lengthy gaps amid the remaining children's births while others are clustered in quick succession. Perhaps some fell victim to a massive 10-month cholera epidemic that swept through Hamburg in 1892, killing more than 9,000. Census and church records list only six alive when Julius decided to go to America in 1898.

There was a massive Jewish migration from Europe in the late 1800s, fed by rising unemployment and worsening anti–Jewish sentiment in the region.[8] During the 1800s, millions of Germans immigrated to the U.S., mostly farmers from rural southern Germany or factory workers from the East. In 1898 the Levy family sold their home and joined 60,000 others sailing for America.

Most emigrants left from Hamburg, the hub for Hamburg American Parcel Joint-Stock Company, the Hamburg-Amerika Line.[9] Their fleet — 163 liners and 223 smaller steam launches — traveled to North and South America, East Africa, the West Indies, Japan, Australia, and Canada.[10] By the 1870s they made weekly trips from Hamburg to New York via Southampton, England; in 1912 their liner *Amerika* warned the RMS *Titanic* of icebergs during a crossing. The company's primary cargo was mail and freight.[11] The journey took two weeks and ships docked in Hoboken, New Jersey, Manhattan and then Ellis Island.

Hamburg-Amerika had a network of local offices throughout Germany and Europe to aggressively court emigrating Jews.[12] Once in Hamburg, the German Central-Committee for the Russian Jews helped travelers by paying for travel and rooms, and offering money. When the Levys left Hamburg, the city was teeming with businesses catering to travelers: shipping companies, hotels and boarding houses, and supply houses.

Travelers had to endure a 14-day quarantine so Hamburg-Amerika built an emigrant city on nearby Veddel Island in 1883. For many, a visit to the port was the first time they ever saw the ocean. As they approached, passing the Reichardt factory and smelling the cocoa, their first glimpse was a forest of masts and a fleet of ships of all sizes.[13] Far from nervous anticipation, most looked ahead to their ocean crossing with a sense of dread.

Once the Levys traveled the mile from their home to the port, they came under the control of a Hamburg-Amerika agent responsible for moving them through the process and onto a ship. Some of the more unscrupulous agents sent their wards to nearby hotels, cafés, or bars where they were encouraged to spend money freely. A portion found its way back to the agents. Hamburg was known for those scams.

At the steamship office, an agent took the family's travel documents and arranged for tickets that cost the equivalent of $400 to $1,000. (In 1902 a one-way 2nd Class ticket was $40 and a 3rd class steerage ticket, $27.) Each person was given a medical examination and required to take a bath while their clothing was disinfected. New arrivals were easy to find in the confusing milieu; for several days they smelled of steam and carbolic acid.[14]

The Levys were sent to the "CLEAN" side and joined the general population. Anyone found with a contagious disease was sent to the "UNCLEAN" side and was either sent home or made to wait until the illness passed. "CLEAN" passengers spent 14 days at Veddel with families staying together in dormitories housing 250 people in rooms of 25. They ate in a huge dining room with 50 large tables set for 1,500. Food was abundant and well-prepared and luxuries like beer and cheeses were also available. For the Levys there was kosher food and a synagogue and their 2nd Class tickets allowed access to better facilities. Hamburg-Amerika bands played regional music and the local tradition was to dance until dawn the day of departure.[15]

The Levy family traveled on Hamburg-Amerika's *Pennsylvania*, not a glamorous ship but quite large. Built by Harland & Wolff in Belfast, Ireland, at 12,891 tons, she was 560 feet long with a beam of 62 feet, had a single large funnel, four masts and four large steam boilers powering twin 35-foot propellers that produced a top speed of 14 knots. She was launched on September 10, 1896, and made her maiden voyage to New York on January 30, 1897. On March 22 she began regular Hamburg–New York crossings. German ships were designated by their use. The *Pennsylvania* was a "Postdampfer" or "Mail Steamer." Her primary cargo was mail.[16]

The *Pennsylvania* had accommodations for 162 1st Class ("Erste Cajute"), 197 2nd Class ("Zweite Cajute"), and 2,382 3rd Class passengers. The 3rd Class–steerage passengers shared space with mail and cargo but the number of those passengers is deceiving. The ship carried more freight than people and never approached their 3rd Class limit. Every remaining passenger manifest lists 375 to 475 people, 75 percent traveling 3rd class–steerage.[17]

Accommodations varied. The 1st Class cabins were not as luxurious as better-known ships like *Amerika*. The only difference between 1st Class and 2nd Class cabins was a little more room and a location on the upper of the two levels above deck. Both levels had a narrow outdoor promenade porch encircling the cabin section. Unacquainted passengers shared rooms for two to six, although married couples berthed together, as did single women and single men. There was little privacy no matter the class; there wasn't a private bathroom on the ship. Cheaper steerage tickets ($18–$20) were the most common and coveted by ship owners because the small space allotted meant they were more profitable than even 1st Class tickets.

On many ships, steerage passengers were herded into the belly of the ship to huge compartments filled with high bed racks. There they stayed except for daily excursions onto the deck. Fresh air circulated only when cargo hatches were open; in cold weather, passengers huddled around steam pipes for warmth. Meals were served from huge cauldrons; the stew-like leftovers from the upper class dining rooms were ladled into small pails for the 3rd Class passengers, who were given mess tins with a plate, mug, knife, fork, spoon and water can.[18] Passengers were fed at 9 A.M., 1 P.M. and 5 P.M.

The *Pennsylvania* was large but the trip was still not comfortable. In good weather, passengers crowded the deck enjoying fresh air but had to navigate cranes, winches, rigging, and dangerous walkways. A winter crossing meant almost two weeks inside cabins or below deck trying to stay warm.

The Levy family did not leave Hamburg together. Archived Hamburg passenger lists are for the most part complete but records are missing for several Levy family members. What remains adds to the confusion. The head of the family often traveled first and made arrangements for the rest of the family; Julius sailed on July 17, 1898, and Henriette on November 29.[19] Julius sailed with Henry and Henriette with Paul and Erna in November. Paul was 8 and Erna, 14. No records were found for Selda or John, who probably traveled together since they were older.

The Levys traveled in 2nd Class, "kajute" accommodations, staying in cabins on the lower level above the deck. Each family member received a U.S. Immigration Card confirming they had passed through the pre-departure process in Hamburg and directing the holder to "Present this card to the U.S. Immigration Officials before landing in [New York]."[20] There they also received an Inspection Card confirming they were vaccinated and instructing them to "Keep this Card to avoid detention at Quarantine and on Railroads in the United States."

Aboard the *Pennsylvania* with Paul were 424 souls from all over Europe,

The *Pennsylvania* carried more freight than passengers and was far from luxurious (from the Don Hazeldine collection).

most from Germany and Austria and some from Poland, Russia, and Holland. Almost 250 were listed as "Hebrews" and there were merchants, laborers, waiters, tailors, and farmers. There were virtually no professionals and one-third traveled alone. Among the anonymous faces was 25-year-old Austrian Rachel Loffel, joining her brother in Manhattan at 89 Prince Street. Leib Olshansky was an 18-year-old carpenter moving in with an uncle at 91 Clinton Street. The oldest, 60-year-old Polish laborer Michal Woncio, was with his wife Krebona, a daughter and a one-year-old grandson. Nobody was waiting for the Woncio family.[21]

Henry and Julius arrived in New York on July 28, a sweltering hot day. Paul, Erna, and Henriette arrived on December 13. It snowed in Manhattan the night before but the day was sunny with temperatures in the teens. None of the Levys could be found in detailed immigration records. This could be for a number of reasons. Hamburg-Amerika ships docked first in Hoboken, New Jersey, before going to Manhattan and Ellis Island and often 1st and 2nd Class passengers disembarked there while steerage passengers were processed by the Immigration Service at Ellis Island.[22] The Levys may have disembarked in New Jersey.

Julius moved into a German neighborhood, renting an apartment six blocks north of Central Park at 56 East 114th Street, a block east of Fifth Avenue near Madison.[23] His daughter Friederike and her husband William Marcus were already living there. Marcus and Julius avoided the teeming lower East Side neighborhood between 1st and 8th streets off Second Avenue known as *Kleindeutschland* or "Little Germany," the greatest concentration of German immigrants in New York.

The block was lined with four- and five-story apartment buildings with 12 to 20 units. The Levy building was smaller, home to seven families, mostly middle-class Jews with school-aged children, from Germany, Russia, and Ire-

land. Theresa Schoeman's four daughters worked as bookkeepers and hair-
dressers, Matthew Starr owned a tobacco store, and Patrick Flanagan owned
a stable.

The only surviving section of East 114th is the 400 block east of First
Avenue next to the Hudson River. In the early 1900s, 114th ran from the Hudson west to Fifth Avenue (where West 114th began) but the blocks from Fifth
to First do not survive. Along with everything else in a three- by eight-block
area, the Levys' building was demolished around 1950 by the New York City
Housing Authority. On the spot are the Sen. Robert A. Taft apartments, nine
19-story buildings with 1,500 apartments housing 3,300 people.[24]

By the time Henriette arrived with Paul and Erna in November, Julius
had opened a small candy shop around the corner. Selda went to work at an
embroidery shop, John as a bricklayer, and the younger children attended
school. At the time of the 1900 Federal census (January), Julius and Henriette were living on 114th Street with Selda (21), John (20), Erna (15), Henry
(8), and Paul (10).[25]

The Levy family lived on 114th Street from 1898 until 1909 in a solidly
working class neighborhood filled with immigrants. It was over a mile from
what was then considered the "city." Nearby Fifth Avenue was lined with
stately homes but the side streets were a mix of brick apartment buildings,
row-houses and tenement buildings. It was still nicer than the crowded neighborhoods in other parts of Manhattan, home to other European immigrants.

The Levys often visited Central Park, created in the late 1850s by transforming 2½ miles of granite-filled swampland into an expanse of fields and
lakes.[26] On weekends there were free band concerts but the Sabbath and Julius'
candy store probably meant family excursions were reserved for Sunday. There
were baseball games, cricket matches, prizefights, archery ranges, and fields
for lacrosse, football and tennis. Small boats were allowed on the lakes and
there were pony and goat carriage rides for children.

Erna, Henry and Paul attended public schools. Paul later remembered
it was during these early school years that he developed his love of reading
and books. When he entered school in 1899, New York City's public school
system was the envy of the world, with 225,000 children at 176 schools in
the city.[27] Most of Paul's classmates were fellow Europeans. It was difficult
for teachers, one writing in 1900, "Here we take them almost out of the
steamships ... with not one who can speak the English language."[28]

The schools were larger than anything that Paul had seen in Germany.
One, P.S. 188 on Manhattan's East Side, was the largest public school in the
world with 5,000 students. The average classroom had 42 children and some
had 50 or 60.[29] In Germany, Paul wore long European trousers to school but
in 1899 New York, boys wore knee-high black ribbed socks beneath knick-

ers, and dress shoes.[30] Classrooms had long, narrow tables with rows of backless benches and the teacher's desk was raised on a platform. Other than an American flag, the walls were usually bare.

Immigrant children learned English by rote with rhymes like, "Mrs. Cutter cut the butter ten times in the gutter" or "Only this devil wears skirts and carries a stick this long." Corporal punishment was common; teachers carried short bamboo staffs or tree branches and used them liberally.[31]

Some time in 1907, Julius Levy probably began to notice bothersome physical symptoms. He may have felt involuntarily muscle twitching, cramping, or stiffness. His arms and legs probably become weak and his speech slurred. He may have begun tripping and stumbling and may have had difficulty buttoning his shirt, writing, or using the key to open up his shop. As he slowly lost the ability to make candy and eventually become weak, a doctor would give him and Henriette the terrible news. Julius was suffering from amyotrophic lateral sclerosis.

Today "Lou Gehrig's disease," named for the New York Yankee who contracted the disease and died in 1941 at the height of his career, is well known. But in 1907 little was known about ALS, a quickly progressing neurological disorder in which nerve cells degenerate and stop sending messages to the muscles.[32] Unable to receive stimulus from the nerves, muscles gradually weaken and waste away and when the muscles in the diaphragm and chest wall fail, patients lose the ability to breathe. It is very rare. Only about 5,000 people are diagnosed in the U.S. each year but death results from respiratory failure often in less than five years. There was no treatment available to Julius in 1907.

His condition gradually worsened during 1908 and he could no longer work. In August he moved to the Montefiore Home at 138th and Broadway, "A Hospital for Chronic Invalids." Montefiore was supported by the John D. Rockefeller family but patients didn't go there for treatment; they went there to die.[33]

For several months Julius was kept in an oxygen tent to force air into his lungs but it was a hopeless battle and at 4:30 P.M. on October 10 he quietly died of "exhaustion due to amyotrophic lateral sclerosis." After a funeral at the Moyers Lev Funeral Home at 54 E. 109th, he was buried at Mount Zion Cemetery, an 80-acre site between 58th and 62nd streets in Maspeth, Queens, near the edge of Manhattan. A large Jewish cemetery that opened on May 5, 1893, it was the primary cemetery for immigrants.[34] On October 13, Julius was buried at the top of a quiet hillside at the very northern part of Mount Zion near Tyler Avenue. His grave is off of Path 44R.

With Julius unable to work for the last year of his life, the Levys had to rely financially on William and Friederike Marcus. Selda and Erna both were married within a year, Selda staying in the Bronx and Erna moving to upstate

New York. John remained in Manhattan, still working as a bricklayer. William Marcus brought Henriette, Henry and Paul to live with his family just over the East River at 3781 Third Avenue in the Bronx, with Friederike and their teenage son Seigbert.[35] The Third Avenue apartment was in a crowded neighborhood of shops and apartments connected to Manhattan by the Third Avenue Elevated Train. Henry went to work at the American Embroidery & Lace Company at 110 West 43rd and Paul found a job as a proofreader at a literary agency. But Paul had bigger dreams.[36] He wanted to be a stage actor.

On August 28, 1884, *The New York Times* reported the "new Lyceum Theater School of Acting, under the management of Steele Mackaye, Franklin H. Sargent, and Gustave Frohman, will begin its first term on the first Monday in October and close on the first Friday in June." The Lyceum was at 18 West 23rd and was the first acting school in America, offering "professional stage instruction similar to the renowned French Conservatoire and Theater Francais schools."[37] After auditioning, most students took rooms at the Fifth Avenue Hotel across the street.

The program was either a one- or two-year curriculum. Students were either Juniors (first year) or Seniors (second year). Still today, students who complete the two-year program are known as graduates while those completing the one-year are called alumni. In the early 1900s, courses were offered in general performance, body training, pantomime and voice. There were also classes in the technical aspects of stage production. As students progressed, they were assigned to small stock companies and given roles or technical assignments based on their expertise. Plays were offered to the public at the Lyceum Theater once the groups were deemed sufficiently accomplished. After graduation, students either joined the Lyceum's professional troupe or joined a traveling theater company.

In 1896 the Lyceum School moved to Carnegie Hall and was renamed the American Academy of Dramatic Arts. Credit for the new name is given to Henry Churchill de Mille, a part-time playwright and Episcopal lay minister who had taught at the Academy until his death in 1893. Two of his sons attended on scholarships and both became well-known. William became a writer after graduating in 1901 and for several years taught at the Academy. Younger brother Cecil B. graduated in 1900 and became a movie producer.[38]

Later Academy students include Pulitzer Prize winner Howard Lindsay (one year, 1908) and actors William Powell (one year, 1912) and Edward G. Robinson (two years, 1912). Dale Carnegie, who wrote *How to Win Friends and Influence People* and became a legendary expert in public speaking, was also among the 1912 graduates.[39]

On September 13, 1909, Paul took the train to Manhattan and auditioned for the prestigious Academy.[40] Most prospective students arrived with an introduction letter from someone in theater; on Paul's audition report there is no name listed next to "Introduced by." He simply arrived and said he was 19 and living at 3781 Third Avenue in the Bronx.

Paul auditioned for Franklin Haven Sargent, who annotated his audition report in a red leather ledger. Sargent noted he was a "German Hebrew" with "dark" coloring and a "Public School" general education, was 5 feet 5 inches tall and 125 pounds and described as having "fair" proportions but "good" physical condition. Not surprisingly his pronunciation was strongly "German." Though there was an "X" next to the query concerning previous training, Paul said he had some "amateur" stage experience. That was probably not true.

His audition went fairly well, considering. Writer Sam Marx said that Paul recited Shylock's speech from *The Merchant of Venice* but audition reports rarely mentioned the piece performed. Sargent thought Paul had a "good" voice although he could not disguise his "native dialect." He had "very good" versatility, pantomime, characterization, and dramatic instinct and overall a "lively" stage presence. He had a "very dramatic and experienced" imagination and he could "learn drama" but Sargent noted he would probably be "handcuffed by [his] size and appearance." A note in the corner read "Accepted, October-Jun," meaning Paul would enter the first week of October as a Junior (first-year student).

It was later claimed that Paul grew up poor but the family always lived comfortably in better neighborhoods than many immigrants. When he entered the Academy, Paul was still living with the Marcus family in a solidly middle-class part of Brooklyn. The AADA 1909-1910 tuition was $400, not an insignificant amount when a dress shirt cost 95¢, a nice men's suit $30, and a new Ford $750. A six- or seven-room house cost about $3,500.[41] That Paul could afford $400 tuition speaks to the relative financial comfort in which they lived.

Paul Levy in 1911, when he was a first year student at the American Academy of Dramatic Arts (courtesy American Academy of Dramatic Arts).

The student plays were offered on Thursday afternoons at the Empire Theater at 1430 Broadway. The Empire was built in 1893 by J. B. McElfatrick & Company for theater impresario Charles Frohman, who wanted to own the first theater in what was then "uptown." Building the Empire eventually led to the Times Square theater district.

Except for the large **EMPIRE THEATER** sign over the entrance, the impressive seven-story brownstone and granite building could be mistaken for offices or apartments. Flanked by two four-story buildings with restaurants on the ground floors, the Empire stood between 40th and 41st Streets directly across from the Metropolitan Opera House. It was among the most prestigious theaters in the country. Its size and compact design — it sat 1,099 — made it a favorite for actors and audiences alike.[42] Plush main floor and upper balcony seats were surrounded by ornately inscribed, three-story-tall gilded columns and ceilings covered with large floral wood-carvings, as were the facings of the private boxes on either side of the stage. Additional private boxes ringed the lower level seats. The light fixtures were intricate gold leaf. It was a showplace that opened on January 25, 1893, and hosted his most successful plays and famous actors of the late 1800s and early 1900s. World-renowned names appeared: John and Louise Drew, Maude Adams, Robert Edeson, and the already-legendary Barrymores; Lionel, John, and Ethel.[43]

Paul attended classes at the Academy building and rehearsals at the Empire during October, and on November 5 he worked behind the scenes with other first-year Juniors when the Senior class gave their first performance of the season. The Thursday afternoon offering was a four-act Jean Webster comedy, *When Dreams Come True.*[44] The Seniors put on three performances in late 1909 and two in 1910.

On February 10, 1910, the Seniors presented Henry Sudermann's one-act *The Last Visit* and Henry Kirk's three-act *The Eye of the Needle.* On March 10, *The New York Times* announced **STUDENTS GIVE LAST MATINEE** before their graduation. Emile Fabre's three-act drama *A House Built on the Sands* and George Thurner's *Second Story Men* were performed for the first time in the U.S. before the Senior Class of 1910 graduated on the 14th. The commencement speech was given by actress Helen Ware.

Interestingly, none of the 1910 class went on to stage careers of any note. Some, like Arthur La Rue and Grant Irvin, appeared in a single play and then disappeared. Margaret Greene appeared in six plays and about a half dozen silent films, including *The Angel Factory* (1917) with Antonio Moreno and *A Sporting Chance* (1919) with Anna Q. Nilsson.[45]

During his first year at the AADA, Paul befriended the son of a successful German grain dealer a few years younger. The friendship would help shape his life. The Levys were successful and lived comfortably but Edward L. Bernays' family was wealthy, well-connected, and from famous stock. The Bernays resided in a fashionable three-story brownstone at 121 West 119th with live-in servants, only about four blocks north of the old Levy home on 114th but a world away.[46]

The Bernays family history fascinated Paul according to Edward Bernays. His mother Anna was the sister of Sigmund Freud and another aunt married the famed psychoanalyst. Bernays explained to biographer David Stenn that "a brother and sister married a sister and brother."[47] Paul spent many evenings with the Bernays discussing Freud, analysis and abnormal psychology. Paul became fascinated with the fields.

During his first year at the Academy, Paul decided to adopt a less Semitic-sounding name, reportedly on the advice of his teachers. In 1910 he took the name Edward Paul Bern in honor of his friend, who is remembered as "The Father of Spin" and became the top public relations person in the U.S.[48]

During his Senior year, Edward Paul Bern appeared in all four Senior class performances and also worked behind the scenes. The first performance of the 1911 spring season (Thursday, January 13) were three comedies beginning with two one-act plays, Margaret Cameron's *The Teeth of the Gift Horse* and Frederick Fenn's *The Convict on the Hearth*. The principal play was *The Aviary* by Marc Sonal and Gabriel Annel. No cast lists have been found.

The second performance was on January 26; Paul appeared in the middle of the three plays, between the one-act *Come Michaelmas* written by Keble Howard and a comedy written by Tom Taylor and Charles Reade, *Masks and Faces*.[49] Paul appeared in the lead role of Virginius in *The Dream of a Spring Morning* (*Il sogno di un mattino di primavera*), by Gabriele D'Annunzio. After Eleonora Duse played the lead in 1897 opposite famed Italian actor Ernesto Zacconi, they began an affair that was something of a theatrical scandal that brought worldwide attention to the play.[50] Paul's appearance was noted in theater papers like the *New York Dramatic News* and the *Musical Courier*.[51]

On February 9, the students' third performance included a one-act dialogue and two plays, Alfred Sutro's *The Man on the Kerb* and Arthur Law's three-act comedy *The Country Mouse*.[52] Paul appeared in the latter; the *Dramatic News* reviews described the strong performance of Edward Bern.[53]

Paul's final performance was on March 12, the evening before the Class of 1911 graduated, playing the lead as Dr. Bruno Martens in *Friends of Youth* by Ludwig Fulda and again receiving good reviews in both the *Musical Courier* and the *New York Dramatic Mirror*. The following day, graduation ceremonies were held at the Empire. Paul was among the thirty-two "possible actors and actresses [who] received diplomas and were sent out into the world to seek engagements."[54]

The graduation speakers were Academy president Franklin Sargent, instructors Dr. James J. Walsh and William de Mille, and English actor Henry Miller. Walsh spoke of the need for actors to develop their personal character, warning that the "power of good in the theater depended upon the character of the players and the earnest desire to give to others what would be best for them." William de Mille offered advice on the struggles of being an actor.

The New York Times noted graduates received **Lessons from the Great Star**; Miller was a popular producer and actor appearing in his 45th play.[55] He suggested actors need the "imagination of a poet, the sense of apprecia tion of a writer, the ear and timing of a musician, the grace of a dancer, the expertness of a fencer, the courage of a soldier, and thick skin of a rhinoceros." Paul took the speakers' instructions to heart; like Walsh, he spent a life looking to do good and Miller's themes surfaced in his writings and directing, particularly the emotion attachment to the audience he invoked.

"Edward Paul Bern, New York City" was the first name on the alphabetized list of graduates including men and women from Wellesley Hills, Massachusetts, to San Francisco to Florida.[56] Like the class before, the Class of 1911 produced no theater stars. A few had minor roles in long-forgotten plays but only Aline McDermott, who appeared in 11 from 1912 to 1944, appeared in a name play; her final appearance was in the well-known *State of the Union* with Billie Burke and C. Aubrey Smith.

What fame Paul's classmates did achieve came from off the stage. James Wheaton Mott was a lawyer and a seven-term Congressman from Oregon. Lucia Bronder became a writer, and one of her plays was made into the 1932 George Cukor movie *Rockabye* with Constance Bennett and Joel McCrea. A few worked in Hollywood. Lucille Arnold appeared in a single film, the 1917 silent *Nuts in May*, the debut of British comic Stan Laurel. George Shelton appeared in 20 films from 1933 to 1947, most minor comedies like *How Am I Doing?* (1935) and *Meet the Bride* (1937).

Mary Alden and Tom Powers had legitimate screen success however Alden appeared with Lillian Gish in *The Battle of the Sexes* and with Wallace Reid in *The Second Mrs. Roebuck* (both 1914); in D.W. Griffith's *The Birth of a Nation* (1915) she played Lydia, a mulatto maid in a sexual relationship with a white politician, one of the most controversial themes in the film. She eventually worked in 125+ films including *The Plastic Age* (1925), *Brown of Harvard* (1926), and *Rasputin and the Empress* (1932), working with greats like Blanche Sweet, Mary Pickford, Will Rogers, and Clara Bow.[57]

Tom Powers went from the Academy to the movies and appeared in 50 silents before returning to the stage in 1917, where he appeared in 35 plays through 1944 including *Strange Interlude* (1928) and *End of Summer* (1936). In 1944 he returned to Hollywood to play the victim of a murderous insurance scam in the Fred MacMurray–Barbara Stanwyck melodrama *Double Indemnity*, and appeared in another 75 films like *Two Years Before the Mast* (1946), *The Farmer's Daughter* (1947), and *East Side, West Side* (1949). He also appeared in the early 1950s television shows *The Lone Ranger* and *Adventures of Superman*.[58]

After graduation, Paul remained at the Academy as a stage manager, a decision that led to a chance meeting that changed his life. It's been suggested that Paul met Dorothy Mellett when they were students at the Academy but he had already graduated when the spring auditions were held for the class of 1912 and Mellett arrived for her audition on May 8. "Mrs. L. Melette," married and living at a nearby hotel, was introduced to Paul by the school's stage director Joseph Graham.[59]

Dorothy Roddy Mellett remains an enigma. We know very little about the woman who would murder Paul Bern and most of what we know is anecdotal, second-hand, or fiction. She was pretty; Paul described her as "breathtaking, enchanting, indescribable, the loveliest girl I'd ever seen ... an ethereal will-o'-the-wisp."[60] But the few surviving photos don't flatter her.

Paul told MGM story editor Sam Marx she worked as an artist's model in New York and was painted by the legendary Howard Chandler Christy, who called her "The Butterfly Girl." Hundreds of his famous wartime recruiting posters and portraits survive but no trace of "The Butterfly Girl" remains. As pretty as Dorothy might have been, it was hard to ignore her oddest habit: Whenever she spoke she had a habit of dropping the lids over her eyes, making conversations uncomfortable.[61] And she always wore extremely high heels and added lifts.

She was born Dorothy Roddy on March 15, 1884. On a later marriage license application she declared her birthplace to be Columbus, Ohio, and her parents to be physician William Roddy and Lillian Johnston Roddy. None of that information appears true; not a single detail can be confirmed by any written record, other than her name. Exhaustive research in Franklin County, Ohio, Birth, Death, and Probate Records uncovered no Dorothy Roddy born in or near Columbus during the 1880s and there are no death records for William Roddy or Lillian Johnston Roddy through 1899, nor are there probate or adoption records for *any* Roddys.[62] Why Dorothy chose Columbus is unknown.

Details of her early life are equally impossible to confirm. The 1890 Federal Census likely would have filled in some blanks but almost all records were destroyed in a January 10, 1921, fire at the Commerce Department in Washington, D.C. Only 1,233 census sheets — records for just 6,160 of the 62,979,766 citizens recorded — survive. Not a single record for any Roddy in the U.S. survived the fire.

Dorothy was also said to have been born in Indianapolis, Indiana, was orphaned and a ward of the court. That may be true but exhaustive research through country birth and death records, adoption records, and probate records throughout Indiana and western Ohio failed to confirm the story of Dorothy's youth.

When children were orphaned, they were often taken in by local families. It wasn't altruism; they were usually listed as "boarders" or "servants" on census records and they were taken in to work. In the late 1800s Roddy was a common name in the lower Midwest in Ohio, Indiana, Missouri and Iowa and among several census records with unrelated Roddy children living with Indiana families in 1900 was a young girl who may have been Dorothy.

"Addey" Roddy was a 16-year-old (born in Indiana in March 1884) boarding with the Harry Whitmer family on a 60-acre farm in Greene Township, a rural area of Madison County northwest of Indianapolis.[63] Later newspaper stories said Dorothy lived in Center or Greene Township. Center Township was part of Indianapolis proper and Greene Township, 40 miles from Indianapolis and 15 miles of dirt road from the nearest town, was the Anderson County seat surrounded by tiny crossroads towns like Prospect, Alfant, and Hardscrabble.[64] Life on the Whitmer farm would have been difficult. "Addey" may have been Dorothy, and she left the Whitmer farm for Indianapolis before she was 19.

In 1906, at 22, Dorothy was living at The Cambridge, a hotel in downtown Indianapolis, and working as a secretary at a coal company. She was a petite, pretty redhead who stood 5' 3" tall and was a little on the heavy side.[65] Only two or three photos of Dorothy have so far been found. One shows a plain, almost expressionless face staring at the camera, her dour expression hiding any prettiness. But another photo shows a dazzlingly cute girl full of energy. Which was the real Dorothy?

Dorothy Mellett was a beautiful red head whom Paul described as "the loveliest girl I'd ever seen."

While living at the Cambridge, Dorothy met Lowell Mellett, a reporter for the *Indianapolis Star* and one of seven sons of wealthy Indianapolis life insurance agent Jesse Mellett and his wife Margaret. Lowell was born on February 22, 1884, in Elwood, a small town to the northeast, but by 1906 the Melletts were in a stately brick mansion at 510 Meridian Street north of downtown Indianapolis.

Six of the seven Mellett sons became well-known newspapermen. Donald, editor of the *Canton Daily News,* was murdered leaving his office during a feud with gangsters controlling the Ohio city in 1926.[66] His murder received national attention.

On June 22, 1907, Lowell's older brother Roland drove him and Dorothy to the Marion County Courthouse in Indianapolis where the couple obtained marriage licenses and were married the same day by a judge. Lowell listed his occupation as "newspaper work." Dorothy left that space blank, but confirmed she had not been an "inmate of county asylum." In the space reserved for parental consent Roland Mellett signed for Dorothy.[67] Dorothy signed "Dorothy Roddy" in a small and simple schoolgirl style.

Soon after, Lowell and Dorothy moved to New York where he worked as a reporter for a Manhattan paper and the United Press Syndicate. Dorothy may have done the artist modeling Paul later mentioned but nothing is known of her activities until her May 8, 1911, audition at the AADA. By then the Melletts had begun divorce proceedings and Dorothy moved into a hotel. Lowell went on to great success: he was later the editor of the *Washington Daily News* and one of President Franklin Roosevelt's closest advisors and head of Roosevelt's World War II film and propaganda office.[68]

Dorothy's audition report noted she was "married, 4 years" and lived at the Manhattan Square Hotel at 50 West 77th Street. She auditioned for director J.M. Edgar Hart.[69] "Mrs. L. Melette" said she was from English and Irish parents and fudged a bit on her age, admitting only to 26 instead of 27. She did not impress physically; at 5'3" she had "medium" coloring and was "heavy" and "stout." She had no previous training or stage experience.

She exhibited little talent and "ordinary" intelligence. Although "intelligent" when reading scripts, her voice was "light," her pronunciation and memory "fair" and her spontaneity "weak." She was "too self-conscious" to show any stage versatility, couldn't pantomime and stood too erect with her "shoulders raised" while performing. Exhibiting only "fair" dramatic instinct, she was nonetheless accepted as an April Junior.

Dorothy is not mentioned in any cast records for fall, 1911 or spring, 1912 and she did not attend the March 15, 1912, graduation ceremonies, when two of the best-known actors in the world—George Arliss and Mary Augusta Davey—spoke.[70] By then she and Paul had entered into a deep relationship that began the moment they met, according to Paul's brother and sister. She was thrilled with a driven and intelligent man who shared her interest in theater.

Among oft-repeated inaccuracies about Dorothy is that she graduated with Paul and was a successful actress. Neither is true. Research at the Academy archives confirmed that she did not complete her first year.[71] By the spring of 1912 she and Paul had left New York. Another fiction is that she was a lead actress for the Ben Greet Players after leaving the Academy. In reality, there's only a single mention of Dorothy working at all and none of her performing *anywhere*, certainly not with the prestigious Ben Greet Players, the most popular company in the world. Ben Greet's "Woodland Players" were organized for Queen Victoria's jubilee in 1887 and put on Shakespeare on outdoor stages. The novel idea — outdoor theater, Shakespeare in the Park — became the rage of European stage.[72] Greet rarely used scenery or sets, forcing his audience to concentrate on the actors.[73]

Greet brought his Pastoral Players to America in 1902 and performed throughout the U.S. and Canada for several years at parks and at colleges like Harvard, Yale, West Point, Wellesley, Vassar, Minnesota, California, Illinois, and Indiana.[74] Greet was a popular attraction at the Circuit Chautauqua outdoor revival events or meetings and on November 14, 1908, performed for President Roosevelt on the White House lawn.[75]

Months of newspaper stories preceded the arrival of the Ben Greet Players, by which time locals knew the cast by name. Greet advertised that his company employed *only* British actors so if *any* American was a lead it would be big news. In thousands of articles about Greet, Dorothy was never mentioned.[76] Quite simply, it's impossible to confirm Dorothy ever appeared on stage anywhere except for a single play, and she got that job later through Paul.

Paul, on the other hand, quickly found work. In the summer of 1912 he auditioned and was invited to join the newly formed Annie Russell Old English Comedy Company, led by one of the best-known actresses of the early 1900s. By 19, she was the lead in the Madison Square Theater Company, the "perfect ingénue," and at 25 was known as "the Duse of the English speaking stage," likened to the great star Eleanora Duse.[77]

Her Annie Russell Old English Comedy Company, supposedly "composed entirely of English players of distinction," offered revivals of Shakespeare and Richard Brinson Sheridan.[78] Sheridan's late 1700s comedies were very popular and Russell offered his most recognizable works: *Rivals*, *The School for Scandal*, and *She Stoops to Conquer*.[79] Russell's calling card was faithful depictions of everything from period speech patterns to costumes, and even exact reproductions of 16th and 17th century furniture. Her sets were painted by Grace Olmstead Clarke, whose extraordinarily realistic backgrounds were well known.

Russell took her new troupe to her vacation home on the coast of Maine for a month before returning to New York for the fall season.[80] In New York the company performed at the 750-seat 39th Street Theater (119 W. 39th), built in 1910 by Lee and J.J. Shubert, who named it Nazimova's 39th Street Theater trying to keep Alla Nazimova from leaving. A few months later she departed anyway and her name was removed.[81]

Russell offered multiple plays simultaneously for one or two weeks. Half the company traveled and half remained at the 39th. Her primary director was Oswald Yorke and the company had about 30 actors like Arthur Barney, Clifford Devereaux, Phillip Edwards, Holland Hudson, Harold Meltzer, Fred Permain, Littledale Power, William Scott, Edgar Ware, Frank Reicher, Edward Longman, John Westley, George Giddens, Sidney D. Carlyle, Beatrice Herford, and Edward Paul Bern, recent graduate of the American Academy of Dramatic Arts.

On October 21 the company began rehearsals for Sheridan's four-act comedy *She Stoops to Conquer* and Edward Paul Bern was now "Paul Bern."[82] The play is a comic love story about a prosperous young man's infatuation with a woman who he believes is a barmaid but who is in fact a wealthy matron. On November 11, Paul debuted (playing Thomas) in *Conquer* with Longman, Reicher, and Russell leading. Russell played both the wealthy matron and the barmaid and reviewers noted the "acting, even with first night nervousness considered, was delightful."[83]

After a three-week run — Russell's popularity was clear, since plays usually ran for a week — the company switched to Shakespeare's *Much Ado About Nothing* on December 10 with Russell and Reicher in the leads.[84] After two weeks the company switched to Richard Brinsley Sheridan's four-act comedy *The Rivals*

Annie Russell, leader of the first theater troupe for which Paul performed.

with Russell, Permain and Reicher leading.[85] *Rivals* was a durable English comedy offered by companies the world over.

Paul was not in the main cast for *Much Ado* or *Rivals* but worked behind the scenes in stage direction and technical duties. At the time there was some heady company in nearby theaters. Nazimova was in *Bella Donna* at the Empire, Douglas Fairbanks in *Hawthorne of the U.S.A.* at the Astor, Billie Burke in *The "Mind the Paint" Girl* at the Lyceum, and George M. Cohan at *Broadway Jones* at Cobans.

In early January, Russell took *Conquer* to the West End Theater (another prestigious New York playhouse) for a month, offering *Rivals* on Wednesday and Thursday. She then moved to the Majestic Theater in Brooklyn until March; Paul reprised his small role as Thomas.[86]

Some of the company traveled to Baltimore in early March to perform *Conquer* for a week ending the 13th. On May 1 the company traveled to Canada for a week-long engagement at the Royal Alexandria Theater in Toronto beginning the 5th. *Conquer* was offered Monday, Tuesday, Friday and Saturday evenings and Thursday and Saturday matinees, and *Rivals* on Wednesday and Thursday evenings.[87] Paul appeared as Thomas in a cast described as the "same to every member as was seen in New York."

After engagements in Connecticut, Providence and Woonsocket, Rhode Island, and Boston, Russell grew weary of travel and in early 1914 disbanded her troupe.[88] There is no confirmation that Dorothy worked at all during this time but it was later claimed that during Paul's travels she performed in Denver, Woonsocket, Wilmington, Delaware, and Glens Falls, New York. Some of the claims matched places Paul worked but there is no mention of Dorothy in newspapers.

Paul returned to New York with a solid résumé as an actor, stage manager, and director and on September 29 was hired to direct a play sponsored by the Sociological Fund of Medical Reviews of Reviews, *The Guilty Man*, at the Lyric Theater beginning on November 14.

The Fund was lobbying for laws to ensure children born out of wedlock were legitimate and entitled to a father's name and allowing physicians to "prevent the coming into the world of unwelcome children." The Fund was addressing "limitation of offspring ... the right of a child to be well born ... and the right of a mother to choose whether and when she shall give birth...." The controversial ideas were espoused by the German Socialist party, which may have been how Paul was originally recruited.[89]

Papers said **PUT ON DARING PLAY TO UPSET OLD LAWS**, warning that the controversial social agenda was "likely to startle many good people,"[90] but backers included John D. Rockefeller, Jr., Mrs. William K. Vanderbilt, Mrs. O.H.P. Belmont and Norman Hapgood, well-known names in New York City society. Among the philanthropists and famous names on the Fund registry was "Paul Bern, Secretary."

The performances were invitation-only, for lawmakers, physicians, social workers and teachers. Lee Shubert donated the Lyric, Holbrook Blinn directed and "Paul Bern, late a member of Annie Russell's Old English Comedy Company, will have charge of all of the technical details of the performance."[91]

There was loud public outcry but Paul said, "I am tremendously pleased at the result.... 'You won't get an actor to play for you,' someone told me after our first announcements. I was just a little afraid that this might be true. But when I approached prominent professionals, I found the attitude of all of them extremely cordial ... we are able to appeal to the dramatic profession only on the ground of helping a notable movement."[92] Paul attracted an impressive cast led by Jane Cowl, Julian L'Estrange, John Barrymore and Georgia Lawrence but public protests delayed the opening until the 21st and by then Cowl and Barrymore left due to scheduling conflicts, replaced by Emily Stevens and Schuyler Ladd.[93] Tyrone Power took over the lead just before the play opened.[94]

Rehearsals for *Guilty Man* began on September 15. The four-act play was based on the novel by Francois Coppee, the story of wealthy French law student and the pregnant girlfriend he abandons. As an adult he is an unforgiving prosecutor when he learns that the young girl died and his son was on trial for killing a man who "taunted him about the stain of his birth." In the play's climax the broken old man admits he is the father of the accused and pleads for a change in the laws that drove the young man to murder. The weeklong run was sold out, leading producer Al Woods to buy the rights and put on the play with Charles Frohman on Broadway.[95]

After *Guilty Man*, Paul was hired by another new company, one founded by Frank Craven, a known but not renowned actor producing the farce comedy *Too Many Cooks*. It was the first play Craven wrote and produced himself. The new company had several well-known actors led by Craven's godmother Jennie Weathersby, Inez Plummer, Martin Mann, and Bessie Osmond.[96] On December 30 the company traveled to Wilmington, Delaware, for rehearsals.

Cooks was the story of the problems young couple Albert Bennett and Alice George encounter building their first home. Relatives feud over who would get to live with them, leading an uncle to hire a girl to steal Albert which leads a jealous Alice to cancel the engagement. Alice's father — a labor union official — calls a strike so the builders quit working but Albert finishes the house himself, defying his in-laws and winning back Alice. Paul was listed in the credits as "Phillip Bern."[97]

Cooks debuted at the Wilmington Playhouse on January 25 with William

A. Brady and Winchell Smith — who wrote the popular play *The Fortune Hunter* — in the audience.[98] On February 8 the company moved to the Trenton Theater (New Jersey) from the 10th to the 23rd before the New York premiere on February 24 at the 39th Street Theater where he had performed with Annie Russell.

The play was called "genuinely amusing ... [and] different from anything else that the season has brought to Broadway...."[99] Fans were awed by Paul's production; during the play, a six-room cottage was slowly built on-stage, starting with a stone foundation and ending with furnished rooms and a front porch. Paul's talents seemed to lay off- rather than on-stage.

Cooks sold-out 225 performances between February and September including a month at the Winter Garden Theater,[100] after which the company went to Toronto for a week at the Royal Alexandria Theater, coincidentally another venue Paul visited with Annie Russell. The company arrived in Toronto on September 12 and the play opened on September 14. Balcony seats cost 25¢ and 50¢ and floor seats 75¢, $1.00 and $1.50, pricey for a touring play.[101]

All theaters were filled with people escaping daily reports of the awful battles in the Ardennes Forest. Papers said *Cooks* "succeeded in lifting the whole of Europe from the consciousness of the big first night house for two and a half hours."[102] The Alexandria performances were all sold out.

Advertisements in the *Toronto Daily Star* caught Paul's eye. The Conness-Till Film Company was holding a Photo Play Contest offering a first prize of $200 in gold, $100 for second and $50 for third (between $1,200 and $5,000 today).[103] The company was looking for movie scenarios with ran ads noting how easy it was; "Wherever you turn IDEAS ARE STARING YOU IN THE FACE. Little happenings in the street, in the home, in the office are prolific sources for photo-play ideas."[104] Contest circulars were sent to every theater in Canada asking for a brief synopsis of no more than 500 words on one piece of paper submitted by September 25. Facing a trip with Craven to Oxnard, California, Paul went to Conness-Till looking for work.[105]

He made his way a few miles southwest of downtown Toronto to the picturesque town of Swansea, a hilly hamlet on Lake Ontario where the marshlands of the Humber River feed into the lake. Paul was about to get into the movies.

Moving pictures evolved from a series of discoveries in Europe dating to 1659, when Dutchman Christiaen Huygens devised a lantern projector using a candle to light glass transparencies through a simple lens. Next, the illusion of motion was created by using image rotation, first the 1826 "thaumatrope" that rotated a card with two alternating images and then the 1834 "Phenakistiscope," a simple "flip book."[106] Finally, to win a $25,000 bet in 1877, California Governor Leland Stanford hired Eadweard Muybridge to prove a galloping horse lifts all four hoofs off the ground at once. Muybridge lined up 24 cameras next to a track with strings attached to shutters and when the horse tripped the shutters for 24 closely spaced pictures, it proved Stanford's contention and moving pictures were a reality.

The new industry — centered in the New York area — was dominated by Thomas Edison. In the 1890s he and William K.L. Dickson designed cameras and worked out of a darkened New Jersey building nicknamed "Black Maria," the first movie studio. In 1895, Edison Manufacturing Co. was selling cameras and projectors and Thomas Armat patented a projector called a "Vitascope" that put Edison's films on a screen.

Also in 1895, French inventors Louis and Auguste Lumière patented the first real projector and camera, the Lumière Cinematographe. The December 28, 1895, screening of a 20-second film of workers leaving the Lumière Factory wowed audiences and later Lumière films of a steam engine chugging toward the camera before swerving away and a cowboy firing a gun often left viewers diving to the floor or screaming out loud.[107]

Edison designed the "Kinetascope" (a free-standing wooden box with an eyepiece) that let viewers watch a short movie for 5¢. His first film was of his close friend Fred Ott sneezing.[108] On April 20, 1896, over a thousand New Yorkers were waiting when Koster & Bial's Music Hall opened, offering Edison films of surf breaking on a beach, a comic boxing match or two girls dancing. *The New York Times* described the experience as "wonderfully real and singularly exhilarating."[109]

There was not much craftsmanship in the films but that changed accidentally when Frenchman Georges Méliès' camera jammed and caused an object to disappear. His mistake was the birth of fade-ins and -outs, dissolves, and animation. Inspired by Méliès, Edison lengthened his movies and in 1902 his cameraman Edwin S. Porter took nine 50-foot-long films (of fires, a favorite Edison theme) and spliced them into the 450-foot *The Life of an American Fireman.*[110]

By the early 1900s, studios were popping up all over New York. Edison was in the Bronx and New Jersey. Biograph was in a converted Manhattan brownstone at 11 East 14th. J. Stuart Blackton and Albert E. Smith ran American Vitagraph from the top floor of the Morse Building, filming on the roof.[111] Europeans soon arrived; Pathé Frères, a French production company owned by Charles Pathé, opened in 1904. He was an innovator much like Edison; he began making movies in 1896, "borrowed" technology from the Lumière brothers and in 1904 opened offices in a dozen cities including Moscow, London and New York. J.A. Berst ran the New York offices and by 1908 had production sites in Jersey City, New Jersey, and throughout Europe. By 1912 he was producing 800 films a year.

Edison was a ruthless businessman and a vicious anti–Semite, and most movie companies were run by Jews. In 1908 he organized the Motion Pictures Patents Company (MPPC), known as "The Trust," a merger of Edison, Biograph, Vitagraph, Essanay, Lubin, Selig, Kalem, Méliès and Pathé. The Trust exerted control over the new industry through Edison's 16 camera and projector patents, a deal with Eastman Kodak for the raw film, a requirement that filmmakers pay a licensing fee to the MPPC, and extorting exhibitors to offer only Trust-produced films.[112]

Edison hired hundreds of spies — "patent goons" — to sneak into studios and sets looking for copy equipment. They simply took whatever they found and often destroyed negatives, stole film, and beat up directors and actors. The Trust also hired snipers to shoot cameras, destroying equipment rather than people because cameras were harder to replace. Director Allan Dwan posted sentries armed with rifles on his sets; side-arms carried by directors like Cecil B. DeMille were not for appearance sake.[113]

Companies defied the MPPC — Thomas Ince's Bison-101, the New York Motion Picture Company, Mack Sennett's Keystone, and Carl Laemmle's Independent Motion Picture Company (IMP) among them — but most couldn't film in New York so traveled to Florida, Cuba, Arizona, Texas, Oregon and California to film in safety. Trust companies only went west during the winter months; diversity of scenery made for better films as well.

Demand far outpaced supply since films were replaced every few days and there was an explosion of thousands of store-front nickelodeon "theaters." In 1910 movie companies were small operations but by 1913 the insatiable appetite meant the industry had to expand.[114] There was also a move underway to longer feature films.

There is a scarcity of information about the early years of Canadian film. The movies arrived in Canada in 1897 when Edwin S. Porter brought Wormwood's Dog and Monkey Theatre to Halifax, showing films during a vaudeville program of jugglers, singers, musical monkeys and dancing dogs.[115] Though American and English companies like Edison, Bioscope and American Mutoscope often filmed in Canada, it was still ten years before Canadian companies began production of their own. Most survived only a short time, unable to compete with U.S. imports.[116]

By 1914, Canada was the second largest importer of films in the world. Toronto was the center of the country's film industry, with twice as many movie houses in Toronto as Montreal, even though it was half the size.

Conness-Till was founded in April 1914, the initiative of Philadelphia-born actor Edward H. Robins, a former Belasco leading man who ran the Robins Players theater company. He enticed American theatrical promoter Luke Edwin (L.E.) Conness, Toronto business investor Louis A. Till, and

Philadelphia financiers James P. and Charles E. Beury to invest in a studio to supply Canadian markets. The Beury brothers put up $150,000 and Conness, Till and Robins smaller amounts. Conness was the president, Robins the vice-president, James Beury the second vice-president, Till the secretary, and Charles Beury the treasurer. New York theater agent Joseph A. Mack handled publicity and the B.C. Feature Film Company was in charge of distribution.[117] In Toronto the most popular movie theaters were the Strand, Garden, Windsor, Maple Leaf and the Photodrome.[118]

Conness-Till would compete with imports by producing "Canadian photo plays with distinctive Canadian settings and written by Canadians" and would produce only "Feature Pictures" which allowed for larger returns than shorter films.[119] They rented three industrial buildings on 2¼ acres next to the Humber River in Swansea at 1 Adelaide Street East (near present-day Palace Pier Court).[120] The area was a checkerboard of brick and wood-frame commercial buildings, lakefront hotels — from luxury to Spartan — and all manner of restaurants catering to locals visiting the nearby beaches.

Conness-Till used a 70' × 150' warehouse for interiors and the land along the river for exteriors. The smaller buildings housed offices, storage, film developing and dressing rooms. June 16 newspaper ads offered "Your Opportunity" to invest in "MOTION PICTURES Manufactured in Canada," noting, "It staggers the imagination when one contemplates the monetary possibilities of the motion picture business. Millions have been made in it and millions are still to be found lurking in its recesses. Beginning with becoming modesty as a struggling industry, laughed at by the press when not openly attacked by it, and scorned by the theatrical world as a clinging parasite, it is to-day an international institution, rivaling in importance and in the amount of capital invested many of the great commercial industries."[121] The company flaunted the "Made in Canada" label and planned to produce one feature a week.

A local investment firm handled the sale of Conness-Till stock, capitalizing the company with the Beury brothers' money and $50,000 from stock sales, 500 shares costing $100 apiece. The stock sold quickly and in a few months the Adelaide Street buildings were a beehive of activity after their August launch, the contest, and a large advertising campaign in Canadian magazines and newspapers.[122] The Swansea buildings were outfitted with $50,000 of new equipment: cameras, developing tanks and machinery, and processing systems.[123]

The chief director was William (A.J.) Edwards assisted by Tom McKnight. Former Pathé director Louis W. Physioc was the technical director. The company was led by Edward Robins and Clara Whipple.[124]

❧ TWO ❧

The Movies

Paul's visit to Toronto with Craven was fortuitous since Conness-Till was looking for writers and Paul could write and also had technical and directing experience. He was hired to produce scenarios and started work the day after *Too Many Cooks* finished its Toronto run on September 24. Dorothy Millette also joined the company.

Paul and Dorothy moved to the nearby Humber Beach Hotel, a brand new three-story hotel on the river near the studio. Conness and his family, director Physioc and actress Clara Whipple also lived there. There was a near-tragedy on October 29 when a fire erupted at the adjacent Humber Machine Company garage just before midnight and spread to the hotel. The hotel was outside city limits so there were no fire hydrants and the blaze quickly engulfed the wooden building. A fireboat chugged from the lake up the river at 2:00 A.M. but got stuck in the channel just out of range as everything except two large chimneys was reduced to ashes. The Conness family, Physioc, Whipple, Paul and Dorothy escaped; Whipple ran back inside, grabbed her jewelry case and threw two large steamer trunks full of costumes out the window.[1]

The next day Paul rented a small house at 1621 Queen Street West, a busy street lined with small apartments and shops.[2] The neighborhood was similar to the neighborhood where Paul grew up, three- to six-flat apartments and two- and three-story brick and wood-framed homes with large porches. The area, called Parkdale, was ethnically diverse and crowded due to its proximity to Sunnyside Beach, a popular spot for day-tripping Torontonians.[3] The section of the beach nearest Paul's home is still called Budapest Park.

Toronto was a busy city, home to 375,000.[4] At the eastern end of the lakefront the Woodbine Race Course perched next to Kew Gardens and Scarboro Beach Parks in the Balmy Beach neighborhood. Toronto Harbor was in the middle, with a dozen large wharves just a block from the train station and a short walk to Queens College Park and the Parliament Building. At the southern end, the Exhibition Grounds and racetrack sat on the lake surrounded by a wide beach. Next to the track was the Stanley Barracks, a 19th century military fort.

Queen Street ran the length of the city from the eastern beaches to Hyde Park in the south. The beautiful park is unchanged from the time John Howard built a home there in 1837; still today the 400-acre park boasts miles of natural woodlands and huge oak savannahs around the original Howard house. Just the other side of High Park was the hamlet of Swansea and the Conness-Till facility.

Toronto probably reminded Paul of Wandsbek and the park-like German cities of his youth. Trams snaked down the middle of wide boulevards, there were dozens of lovely parks and the city had defined ethnic neighborhoods offering a taste of Europe. Near the city center, a neighborhood called "The Ward" boasted a large Jewish presence from Germany, Czechoslovakia and Russia that by the early 1900s controlled the city's clothing trade.[5] They shared the area with Italians working as food vendors, innkeepers and shopkeepers, and many Greeks and Syrians who worked the docks.[6]

The area around Paul's Queen Street house was a checkerboard of even more tightly packed ethnic enclaves. A mile to the east, Queens Street was the middle of Claretown, the Irish neighborhood. Closer to Paul and Dorothy were Polish and Ukrainian quarters, and south toward the water the Portuguese lived in an area near the docks where many worked.

The Bern house is long gone. Queen Street to the east is today the center of Toronto's broadcasting, music, fashion and art worlds, and Paul's neighborhood plunged into poverty when it was cut off from the beaches by an expressway in 1955. Stately early 1900s mansions are now apartments surrounded by large low-income apartment buildings. A six-story apartment building stands where Paul and Dorothy lived but in 1914 it was a short walk to Swansea where Conness-Till made movies. Swansea's hilly terrain, dense woods and winding roads probably also reminded Paul of Germany.

The Photo Play Contest brought in 500 story entries from Toronto alone, and during the fall Conness-Till made several newsreels, filming a rugby match and then Prime Minister Robert Borden reviewing the 2nd Canadian Regiment in their lakefront encampment and maneuvers at the Toronto Exhibition Grounds. In exchange for access to the 4,000 soldiers, the company agreed to produce a recruiting film.[7] No details remain about the newsreels except newspaper notes that they were well-received and ran from December to April.[8]

As was the custom at the time, director Edwards filmed all manner of public gatherings for backgrounds. Parades, crowded beaches, and sporting events were popular choices. So many scenes had to be scrapped due to over-eager gapers watching their first filming, the company placed appeals in papers to keep passers-by from ruining shots.[9] In the fall, production began on the

A turn-of-the-century view of downtown Toronto during the annual Pretoria Day celebration.

first feature, *On the King's Highway*, a Mountie-themed film featuring Robins and Whipple. After its January, 1915 release it was described as the "first feature film even made in Canada by a Canadian company" and "very well-acted and well-photographed."[10]

Between January and April the company released seven features and several newsreels. *Canada in Peace and War* was a three-reeler with Robins and Whipple; for one scene, the company arranged a rugby match between the Parkdale Canoe Club and the Balmy Beach Club before 2,000 spectators. The clubs were promised a private viewing of 1,000 feet of the footage as a fundraising event at a local theater and each player received souvenir Conness-Till medals.[11] *Peace and War* was released in late February.

Only sketchy details remain about the Conness-Till releases. *The Better Man* was made in late December or early January and released in late February. *Motto on the Wall* was done in January and released on March 15, *To Err Is Human* made in February and released April 7, *A Soul's Affinity* also in February or early March and released in April, *The Moreland Mystery* made in March and released on April 16, and *The Faithful Servant* filmed in March and released in April.

On March 12, Edwards set up a camera in the city and produced 2,000 feet of film of the Canadian Expeditionary Force marching through downtown. He worked through the night and delivered three finished reels to the Photodrome and Strand theaters the next day. It ran five times a night for over a month to standing-room crowds and dignitaries like the lieutenant governor and the cream of Toronto society.[12]

One film for which there is anecdotal and newspaper records is *His Awakening*, written by Paul. It was the story of an artist who falls asleep and dreams he is a great lover during the era of Egypt of the Pharaohs. It starred Robins and Whipple and was directed by McKnight, was filmed in February and released in April.

Snippets of plots and themes of some Conness-Till films were found in the records of the Provincial Board, which in 1913 began censoring films and newsreels to keep military enlistment from falling as Canada was slowly being dragged into the war in Europe. Canadian films were censored and hundreds of U.S. films were denied distribution for any number of frivolous reasons. Records of the Board summaries offer tidbits as to the films' plots.

Among Conness-Till films refused initial screening permits was the Bern-scripted *His Awakening*, the government saying simply, "Complying with instructions from the Federal Government, this film is refused on account of the war." *To Err Is Human* was denied because it was "Immoral" and had references to "dope, murder, false imprisonment, gambling and theft." *The Moreland Mystery* was denied because it featured "Infidelity of a wife" and "murder," and had "no redeeming feature."

Many notable U.S. films ran afoul of censors due to anti–American sentiment. *Taps* (1913), the classic Bison saga of the Battle of Bunker Hill, was ordered edited because there were "far too much [*sic*] flags; cut flags of U.S. war. The American flag is flaunted from first to last." Wallace Reid's Philippine War saga *The Spirit of the Flag* (1913) featured "too much flag. Simply waving American flag and nonsensical gun play ... [are] very foolish and silly...." Interestingly, it was directed by a Canadian, Allan Dwan. Other classic films censored were *Broncho Billy's Elopement* (Essanay, 1913), Mary Pickford's *Tess of Storm Country* (Famous Players–Lasky, 1914), Roscoe Arbuckle's *Fatty's Gift* (Keystone, 1914), and D.W. Griffith's *Intolerance: Love's Struggle Throughout the Ages* (Triangle, 1916).[13]

Conness-Till's April 1915 releases, *The Moreland Mystery* and *The Faithful Servant*, were the last films made by the company. Trouble began brewing months earlier, and January papers warned **CONNESS-TILL COMPANY HARSHLY CRITICISED** for unfair treatment of employees.[14] Although there was significant start-up money from the partners, within six months the Beurys' demand for faster returns led to cost-cutting that turned the company upside down.

A Canadian weekly, *Jack Canuck*, first publicized the problem in January, noting "[I]f the story as told by a number of their disgruntled actors is anywhere near the truth, we can well understand how big profits are made in the motion picture business."[15]

The actors were often paid late and their earnings well below typical salaries. Clara Whipple worked for two weeks on one film and received $13.50 and by late December actors were being told they "would be paid next week."[16] Even the dressing rooms were sub-par, "lacking the ordinary accommodations which decency demands where men and women are constantly changing their costumes."[17] The *Jack Canuck* writer mused that if their case were aired in court, it would "give some interesting sidelights on motion picture methods."

The problem was the investors demanding unreasonable returns too soon. The untenable situation reached a head in March 1915 when the Beury brothers stepped in, fired Conness and Till and released most of the employees just before the releases of *The Moreland Mystery* and *The Faithful Servant*.

James Beury took charge of the renamed Beury Feature Film Company with Edward Robins staying on to act. Also remaining were McKnight, Physioc, Ned Van Buren, Harry Mainhall and Phillip Van Loan.[18] No Beury credits survive but Mainhall later recalled working for Beury and "...Paul Bern ... was my scenario writer."[19] Paul stayed with Beury until June and then he and Dorothy returned to New York and took an apartment at 132 West 78th.[20]

Paul wanted to stay close to the movies so went to work for Joseph Schenck managing the Yorkville Theater at 157 East 86th, just east of Park Avenue. The Yorkville was one of hundreds of theaters controlled by Adolph Zukor and Marcus Loew and their massive Loew's Theater Booking Office. The Yorkville was built in 1902 by Meyer Bimberg; known as "Bim the Button Man," he made a fortune manufacturing button pins affixed with political slogans. He leased to the Shuberts before Loew took it over in October, 1909.[21]

The Yorkville was typical of New York theaters: a floor section, two large, separate balconies and five tiers of private boxes flanking both sides of the stage to a height of 60 feet. It was a medium-sized theater seating 575.

In March, 1914, Zukor made a deal that jump-started the modern movie industry when he bought the huge Sullivan and Considine theater circuit, hundreds of theaters hosting vaudeville shows that Zukor would turn into movie theaters for his Famous Players Film Company. He bought the Sullivan-Considine holdings after the death of Timothy Sullivan, with Marcus Loew (described somewhat derisively as a "small time vaudeville magnate"[22]), Joseph M. Schenck (general manager of Loew's booking offices), and Aaron Jones (owner of a large Chicago-based circuit). With Loew's theaters in the east, Jones' in the mid west, and Sullivan's western holdings, the syndicate controlled almost all of the theaters in the U.S.

Paul's theater was in Yorkville, a neighborhood bordered by 72nd and 96th streets and Lexington and the East River. Side streets were lined with five- and six-story brick apartments with shops on the ground floors. The Astor Hotel and the popular Berliner Bar stood on the corner at Third Avenue and the area was distinctly ethnic. East 86th was called "German Broadway" and the surrounding blocks filled with working-class immigrants from Czechoslovakia, Germany, Hungary, and Poland.[23]

Along German Broadway were dozens of ethnic German restaurants and stores and two theaters catering to Germans, the Palast and the Yorkville. Many residents moved to Yorkville from the lower East Side German enclave after the 1904 *General Slocum* disaster, when the ship caught fire in the East River off Yorkville, killing virtually all of the 1,446 passengers, most of them Germans enjoying the annual end-of-school outing.[24]

The Yorkville offered American films but catered to locals with German-themed movies, burlesque, and vaudeville. Popular German stage performers like August Neihardt, Lotte Engel, Adolf Philipp and Mizi Gizi performed there. Paul managed the Yorkville from June 1915 until mid–1916. He was responsible for everything at the theater and dealt with the studio representatives frequently. Nothing is known of Dorothy's activities during that year.

In late 1915, Zukor and Schenck built a larger theater — the Orpheum — down the block and leased the 86th Street Theater directly across the street. On April 16, 1916, the Yorkville was sold to German producer Stephan Rachmann and his partner Adolph Philipp, who renamed it the Yorkville Deutsches Theater and tailored programs even more toward German tastes.[25] The sale was fortuitous for Paul since it led him back to the movies. That July, he went to work for Benjamin C. Chapin in Ridgefield Park, New Jersey.

Ohio-born Chapin's startling resemblance to Abraham Lincoln led to a vaudeville career performing *A Day with Abraham Lincoln* to packed turn-of-the-century theaters. Like Lincoln, Chapin was tall, thin, a bit stoop-shouldered, and had dark, deep-set eyes and a high forehead. He read voraciously about Lincoln, was a popular speaker on the Chautauqua circuit and he wrote a play, *Lincoln*, that he debuted in Hartford, Connecticut, in January, 1906.[26]

Each act was a different Civil War event: the fall of Fort Sumter, the Battle of Gettysburg, the end of the War, and the last day of Lincoln's life. Lincoln's story was told amid a tale of two soldiers in love with Mrs. Lincoln's niece Kate Morris, one a loyal Union soldier and the other a Confederate spy. Because of the spy, the loyal soldier is convicted of espionage and sentenced to death but Chapin's clever and intelligent Lincoln alone proves

the man's innocence, the guilt of
the Confederate spy, and restores
his niece to her sweetheart. The
play was known for its powerful
final scene, set in the White House
as the Lincoln family embraces
peace and the war's end and Lincoln makes the ordinary farewells
to his family and long-time butler and quietly walks out to see a
play at Ford's Theater.[27]

In March, 1906, Chapin
brought the play to the Liberty
Theater in New York and moved
every month for a year to a different large venue like the Grand
Opera House, the Alhambra, and
Keith & Proctor's 58th Street
Theater. Chapin often ran against
a racist Civil War play, *The Clansman*, based on North Carolina
minister Thomas Dixon's anti-
black trilogy that disgusted most
people.[28] Critics called Chapin's
Lincoln an "excellent antidote [to
the] contemptible *Clansman*."[29]

After touring until 1916,
Chapin rented a building across

Benjamin Chapin turned his startling
resemblance to Abraham Lincoln into a
career on the stage and in film (from the
Billy Rose Collection, New York Public
Library).

the river from Manhattan in Ridgefield Park, New Jersey, and started Charter Features Corporation with daughter Lucile as his assistant.[30] He turned
his play into a serial of four films expanding Lincoln's story further. He eventually made 10 films.

It's not known how Paul found Chapin. Perhaps Chapin brought *Lin-
coln* to the Yorkville or perhaps Paul simply sought him out but when Paul
registered for the draft on June 5, 1917, he listed his profession as "Motion
Picture Director" and his employer as "Benjamin Chapin, Ridgefield Park,
New Jersey." He and Dorothy were still on West 78th Street and Paul listed
Dorothy as his "wife" and confirmed he was her sole support.[31]

From March through May, Chapin produced a series of two-reelers based
on Lincoln's life that Paul wrote and helped direct. The first four, packaged
as *The Lincoln Cycle*, included *My Mother, The Spirit Man, My Father, The*

Physical Man, Myself, The Lincoln Man, and *The Call to Arms, Humanity's Man*. They were released two a month but were often shown as a single lengthy feature showing "the life of Lincoln from boyhood until his death, following through his rail-splitting career, his marriage, his election as president, his conduct of the Civil War and other memorable events in his life." *My Mother, The Spirit Man* was the story of Lincoln's relationship with his mother Nancy Hanks. *My Father, The Physical Man* was about his father's attempts to steer a young Lincoln away from the education that eventually saved the family farm. There is nothing known about *Myself, The Lincoln Man*, but *The Call to Arms, Humanity's Man* detailed Lincoln's personal struggles during the early days of the Civil War.[32] The first of the series debuted at the Strand Theater in New York on May 24, 1917.

The patriotic fervor at the time added to the films' popularity and Chapin became a celebrity, appearing at benefits for groups like the Patriotic Service League, always seated in a private box in Lincoln regalia.[33] On July 10 he appeared with bandleader John Phillip Sousa at a large military enlistment rally in Manhattan.

Chapin was credited with writing and starring in American Film Company's *Her Country's Call* that was made at the same time and released on May 24, 1918. Chapin supposedly reprised his Lincoln role with Mary Miles Minter and the film is said to be the fourth of Chapin's cycle but that doesn't appear to be the case.[34] No records remain to confirm the work.

The Lincoln series caught the attention of Famous Players–Lasky, which bought the films from Chapin and bundled 10 shorts as *The Son of the Democracy* in early 1918.[35] The serial included the four original 1917 films and new chapters *His First Jury*, about Lincoln's childhood, *The Slave Auction*, about the life of a slave family, *A President's Answer*, about Lincoln's response to Southern secession, and *Down the River, Tender Memories,* and *Under the Stars*. The 1918 version was also known as *The Lincoln Cycle*.[36]

Lasky hired Chapin to produce a Lincoln feature for Famous Players but as he began writing in the spring he fell ill with tuberculosis. After several months at the Loomis Sanitarium in Liberty, New York, Chapin died on June 1. He was only 43 years old.[37] The Lasky feature died with him as did Paul's job at Charter Features.

When Charter Features closed, Paul joined United Picture Theaters, Inc., an affiliate of Charles Pathé's huge Pathé Frères organization. United was run by J.A. Berst and Paul was hired as a scenario writer. Paul was introduced to Pathé by principal director John M. Stahl, who directed most of Chapin's *Lincoln* work that Paul wrote.

Berst knew movies. He was the general manager of the Pathé Exchange and developed the U.S. markets for Pathé in the early 1900s.[38] He distributed

Hal Roach and Mack Sennett films and when Pathé began making movies in 1910 he developed a program of American-style pictures that Pathé sold around the world, among them the Pearl White serial *The Perils of Pauline*.

In April, 1918, Pathé created United Picture Theaters of America, Inc., as a production arm with Berst the president and Lee A. Ochs his vice-president.[39] The company attracted popular stars and respected technical people, with casts that included Florence Reed, Dustin Farnum, Herschall Mayall, and Conway Tearle. Their directors were Stahl, Wallace Worsley, Colin Campbell, and Ernest C. Warde, cameramen Clyde De Vinna, Dal Clawson, and William C. Foster, and writers Jack Cunningham, Catherine Carr, Fred Myton, and Paul.[40]

When Paul arrived, United was making their first film, the seven-reel feature *The Light of Western Stars* with Dustin Farnum and Winifred Kingston.[41] Paul likely had little to do with the movie; it was made in Hollywood and filmed in Mexico, New Mexico and in the mountains south of Tucson, Arizona.[42] Between fall, 1918 and June, 1919, United released five films, most of which Paul probably worked on. Studios often omitted credits for writers or assistant directors but in a small company like United it would be unusual had Paul not been involved. In November and December, Robert Brunton produced two in Hollywood: *Adele*, released January 26, 1919 and *A Man in the Open*, released February 23. These were followed by *Her Code of Honor*, April 6, *The Stormy Petrell*, May 9 and *Playthings of Passion*, June 8, all filmed in New York.

After the *Playthings* release, United invested $3,000,000 to form a production company, United Picture Productions Corporation, with Berst as president.[43] During the second half of 1919 the unit released another half dozen five- or six-reel features. On June 29, Florence Reed's *The Woman Under Oath* debuted followed by Dustin Farnum's *A Man's Fight* on August 11 and Reed's *Her Game* on October 19.[44] Paul probably assisted or created scenarios for some of these films; there were only four writers on staff.

Two United films have no writing credits at all; one —*Her Game*—has striking similarities to later scenarios written by Paul, a circumstantial connection that bears mention. *Woman* is about a woman who saves her family from ruin, told in a later letter to her father. She tricks the heir of the man who ruined the family into marrying her and survives several encounters with other dishonest family members at a remote farmhouse, before saving the day and keeping her husband.[45]

The distinct similarities in theme and plot to Paul's later scenarios lead me to believe he was involved in *Her Game*. His later 1920 scripts are almost all based on family misunderstandings and feuds and pivotal scenes in those stories all take place at remote locations like roadhouses or out-of-the-way homes, all similar to *Game*. Paul's *The North Wind's Malice* is about feuding brothers with one coming between the other and his wife amidst business entanglements. *Suspicious Wives* is about a couple, separated over family arguments, who end up together at her hideaway farm, and *Greater Than Love* is about a couple that separates due to family issues and wind up in the faraway house where the wife had been hidden. It's certainly not conclusive but *Her Game* appears to be a Paul script.

Although organized scenario departments first appeared in 1915, writers were just beginning to come to the fore but still often not credited. Until Jesse Lasky, producers purchased plays and books because they didn't think writers used to crafting 8- to 20-minute scripts could create stories an hour long. Lasky convinced the Academy of Dramatic Arts' William C. de Mille to assemble Hollywood's first story department. Lasky was also a successful New York playwright and he persuaded Robert E. MacAlarney and siblings Margaret and Hector Turnbull to join him writing scripts in a small house with screen doors and a little porch. De Mille's daughter Agnes remembered, "Pop got a studio painter to make him a sign he hung on the doorknob, SCENARIO DEPARTMENT ... the first time those words appeared in Hollywood."[46]

Paul's studio was growing quickly. In October, 1919, United Picture Theatres of America and United Picture Production Corporation were combined under the American Cinema Corporation banner.

During the fall, Paul and Dorothy moved from 78th Street to a larger apartment on the ground floor of a three-story brownstone at 5 West 39th. It was a step up, just a few blocks west of Park Avenue in the heart of the city in a more impressive building in a nicer neighborhood. Paul also reached a milestone, completing the first scenario for which he received writing credit. *Women Men Forget* began filming in December and was completed in mid–January, 1920.

By 1920, moviemaking was the fastest growing industry in the world. Stars were larger than life and Hollywood seemingly the center of the universe. Theaters by the thousands were converted to movie houses. When New York's Criterion Theater was upgraded to a Paramount-Artcraft theater, three huge signs — 62' × 35', 31' × 35' and 12' × 54' were built that held 70,000 light bulbs shining at 150,000 candle power.[47]

When the Federal census taker visited West 39th in January, "Dorothy Bern" said she was born in Paris in 1895 to French parents, emigrated in 1899 and was a naturalized citizen and an "actress, stage." Paul also fudged, saying he was 29 instead of 31, and was listed as a "Director, Motion Pictures."[48] Dorothy was evidently not working; no mention in cast lists, credits, or in extensive theater news was found. She was, however, in the early stages of a mental breakdown that might have prevented her from working.

To the question "Single, married, widowed or divorced," Paul and Dorothy both responded "married," the same answer Paul gave during his 1917 draft registration. The seemingly insignificant comment later caused immeasurable grief but it wasn't a surprising admission. Paul's associates and their intimate friends all knew Dorothy as his wife, and his close friend and attorney Henry Uttal later said, "They came to my house often, and I knew her as Paul's wife. She was a very pretty woman, very intelligent.... [Paul] told me he had found the ideal wife." At the time, Paul had Uttal draw up a will specifically designating Dorothy as "Mrs. Paul Bern."[49]

They were together long enough that he was legally bound to her by the laws of New York, considered married in common law though no record remains of a legal marriage anywhere they lived — New York, New Jersey, Toronto — or anywhere they are known to have visited. They probably considered themselves married but that innocent assumption came to haunt Paul.

Most of Paul's family was nearby. After Julius Levy's death, Henriette moved with her daughter Friederike's family to a series of Bronx apartments, first at 3781 Third Avenue and then farther north at 946 East 181st Street where she was living in early 1920.[50] The apartment on 181st was in a large building a block south of the 800-acre Bronx Park, more celebrated than Central Park with its renowned 275-acre Botanical Garden and 250-acre Bronx Zoo, one of the largest in the world.

Friederike's husband William Marcus owned several flower shops and Henriette was sufficiently well-off to travel to Germany regularly, the first a month-long trip a year after Julius died. She went to Hamburg in March, 1910 and returned on April 23 aboard Hamburg-Amerika's premier liner *Amerika*. Friederike's son Siegbert was a laboratory chemist for a motion picture company in Long Island City — a job Paul probably arranged — living with his wife on Morris Avenue in the Bronx.[51] Henry Bern was still working for an embroidery company and living in Manhattan.

Paul's *Women Men Forget* began filming in December, directed by John M. Stahl and filmed by John K. Holbrook. Paul's scenario was from a story by Elaine Sterne Carrington. Mollie King and Edward Langford starred in the story of Mary Graham (King), whose old school friend Helen visits the home she shares with her husband Robert (Langford). Helen begins an affair with Robert, who tells Mary of his love for Helen, not knowing that Mary is pregnant. A heartbroken Mary confides to loyal friend James that her husband does not know so James arranges for her to stay in the country with his aunt. When Livingston learns Robert intends to divorce Mary, he ruins him financially and demands the unfaithful husband repay notes he now holds. Robert is unable to pay and Helen leaves him but Mary offers to sell her jewelry to help her husband and Robert realizes his wife's true value and they are joyfully united as Mary introduces her husband to his son.[52]

Paul's story was well-received after its March 21 premiere. It again revisited several of Paul's common themes: family entanglements, infidelity, business problems, and a resolution taking place at an out-of-the-way house.

In the spring, Paul joined Stahl at Trojan Film Company to make Paul's *Greater Than Love* for World Film Corporation, which was owned by Lewis Selznick. Paul's script was based on a story by Robert F. Roden; Stahl directed the six-reeler and production began in March.[53] Mollie King starred with Louise Glaum and Donald MacDonald.

It is the story of beautiful young Grace (King), who must choose between two suitors, James Brunton (MacDonald) and Bob Standing. She picks James, whose wealthy father hosts an extravagant wedding that is interrupted when he (the father) is shot through a window by a mysterious assassin. Before dying, he makes his son promise *not* to apprehend his murderer. Several years later Grace discovers James is giving money to a woman named Helen and thinking he's having an affair flees to another town and has a miscarriage. James thinks she has run off with Bob and some months later has a car accident and is taken unconscious to Grace's nearby house. The mystery is solved when Helen and Bob arrive and Grace learns Helen is James' sister, that their father abandoned their mother years before and that the senior Brunton knew it was she who shot him, the reason he asked James not to find her. Bob and Helen become a couple and James and Grace are reconciled.[54]

Greater Than Love stayed in theaters for several months. The film again features Paul's common themes: feuding suitors, family machinations, separations, pregnancies, and another secluded house where most of the final scenes play out. After finishing the film, Paul joined Goldwyn Picture Company as a cutter and in just a few months he began directing. He was earning $200 a week.

Goldwyn was built by Samuel Gelbfisz, born in Warsaw in 1879. After his father died when Samuel was 15, he toured Europe for a year, worked in England and Canada as a blacksmith, and settled in Gloversville, a small upstate New York glove manufacturing mill-town. By his mid-20s he owned a successful glove business but a month after a 1913 visit to a nickelodeon he vacationed with his brother-in-law Jesse Lasky and badgered him into forming the Jesse L. Lasky Feature Play Company with him. Cecil B. DeMille directed their first film, the western *The Squaw Man*.

Using the Americanized Samuel Goldfish, he was the business brains at Lasky, selling films and raising money while DeMille directed and Lasky produced. Lasky merged with Adolph Zukor in 1916 to form Famous Players–Lasky Studio but Zukor never liked Goldfish — "a very crude man ... loud and not the most pleasant man to have anything to do with..."[55]— and when Goldfish squabbled with Zukor's star Mary Pickford *and* divorced Lasky's sister just after the merger, he was thrown out. But his $7,500 equity earned him a $900,000 buyout ($15,000,000 today) and he joined the theatrical Selwyn family to start Goldwyn Pictures, a name he liked so much he legally changed his name to Goldwyn in 1918.[56]

Goldwyn believed the public loved stars and filled his company with highly paid talent, actors like Mae Marsh, Madge Kennedy, Rex Beach, Jack Pickford, his crown jewel, comedienne Mabel Normand, and writers and directors like Clarence Badger, Victor L. "Pops" Schertzinger, and Hobart Henley.[57] He also employed a novel startup strategy of completing 12 films before releasing the first. It worked. Demand grew during production and resulted in big crowds. The first film — Mae Marsh's *Polly of the Circus*— was released on September 9, followed by Madge Kennedy in *Baby Mine*, Maxine Elliott in *Fighting Odds*, and Jane Cowl in *The Spreading Dawn*.[58] Goldwyn's early films were hits but when Paul arrived the studio was in the midst of major upheaval.

Earlier events in 1918 and 1919 had already conspired to weaken Goldwyn. A worldwide influenza epidemic in 1918 kept thousands of theaters closed and Goldwyn was hit particularly hard due to his huge payroll. By 1919 his precarious financial condition led him to move to Culver City, 15 dusty miles west of downtown Los Angeles and 20 from Hollywood. In 1915 Harry Culver had offered free land to anyone building a movie studio in his new city and D.W. Griffith, Thomas Ince and Mack Sennett were the first, moving to 16 acres at the end of a long dirt road named Washington Boulevard. However, after they disbanded Goldwyn purchased their site for $325,000 in 1919.

Goldwyn's lot had a three-story office building, six glass soundstages and dozens of small buildings for prop-making, costume design, film developing, stables, etc. He loaned a small shed to Will Rogers for his personal stable and remodeled the site to look like an English manor, rolling sod on top of the sand and planting rose gardens.[59]

A break-even 1918 and loss in 1919 suggested Goldwyn was in trouble, since the rest of the industry was growing exponentially; there were 15,000 theaters in the U.S. holding 8,000,000 seats and in 1919 over $800,000,000 was spent on tickets.[60] Ominously for Goldwyn, the public lost interest in most of his stars; worse, big producers like Fox and Zukor were widening the gap between them. Zukor's empire included a dozen studios and hundreds of the big-name stars, and Marcus Loew owned a growing theater chain and the successful Metro Pictures.[61]

Goldwyn's temporary savior was slick deal-maker Frank Joseph Godsol, who brokered a large investment from a group including the du Pont family, but his help came at a cost. By the time Paul joined Goldwyn in New York in the spring of 1920, Godsol was already working to take Goldwyn's studio from him. Everyone carried on amidst a titanic power struggle.

Paul's first assignment was co-directing *The North Wind's Malice* with Carl Harbaugh. *Malice* was a seven-reel feature based on a Rex Beach short story, a complicated shoot with outdoor winter scenes, blizzards, and fires. Robert B. McIntyre — Goldwyn's first casting director — was the production manager and filming was done by Lucien Tainguy, Oliver Marsh, George Peters, and Roy Vaughan. Tom Santschi and Jane Thomas starred in the film, shot in Port Henry, New York, a small village on the shores of Lake Champlain.[62]

Tired of bickering with his wife Lois (Thomas), Roger Folsom (Santschi) leaves her and she takes up with Henry Carter. Roger's brother Tom is also angry at Lois because she fouled up his relationship with Dorothy Halstead, the lovely ward of Jewish storekeeper Abe Guth. To get even, he tells Roger of Lois' affair with Henry. Roger gets so angry he joins an Alaskan mining expedition, not knowing Lois is pregnant, desperate and penniless. After the Guth store is destroyed by fire, Tom is forced to steal food for the family and is caught and jailed. Lois has her baby and Henry searches for Roger and tells him, after which Roger returns to Lois and frees Tom from jail and Tom admits to his lies and wins Dorothy's heart.[63] Throughout the film a diaphanous character known as Malice drifts in and out of relationships and situations.[64]

To recreate realistic winter scenes, Paul and Harbaugh rented two large Curtiss airplanes to blow simulated snow across the sets. After its August 8 premiere, reviewers praised the acting and the characters, particularly storekeeper Guth and his wife, described as "...sympathetically and humanly presented."[65] Paul probably modeled those characters on his own parents.

The summer of 1920 should have been a time of great celebration for Paul. He was moving up at Goldwyn, where his first assignment was directing a major feature. But at his moment of triumph he was hit with a one-two punch that doubtless sent him reeling. His mother Henriette was found dead in the ocean off Long Island. And he had to commit Dorothy to an asylum.

Some of the timing is hard to confirm. Henriette's body was discovered off Rockaway Beach in the early morning of September 15 and by early October, Paul was living in L.A. so it appears Dorothy's problems arose before Henriette died.

During 1920, Dorothy began to exhibit symptoms of mental illness. Mike Mindlin, who had known Paul and Dorothy since 1912, said her "mind seemed upset by worries. She brooded almost constantly. She had few friends and was often ill but never saw a doctor, adhering to the Christian Science teachings she had taken to."[66] During the summer, she became more and more obsessed with God and religion, babbling incoherently about the subjects. Voices spoke to her and she to them, and she became convinced she was a member of the inner circle of God. She became fanatical about God and (according to Paul's brother Henry) by August no longer recognized Paul.[67] She was psychotic; schizophrenic, paranoid, or both.

Paul's sister Friedericke described her ailment as "dementia praecox," a catch-all at the time to describe the psychotic disorder that became known as schizophrenia.[68] It is the rapid disintegration of mental processes usually starting in the late teens and characterized by delusions, inappropriate processing of feelings or perceptions, and hallucinations.[69] Sufferers also tend toward solitary lifestyles, lose interest in relationships and become secretive. In 1920 it was considered incurable and there was no treatment regimen; the disorder was not formally identified and writings published by Eugen Bleuler and Emile Kretschmer until 1924.

In August, Paul committed Dorothy to the Blythewood Sanitarium in Greenwich, Connecticut, a few hours from the city by car. Greenwich was and still is a quiet seaside village in the southwestern part of the state with beautiful rocky beaches, a quaint downtown, and acres of pristine rolling woodlands filled with creeks and dotted with pastures bounded by stone fences.

There were other sanitariums in Greenwich — Brooklea Farm, Crest View Sanitarium, and the Westport Sanitarium — but Blythewood was the most exclusive and most expensive and the only fully private facility. Money was needed to stay at Blythewood. Paul was by no means wealthy so a good part of his $250 weekly Goldwyn salary went to Dorothy's care.

Blythewood's ten acres was surrounded by several hundred acres of woodlands dissected by a wide stream running through the groomed grounds. The manicured lawns and hilltop Forrest Building were more reminiscent of an exclusive golf club than a mental hospital, but the bucolic setting belied the seriousness of the residents' mental problems. The Forrest Building was the main residence and services building, accessed via winding gravel drive leading to a large circular court. It was a large three-story clapboard building with huge brick chimneys at each end, green awnings above the windows, and a large porch. There was a unit housing medical facilities and a one-story Occupational Building lined with windows and filled with tables for arts and crafts and several pianos. Residents spent most of their days in the Occupational Building.

No matter how pastoral the setting, Blythewood meant Dorothy had serious mental problems. Her Blythewood treatment records are lost; the facility closed in the 1960s.[70] Paul's brother Henry later claimed Dorothy stayed "eight months and was discharged. Not cured. Just as harmless."[71] Jean Harlow biographer David Stenn theorized Dorothy was at Blythewood a few months but it was probably much longer.

When she did leave Blythewood, she moved to a top-floor room at the Algonquin Hotel in New York, an apartment paid for by Paul. In 1932, the hotel manager said she lived there "almost ten years," meaning she left Blythewood in 1923 or 1924.[72] Circumstantially it would seem that if she was released after just a few months, Paul would have reunited with her. Paul's few friends who knew about Dorothy were told he never married because, "How would she feel if she ever regained her reason and learned I had married?"[73]

Paul's sister Friederike said Dorothy's illness left him devastated and "heartbroken. He went around like a shadow." His nephew Sig said after placing Dorothy at Blythewood, Paul "mourned like he mourned for a dead one. He would not think of putting her in a cheap sanitarium, although he could not afford to keep her in such an expensive place."[74] He also opened a bank account for "Mrs. Paul Bern" and supplied Dorothy with $175 a month for insurance, hospital bills and living expenses.

After she left Blythewood, Paul continued supporting her, apparently with the understanding that she would stay in New York and get on with her life and he would continue on with his. But Dorothy was unable to effectively move on, remaining a recluse at the Algonquin waiting for Paul's letters and checks. For the next decade she remained a mystery at the hotel, taking almost all her meals in her room and venturing outside only for brief neighborhood walks. When she did go out, she kept strictly to herself, eyes downcast, refusing all attempts at conversation.[75]

There may be some truth to Harlow biographer Eve Golden's theory that after Dorothy's illness Paul simply excised her from his life. But if he did so, he made sure she was well taken care of. On August 30 he went to the 521 Fifth Avenue offices of lawyer and good friend Henry Uttal and had Uttal draw up a will leaving everything to his wife, "Mrs. Dorothy Bern."[76] Uttal and his wife had known Dorothy and Paul since 1918 and socialized with them often.

Paul immersed himself in work and on September 4 was tabbed to replace director Mason N. Litson as the studio's continuity editor. Litson had spent 1920 directing a 12-part serialization of Booth Tarkington's Edgar Pomeroy character. It was a stunning promotion for one so young even in an industry of young executives—Goldwyn's Clarence Badger was among the movies' oldest directors at 40—and Litson was 10 years Paul's senior and more experienced.[77] He was apparently not assigned anything significant right away, perhaps due to the upheaval in his personal life.

Henriette was still living with Friederike's family on East 181st and during the summer of 1920 she joined the throng of city dwellers escaping the stifling heat by renting a house at 259 Rue de St. Felix near Far Rockaway's large beach. The tidy bungalow was just three blocks from the Atlantic Ocean.[78]

Rockaway Beach was only about 20 miles from East 181st but it took most of the day to get there. She took a ferry and a series of Brooklyn Rapid Transit Trains south and east around Jamaica Bay to the south shore of Long Island at Rockaway. At Jamaica Avenue in Brooklyn she boarded an elevated train to connect with the Long Island Railroad to travel along the Atlantic Branch to a Rockaway Beach line that took her to Rockaway Beach Station, a small three-story building next to the tracks, and either took a carriage or a cab to her rental house a half mile away near the beach.[79]

Rockaway Beach and nearby Seaside was the "The Playground of New York" back to the 1880s. Huge summer mansions built by the Vanderbilts and Astors shared ocean views with small bungalows and row upon row of 25-foot-square canvas tents lined up on the beach and rented by the week. Not far from Henriette's rental, the Rockaway Beach resort and pier offered amusements and rides in George Tilyou's Amusement Park and the huge Rockaways' Playland. Built in 1901, Playland was world-renowned for its Cinerama roller coaster, the biggest swimming pool in America and a $1,000,000 midway.[80] Rockaway's boardwalk stretched six miles and was also home to dozens of brothels.

Many of the bungalows around Henriette's rental were built for returning soldiers and originally stood in nearby Gravesend but after World War I ended they were hauled by barge around the bay from Bensonhurst and lined up on streets near the beach. Rue de St. Felix was in a middle-class, blue-collar neighborhood and has since been re-named Beach 14th Street.[81] Henriette arrived in late June and presumably spent the summer enjoying the beach.

Early on the morning of September 15th she left her bungalow and walked south the three blocks to the end of Rue de St. Felix, continued across Bay Avenue and then a short distance across the grassy dunes. Just beyond the dunes she climbed a rocky embankment that looked over the cold water of South Oyster Bay.[82] She would have seen the trees and beaches of remote Silver Point Park barely 1,000 feet across the open ocean.

We don't know what happened that cool Wednesday morning nor do we know what Henriette was thinking. All we know with certainty is that late that afternoon a couple walking along the dunes noticed a fully clothed body floating in South Oyster Bay. Police pulled the body of Henriette Levy out of the cold water. She had tumbled off of the embankment and drowned.

There was no obituary for Henriette, just a short article in the *Queens Daily Star* about the discovery of her body. The paper listed her in the end-

View of Tent City, Rockaway Beach, N. Y.

Rockaway Beach was a popular getaway in the early 1920s, its long beach covered with miles of tent cities. Families rented tents by the week.

of-the-month death summary with the other 20 people who died in Queens that September, stating simply, "LEVY, Henrietta [*sic*]..72 years..259 Rue St. Felix, Far Rockaway."[83] The coroner assumed her rental was her home. On September 17, Henriette was buried next to Julius on the quiet hilltop at the north end of Mount Zion Cemetery.

Henriette's death certainly had a profound impact on Paul, particularly coming so soon after Dorothy's commitment. A decade later the circumstances would be discussed and facts assumed as truths. But did Henriette commit suicide or die in an accident? She certainly could have killed herself; medical records don't offer a conclusive determination. Her death certificate lists the cause of death as "Drowning by falling off embankment, accidental."[84] *Accidental.* No note was found at her rental nor was she perceived as suicidal by family who would not have left her alone in Rockaway Beach if they thought she was self-destructive. Absent confirmation she was suicidal, it can't be assumed she committed suicide.

When Henriette's death was described as a suicide a decade later, rumors followed of rampant mental illness and a rash of Levy family suicides. If Henriette was mentally ill, Paul would likely have made the same arrangements for her that he made for Dorothy. One biographer suggested Henriette committed suicide after learning of Paul's relationship with a Gentile and that guilt over Henriette's death led to Dorothy's breakdown. But Henriette knew all about Dorothy. Paul was with her for a decade. Paul's sister later confirmed the family's awareness of and acceptance of Dorothy as his wife.[85] It's equally questionable that a non–Jewish relationship would be enough to prompt Henriette's suicide or that Henriette's death would have had such a profound impact on Dorothy. The tragic events were unrelated.

During those two awful months, Paul began his new job as continuity director. It was a tumultuous time for Goldwyn as well — the studio and the man. Frank Godsol's assault on Goldwyn had continued and on October 31 the Board re-elected Goldwyn to his old position as president but stripped him of power by naming Godsol Chairman. Goldwyn was still at the studio, but powerless.[86] Most of the Culver City writing staff joined less battle-weary studios, and not long after Dorothy's commitment and his mother's death, Paul left for California in early October.

In 1920 Culver City was home to the largest studios in the world, but Hollywood was the public center of the movie universe, recognized by millions of fans as the place where the new magic was conjured. The world knew Hollywood from images of stars in limousines living in luxurious mansions surrounded by palm trees. They knew little of Culver City.

Los Angeles itself was a contradiction. Dorothy Parker described it "72 suburbs in search of a city."[87] The hills around the city were dotted with thousands of oil wells left from the early 1900s L.A. basin oil boom, most of them around Culver City. They were everywhere, a forest of tall, ugly metal trees, visible for miles. There were 40 small towns scattered within 30 miles of downtown, so many it was impossible to tell where one ended and another began. As far as the eye could see, the landscape was a patchwork of lemon and orange groves, pueblos, hotels and apartments springing up like flowers, expanding business blocks, and impressive homes for retirees coming to California.

The area was still traversed mostly by dirt roads. Only some main streets near downtown were paved. The well-organized Red Car trolley line ran from downtown to the beaches at Santa Monica, to the San Fernando Valley and Tropico (now Glendale), south down the coast to Newport Beach, and as far east as Riverside. Hollywood from downtown was a 40¢ ticket and passengers had to change cars three times. Going to Culver City cost 30¢ and only meant one transfer.[88]

Hollywood and Culver City were both a distance from downtown. Hollywood was just a large ranch when studios arrived in 1913. In the 1800s the area was divided by the Spanish government into the Rancho La Brea to the west and Rancho Los Feliz to the east and in 1886, Ohio-born millionaire and religious fanatic–Prohibitionist Horace Wilcox and his wife Daeida bought most of Rancho La Brea, laid out a grid and sold lots. Mrs. Wilcox named it after a friend's Ohio estate and planned a Christian community with a Methodist, Prohibitionist church on every block. It turned out quite differently when the movie people began to overrun Hollywood.

The first movie companies grabbed land in the eastern reaches of Hollywood north of Elysian Park (now Silverlake) in an area called Edendale, a town surrounding Echo Park Lake, where sound was said to echo off the lake for miles. Edendale was mostly empty hills and a main street dotted with a half dozen stores and the Clifford Street School.[89]

Hollywood was not very glamorous either. The main street was Prospect Avenue (today Hollywood Boulevard), a long dirt boulevard shaded by pepper and palm trees and lined with large Victorian mansions set back 100 feet from the curb. There were only a few buildings over a single story, the most prominent being artist Paul de Longpre's Moorish castle at Prospect and Cahuenga with its acres of flower gardens. Nearby was the huge, wooden Hollywood Hotel. When Hollywood became too crowded with studios and land too expensive — an acre cost $500 in 1910, a *quarter* acre was $150,000 in 1920 — studios looked elsewhere and were drawn to even less glamorous Culver City. Stars didn't live in Culver City; in fact, almost nobody lived there in the early 1920s.

Movie wealth was becoming visible around Hollywood as actors moved from bungalow court apartments to mansions hidden by palm trees, hedges, and flowers. A mishmash of Swiss chalets, flat-roofed adobes, English cottages, Norman castles, and Mesopotamian mosque-styled mansions sprung up. There were also plenty of redwood California bungalows and every house, big or small, seemed to be covered with vines and shrubbery and surrounded by orange trees.[90]

The fastest-growing area was Beverly Hills, what locals called "Morocco Junction." Development began accidentally in 1907 when oilman Burton Green sold lots to retirees to recoup money lost in dry oil wells. Borrowing the name of his hometown of Beverly Farms, Massachusetts, he built a hotel and mapped out a subdivision. His first model home still stands unchanged at 515 Canon Drive and in 1911 his crown jewel, the Beverly Hills Hotel, opened in pink splendor amid an expanse of bean fields dotted with a few houses. Its green tiles visible for miles, it squatted under the Santa Monica Mountains which locals began calling the "Beverly Hills." The area was desolate. As late as 1923, Charlie Chaplin said it looked like "an abandoned real estate development" with sidewalks disappearing into bean fields.[91]

In Hollywood, every morning dozens of real cowboys and authentic Indians gathered at the bottom of Gower Street at Sunset — "Gower Gulch" — hoping for a day's work.[92] Another gathering place was in the middle of Vine

Lasky and Paramount's Hollywood studio in 1920, offering an idea of the undeveloped nature of Los Angeles the summer that Paul arrived.

Street, another dirt road with a row of pepper trees down the middle shading benches filled with people looking for work.[93] In Culver City, the line of hopefuls outside Goldwyn formed on Washington Boulevard at the door to the Casting Office and stretched down the block.

The entire L.A. basin was growing. Between 1900 and 1920, Hollywood's population surged from 500 to 70,000 while L.A.'s soared from 125,000 to over 650,000. Culver City had more businesses than people. In 1920 only about 1,000 people lived there.[94] In Hollywood, Prospect Avenue and the side streets were lined with fashionable retail stores, restaurants, cafés and taverns. Most evenings the promenade was crowded with locals wandering among the new shops.[95] The year Paul arrived in L.A., 62,458 building permits were issued.[96]

❧ THREE ❧

Hollywood

Arriving in Los Angeles in September, 1920, Paul moved into the Crawford Apartments at 941 Georgia Street, in a neighborhood southwest of downtown.[1] No 1920s-era structures remain in that part of Georgia; they've been replaced by commercial buildings and parking lots serving the Staples Center. But in the early 1920s it was a neighborhood of apartment buildings and bungalows. The 900 block was between 9th Street and West Olympic Boulevard, main streets lined with commercial businesses, apartments, restaurants and taverns. Paul's block was quiet and dominated by twin apartments on opposite sides of the street in the middle of the block, the Crawford at 941 and the Spier at 916. Around each were a half dozen bungalows.[2] It was about a mile and a half west of Goldwyn.

The Crawford was a three-story wooden building with 29 apartments. It was not luxurious, with apartments renting for $10 to $30 a month.[3] The building filled the lot; there was no yard or parking but few residents probably owned automobiles anyway. On each floor a hallway ran the length of the building with five one-bedroom apartments on either side. Each apartment had two windows, one in the living room and another in the bedroom. There was a fire escape at the rear and no elevators.

Paul's neighbors were blue-collar: locksmiths, electric train conductors, store clerks and a few teachers. The area around Georgia Street was not a movie star enclave. There were actors, a few extras like Olive Swan (1005), Fanny Beers (1009), and Louie St. Cyr (1116).[4] The Crawford was two blocks from the site of D.W. Griffith's first California studio, a vacant lot at 1200 Georgia he lined with dressing room tents in 1910. In the 1921 L.A. City Directory, Paul was listed simply as "author."[5]

After his arrival, Paul received some important assignments, first to co-direct the Mabel Normand film *Head Over Heels* and then to assist writing and directing several chapters of an ongoing serial based on the Booth Tarkington character Edgar Pomeroy. Normand had worked for Goldwyn since

49

1917 and was the studio's biggest asset and most popular star. The daughter of a Staten Island carpenter, she entered films in 1909 with Biograph and by 1920 was a star, but she lived a completely reckless life and was — for good reason — known as Hollywood's "I Don't Care Girl."[6] Larger than life, the "Queen of Comedy" was barely five feet tall and 95 pounds. An irreverent quick wit, she once told a reporter her hobbies were to "pinch babies and twist their legs. And get drunk."[7] Her personal life was a mess.

Goldwyn advertised her as the studio's "cyclonic comedienne" and she lived her life like a tornado, not cashing paychecks for months at a time. Like Paul, she was obsessively generous, routinely tipping working women with $100 bills.[8] Her love life was equally unrestrained. Men loved her. Charlie Chaplin and Sam Goldwyn both tried to win her and her decade-long here and gone relationship with Mack Sennett tortured both for years after it ended. Between 1909 and 1921 the tiny dynamo made over 150 shorts and dozens of features and was known the world over but she was mired in a massive drug problem. She and Paul became close friends.

There's been much conjecture about Paul's relationship with Mabel. Normand biographer Betty Fussell dismissively asserted he "promptly fell head over heels in love" with her.[9] That may have been true but it's a weak indictment, and given the timing — he had just lost his mother and put his wife in an institution — it's hard to imagine he would fall head over heels in love with *anyone*. It's possible, though.

Normand was one among many beautiful women who were attracted to the urbane and witty Paul but whom Paul was somehow later judged to be inadequate. His friend Al Lewin later said, "He's got that goddamned Pygmalion complex; he's hellbent on finding someone to make over and fall in love with."[10] John Gilbert, another close friend, said, "He has a Magdalene complex. He does crazy things for whores."[11] Both may be accurate descriptions of Paul's relationship with Mabel.

When Mabel and Paul met, she was already falling. As early as 1918 her health was failing after years of alcohol and drug issues and by 1919 her acting became uninspired as she was less able to work. After starring in eight features in 1918, she appeared in just five in 1919 and would only do three or four in 1920. By 1921 she could barely finish two. When *Head Over Heels* filming began, her drug addiction was an open secret and a once healthy countenance had become tired, worn, and "wasted."[12]

But in the public eye she was still a star and the five-reeler *Head Over Heels* offered a tomboy character similar to *Mickey*, the 1918 hit that made her famous. Paul shared directing duties with Victor Schertzinger, one of the few directors left to whom Mabel would listen. He had directed 40 features including a dozen Charles Ray titles and seven other Normand hits including *Jinx*

Mabel Normand was among Paul's closest female friends during his early years in Hollywood.

(1919), *Pinto* and *What Happened to Rosa* (both 1920).[13] *Heels* was based on Nablro Isadorah Bartley's story "Shadows" and a popular stage play by Edgar Allan Woolf.[14]

Normand plays Tina, an Italian trapeze artist brought to the U.S. by her manager. She arrives timid and untidy and moves in with elderly patron Papa Bambinetti, who is told by a slimy agent he will make her a star. Taken against her will to a beauty parlor, Tina emerges predictably beautiful and her manager's assistant Lawson (Hugh Thompson) falls in love with her. Tina cannot chose between love and her family in Italy and decides to return, but when Lawson takes up with another actress she stays and they marry.[15]

Paul's challenge was to show the inner artistic temperament of Normand's acrobat character and effect a Pygmalion-like transformation into a beautiful, sensitive woman. Normand's diminishing looks were hidden with camera angles but she still showed flashes of her athleticism, performing on a trapeze, entering one office by climbing through the transom above the door and physically ejecting a half dozen stenographers to get into another. Paul also effectively used camera and expression to interject feminism and sexuality into an otherwise boyish character.

No amount of directorial expertise could salvage the film, however. Camera angles or back-lighting couldn't hide Normand's decline from coquettish comedienne to tired drug addict. Even though she was Goldwyn's most recognizable star, the film would not be released until 1922, and then without publicity.[16] Not long after filming ended, she disappeared from Hollywood and was rumored to be resting in Europe or New England rebuilding her "wrecked nervous system."[17] She would not return until August, 1921. In truth, her friend William Desmond Taylor put her in a sanitarium in the East for treatment. Taylor tried to save Mabel from herself until his own death in 1922. Paul tried until her death in 1930.

During the fall of 1920, Paul also worked on Goldwyn's Tarkington project, the serial *The Adventures and Emotions of Edgar Pomeroy*. Individual *Pomeroy* films were made and released monthly from March 1920 to April 1921.[18] The earlier chapters were directed by Mason Litson or E. Mason Hopper.

It's not known why Paul replaced Litson as continuity editor before coming to California or why he replaced him directing the final chapter in the serial but he was assigned *Edgar, the Detective* just before November filming began. Edward Peil, Jr., played the title role with Lucille Ricksen, Buddy Messinger, and another half dozen child actors.[19] Filming lasted two weeks and the film was released on April 10, 1921. On May 1 the studio announced it would continue the series but nothing came of it.[20]

The child actors in the *Edgar* troupe looked upon Paul as a favorite uncle. One morning, Eddie Peil told Paul he was scared he "looked too old now to go on playing Edgar," worried because the character was 11 and he was turning 12 that day. Paul reassured him he was fine and quickly arranged a birthday party for his young star.[21] His worries were soon forgotten.

Paul also became close to 11-year-old star Lucille Ricksen, a lovely (5' 2" and 110 pounds) child found by a Goldwyn agent in Chicago. She and her mother Ingeborg were brought to California and she was given the female lead in the Edgar serial. She quickly showed an immense talent, as "one of the most promising of the younger actresses in Hollywood" and was among the best-known child stars.[22] She went right to features in *The Old Nest* which was released in early 1921. From their introduction, the Ricksen women came to Paul for career and personal advice.

Thoughtful and erudite, Paul had strong beliefs about moviemaking. His discussions with Edward Bernays about Freud and psychology led to a deep interest in reasons why people think and act the way they do, and his ideas were at the forefront of a shift in how movies were made. Moviemakers had only lightly experimented with expressing thought on film, most films just simple streams of physical action. Situations involving psychological processes had for the most part been shunned by filmmakers.

Paul believed the next step would be a photographic presentation of characters' thoughts or feelings. In a 1920 interview he said, "The big development in motion pictures is the field of expressing thought. To some extent this has already been done."[23] He offered an example of a quick cutaway to images of flowing lava to infer anger, simple-sounding today but innovative in the 1920s. He used the process in his first *Edgar* film: As Edgar watches his father working around the house, Paul switched back and forth between Edgar's facial expressions and views of the father, allowing viewers to intuitively recognize they were being shown that Edgar was proud of his father. Paul continued:

> Dr. S.P. Goodhart, a New York alienist and specialist in mental diseases, and I were recently discussing the fact that when thought is entirely freed from inhibitions it takes what may be called visual form, as in dreams. The dream, as Freud says, is a series of pictures, fantastic, kaleidoscopic, mysterious, with emphasis on essentials, and rather frightening to our consciences. Dr. Goodhart thinks that if the screen can ever present a dream as it really occurs (not, as we do today, by simply continuing normal action), science may be able to develop theories and truths of great importance from it. I hope that some day we will create a dream-picture, made of the stuff that dreams are really made of. Here will be pure thought, visualized as only the camera can visualize it.[24]

Paul was already known as the resident intellectual at Goldwyn, consulted about everything from writing to direction. But he was also showing a knack for production supervision. He worked on dozens of Goldwyn films in late 1920 and early 1921 as a production supervisor or continuity editor, but shunned credit. His next confirmed credit was not until 1921 for a script he wrote earlier, *Suspicious Wives*, made by old friend John Stahl and Trojan Film Company in New York. His next credited Goldwyn work was *The Man with Two Mothers*, which would film that summer.

Paul's arrival in Hollywood coincided with an increase in public awareness that all wasn't perfect in screenland. In Hollywood, most early–1920s problems were drug-related. Cheap Oriental drugs had flowed into L.A. for a decade but most people didn't yet understand the real dangers. Drugs were used liberally to cure hangovers caused by "bathtub gin" or punch made with 200-proof medicinal alcohol. Cocaine, an active ingredient in Coca-Cola and not even illegal until 1914, was easy to find, as was heroin, opium and morphine.

Each studio was serviced by its own dealer that hired low-level studio workers as couriers so deliveries could be made in minutes. "Mr. Fix-it" served Fox, "The Man" was at Paramount and "Captain Spaulding" at Lasky. Captain Spaulding was once arrested but charges were dropped when he threatened to "name names."[25] The best-known dealer was "The Count," who put heroin in peanut shells and gave potential Sennett and Goldwyn clients their first dose free. Among his famous addicts were Mabel Normand and Wallace Reid.[26]

The public first became aware that something was amiss in Hollywood after the strange deaths of Robert Harron and Olive Thomas. Harron was a former child star who battled depression that worsened after his brother died in a 1915 car accident and a sister died during the 1918 Spanish flu epidemic. Even though he signed with Metro for $5,000 a week in 1920, drugs were deepening his depression and on September 5 he shot himself in the chest in a New York hotel room. Metro claimed that before he died he told doctors it was an accident, but it was likely a suicide. D.W. Griffith's classic *Way Down East* was premiering the next day and he had been devastated that Griffith had given the lead to Richard Barthelmess over him.

There was an even more bizarre incident that same day when gorgeous actress Olive Thomas somehow poisoned herself in Paris. Violet-eyed Thomas ran away from a Pennsylvania mining town to get married at 14 and by 17 was a famous Ziegfeld Follies headliner and the first "Vargas Girl" painted by renowned artist Alberto Vargas (he called her "The Most Beautiful Woman in the World"). She married Mary Pickford's younger brother Jack in 1916 and appeared in several dozen films and was a rising star when she and Jack sailed for Paris on a second honeymoon on August 12.[27]

On September 5 she was found near death in the luxurious Ritz Hotel in Paris and early papers said maids found her lying nude atop a pile of furs holding an empty bottle of bichloride of mercury. Jack told police she mistakenly ingested the drug in a darkened bathroom but friends knew she was despondent over their drug addictions and that Jack had infected her with syphilis. It was incurable; the only regimen was a topical mixture of bichloride of mercury and water. She probably drank the mixture accidentally thinking it was plain water and after five days of agonizing pain leading to deafness and blindness she died on the 10th.

Jack — known to female studio workers as "Mr. Syphilis"[28] — auctioned off her belongings a few months later and Mabel Normand bought a 14-karet gold cigarette case for $50, a 20-piece toilet set for $1,425, a diamond and pearl brooch and sapphire pin for $500, and a platinum set with a star sapphire for $425.[29]

Thomas' death led to the rebirth of year-old rumors about her sister-in-law Mary Pickford's 1920 wedding to Douglas Fairbanks. It was widely known in studio circles that their relationship began as an adulterous affair; when Mary's husband Owen Moore threatened to kill him, Fairbanks moved to Arizona for a month and even considered going to South America for another six.[30] Moore was paid $100,000 ($2,500,000 today) for a quiet divorce.

During Paul's first months in Culver City, the industry was coming under ever-increasing scrutiny from fans, writers, and community groups. The deaths of Harron and Thomas were the first chinks in the armor.

Paul quickly developed a wide circle of friends from actors and cameramen to writers and studio executives. His closest friend was Carey Wilson, a 30-year-old Philadelphia-born writer who began writing for Jans Pictures in

1919 and Metro in 1920.[31] They met just after Paul arrived in L.A. and remained close for the rest of Paul's life.

In the spring of 1921, Wilson invited Paul to share his house in the 1400 block of Kings Road in the hills above Sunset Boulevard. Paul moved in during April or May but kept his Georgia Street apartment. Wilson's aging two-story, tile-roof Spanish hacienda hung precariously to the edge of a hillside with a long second floor balcony overlooking a canyon below and the Hollywood Hills above. Colleen Moore described the shabby house as "a miserable, run-down place."[32]

Kings Road became the most notorious bachelor hang-out in Hollywood, a reputation cemented later that summer when John Gilbert moved in with one of his Philippine houseboys.[33] Gilbert—Jack to his friends—had already done 50 films and was a rising star and he and Wilson became Paul's closest friends. It was an odd pairing, Paul the cultured thinker and Wilson and Gilbert acknowledged cocksmen.

Years later, Paul was unfairly criticized for problems with women but Gilbert's tortured relationships were legend. His obsessive affair with Greta Garbo—who flip-flopped over her feelings for him and twice left him at the altar—lasted for years and eventually drove him to an alcoholic death. First wife Leatrice Joy was devoted to director Cecil B. DeMille, who controlled his stars on- and off-screen, and whenever DeMille (who hated Gilbert) suggested to Joy she should separate from her husband, incredibly she did. During one of the frequent DeMille-orchestrated separations, Gilbert moved in at Kings Road.[34]

With the addition of the hard-partying Gilbert, the bachelor house on the hill above Sunset was soon known for wild parties and the strange goings-on of its crazed inhabitants. Known at the studios simply as "Kings Road," the house, residents, and activities

Paul shared a Kings Road hacienda with Carey Wilson and John Gilbert (pictured) in 1921.

became legend. According to Colleen Moore, "[T]hose three *nuts* lived there. They were very witty and very bright. The parties were incredible. *The ordinary days* were incredible. Once they almost blew up the place experimenting with aniline dyes. There always seemed to be a near-fatal accident in that place but things always turned out all right."[35]

The three were always fiddling with *something*. The aniline (purple) dye experiment left the house reeking of rotting fish for a month. They probably didn't know that prolonged exposure to aniline fumes can be lethal. Another project involving roulette wheels; two dozen of them were set up throughout the house in an effort to figure out how to beat the game. At Kings Road, it was always something, and it usually involved women and liquor- or drug-fueled parties.

Charlie Chaplin lived just down the hill and was a constant visitor. Almost nightly he wandered up to check the in-house gin distillery or thumb through Paul's massive book collection to research the afterlife. Chaplin and Paul spent many evenings at Kings Road discussing Chaplin's fascination with death or communing with the dead via spirit-writing, séances, mediums, and Ouija boards.

During July, 1921, Harry Houdini was in L.A. working on *The Soul of Bronze* when he met Gilbert and was invited to Kings Road to explore the Ouija board and spiritualism with them. Houdini spent his life exposing fake spiritualists and agreed to host a séance for a group that included the housemates, Chaplin and Gilbert's wife Leatrice. During the séance the heavy teak table lifted off the floor, shook and finally crashed into the wall, pinning a terrified Gilbert.[36] After Gilbert ran howling from the house, Houdini showed the group how he had rigged the table with a method used by fake mediums.

Paul fit in perfectly with Wilson and Gilbert. He was well-liked and had a sparkling sense of humor, evidenced by a later letter to Goldwyn Studio business manager H.E. Edington:

My dear Harry,

The unfeeling Tax Department of the State of New York insists on my paying a tax to that noble Commonwealth for the year 1920. Unfortunately, the money which the Goldwyn Company paid me that year was so little that the distance of two years has caused the amount to disappear entirely from my mind. I must, therefore, ask your good offices to let me know how little I received that year so that I can make the proper report.

Best, Regards, Sincerely,
Paul Bern.

He later wrote Edington mentioning *What Ho!—The Cook!*, "Please be sure and do not include the bonus I received for helping to launch *What*

Ho!—The Cook! upon an unsuspecting and defenseless world."[37] He was well known for his sense of humor and whimsy and had many friends.

That summer Paul met another woman whose legacy would be tied to him forever. Unlike his unconfirmed relationship with Mabel, Paul did fall in love with Barbara La Marr, who first arrived at Kings Road on the arm of John Gilbert in June, 1921. Gilbert was enduring another DeMille-choreographed separation from Leatrice and took up with La Marr, who was a fixture at Kings Road that summer. Barely 24, she was still married to her fourth husband (actor Ben Deeley) when her affair with Gilbert began.[38]

She was born Reatha Deane Watson in 1896 in Yakima, Washington, and her life was marked with scandal.[39] After her family moved to the remote border town of El Centro in southeastern California, the 16-year-old accused her married half-sister and a friend of kidnapping her. Just a month later she eloped with nearby rancher Jack Lytelle and moved to Arizona, returning three months later claiming that Lytelle had died.

In early January 1914 she ran away to L.A., moved into the downtown Rockwood Apartments and got a job as a burlesque dancer, but was arrested on the 23rd for being underage.[40] A social worker said, "There is no charge against Miss Watson unless it is that she is dangerously beautiful.... There is a constant danger hanging over girls of such remarkable beauty as Miss Watson who are alone in the city." A juvenile court judge told her, "You are too beautiful to be allowed alone in the big city. You are too beautiful to be without constant protection from your parents at your age." He ordered her to return home or be named a ward of the court and headlines blared **BEAUTY TOO DANGEROUS — GIRL ORDERED FROM CITY.**[41]

Los Angeles Herald beat writer Adela Rogers St. Johns was at the courthouse that day and described Watson as "the most beautiful girl I or anybody else had ever seen" and wrote that the first time she saw her, "[I] lost my breath."[42] St. Johns took the young girl back to the paper's offices and the *Herald* ran a three-page story about "The Too Beautiful Girl." Her tale was told across the country.

Three months later, on June 2, 1914, Watson married Max Lawrence, a man she'd met a week earlier. St. Johns was invited to the wedding and pictures ran in papers; it was soon discovered that Max was Lawrence F. Converse, a married man with three children. The enraged Mrs. Converse called police and the honeymooners were met in San Francisco; he was arrested and charged with bigamy. Headlines blared **ONE WIFE TOO MANY!** He knocked himself unconscious banging his head against his cell door and told the court he had no recollection of the wedding.[43]

Watson wanted to be a movie actress but her notoriety left her *persona non grata* at studios. In an unusual move, several studios publicly announced "the doors of the studios in and around L.A. have been closed ... and her escapades too widely advertised." One studio manager said, "We don't want public characters or limelight beauties in our pictures...."[44] Reatha left L.A. for San Francisco and became a cabaret dancer known as Folly Lytell.[45] She and partner Phillip Ainsworth were the hit of the 1915 San Francisco World's Fair and they married October 13, 1916, but he left three months later because of her affairs.[46] She toured the Orpheum circuit as Barbara La Mar with Carvelle, La Mar and Carvelle (the second "r" in La Marr wasn't added until she returned to the movies) before moving to New York with entertainer Ben Deeley and marrying him in September, 1918, in Fort Lee, New Jersey. Her divorce from Ainsworth was not yet finalized.[47]

As Barbara La Marr Deeley, she wrote six scenarios for Fox before moving to L.A. in late 1919 and into a downtown apartment at 106 East Washington.[48] She hid her identity and worked as a $10 daily extra on films like Anita Stewart's *Harriett and the Piper* and Shirley Mason's *The Flame of Youth*. She caught Douglas Fairbanks' eye filming *The Nut* in early 1921 and he tapped her for the role of Milady de Winter in *The Three Musketeers*. Fans learned she was the "Girl Who Was too Beautiful" and they adored her, literally gasping during on-screen close-ups.

She took up with Gilbert during *Musketeers* filming and during her Kings Road visits became friendly with Paul. *Musketeers* propelled her to stardom amid stories of her healthy appetite for men, sex and parties. She rarely slept more than two hours a night, saying, "Eight hours of sleep out of twenty-four — how ridiculous. When life is so short and so delightful, why should we spend a third of the precious hours in a coma?"[49] Her hillside Spanish hacienda at 6672½ Whitley Terrace in Whitley Heights had several passageways from her bedroom, one to the chauffeur's quarters and another to the street-level garage above the house.[50] She reportedly kept her cocaine stash in a miniature gold-plated piano.

Gilbert and La Marr quickly tired of each other and he returned to Leatrice but Paul remained fascinated by La Marr. Through the late summer and fall of 1921 he pursued her with gifts and flowers. They were a couple for most of 1922. According to St. Johns, La Marr considered Paul "her best, her only, man friend,"[51] a telling comment given La Marr's complete disregard for and chronic mistreatment of most men in her life. St. Johns said La Marr rejected romantic involvement with Paul but they did have a very strong relationship. According to Paul's brother Henry, if it weren't for Dorothy — who Paul perhaps still believed might be somehow cured — Paul would have married La Marr.[52]

La Marr no doubt realized the incongruity of her love for a man like Paul, so different from her previous lovers. She gave him a silver cocktail shaker engraved, *To Paul, May the phantom hand of memory soothe thee now though tomorrow you mayeth regret me. B. La Marr 1922.*[53]

She knew her life was a roller coaster that often spun out of control. As a teenager she complained that "people watch her rather than watching *over* her" because of her looks.[54] The romance with Paul lasted late into 1922 but she was described by Paul's friend Al Lewin as just another "Pygmalion" for Paul. If *any* of his female friends needed transforming it was the tragic La Marr.

The year had been a financial disaster for the industry, described by Goldwyn biographer Scott Berg as "a tide of recession" washing over the movies.[55] Goldwyn was on perilous financial footing. He owned hundreds of under-performing theaters and was reeling from Godsol's ongoing palace coup. Releases were only marginally successful, mostly forgettable films like *A Voice in the Dark*, *The Ten Dollar Raise*, and *The Old Nest*. Revenues were less than half of expenses; the Kodak film delivery man would not leave film unless he was paid in cash.[56]

To increase revenues, Goldwyn contracted with Italian film company Inione Cinematrografica Italiana to distribute their films in the U.S. The first, *Theodora*, was a commercial success, earning $10,000 premiums from the 55 largest exhibitors, but the temporary elixir didn't stop the problems.[57]

The beautiful and volatile Barbara La Marr.

Payroll was paid late, vendor payments delayed, and virtually every contract was either cancelled or allowed to expire. Goldwyn said, "Stars are to be eliminated from this company's program" and he would make "pictures at a lower cost. Salaries are being reduced and expenditures watched with a careful eye ... so motion pictures remained a popular priced amusement."[58] He said the studio needed to "use scenic suggestion instead of realism.... Instead of building a whole new town, show an atmospheric bit of town, which because of the power of suggestion will be more effective than the complete town. That is the method of the artist who paints pictures instead of photographing them."[59] He was less concerned with affordable moves than with salvaging his studio but he was little more than a lame duck due to Godsol's machinations.

Departments were reorganized and on August 13, Paul was promoted to editor in charge of the scenario department, succeeding J.G. Hawks. Ralph Block and Clayton Hamilton were his assistants.[60] He was responsible for the entire scenario department (the writers, all script development and script approval). It was a huge promotion after a short tenure. He was also consulted on production and direction questions.

Goldwyn's difficulties were *helping* Paul. He was given promotions while others were let go. If he could wait out the industry downturn and the Goldwyn-Godsol civil war, he would be in a good spot.

Paul's talented staff included Rupert Hughes (uncle of Howard), LeRoy Scott, Thompson Buchanan, Clayton Hamilton, Alice Duer Miller, and Kathleen Norris.[61] The directing staff featured Frank Lloyd, Clarence Badger, Harry Beaumont, T. Hayes Hunter, Victor Schertzinger, and Reginald Barker. There were a few name stars left like Irene Rich, Betty Compson, Mabel Normand, Jack Holt, House Peters, and Tom Moore but most roles were assigned to lower-priced stock company actors like Helene Chadwick, Cullen Landis, and John Bowers.[62]

At the time of his promotion, Paul was directing *The Man with Two Mothers*, which began production in July. Tom Moore was originally slated for the lead but at the last minute was replaced by Cullen Landis, a lower-cost stock player. The original female lead — never publicly identified — was also replaced by Sylvia Breamer, who was "recalled from her New York vacation."[63]

Mothers was a reunion for Paul and Mary Alden, a classmate from the American Academy, which was mentioned in the papers.[64] She was one of the few successes from Paul's class, a veteran of 60+ films when she signed with Goldwyn in 1920.

Irishman Dennis O'Neill (Landis) lives with his widowed mother (Alden) and learns his American uncle left him a fortune. But he must go to New York to live with and care for his aunt to receive his inheritance. When they arrive, his aunt — an Irish immigrant pretending she is not from humble origins — tells O'Neill his mother can't stay but he sneaks her into an apartment with his friend Tim Donohue. She goes quietly, knowing Bryan's "second mother" offers her son a life she cannot. Dennis falls in love with distant cousin Clare Mordaunt (Breamer) and learns the manager of the family business and his assistant are stealing from the company. The manager tells Clare that Dennis is keeping another woman at an apartment and after Dennis beats the man in a tremendous fistfight, saves the company, introduces his mother and wins Claire.[65]

Goldwyn surprisingly allowed Paul free rein making *Mothers*. Amid the studio cost-cutting, Paul built an Irish fishing village on the lot, a strange accommodation given Goldwyn's position on spending and the fact that the village was only featured in a few scenes early in the film.[66]

The climactic fight between Landis and William Elmer took place on September 23, the last day of filming. Paul told them a realistic fight was important and they shouldn't overtly fake punches. The fight between the athletic Landis and Elmer — a boxing aficionado who sparred with Jim Corbett — provoked lively betting among studio workers. Hundreds surrounded the soundstage and watched from every window, walkway and rooftop. They were not disappointed; for six minutes the actors beat each other without quarter. When Paul finally yelled "cut!" both were disheveled and bloodied. Landis had two black eyes, a bruised cheek and a dislocated thumb and Elmer black eyes and deep cuts in his forehead that required a dozen stitches to close.[67]

Mothers was scheduled for release in early 1922 and for the first time ads noted a film "directed by Paul Bern, now Editor in Chief at the Goldwyn Studio."[68] While he made *Mothers*, his year-old screenplay *Suspicious Wives* was released by Trojan Film Company. His friend John Stahl directed the six-reel feature that starred H.J. Herbert and Mollie King, who also starred in Paul's *Women Men Forget*.[69] The plot features the themes common in Paul's early writings: infidelity, family misunderstandings, and a secret location where the climactic action takes place.

In *Women Men Forget*, the feuding couple is James (Herbert) and Molly Brunton (King), who split up because Molly wrongly believes her husband was unfaithful. She finds sanctuary with an elderly couple in their remote farmhouse without learning the other woman was James' sister-in-law. While searching for Molly, James is injured and temporarily blinded in an automobile accident and coincidently is carried to his wife's farm where she nurses him back to health. He isn't aware it is Molly until his sight is restored when his sister-in-law arrives to clear things up and they are reconciled.[70] The film earned good reviews after its New York premiere on September 1.

Paul's rapid ascent at Goldwyn was chronicled in papers and magazines. He'd only been directing for a short time but was featured in a half-dozen interviews about the technical side of filmmaking. He also wrote a long article for the respected *Photojournalist* magazine in the summer of 1921.[71]

In a September interview he explained that Goldwyn was "in the market and particularly anxious to secure some stories."[72] That's not surprising since most of the writing staff either quit or was let go during the previous eight months. Paul never told writers what kind of stories he wanted because that led them to produce what they thought the studios wanted. He said Goldwyn would "make really big pictures" but no light comedies, nothing designed for a specific star (Goldwyn had few of those anyway), and no costume stories or westerns. In short, nothing expensive.

Paul suggested a need for "inventiveness" from writers who recognized the "fundamental human relationships" that resulted in "terrific dramatic clashes," but he warned that drama should never lead to heaviness or morbidity that loses the viewer's interest. Stories should be written, he thought, as an "original effort expressed in picture terms and born of a picture mind." He summed up by saying, "No formula can be written to express (how to appeal to audiences), for any formula would merely act in a limiting, repressive manner, and would defeat our purpose of trying to secure fresh, untrammeled, novel stories, ideas and twists." Goldwyn's financial situation meant *finding* stories because the cost of buying star features was out of the studio's financial reach.

Paul was leading a change in writing style for movies, opining that scenarios should be created expressly in the language of the screen, that "the new sort of writer must be born ... to satisfy the demands of the screen. With few exceptions everything ... screened to date was originally written in a form of expression for centuries past — stage, novel, short story, etc. In many cases of works written directly for the screen, the writers have been so under the domination of these earlier forms of expression that scenarios were written [as if they were for] books while movies were a subsidiary consideration."[73]

He knew movie writers had to be *developed*; they weren't born and studios needed "a school of writers who will throw away completely the idea of writing novels and write screen material purely.... This will need a complete change of training, and, even more, a complete liberation from the technical forms being taught." Paul believed that there was not yet a "single screen writer, in the pure sense of the word, existing today, because even the best of those who have written excellent screen material have done it by adaptation of ideas which have been formulated [in books or plays]. The great screen play will be written only when it is purely original effort, expressed in picture terms, born of a picture medium.... [T]he potential of the camera [is] enormous, and we should tell our stories thru some of the, as yet, secret ways which are possible only on screen."

Paul saw movies as a medium in its infancy. His writing and directing style — telling a story through the eyes of more than one actor, sometimes as many as three or four — was innovative. But he understood film's ability to present a new perspective to audiences, one he described as "the possibility of seeing life as the blind man 'sees' it, without perspective, with the object terrible and distorted. We can also see life as it appears to the child, with a world of gigantic adults walking about among enormous buildings and objects." He understood film could show thought, a new avenue, and his films began to evidence that. He was described as "one of the most progressive motion picture directors"[74] in Hollywood.

Technically he believed a movie should be a "straight-running story" done a new way; that, "when motion pictures were in their infancy, using retrospect to fill in gaps ... cutting back to years previous ... confused viewers. Directors should use as little retrospect as possible...." Paul thought viewers liked well-developed stories told somewhat chronologically without a lot of cutbacks to remind them of plot. He thought audiences were smart enough to follow without coaching and had become an adept story-teller.

He looked for stories everywhere. He had dozens of small-town papers sent to the studio for script readers to study because local reporters were "much closer to people and events than big metropolitan journals. There is enough drama and comedy in every issue of newspaper to make a good photoplay if the reader can only see it."[75]

In late 1921 the industry and the Goldwyn Studio were at a crossroad. Over 85 percent of the world's movies were made in the U.S. but for several years cost pressures, legal investigations of industry trade practices, and rising public resentment were all taking heavy tolls. It came to a head on August 30. The Federal Trade Commission charged Jesse Lasky with restraint of trade for block-booking policies that forced distributors to buy low-quality films to get popular titles. Studio theater ownership also came under scrutiny.[76] Worse, a tide of censorship fervor was rising. Many stars — like Francis X. Bushman, Bessie Love, Clara Kimball Young, Mae Marsh and Carlyle Blackwell — went back to the stage to wait out the upheaval.[77]

A major studio problem was a change in the public acceptance of what their stars did. Stars had always been bulletproof; they could do anything they wanted without repercussion. The public had turned a blind eye until the late 1920 deaths of Robert Harron and Olive Thomas because few stories actually leaked out of Hollywood but by September, 1921, almost 40 states were considering censorship laws. Peccadilloes that had remained private were discussed openly in papers. Jesse Lasky said, "Churches, women's clubs, and reformers had blood in their eyes over Hollywood's sinfulness and the moral laxness in some films."[78]

The six months beginning that September were pivotal in movie history because of several events that altered forever the studio landscape and the public perception of stars, leading to a massive industry realignment. The deaths of Harron and Thomas were like lights going on for movie fans, but the litany of smaller problems climaxed with the Roscoe Arbuckle scandal and the murder of William Desmond Taylor, two events that brought the industry to its knees.

Roscoe Arbuckle — "Fatty" to fans but never to his friends — was a $3-

a-day extra in 1913 but by 1921 earned $3,000,000 a year and owned a 649 West Adams mansion and a $250,000 custom-made Pierce-Arrow equipped with a bar and toilet. His first 12 films for Jesse Lasky and Adolph Zukor made millions but Lasky still bristled at paying the biggest contract in history: $7,500 a week for three films a year. Arbuckle deserved it but Lasky and Zukor somehow felt extorted.

Exhausted after completing his three films, Arbuckle drove to San Francisco for a Labor Day stay in a three-room 12th floor suite at the St. Francis Hotel overlooking Union Square. One uninvited guest to his weekend party was actress Virginia Rappe, who became violently ill and was rushed to nearby Wakefield Sanitarium. A concerned Arbuckle phoned and said, "She'll be all right. I'm leaving by steamer for L.A. tomorrow morning. If everything doesn't go smoothly you know where to call me. And send the bills to Anger."[79] He paid his $611.43 hotel bill and left for L.A. on the S.S. *California*.[80]

On Friday, Rappe died from peritonitis caused by an infected bladder, probably from a botched abortion (her sixth). Wakefield was a maternity hospital, supporting the theory she underwent an abortion, performed by the same doctor who cared for her and assisted in her autopsy. When Arbuckle got home, police returned him to San Francisco and he almost fainted when told he "was to be held without bail for the murder of Virginia Rappe."

He was pilloried in the press. Unfounded rumors that Rappe was violated with a Coca-Cola or champagne bottle or a piece of furniture and infected with gonorrhea are still believed today (she did have gonorrhea when she died).[81] Headlines screamed **TORTURE OF RAPPE CHARGED** and **ARBUCKLE DRAGGED WOMEN TO ROOM**.[82] But Hollywood knew her reputation; Mack Sennett fumigated his studio *twice* to remove "crab" infestations after the amoral Rappe's visits.[83] Before she took ill, she had sex with the hotel detective.

Arbuckle was indicted for manslaughter and Lasky and Zukor let him hang even though they had millions invested in movies ready for release. His blockbuster *Gasoline Alley* was pulled from 3,200 theaters while Rappe's 11 awful films were featured. Theaters offered **SPECIAL ADDED ATTRACTION!!! Virginia Rappe in *A Twilight Baby*.**[84] The meaningless film had been out of theaters for over a year.

At Arbuckle's legal proceedings, witnesses lied embarrassingly. The worst was ugly, disagreeable Bambina Maude Delmont, a con woman with 50 arrests for prostitution and bigamy who sold herself to lawyers as bait to trap married men in adultery and who wired her lawyers, "WE HAVE ROSCOE ARBUCKLE IN A HOLE HERE. STOP. CHANCE TO MAKE MONEY OFF HIM. STOP."[85] Over 30 of the 40 prosecution witnesses weren't even at the party and even with all the perjured testimony the jury still wouldn't convict Arbuckle; on December 2 the jury hung voting 10 to 2 for acquittal. Corrupt D.A. Matthew Brady announced a second trial for January 11, 1922.[86]

As 1921 came to a close amidst the tumult, Paul was involved in several projects, the E. Mason Hopper-directed *Hungry Hearts* and the Carey Wilson scenario *Broken Chains* among them. Both were scheduled for production later in the spring of 1922. In December he traveled to New York to meet with Goldwyn's East Coast writing and casting departments. It's unknown whether he visited Dorothy, even whether she was still at Blythewood or had moved to the Algonquin, but his New York trips usually meant a trip to New Rochelle to visit Henry, his wife Miriam, and their children Gerald, Gordon, Raymond and Barbara, who looked forward to "Uncle Paul's" visits.[87]

Heading into 1922, the second Arbuckle trial was front page news. D.A. Brady couldn't even call his original witnesses, so many had recanted and admitted they were told to lie. On February 3 another jury hung amid rumors Brady paid for the guilty votes. Looking more and more like a criminal himself, Brady said he would try Arbuckle yet again.

The trial was pushed from the headlines by perhaps the biggest Hollywood scandal to that time and Paul was dragged into the tumult due to his friendship with Mabel Normand. On February 3 the headline **Arbuckle Jury Still Held Up** ran below the more urgent **MYSTERY GUNMAN KILLS FILM DIRECTOR TAYLOR!!!**[88]

On the day Virginia Rappe was buried, the new president of the Motion Picture Directors Association had promised that Hollywood would "clean house" and make "the cleanest of films."[89] He was Lasky's chief director William Desmond Taylor, "a cultured, dignified gentleman with a charming personality and considerable magnetism." His Paramount bio said he was born in Kansas, prospected in the Klondike, served in the Canadian Army and earned medals for heroism at Dunkirk. But in truth he was William Cunningham Deane-Tanner, owned a New York antique shop, was married to ex–Floradora actress Ethel May Harrison and had a daughter named Daisy. He walked out on all of it in 1908 but when his family saw him in a 1916 movie and tracked him to Vitagraph, he secretly supported them from Hollywood.

On February 1 he spent the afternoon with Lasky discussing a Mary Miles Minter film and the next morning his butler found him on the floor in his Lake Terrace Court bungalow at 404 South Alvarado.[90] Lake Terrace was filled with movie people. Chaplin actress Edna Purviance lived on one side and comedian Douglas MacLean the other, separated from Taylor by a dark, eight-foot wide alley from the courtyard out to the street.

Police thought Taylor suffered a heart attack but two hours later his body was rolled over and a bullet hole found in his back and a pool of blood on the floor.[91] Minutes after police arrived, Taylor's friend and Paramount manager Charles Eyton arrived, gathered papers from the bedroom, burned some in the fireplace and left with the rest.[92] Teenager Minter arrived in her robin's-egg Cadillac roadster, doors emblazoned with her signature butterfly emblem in gold. She wailed over the body, ran upstairs and rummaged through his desk.

In his bureau, police found a pink nightgown in a box and in his riding boots a lace handkerchief monogrammed "M.M.M." and love letters scribbled in schoolyard code signed "Mary," written on Minter's butterfly stationary. Three strands of long blonde hair under the collar of Taylor's coat matched hair from Minter's brush.[93] Taylor's valet laundered his suits daily so police knew Minter was with him the day he was killed.[94]

McLean's wife told police she heard a gunshot the night before and saw someone hurry out the alley in a long coat with a high collar, scarf and a hat.[95] There was no shortage of suspects. His first wife. Chauffeur Dennis (or Denis) Sands, who may have been his brother, a career criminal. Drug dealers angry with Taylor for public anti-drug posturing. Even director Marshall (Mickey) Neilan, who was in love with Minter. Of course, Minter herself. The chief suspect was her mother, Charlotte Shelby, who knew that her daughter and 50-year-old Taylor were having a relationship. Unfortunately for Paul, Mabel was also a suspect. Mabel was the last person to see Taylor alive, leaving Lake Terrace just before he was shot. Two pictures were on his piano, one signed by Mary Pickford and the other by Minter. ("For William Desmond Taylor, artist and gentleman, Mary Miles Minter.")

At a 1996 symposium at the University of Southern California, Budd Schulberg (son of Paramount executive B.P.) described the pervasive corruption in L.A. in the 1920s: "I always thought of Hollywood like a principality ... and the people who ran it really had that attitude.... Their power was absolutely enormous.... They could cover up a murder. You could literally have somebody killed and it wouldn't be in the papers." The D.A.'s office had effectively been for sale for years. Thomas L. Woolwine was certainly not the first dishonest D.A. but his tenure (1914–1923) coincided with huge industry growth and he oversaw and profited from hundreds of cover-ups. He kept the Taylor evidence at his home and told the grand jury he "lost" it. He lost the only copy of Shelby's grand jury testimony. Incredibly, in 1926 what little remained was stolen in Chicago. His successor Asa Keyes was carrying it around in a briefcase.[96]

The Minter revelations were a bombshell but strangely Shelby was never formally questioned. When Woolwine was run out of office in 1923, his relationship with Shelby was uncovered. Her alibi, provided by Woolwine's top investigator Jim Smith, didn't come cheaply. Shelby told her accountant that Woolwine's replacement "would require a lot more money than Woolwine."[97]

The firestorm from the Taylor revelations washed over the industry like a tidal wave and splashed Paul because of his friendship with Mabel. Like Paul, Taylor cared for Mabel and tried to get her off drugs, even arranging the year-long East Coast exile from which Normand had just returned. Public criticism was directed at her because of her raucous lifestyle. Paul knew she would be targeted and as soon as he heard about Taylor's death rushed to Mabel's Vermont Street mansion and waded through a throng of reporters and photographers waving his cane and threatening to kill them if they didn't leave her alone for a few hours.[98] It would only be a temporary reprieve, however.

Woolwine allowed papers to identify Mabel as a suspect to help distance the Minter family from suspicion, and one headline said **Drug-Crazed Film Queen is Murder Suspect**.[99] Paul's relationship with Mabel was well-known so his name arose in the middle of everything as, of all things, a fellow suspect! On February 14, Wallace Smith, writing for the sensationalist *Chicago American*, was the first to mention rumors linking Mabel and Paul:

One of filmland's leading actresses, the adored darling of thousands of movie fans throughout the country, will be placed under arrest within a week in connection with the murder of William Desmond Taylor.... With her will be arrested — and charged directly with the crime — a man high in the moving picture industry and one whose name before today was shielded in the tragic puzzle.... [She] is known as a woman who for a long time conducted an affair with one of the star producers of moving pictures ... wanted to tell his story of the actress' affairs and especially her associations since she took up the morphine habit and became a leader in Hollywood's "dope parties."[100]

Paul was the "man high in the moving picture industry" mentioned as a suspect. Interestingly, the relationship was described as "...a weird narrative of love and an insane jealousy that was known to but few of the film folks...." Papers said he was to attend the annual ball of the American Society of Cinematographers on February 4 at the Ambassador with Mabel but went alone as she avoided "THE social event of the season."[101] Her seclusion only added to the suspicion surrounding the pair.

Scandals big and small left the industry reeling as cries to clean up Hollywood grew louder. On February 9 the *Chicago American* noted, "Stars of the movies, idols ... beautiful women and athletic men, are being destroyed by the use of drugs."[102] Pulpits and papers demanded reform. Stars were no longer immune from accountability. They were under attack.

The industry tried to deflect the criticism with stories of their own. Adela Rogers St. Johns described life in Hollywood as "pretty dull ... a good place to rest up. No cabarets. No place to dance. An occasional party...."[103] Addressing Taylor and Minter she asked, "[W]ho shot Bill Taylor? Suppose Mary

Miles Minter was in love with him. She's an unmarried girl.... Bill Taylor was a big, fascinating, strong man. No wonder."[104]

Something had to be done or public devotion could be mortally injured. Louis B. Mayer quietly led the formation of the Motion Picture Producers and Distributors of America, which inserted morals clauses in contracts and wrote a Code of Conduct. Indianan Will H. Hays — the ex-postmaster general who was himself scandal-ridden after taking bribes during the Teapot Dome scandal[105] — was paid $100,000 a year to run the MPPDA. His office had no real "teeth." Mayer actually brought him in to avoid looming state censorship. Even so, it would be five years before Hays released his list of 11 "don'ts" and 27 "be carefuls."[106]

Normand was understandably crushed by the death of her close friend and, hounded by the press, hid out at Kings Road for a month with Paul. After completing *Susanna* for Mack Sennett she escaped to Europe for six more months while Goldwyn took advantage of the scandal by finally releasing *Head Over Heels* in April. The uproar resulted in better box office than the film would have earned but as biographer Betty Fussell noted, by then she was "dying by inches." So apparently was Goldwyn.

Goldwyn's cost-cutting couldn't stop the climax of the Godsol-orchestrated coup. After a 1921 loss of $686,827, on March 22 the Godsol-led board of directors ousted Goldwyn from the studio that carried his name. He took his $600,000 severance to New York.

Just before Goldwyn's exit, Paul's film *The Man with Two Mothers* premiered to good reviews, described as "well acted and cleverly made, [and holding] interest from beginning to end."[107] Paul received kudos for bringing "out the comedy and the Irish characterizations with deftness and sympathy."[108] It remained in theaters as late as September.[109]

During Paul's late 1921–early 1922 visit to New York, he met with casting director Robert McIntyre, who was working with the winners of his nationwide "New Faces" contest, William Haines and Eleanor Boardman. She was starring in the play *The National Anthem* when she lost her voice. Assuming her stage career over, she entered Goldwyn's contest and won over 1,000 entrants.

Paul was present for her screen test, which went poorly. Nerves and inexperience left her utterly unable to emote for a camera. McIntyre was ready to audition another actress when Paul stepped in, tutored Boardman on acting for a camera and convinced McIntyre to give her a second test. The retake went better and in March she and Haines left for Hollywood, each with a $50-a-week contract in hand. If not for Paul, Eleanor Boardman would not have become a star.

While in New York, Paul also spoke to film production and cinema composition classes at the prestigious Columbia University film school with fellow Goldwyn writer Rupert Hughes.[110] Paul was described as "one of the most progressive of motion picture directors" and was already known for experimenting with new and different story-telling techniques.[111] He was still preaching his gospel of avoiding retrospective to coach viewers: "Retrospect tends to confuse the sequence of the picture. Now that the art is becoming more finished, it is the object of the director to make pictures with as little retrospect as possible. The straight running story, especially in the comedy type of picture, is the one the audience enjoys best, I believe."[112]

Goldwyn production had come to a virtual standstill while Godsol reorganized and then proceeded only in fits and starts. In May a freer hand and more responsibility for the film editing process was given to the edit staff and since Paul was the *de facto* leader of that group, Godsol was recognizing him by redesigning processes to fit Paul's strategies. Before, the editor reported to and received direction from the production supervisor, limiting editor input and limiting new ideas. Going forward, films would be assigned to specific editors, who were given considerable latitude creating the final product. Paul's first assignments under the new guidelines were *The Christian* and *Under the Skin*.[113]

Paul became the public voice of the studio, giving regular newspaper and magazine interviews about all aspects of filmmaking. He believed better stories meant better movies and as simple as it sounds, some studios still didn't even have separate scenario departments. Even though Jesse Lasky formed the first scenario department in 1915, other studios were slow to follow. A milestone was reached in 1919 when Joe Schenck hired John Emerson and Anita Loos to write for Constance and Norma Talmadge.[114] It was "a significant new direction in motion pictures" because Emerson and Loos were consulted during filming and had approval over the final product.[115]

Paul drafted a detailed memorandum to his writers describing his theories about audiences. He believed domestic films were more popular than imports because they showed "life more truly as it is being lived by the people." European films were often showpieces for the directors' artistic ideals.

Paul believed moviegoers went to theaters to "purchase the riddle of the Universe" and "solve all the problems that afflict mankind by escaping from them." His romantic notion was that audiences wanted to feel that theirs was the best possible world and that "everything comes out right in the end." When writer Jim Tully asked him why the beautiful film *The Girl I Loved* was not a financial success, Paul said simply, "[T]he picture was a thing of beauty and emotion, but failed *because the boy did not get the girl*."[116] To Paul, moviemaking was a simple thing: produce a beautiful product with a happy ending.

He said a "background [in the people] is invaluable in making a picture commercially acceptable,"[117] that "some resemblance to life as it is" needed to be present and "the use of fundamental human relationships, resulting in terrific dramatic clashes, is definitely desirable." His films were relationship stories that appeal to the masses.[118]

His ideas about character development offered a view of how he thought and his interest in the mind, harkening back to his discussions of Freud and psychoanalysis with Edward Bernays. Paul believed developing character motivation and getting "into a character's mind and to picture what is going on there" should be the writer's goal, using a confused wife as an example: "All her inner life is conflict, a surging maelstrom of passionate cross currents. And yet, in pictures, we get only the facial expression to indicate the struggle. But suppose you could get into this woman's mind and visualize the conflict. On the one hand, thoughts of herself and her lover together; a vision of herself at the altar, making the sacred promise; again the urge of passion; then the thought of her baby.... The possibilities are immense."[119]

He said, "[I]t is almost impossible to transfer a book to the screen without losing much of its essential flavor.... [A] novel is expository, largely concerned with the inward development of the character, the motives, the impulses which influence their actions. Up to now it has been necessary to discard practically all these delicate shadings and confine the motion picture to a record of actions."

Paul was describing the evolution that began when feature-length films replaced 10-minute shorts. He believed better story-telling and subtle character development were keys to the acceptance of longer films. His use of subtlety was seen in Mabel Normand's transformation in *Head Over Heels* two years earlier when her tomboy character enters a beauty shop and quietly exits a beautiful woman, *visually* showing the audience there was a woman underneath the character mature enough for the love that was key to the plot.

Paul believed visual tools scratched the surface, and that "psychoanalysis will open the way to a picturization of dream action," making film a better story-telling vehicle than stage or books. He believed neither allowed the interpretation of dreams that could be visualized in film, that it "...is the key to the door through which we may envision the workings of the human mind, the most fascinating, the most absorbing of all action. The motion picture of the future will be a medium infinitely expressive which will need no words to convey its meaning. It will speak in a language of symbols which are older than race itself and which will be clear to the simplest mind."

Lack of character development was a common critique of early film. When *London Post* art critic Walter Bayes admonished filmmakers for their inability to "show things through a character's eye," he singled out Paul as among only a few filmmakers willing to try doing so.[120] Whether Paul's interest in psychoanalysis and the human mind grew from the circumstances of his mother's death, his deep interest was clear from interviews. Above all he believed creativity should reign, that no "formula" could be created.[121]

He was always looking for writers and actors and was free with his help. Late that spring, Kansas City–born Stanley Smith walked into his office. Smith grew up in Hollywood and answered mail for actor Elliott Dexter but couldn't get an entrée into the studios, writing letters to everyone from D.W. Griffith to Cecil B. DeMille. He visited Paul, who arranged a meeting at Pathé (and a role in *The Sophomore*) and then Paramount, where he would appear in almost 40 films opposite stars like Clara Bow, Nancy Carroll and Ginger Rogers. He credited Paul for his career.[122]

Paul was working on the immigrant saga *Hungry Hearts*, was in pre-production for *The Christian* and *Under the Skin*, and was helping Carey Wilson writing and pre-production for *Broken Chains*. All were scheduled for summer filming.

Hungry Hearts was based on a 1920 novel by Anzia Yesierska and Paul was credited as post-production supervisor. Credit for the scenario went to Julien Josephson but given the theme — hardships faced by Jewish immigrants living on New York's Lower East Side — it would be surprising if Paul were not involved.

Abraham and Hannah Levin and their children come to New York and experience the challenges of immigrant life. Everyone in the family works but they still face enormous financial pressure and when their landlord raises their rent an enraged Hannah destroys much of their apartment and is promptly arrested and put on trial. Daughter Sara's (Helen Ferguson) beau, lawyer David Kaplan (Bryant Washburn), represents the family even though he is the landlord's nephew, and Hannah is acquitted. He marries Sara and moves the Levin family out of the city into his large suburban estate.[123] *Hearts* was released on November 26.

During that same period, Paul worked with Wilson on another family drama, *Broken Chains*. Paul is not credited as a writer — Tay Garnett, Winifred Campbell and Wilson were — but period newspaper stories listed Paul as among the writers. *Chains* was directed by Allen Holubar,[124] assisted by Nat Salmon, and Byron Haskin did the filming in the mountains near Santa Cruz in Poverty Flat and Boulder Creek.

Peter Wyndham (Malcolm McGregor) is disgusted with himself after cowardice stops him from helping beautiful Hortense Allen (Claire Windsor) during a jewel robbery. He retreats west and is quickly beaten by brutish local bully Boyan Boone (Ernest Torrence), but rallying his manhood he later beats up Boone and frees Boone's daughter Mercy (Colleen Moore) from his clutches.[125] The film premiered in New York and L.A. on December 10 and was well-received.

At Kings Road, things reached something of a climax that spring. At the end of May the housemates were invited to a housewarming at director Arthur Rosson's 233 Carmelina Avenue house in Brentwood. Coincidently, Leatrice Joy, who had just completed *Manslaughter*, was also invited. Joy and Gilbert were again separated and Jack arrived at the party with the lovely Bebe Daniels.

Gilbert was no longer seeing Barbara La Marr, who dated Paul for most of 1922, and he and Joy re-connected at the party and tried to leave quietly for Kings Road but were surrounded by cheering guests throwing rice. The next morning a laughing Paul woke the couple up by handing them a paper with the headline **THE GILBERTS DEFINITELY SEPARATE**.[126] She moved into Kings Road and become a surrogate den-mother to the men.

One morning not long after, Leatrice answered the door and found a tiny blonde on the doorstep. She introduced herself as Wilson's wife Hopie, from whom Carey separated before leaving New York a year earlier. The irrepressible Wilson had described his former wife as everything from a "blood-sucking, life destroying bitch" to a "monster ... a behemoth" who tried to kill him with an umbrella, quite the opposite image of the fragile beauty standing at the front door.[127]

Learning she was there, Wilson vaulted over the back porch railing down to the yard, slashed through the canvas roof of his convertible and roared down the hill. But a few days later he and his ex-wife reconciled and he moved out of Kings Road. When the Gilberts moved to an English bungalow at Sweetzer and Fountain a few months later, Paul returned to his Georgia Street apartment.

His next project was a scenario for *The Christian* he based on the play by Sir Hall Caine.[128] Maurice Tourneur directed one of the first all-star casts at Goldwyn since the 1921 upheaval, assisted by Cedric Gibbon and Charles Dorlan.

Childhood sweethearts Glory Quayle (Mae Busch) and John Storm (Richard Dix) leave the Isle of Man for London, where she wants to become a nurse and he — a Christian socialist who tries to live as Christ would have — is entering a monastery. But she becomes a famous stage star and he leaves the monastery and renounces his vows because he loves her. Lord Robert Ure becomes infatuated with Glory even after having an affair and betraying her friend Polly Love. To keep Glory from John, he incites the populace against John, claiming he has blasphemed by predicting the world will end soon. John believes he can only save Glory's soul by killing her and goes to do so but she convinces him of her love. A confused John then wanders the streets where is he is mortally beaten by an enraged mob. But before dying in Glory's arms, he marries her.[129]

The Christian premiered the following January 14 in Kansas City and opened nationally a week later. Crowds were awestruck by the exteriors filmed in London and the lavish interiors filmed in Hollywood. One critic described it as "one of the notable screen achievements of the year" and "the top of the list" of great films to see in 1923.[130]

Paul's next film had been originally titled *Under the Skin* but that was changed to *Captain Blackbird* to avoid confusion with another Goldwyn effort, *Brothers Under the Skin*.[131] The title was changed yet again to *Passions of the Sea* and then to *Lost and Found* before the final *Lost and Found on a South Sea Island*. It was filmed in the fall, directed by Raoul Walsh and based on a scenario written by Paul and Wilson. It was supposedly filmed in Tahiti but that seems unlikely given Goldwyn's financial pressures; also, no period stories mention any such trip. What *was* written described sets at Culver City.[132] It may have been filmed at Catalina Island since a complete Pago Pago jungle village sat above the Isthmus surrounded by an intricate rain-making system that was used for hundreds of films.[133] The filming was done by Clyde De Vinna and Paul Kerschner.[134] Lead actor House Peters' stunt double was William Haines.

Conniving white trader Faulke cruises the Pacific exploiting native tribesman but convinces Madge (Rosemary Theby) to take one of her daughters, Lorna (Pauline Starke), and leave her husband Captain Blackbird (Peters). She leaves another infant daughter with Blackbird and moves to a small island near Pago Pago with Faulke. Faulke wants Lorna to marry the native chief to further his ill-gotten commerce but she loves local sailor Lloyd Warren (Antonio Moreno) and flees with him to avoid the forced marriage. Blackbird sails into Pago Pago and is approached by Lloyd and Lorna for help but doesn't recognize his long-lost daughter at first. When he does, he returns to Faulke's island with his crew (Haines also appeared as a crew member), rescues Madge from the warring natives and reconciles with his wife.[135]

Moviegoers were fascinated with stories of island paradises and nearly naked natives, leading to dozens of "island films" in the 1920s and 1930s. The theme of *Lost and Found*—heartless white traders exploiting peaceful natives — was retold in classics like Maurice Tourneur's *Black Paradise* (1926) and Woody Van Dyke's *White Shadows in the South Seas* (1928).[136] *Lost and Found* premiered in L.A. the following February 25 and Walsh was praised for the film's beauty but most of the publicity came from a scene that caused something of a scandal: Pauline Starke swimming in a jungle pool apparently naked.[137] The scene, which was seen in the U.S., was banned by German film censors.[138]

Lost and Found was William Haines' second role after arriving in March with Eleanor Boardman.[139] He, Boardman and Paul became good friends.

Discussing that friendship, Haines biographer William Mann described Paul as suffering from a "severe inferiority complex..." and said that he "fell obsessively in love with beautiful women, but ... was also drawn sexually to men."[140] That doesn't seem to be the case. Nowhere in my research was there any reference at all to such leanings. It's not surprising that Paul befriended Haines; Haines was an interesting, intelligent, fascinating man. He was also completely open about his homosexuality and infuriated his studios by flatly refusing to allow them to pair him with women for publicity.

Paul introduced Haines to Barbara La Marr that summer. His romantic relationship with La Marr had cooled but the two remained very close. If Paul still held a romantic candle for her, he would not have been threatened by the homosexual Haines. But Haines surprisingly fell in love with La Marr and according to contemporaries had a physical relationship (he had several affairs with women including one with Norma Shearer while filming 1925's *A Slave of Fashion*). La Marr spoke of marrying Haines and the three socialized frequently from late 1922 into early 1923.

❧ FOUR ❧

Director and Father

In the 1922–1923 *Motion Picture Studio Directory*, Paul was described as "Stage manager, actor and director. Stock work: Lowell [apparently Massachusetts]; Screen career: publicity writer, laboratory manager, cutter, scenario writer, director, editor. His first pictures were made in Canada in 1915. At present editor at Goldwyn Studios, Hollywood." Paul was obviously a man on the move.

In January 1923, *Film Daily* announced, "Paul Bern, formerly Scenario Editor of the Goldwyn Company, has become Production Supervisor of the Universal productions."[1] He was probably brought to Universal by production head Irving Thalberg. Thalberg was born in 1899 and spent summers at his grandmother's cottage at Edgemere on Long Island, next to Universal chief Carl Laemmle's beach house. Laemmle hung a sheet over his front porch and screened movies for neighbors to get their opinions; noticing young Thalberg's intuition about movies and audiences, he hired him in 1919. Laemmle's *lassez faire* management — he called his own bureaucracy the "Bottomless Pit"[2] — allowed Thalberg great responsibility. Traveling to Hollywood with Laemmle in July to check the California lot, Thalberg was left there to reorganize the operation as *de facto* general manager. He was barely 20.

By the time Thalberg met Paul in late 1922, he had supervised 100 films, was known as "The Wunderkind" and acknowledged among the smartest men in movies. But he eschewed having his name on screen, saying, "If you are in a position to give credit, you don't need it."[3] And unlike most executives, he did not surround himself with "yes men," preferring an inner circle of trusted confidantes, each with a separate expertise. He kept his tightly knit, hand-picked coterie together for the rest of his life; it was made up almost entirely of German Jews, most older, most well-educated, and interestingly most short like him. Bernie Hyman was his editor and production assistant who with Harry Rapf made the low- to mid-budget films, Al ("Arlie") Lewin was his resident intellectual, and Hunt Stromberg a former reporter and pub-

75

licist who worked with the writers. During meetings, Thalberg paced back and forth absent-mindedly flipping a silver dollar.

However, just after Paul arrived at Universal in January, Thalberg left. The previous December, Thalberg met Louis B. Mayer at his lawyer Edwin Loeb's house. Mayer wanted Thalberg. Louis B. Mayer Productions was a step down from Universal but Thalberg would be second in command, vice president in charge of production, and Mayer promised to "look after [you] as though [you] were my son."[4] Thalberg joined on February 15. He must have known he was leaving and still brought Paul into Universal during his negotiations with Mayer, perhaps intending to bring Paul to Metro later.

Paul worked for several studios during 1923. An April article in *The New York Times* noted he "joined the John M. Stahl unit at the Louis B. Mayer studio to prepare continuity for Stahl's next First National attraction and supply an original story for future production by the editor."[5] Thalberg likely made this arrangement as well. The film was *The Wanters* which would begin production later that spring. He worked at Warner Brothers that summer and was also involved with a number of Famous Players–Lasky and Paramount projects.

Paul was still a sought-after interviewee and still stressing the need for more creative writing. He wrote a newspaper article "The Type of Story in Demand" detailing the process:

> The day has gone when the demand for stories is so great that any string of incidents is acceptable. The stories must have some extraordinary feature ... greatness of characters, of dramatic situation, of physical thrill, greatness of theme, of idea.... Great stuff can not be labeled or pigeon-holed. It must be unusual and impressive, not because it falls into the category of "society drama" or "melodrama" but because it is a true, sincere, big and impressive through some intangible quality in it.[6]

Story development was one of Paul's strengths. He believed a great scenario could be developed from a single good idea; that a great plot could be built around a single situation or character.

He was still at the Georgia Street apartment and hanging out with Carey Wilson, Jack Gilbert, Billy Haines and Barbara La Marr, but something happened in early 1923 that abruptly ended both the Haines–La Marr relationship and the Haines-Bern friendship. Haines was usually very open about his personal life but remained tight-lipped about the La Marr quarrel that took place after he worked in her *Souls for Sale* at Goldwyn. His actions were out of character; his friendships, particularly to female friends like Carole Lombard and Joan Crawford, lasted for life. But *something* happened with La Marr; he never spoke to her or about her again. It had to do with Paul.

Barely two years from rocketing to stardom after *The Three Musketeers*, La Marr already had uncontrollable addictions to alcohol, drugs and sex.

Early 1923 was a window into her life. In January during *Souls for Sale* filming she became addicted to morphine after having the drug prescribed for a sprained ankle. On March 3 she became engaged to Wallace Beery and on March 6 she adopted a baby in Texas. She then broke off the Beery engagement but Hollywood was already abuzz that the baby was her own.[7]

Pregnancy whispers arose in the late fall and grew louder when she stopped working after *Souls for Sale* and completely disappeared from Hollywood nightlife. Her work schedule was admittedly spotty due to increasing drug use but it never affected her social schedule. She was absent from the studios until the late spring filming of *Strangers of the Night* and *St. Elmo.*

In early March, during a trip to Dallas, La Marr visited the private orphanage Hope Cottage with a phalanx of reporters, one later writing "[T]his one particular baby touched her heart." La Marr adopted the seven-month-old boy and named him Marvin Carville La Marr. People in Hollywood whispered that La Marr had given birth secretly and somehow arranged to adopt her own child.[8]

Haines biographer William Mann touched on the reason for Haines' anger toward La Marr and Paul when he mentioned that friends "claim a distinct resemblance to Bern in later photographs of La Marr's son."[9] The Hollywood rumors were true. La Marr did indeed adopt her own son. Paul's son.

From his earliest memories, Marvin (renamed Don Gallery) understood Paul to be his father.[10] According to Gallery he was born July 29, 1922, in L.A. His birth certificate does not mention La Marr but he said his adoptive parents and their famous friends (including Douglas Fairbanks, Jr.) "always told me that [La Marr] was my birth mother and Paul my father."

After his birth he lived secretly with family friends while his mother engineered his adoption. In February, 1923, the seven-month-old was sent to Hope Cottage. La Marr picked Dallas because of a pre-arranged trip in March to serve as queen of a large automobile show. While in town she arranged the orphanage tour, brought some photographers, and picked out her own son. She brought him home in early March and said she would raise him to be the kind of man she wanted for a husband. To the many who questioned her parenting abilities, she curtly said, "[T]here is more motherhood in my little finger than in the whole body of the majority of mothers."[11]

Gallery was told his biological father was Paul; "I have no idea who my real father was, but I can guess; Paul Bern." Gallery told this writer that when he was very young he thought Paul was his godfather and that Paul visited him every Sunday, rarely missing a visit. He brought presents for Don and his sister (who was about the same age), played with them, and often took them out for afternoon trips. Later, Paul brought Jean Harlow along with him; Don and his sister knew her as their godmother. The kids loved canine star Rin Tin Tin, who lived with his owner Lee Duncan across the street from Jean, who arranged for the children to visit the canine star several times.[12]

Paul kept tabs on Donald through the children's nannies, writing regular letters instructing them to contact him if Donald was ever in trouble or hurt, or needed anything. Paul fathering a child by La Marr is a bombshell that directly contradicts later studio fiction describing him as impotent and unable to have normal sexual relations. Fatherhood obviously refutes the most damaging fictions passed on about Paul after his death.

The baby didn't end La Marr's bizarre spring. A month after returning from Dallas, her fourth husband Phil Ainsworth was sent to San Quentin for passing bad checks to buy presents intended to win her back. A week later she married comedian Jack Dougherty even though her divorce from Ben Deeley, who left her over her serial adultery, wasn't finalized. Dougherty was the "fifth husband the pulchritudinous Barbara has promised to love, honor, and obey."[13]

The night of the wedding, she called Paul at 2 A.M. and asked him to awaken a friend who owned a jewelry store to buy wedding rings (that Paul paid for). He was unable to obtain a wedding license in L.A. so drove the couple to Ventura, got a license, found a minister at the First Congregational Church and acted as best man.[14] He also paid for everything and arranged for a bootlegger to deliver liquor for a reception when they returned to L.A. None of La Marr's friends knew about the wedding; most didn't even know she was seeing Dougherty. Years later Adela Rogers St. Johns used Paul's favors to "prove" some bizarre alleged obsession.

La Marr had no more success with Dougherty than with her previous husbands. Six months later she was named a co-respondent in a divorce case and Dougherty moved out.[15]

While Paul was dealing with the various La Marr situations that spring, his script *The Wanters* was in production at Metro, directed by John Stahl.[16] The film is the story of wealthy Elliot Worthington's (Robert Ellis) love for Myra (Marie Prevost), his sister's maid; the sister fires Myra when she finds out. But Elliot marries Myra and returns home to the dismay of his family and friends. Myra is snubbed and becomes disillusioned with the hypocrisy of her husband's wealthy friends and runs away to a small apartment. After upbraiding his so-called friends, Elliot searches for Myra, arriving just in time to save her from being hit by a train after her foot gets caught in a switch.[17] *Wanters* was released in November.

That summer Paul joined Rex Ingram, Ernst Lubitsch, Hugo Ballin, and Robert Wagner as a founding member of Little Theater Films, which would develop regional theater groups and university drama societies to provide an avenue for new movie scenarios. The group was led by *Movie Magazine* editor Curtis Melnitz and noted New York drama critic Kenneth Magowan the group's eastern representative.[18]

Two of Paul's scenarios were produced in the fall, *Name the Man* for Goldwyn and *The Marriage Circle* for Warners. *Name the Man* was based on a Hall Caine novel and was the first American film for Swedish director Victor Seastrom.[19] Real name Victor Sjostrom, the one-time donut salesman became the father of Swedish film. Paul was thrilled that Seastrom directed his script; Seastrom was legendary for his mastery of the psychology of characters and his films were showcases for themes like guilt and redemption, which were prominent in Paul's writings. June Mathis assisted Paul with the editing.[20]

On the Isle of Man, Victor Stowell (Conrad Nagel) — son of the island's judge (Hobart Bosworth) — is engaged to Fenella Stanley (Patsy Ruth Miller) — daughter of the island's governor — but becomes involved in the life of Bessie Collister (Mae Busch). Victor offers Bessie a place to stay after her brutal stepfather throws her out and after a night together — and apparently having sex — Victor decides he must marry her. But his father dies and he must take over as judge, as his best friend Alick Gell falls in love with a now-pregnant Bessie. She is unfairly charged with murder after suffering a miscarriage and refusing to name the father, and Victor presides over the case and betrays her by sentencing her to death. Realizing his sin, he helps her escape from jail and flee with Alick and after a mob gathers he admits his guilt and his fatherhood of the child. He is jailed for two years but arranges for a private tutor to complete Bessie's education and in the end is freed and marries Fennella.[21]

Fans flocked to see *Name the Man* after its release in early January, 1924; it was called "a truly great picture with a heart appeal from which even the most callous cannot escape." Seastrom's films were described as "art as well as entertainment"[22] and critics complimented Paul: "[T]hrough relentless reaping of what characters have sown is seen a sympathy and understanding of the human heart which is seldom found on the screen. This is due to the skillful adaptation ... made by Paul Bern" with "simplicity, sincerity and intelligence."[23]

Today much of the film is missing, including the last two reels, but viewing what remains, it's difficult not to find it muddled; what appears to be a comedy bedroom farce changes to tragedy-melodrama (more typical of Seastrom). It's hard to decide what you're watching. There are also obvious casting issues. Busch was more suited to comedy and over-pantomimed her dramatic role and Nagel didn't have the presence to pull off such a layered role. Even so, 1924 audiences loved it.

Paul's second late 1923 scenario was *The Marriage Circle*, made at Warners that fall. What papers called a "Viennese-set piece from the pen of Paul Bern" would be Ernst Lubitsch's first production for Warners.[24] Lubitsch was another famous European director new to the U.S. He was imported by Mary Pickford to direct her in *Rosita* but audiences hated her in a sexy role and the film was widely panned. He had better luck with *Marriage Circle*, which Paul loosely adapted from the Austrian play *Only a Dream* by Lothar Schmidt.

Paul's script, a peek into married life, was about a young married woman intent on stealing her best friend's husband because she is bored with her own. Professor Josef Stock (Adolphe Menjou) and his jazz-baby wife Mizzi (Marie Prevost) do nothing but bicker and she wants Franz Braun (Monte Blue), happily in love and married to her best friend Charlotte (Florence Vidor). Stock sees this as his chance to divorce Mizzi and hires a detective to follow her but his plan is complicated because Charlotte is also being pursued by Franz's medical partner Gustav Mueller. On top of everything, Charlotte mistakenly believes her husband is having an affair so she begins an affair and asks Mizzi to keep her husband busy, not knowing Mizzi desires him. Amidst all the confusion, Mizzi and Gustav Mueller turn their attentions to each other.[25]

The Franz Braun role was initially given to Warner Baxter but after eight days Lubitsch turned to his assistant Henry Blanke and said, "He looks like a detective," and replaced him with Monte Blue.[26] Lubitsch's direction infused palpable tension amidst the various romantic entanglements. The final scene, a crowded garden party attended by the various pursuers and those pursued, is full of Lubitsch-designed sexual tension and in the end everyone goes off with someone new, each the person they desired.

After its February 1924 release, critics praised the film and Lubitsch for bringing out the finest from the actors and making "a new star of the first magnitude" out of Prevost (though she had done 60+ films).[27] *Photoplay* said "[T]he characters themselves reveal the story, which runs smoothly along to its logical ending. There is no straining for effects.... [I]t's all very simple, very human and intensely entertaining."[28] Paul's input was noted as the film was described as "a thorough study of American people's psychology...." Lubitsch said *Marriage Circle* was his favorite film because "I was experimenting ... to create a story that would reflect life as it is lived by thousands of married couples — just everyday people that we meet all around us."[29]

Lubitsch gave an entertaining interview discussing apparently confirmed bachelor Paul writing a script about relationships and marriage. Everyone in the film was having marriage issues: Monte Blue and Marie Prevost divorced during filming, Adolphe Menjou, cameraman Charles Van Enger and

Creighton Hale shortly after, and finally Lubitsch himself. He observed, "Everybody is divorced but Paul Bern, who wrote the script. And he isn't married."[30]

In early 1924 Paul was hired by Jesse Lasky to write for Famous Players–Lasky, paying him $250 a week ($5,000 today). But he continued to live frugally, loath to spend money on himself but showering it on friends. He was still living on Georgia Street, sending twice-monthly checks to Dorothy at the Algonquin, and helping Barbara La Marr and Mabel Normand through their personal travails.

In March, La Marr caused a furor when she said "a woman must be immoral in order to be a movie vamp." Other movie "vamps" like Theda Bara, Nita Naldi and Gloria Swanson criticized La Marr and women's groups called for a ban on her films that "have a demoralizing effect upon the young people."[31] Her worsening addictions made it harder for her to work; she appeared in just four pictures that year: *White Moth* for Maurice Tourneur in February, *Hello 'Frisco* for Universal and *Sandra* for First National in the summer, and she began *Heart of a Siren* in November.

She was fading fast and needed cash, so she asked Paul to sell the last vestige of her wealthy lifestyle: her Rolls Royce. He pretended to broker a deal to sell the car for twice its value, gave her the money and put the Rolls in a garage.[32]

Like Barbara, Mabel too was fading. The public outrage after the Taylor murder was re-ignited after a January 1, 1924 party when her long-time chauffeur got into an argument with wealthy playboy Courtland Dines at Dines' North Vermont bungalow, pulled a gun and shot Dines. The scandal worsened when it was leaked that her chauffeur was an escaped convict, the people at the party were drunk (Edna Purviance was with Mabel), and the gun was Mabel's. Censorship boards called for a ban on her films while Paul vainly tried to keep her working.

During this period Paul escorted Mabel to numerous industry functions, private gatherings, and premieres like Douglas Fairbanks' *The Thief of Baghdad* on March 18. Their frequent dates were noted in the press, but whether they were a couple or Paul was simply helping her weather the storm is hard to confirm. However, a note he sent her from the Ambassador on their pale green stationery offers a hint at romance:

> There is nothing in the world about which a man is as stupid as the purchaser of a gift for a woman — unless he happens to be in love with her — and then he makes the most senseless present it is possible to desire. Would you mind very much if I ask you to get your own gift, as useless and unnecessary as your mind may dictate? Many thanks for favors and kindnesses — and best wishes for the New Year — Paul Bern.

The note indicates a more personal relationship but still puzzles, at once romantic and at the same time formal. He mentioned being in love but then he offers "best wishes for the New Year" and signs his full name. It should also be noted that by early 1924 Mabel was a full-out alcoholic, something Paul would not have found appealing.

Paul's first Lasky-Paramount assignments were the important Pola Negri vehicles *Men* and *Lily of the Dust*. After arriving in the U.S. with great fanfare, the demanding diva's first films were dreadfully uneven. *The Cheat, Bella Donna* and *The Spanish Dancer* left Lasky worried she would be a bust so he hired Dimitri Buchowetzki, who directed Negri in Berlin, to try to work with her. *Men* was a story Buchowetzki carried for years in his head with Negri in mind. Paul brought the story to life. The scenario was originally titled *Compromised*. Negri starred as Cleo, a waitress in a waterfront Marseilles café tricked into moving to Paris by a wealthy man. Her anger at men controls her life, using them when and however possible as she ascends to a life of wealth and luxury and becomes a well-known stage star and café habitué. She has a chance meeting with impoverished Georges (Robert Frazer), whose honesty and love restores her faith in men.[33]

Men was released on May 26, with ads reading, "You know Negri can act! But *Men* is Negri at the pinnacle of greatness! For here the story is a real match for her magnificent art. See her as the dancing pet of Paris — matching her wits against the kind of men who bargain for souls, reveling as she makes them pay the price of her youth. Only then will you see the full fire of her genius!"[34] The film was well received as a "vivid picture of life in the Parisian half-world [and] one the month's best offerings."[35] It did well but Negri was not as well-received as Lasky hoped; her acting was still stiff and overly stagey.

On March 28, just after *Men* was finished, Lasky announced that writers R.H. Burnside, Paul Sloane, Frank Tuttle, and Paul would now direct, saying, "[M]aking these four men directors ... [follows] our policy of striving to keep the quality of our product steadily advancing by incorporation [of] new ideas and new blood."[36] The directing roster already included Cecil B. DeMille, George Fitzmaurice, Herbert Brenon, Thomas Meighan, and Allan Dwan.

Paul's first directing assignment would be a Jetta Goudal vehicle *Open All Night* in June or July. Lasky also announced, "Ernst Lubitsch, who made Miss Negri's greatest European success, *Passion*, will direct her in *Forbidden Paradise* based on a story by Paul Bern."[37] *Paradise* has never been attributed to Paul but he was identified as the writer in papers and in April studio releases listing Paramount's 40-film production schedule.

In the meantime, Paul worked on his second Paramount script for Negri,

Lily of the Dust, a tragic love story set in Germany that Buchowetzki again directed.

Impoverished bookstore clerk Lily Czepanek (Negri) lives in a small Army garrison town and falls in love with officer Richard von Prell (Ben Lyon). His commanding officer Colonel von Mertzbach (Noah Beery) forces her into marriage so a shattered von Prell follows them on their honeymoon, and when von Mertzbach sees Lily speaking to Richard, he divorces Lily and wounds von Prell in a duel. Thinking her love is dead, Lily turns to wealthy businessman Karl Dehnecke (Raymond Griffith) but Richard returns and agrees to take her back if she leaves the trappings of wealth given her by Dehnecke. Too poor to support her, von Prell depends on a wealthy uncle for money and the uncle must first approve of Lily so a climactic meeting is arranged.

Buchowetzki fills the climax with tension as they await his answer. Does Lily love von Mertzbach? Does she love Richard? Will Walter accept her? In a shocking twist, Walter indeed refuses to accept the wayward girl and she dejectedly returns to Karl.[38] The unexpected ending — not in the original Hermann Sudermann novel or stage adaptation but written by Paul — made this one of the most talked-about films of the summer. The film was based on a real-life incident: A 10-year-old Buchowetzki stumbled on an actual duel while hunting for bird eggs in the woods and watched transfixed as one of the combatants shot and wounded the other.[39]

It would be a busy six months for Paul. He directed his first three Paramount films — *Open All Night*, *Worldly Goods*, and *Tomorrow's Love* — and two of his scenarios — *Forbidden Paradise* and *Vanity's Price* — were produced.

Lasky tried to make a star of the demanding but untalented Negri. He next brought Ernst Lubitsch from Warners to work with her in *Forbidden Paradise* in mid–July. Lubitsch and Negri had history. He was as intolerant of her temperamental outbursts as she was of his attempts to bridle her, which made for a loud, argument-filled set. But the film is beautifully done.

Hans Kraly and Agnes Christine Johnston are credited with the script — based on the 1913 Lajos Biro novel *The Czarina* — but newspapers credited the story to Paul. Charles Van Enger did the filming on lavish European sets designed by Hans Dreier. Negri demanded her friend and lover Rod La Rocque star with her; like her, he had looks but limited skills.

Like *Marriage Circle*, Lubitsch's film is full of sexual tension and illicit relationships. Alexei (La Rocque), a dim army officer, saves the czarina (Negri) of a small European kingdom from revolutionaries and she rewards him with what he thinks is love. In his naïve infatuation he leaves his sweetheart Anna, the czarina's lady-in-waiting, only to discover the sexually voracious czarina can't be faithful. He becomes so angry he joins the rebels and plots against her but when her chancellor ends the uprising by bribing the insurgents, she orders Alexei's arrest. She is tormented by guilt and releases him to return to Anna. The czarina slips back into the arms of the French Ambassador.[40]

The film includes some wonderful Lubitsch touches. He hints at the czarina's sexual appetite during a banquet after she seduces the dense Alexei; dozens of men at the table are wearing the exact same medal she had just given him! At the end of the film, after the czarina meets with the French Ambassador behind closed doors, he exits her office wearing the same medal as the rest of the men at the dinner. A young Clark Gable had a small role in the wonderful film.

Paul's second script, *Vanity's Price*, for Gothic Pictures and Film Booking Offices of America began production the last week of August.[41] Preoccupied with fame, American actress Vanna Du Maurier (Anna Q. Nilsson) lives in a huge mansion with footmen, butlers, Russian dancers and Ethiopian servants. She meets millionaire Henri De Greve (Stuart Holmes), who somehow doesn't realize he was once married to her and fathered her son, Teddy. The shock of seeing him ignites fear of losing her looks so she has an operation in Vienna to restore her beauty, but a side-effect from the operation is that she remembers nothing from the weeks before and becomes obsessed with men. She has an affair with De Greve, who is also pursuing Teddy's fiancée Sylvia. When Sylvia tries to drown herself to get away from De Greve, Vanna regains her wits and lures him to her bedroom where she tells him of their past and beats him with a riding crop. For good measure her long-time admirer Richard Dowling beats up De Greve himself before proposing to Vanna. Everyone is reunited and Vanna recognizes the folly of vanity.[42]

The art direction and set design were spectacular; the massive mansion set reminded critics of St. Patrick's Cathedral but reviews were middling after the film's September 7 release. R. William Neill's direction was criticized as pedestrian and "inexperienced" and it was warned that the film "would not set the world on fire." But one critic loved that Paul's scenario "[swept] along irresistibly"[43] and another wrote, "[T]he story was written by the imaginative Paul Bern, and it would have been a superior effort if he had directed it."[44]

Vanity reunited Paul and Lucille Ricksen, whom he had mentored since first meeting her on the *Edgar* serial in 1920. By 1924 she had already had high-profile roles in 25 films like Dorothy Davenport Reid's *Human Wreckage* (1923) and *Those Who Dance* (1924), working with stars like Conrad Nagel, Bessie Love, and Cullen Landis. She was only 14 but played characters much older and was named one of the 1924 WAMPAS Baby Stars (the Western Association of Motion Picture Advertisers annual selection of 13 women on the threshold of stardom). Named with Ricksen were Clara Bow and Dorothy Mackaill.

Unfortunately, Lucille had fallen ill weeks earlier while making *The Galloping Fish* with Chester Conklin and was diagnosed with tuberculosis just before *Vanity* began filming. Within two months her health declined and she could work no more. Paul visited her every week for the rest of 1924.

At the same time, Jack Gilbert asked Paul to help save his bizarre marriage to Leatrice Joy. They had endured dozens of separations — some suggested by Cecil B. DeMille and some due to affairs — but that summer a pregnant Joy learned of his latest affair with Leatrice Taylor and moved to a Long Beach apartment with her mother and filed for divorce. Gilbert asked Paul (along with Lois Wilson and writer Barney Glazer) to persuade her to reconcile. Their efforts were initially successful but when she returned to their former home and found evidence of his affairs, she went back to her mother. When Joy gave birth to their daughter a month later, Gilbert sent her 1,000 roses.[45]

During the summer and fall of 1924, Paul directed three Lasky films, *Open All Night*, *Worldly Goods*, and *Tomorrow's Love*, cementing his reputation as a first-rate director and master story-teller. Starting *Open All Night*, he was called "the sensational graduate of the Lasky scenario department" and by *Tomorrow's Love* he was "hailed as the successor to Cecil B. DeMille at the Famous Players–Lasky studio."[46] He was recognized as one of the most creative directors in Hollywood and an erudite spokesman in demand for interviews. He was also a popular speaker, chosen with Rupert Hughes, Rex Ingram and William de Mille to address students at the new Columbia University School of Film's photoplay composition classes.[47]

Paul persuaded the studio to give his friend Viola Dana the lead in *Open All Night*. Tragedy seemingly followed the Metro and Lasky star of over 100 films. She married director John H. Collins at 16 but he fell victim to Spanish flu contracted days after his induction into the Army and died in 1918. In 1920 she became engaged to Ormer Locklear, the best-known stunt pilot and barnstormer in the world, brought to Hollywood after Sydney Chaplin saw him walk from one plane to another high above an airfield he owned. On July 26, 1919, he became the first man to successfully transfer from a car to an airplane filming Universal's *The Great Air Robbery*.

Dana had only recently begun dating after the death of her first husband; during her sabbatical, Paul was often her escort but she and Locklear began a heated affair even though his wife Ruby was back in Texas. He often buzzed Dana at the Metro lot with a "Locklear Bounce," ricocheting off the roof of a soundstage above his girlfriend. In 1920, Fox starred him in *The Skywayman* and on August 2, 1920, he filmed a stunt at an oil field near DeMille Airfield (present day Wilshire and Crescent). Illuminated by blinding searchlights, Locklear's plane was put into a spinning dive as Locklear waited for the lights to be shut off as a signal to level off. But they were not dimmed and Locklear and Milton Elliott were killed when his Curtis Jenny slammed into the ground and burst into flames. Dana witnessed the crash, which Fox included in the film, along with views of the gruesome remains.

He had a Hollywood movie star send-off with thousands of fans outside the funeral home and his movie star girlfriend weeping over his coffin. Then his body was taken to Texas for another funeral, this time with a weeping wife.[48]

Open All Night was a farce comedy written by Willis Goldbeck based on short stories by Paul Morand. The cast was led by Dana, Adolphe Menjou, and Jetta Goudal. Goudal was a late addition to the cast; she was supposed to co-star with Rudolph Valentino in his final Lasky film *A Sainted Devil* but was replaced at the last minute by Dagmar Godowsky.[49] Paul also arranged for Goudal's role.

Night reminded critics of *The Marriage Circle*, revolving around a strained marriage and a discontented wife yearning for excitement from her "mild-mannered husband."[50] Therese Duverne (Dana) wishes her husband (Men-

Paul and Viola Dana have lunch with Ernst Lubitsch on the set of *Open All Night*.

jou) would show some manliness but he is afraid of losing her respect if he treats her badly. Her friend Isabelle introduces her to famed bicyclist Petit Mathieu at the Cirque d'Hiver six-day race in Paris and she is infatuated with Mathieu. Edmond is equally interested in Mathieu's girlfriend Lea, who is tired of *her* husband's brutish treatment. But when Edmond discovers his wife with the handsome cyclist he develops a temper and beats him up, leading to a reconciliation.[51]

Open premiered on September 8 to conflicting reviews, but Paul's direction received kudos. Although described as "a newcomer in the ranks of directors," he was called "a shrewd director, smart and sophisticated" who showcased "sexual magnetism in the play of characters with a dash of subtlety." But the film was dismissed as "a frothy sort of affair, so absurd that one wonders why it was produced."[52]

Paul artfully depicted the dichotomy between the two women's lives and their conflicting desires as they secretly envied the other's relationship. To show Therese's disdain for her husband, Paul filmed her soaking in an ornamental bathtub responding disparagingly to her husband's timid knock. He spent the entire first day filming the bathtub scene; Dana said she lost three pounds. He also set the story to take place in a single day, adding to the film's movement.[53] Goudal, whose performance was described as "perfection," became another of Paul's projects, a close friend to whom he gave advice and whose career he actively helped develop.

Goudal's career was at a crossroad when *Open All Night* was cast. After her 1923 performance in *The Bright Shawl* she was assumed to be on a fast track but she was a temperamental diva and studios began blackballing her. She asked Paul for help and he cast her in *Night* and helped her get work for another five years.

Night writer Willis Goldbeck was also a close friend of Paul's. In a later 1924 interview Paul said Goldbeck was one of the few writers who understood his coda that audiences were intelligent and scenarios should reflect that. "Directors who thought motion picture audiences were not intelligent are into the discard," he said, "put there by the public together with the product that resulted from that mistaken idea. The [belief that] theater-goers accepted their entertainment without consideration for its quality was repeated so often that many directors believed it. They woke up to find that they had no audience."[54] Paul knew audiences could follow complicated scenarios and characters and his work evidenced that belief.

Paul befriended Ernst Lubitsch after his arrival at Goldwyn and oversaw his *Forbidden Paradise* script. They joined a loosely organized group of German émigrés in the movie business that called themselves "The Foreign Legion." Other members included Fritz Lang, the Laemmle family, Henry

Blanke, and Salka and Peter
Viertel. Lubitsch visited the
Open All Night set and sat for
publicity stills with Paul, whose
respect for Lubitsch led to accu-
sations that he copied the
Lubitsch style. It was a common
accusation; Monta Bell and
Harry d'Arrast were accused of
the same thing.

Lubitsch thought the
script was everything, that a
well-done script could be easily
translated by a director into a
visual created *by* the script. Paul
was similar to Lubitsch in that
belief but it is unfair to say Paul
copied Lubitsch's style since Paul
always believed the script and
character development drove the
film. After Lubitsch viewed a
script, the filming process was
already in his head. He said at
that point, "I've finished the picture. All I have to do is photo-

Paul's close friend and one-time girlfriend
Jetta Goudal, on the set of *Open All Night*.
Paul arranged for Goudal to get a role in his
film.

graph it.... For me, it is virtually all done in the script."[55] Paul reached the
same place from a different direction, creating the script to accomplish that
goal and was talking about that process before Lubitsch arrived.

In September, Paul began directing the farce comedy *Worldly Goods*,
based on a Sophie Kerr story serialized in *Ladies Home Journal* in early 1924.
Eleanor Lawson (Agnes Ayres) refuses the marriage proposal of wealthy Clifford Ramsay because she is drawn in by Fred Hopper (Pat O'Malley), a fast-
talking car salesman with big ideas and small results who rarely works. She
is forced to get a job when the electricity and telephone are shut off. Fred
overhears Ramsey's plans for a real estate deal and engages in a breezy affair
with wealthy Letitia Calhoun so she'll lend him $70,000 to steal the deal.
Eleanor discovers Fred's manipulation of Letitia and starts divorce proceedings but changes her mind when Fred promises to mend his ways, admits to
Ramsey his duplicity, and is rewarded with a job.[56]

The success of *Goods* was "due to Paul Bern's gentle and imaginative
direction, which helps the flow of the story and aptly delineates a variety of

interesting characters"; "weak spots in the script" were hidden because the movie was "so aptly directed."[57] To visualize Fred's dishonesty, Paul crafted a scene where he finds several bills he knows fell from someone else's wallet but pretends they fell from his. The marvelously subtle depiction clearly showed Fred's personality flaws.

Next was another farce comedy, *Tomorrow's Love*, again with Ayres and O'Malley, which began on November 2. It was written by Howard Higgin based on the Charles Brackett *Saturday Evening Post* short story "Interlocutory."[58] Like *Open All Night* and *Worldly Goods*, *Tomorrow's Love* was a story of uninspired marriage, unreasonable expectations, outside love interests and reclaimed love.

Judith (Ayres) and Robert Stanley (O'Malley) are in love but his stubborn streak irks her; he leaves windows open in the cold, drives an open car when he's sick and won't wear an overcoat. When his car breaks down, he is picked up by Bess Carlysle, an old girlfriend who insists he return to her apartment to dry off. Judith learns he is there and arrives to find her husband having a whiskey and enjoying a foot bath. He is too stubborn to explain so Judith secures a divorce decree and leaves for the Orient to wait the year for it to take effect. Robert still loves Judith and knows Bess is shallow but obstinately becomes engaged to Bess as the film follows Judith's travails with men during her travels and the realization she still loves Robert. She returns home and frantically races to a party he's given on the last night of the waiting period, leaping her car over a gap in a drawbridge and darting in front of a train before arriving just before he is to marry Bess. In the 24th hour of the 365th day they realize they are still in love and they invalidate the divorce decree and regain their lost happiness.[59]

Writers found it interesting that Lasky assigned his "resident bachelor" to another movie about married life but commended Paul for creating another excellent domestic film.[60] He "denied to reporters that his remarkable understanding of the trials and tribulations of married life [was] responsible for his bachelorhood."[61]

The lavish costumes were created by Howard Greer, who made the costumes for Paul's earlier *Lily of the Dust* and for *Men*. Paul convinced Lasky to appoint Greer the head of all fashion design and costuming for the studio, which Lasky did as *Love* filming began.[62]

On November 9, Lasky announced the production schedule for the first half of 1925, 40 films culled from 14 famous books, 12 magazine stories and five popular stage plays. Paul would direct Leatrice Joy twice in an adaptation of the Richard Pride novel *Marqueray's Duel* (entitled *Modern Babylon*) in March and *Grounds for Divorce* in June. Another film mentioned was *The Dressmaker from Paris*, assigned to Raoul Walsh.[63]

During the fall, Paul moved from Georgia Street to an upper floor room at the Ambassador Hotel.[64] The Ambassador was a luxury hotel with hundreds of well-appointed rooms and several dozen bungalows dotting a lush 10-acre site at 4121 Wilshire; it was home to dozens of studio executives and stars like D.W. Griffith, Howard Hughes, Paul's friend Irving Thalberg, Cecil B. DeMille's assistant and girlfriend Jeanie MacPherson, and John Barrymore, who lived in the hotel's Siesta Cottage bungalow for years. The hotel was also a hub of Hollywood society. Friends described Paul's room and bath as a "monk's room" but he enjoyed the solitude.

The week Paul moved to the Ambassador, the news of the strange death of 42-year-old Thomas Ince filled papers. After 500 films he was already an icon known as the "Father of the Western." Ince accepted an invitation from William Randolph Hearst to spend the weekend aboard Hearst's 280-foot yacht *Oneida* along with Hearst mistress Marion Davies, her friend Charlie Chaplin, Hearst production manager Dr. Daniel Carson Goodman, Davies' secretary Abigail Kinsolving, Davies' two sisters, a niece, and actresses Aileen Pringle, Seena Owen and Julanne Johnston. Also aboard was Ince's business manager George H. Thomas, Louella Parsons, a minor Hearst columnist from Chicago, and Margaret Livingston, Ince's long-time mistress. Ince's wife Nell stayed at home.

Ince attended the premiere of his film *The Mirage* in L.A. and then joined the group in San Diego on Saturday. Sunday evening they celebrated Ince's birthday but early Monday he was removed from the yacht accompanied by Dr. Goodman and taken to his Beverly Hills estate, where he allegedly died Tuesday, November 18. According to the death certificate (signed by Ince's private physician), he died of heart failure and after a hastily arranged Friday funeral attended by Davies, Chaplin, Mary Pickford, Douglas Fairbanks, and Harold Lloyd, Nell had him cremated. A few days later she left for Europe for a month.[65]

Early papers and witnesses aboard the *Oneida* described a vastly different version. The bulldog editions of San Diego papers led with **Movie Producer Shot on Hearst Yacht!** But as those headlines mysteriously vanished, Hearst claimed Ince fell ill visiting his San Simeon castle with Nell and their children and died of acute indigestion. He would tell so many lies, people didn't know what to believe.

Chaplin's long-time chauffeur and assistant Toraichi Kono said Japanese servants on board saw Ince removed, bleeding profusely from a head wound. It was rumored that Hearst, who knew of a Davies-Chaplin affair, grabbed the pearl-handled, diamond-encrusted pistol he used to shoot gulls and took a shot at a man he believed was Chaplin but was Ince. Different versions arose — Ince was shot as he happened upon Chaplin and Davies, Ince (lying in bed) was hit by an errant shot fired by Hearst, Ince and Davies were in the galley looking for something for Ince's stomach when Hearst shot him, etc. — but none were confirmed. Ince was obviously shot; numerous witnesses saw his head wound.

The San Diego D.A. called only one witness at his inquest — Dr. Goodman — who concocted perhaps the most farcical story, that he and Ince left the boat after Ince took ill and took a train toward L.A., before disembarking at Del Mar and checking into a hotel to wait for Nell. Goodman then claimed to have left before she arrived. His ridiculous yarn somehow satisfied the D.A.

Controversy swirled for decades, most caused by those aboard the *Oneida*. Chaplin denied being there but insisted he, Hearst and Davies visited Ince at home before he died. Marion Davies denied Chaplin, Goodman and Louella Parsons were even on board and said Nell phoned her Monday to tell her Ince had died even though he didn't die until Tuesday. Parsons never said anything about the weekend and within a few weeks was writing a syndicated Hearst column, making her the most powerful writer in Hollywood. Insiders liked to say, "Give Louella an Ince and she'll take a column!"

Abigail Kinsolving's story was equally bizarre, telling police Ince raped her Saturday night (even though his mistress was on board). Strangely, however, nine months later she gave birth before dying in a mysterious car accident near Hearst's San Simeon estate. A strange suicide note found in the car was obviously written by *two* people, the car found by Hearst's bodyguards, and no police reports survive. Baby Louise was raised in an orphanage paid for by Davies.

Nell received a large trust fund and a former Hearst property in Hollywood, the Chateau Elysee Apartments, where she lived for years.[66] The *Oneida* was called "William Randolph's Hearse" and D. W. Griffith said, "All you have to do to make Hearst turn white as a ghost is mention Ince's name." Louella Parsons would later lead a Hearst-MGM cover-up after Paul's death.

Paul's first 1925 assignment was *The Dressmaker from Paris*, originally assigned to Raoul Walsh but given to Paul after his 1924 successes. It was originally scheduled for summer but moved up to January. "Paul Bern's super-production" featured gowns by Parisian designer Travis Banton costing $50,000.[67] Leatrice Joy starred with Allan Forrest, Ernest Torrence, and Mildred Harris.[68]

Doughboy Billy Brent (Forrest) meets beautiful shop-girl Fifi (Joy) lighting a cigarette for a one-armed soldier in 1918 Paris but as they fall in love he returns to the front. After the war he manages the Emporium clothing store in Clarion, Illinois, for stubborn Scottish owner Angus McGregor (Torrence) and is dispassionately engaged to McGregor's young daughter Jean (Harris). With McGregor away on business, Billy invites famed but scandalous French designer Madame Louise to present a fashion show. She arrives with 14 gorgeous models and he realizes she is his lost love Fifi. Jean and the models are caught in a raid at a local roadhouse, and townspeople demand the "The Dressmaker from Paris" leave town. But when Jean is discovered in an affair Fifi takes the blame. McGregor returns and, impressed with Billy's business acumen and thankful that Fifi sacrificed herself to protect his daughter's good name, makes him a partner. Billy and Fifi marry.[69]

Dressmaker was released on March 25 and called an "unusual combination of human interest story and rare, dazzling beauty." Viewers liked the lavish costumes and startling new "bob" haircuts that caused as much excitement as the film. Theaters held their own fashion shows along with the film, a financial windfall for Lasky. Paul was commended for "sophisticated direction in which [he] ably and subtly balanced his restrained comedy and pathos." Lasky called him "one of the directorial sensations of the year" and after *Dressmaker*, "the reason was apparent."[70]

During *Dressmaker* pre-production, almost 75 people approached Paul asking for work, each with their own tale of need. He found spots for each one, among them Olive Borden, who was given a small role. When she couldn't afford the dress for the extra role, Paul bought one for her.[71]

Not long after starting *Dressmaker*, Paul met 19-year-old Lucille Fay LeSueur, who was discovered in Kansas City by Harry Rapf.[72] Her affair with Rapf— in the 1920s and 1930s it was almost impossible for young girls to find work in Hollywood *without* sleeping with someone — earned her a $75-a-week MGM contract. Sex with male authority figures probably seemed normal to her; her second stepfather molested her for years.

Rapf thought her name sounded like "sewer" so fans were asked to name her for a $500 prize. For a month she was "Joan Arden" before MGM learned two entries submitted the name and to avoid paying two $500 prizes she became Joan Crawford. Rapf invested an inordinate amount of time and money in grooming her. She was a dancer with no experience yet received star treatment, given roles right away and even filmed at a costume fitting with designer Romaine de Tirtoff Erte. But she was a handful, a well-known bisexual with a voracious sexual appetite. In the early 1920s she was arrested in Detroit for prostitution and later frequented Harlem's lesbian clubs and live sex shows with lesbian friends Bea Lillie, Tallulah Bankhead, Estelle Winwood, Barbara Stanwyck and Marjorie Main.[73] At MGM her escapades became known simply as "Joan stories."[74] Eddie Mannix spent months searching for a pornographic movie she made in New York and paid $50,000 for the negative. Harry Rapf's son Maurice said the New York office was engaged to find any copies and confirmed Mannix's purchase.[75]

Crawford wanted to further speed up her career and hung around stages watching established stars work, learning everything she could about filming and pestering Rapf for bigger roles. She also befriended Paul and sought him out often for advice. They were also rumored to have been sexually involved.

When she requested Paul's help, he asked her, "What have you done to improve yourself?" He tried to add culture to her life, furnished dresses for public appearances and reportedly sent her an ermine wrap she supposedly returned.[76] Paul did help her, later getting her a role in Edmund Goulding's *Paris* and six other films in her first eight months at MGM.

Even with his hectic schedule, Paul still visited young Lucille Ricksen every week, bringing magazines and presents and comforting her as tuberculosis ravaged the beautiful teenager. For hours he sat by her bed and read to her or just held her hand. He also paid for doctors and nurses and the family's bills.

Her last weeks were tragically horrific. On February 26, her distraught mother Ingeborg suffered a fatal heart attack and collapsed, falling dead on top of her bedridden daughter. For the next three weeks, Paul came every day, talking and helping her accept her approaching death. On March 13 the 16-year-old died in her bed with Paul still holding her hand. He remained distraught even as funeral home attendants took away her body for a funeral he paid for. He also paid for the headstone for Lucille and her mother.[77]

Paul was so upset that he left Hollywood for two weeks, the first vacation he had ever taken. He traveled by train to Arizona and the Grand Canyon and stayed at the El Tovar, a turn-of-the-century hotel (fashioned after a European hunting lodge) sitting on the rim of the canyon.[78] He read scripts and took horseback expeditions into the canyon; after falling several times, he said, "I'm afraid I shall never be a Tarzan. It's an electric horse for me in the future."[79] He returned to Hollywood at

Young actress Joan Crawford, who sought out Paul for career advice and became a good friend.

the end of March and traveled to Lasky's New York offices for two weeks, during which time he visited with Dorothy at the Algonquin. His brother Henry said he visited once a year until Dorothy's worsening psychosis became too much for Paul to handle.

When he returned in April, he began *Grounds for Divorce*, a farce comedy expected to be a big Lasky hit. Papers said the assignment was "one of the most important stories of the Paramount program ... a reward for his success with *The Dressmaker from Paris*."[80] Filming began on April 13.

Grounds is the story of Maurice Sorbier (Matt Moore), a Parisian divorce lawyer obsessed with his work. His wife Alice (Florence Vidor) leaves him, thinking that's the only way to get his attention. Instead of dashing aviator Guido, Alice marries Count Zapata even though she doesn't love him. Zapata refuses her a divorce so Guido suggests she ask her ex-husband for help and then takes Zapata flying to scare him into signing divorce papers. Guido does a dozen loops, spirals and barrel-rolls to intimidate Zapata, who still refuses to sign. Spying a parachute at his feet, he dons it and jumps. A title card reads "I'll scoop you up if you try!" and as Zapata floats down, Guido cuts him off and actually catches him. Zapata signs the papers. Guido lands expecting to find a waiting Alice but she has reconciled with Maurice and the two have run off to get married.[81]

Paul crafted an excellent film but *Grounds* suffered from the casting. Moore was said to be too "Anglo-Saxon ... impossible to think of as Maitre Sorbier."[82] Vidor was too old to play the young Alice. But Paul was featured in ads reading "Don't forget, the man who made *Dressmaker from Paris* made this one too!"[83]

Paul and cameraman Bert Glennon used a new German gyroscope camera letting them follow the actors as they advanced or retreated from view, and used sepia for the night scenes instead of the usual exaggerated blue. The result was a clearer picture with more movement. Some archives list the release on July 27 but newspapers confirmed it was in theaters as early as June 6.[84]

My Wife and I has not been credited to Paul but when Warners announced the production schedule at their regional exhibitor meetings the previous July, it noted "*My Wife and I* written by Paul Bern."[85] Since he was no longer with Warners when the film was made, they probably simply removed his name from the credits.

Paul's story is about the infatuation of young spendthrift Stuart Borden (John Harron) with Aileen Alton (Constance Bennett), a beautiful but mercenary siren. When Stuart buys her a mink coat, his father (Huntley Gordon) refuses to pay for it and cuts him off so she discards him. His father then becomes infatuated with her and gives her the same mink and begins to neglect his family even as he and his wife are feted at a 25th anniversary party.

Enraged that his father is destroying the family, Stuart rushes to Aileen's house intent on killing whatever man he finds but his mother arrives in time to prevent him from killing his father. The entire Borden family is chastened by the experience and vow to start a new life together.[86]

The scenario is similar in theme and setting to several of Paul's creations during that period, lending more credence that *My Wife and I* was his. The convoluted family relationships, infidelity, and the remote location of the climactic scenes are reminiscent of his earlier 1920 stories *The North Wind's Malice, Suspicious Wives* and *Greater Than Love.*

In late July, Paul took a large crew by train to Sacramento and six hours by car north into the mountains for *Flower of Night*, a Pola Negri drama set in 1856. A large camp was built near the mining town of Red Dog, 12 miles east of Grass Valley (made famous in Bret Harte's stories). The area was settled during the 1848 gold rush and grew from 20 cabins to 150 buildings housing 50 saloons and brothels but by 1925 it was abandoned. A single mine 20 miles away remained.

Wealthy miner Don Geraldo y Villalon (Joseph Dowling), descended from Spanish nobility, is cheated out of the family's Flor de Noche gold mine by Derck Bylandt. Don Geraldo is devastated when his daughter Carlota (Pola Negri) falls in love with John Basset, Bylandt's assistant manager, and she sneaks out to attend a ball with him. After being accosted by a drunken Bylandt, Carlota returns home and confesses she has dishonored the family name. When her disgraced father commits suicide, she flees to San Francisco and becomes a dance hall girl and meets Luke Rand, the sinister head of the local Vigilance Committee, who will recover her mine if she will marry him. She agrees but when she learns his plan involves killing Bassett she warns him, he kills Rand in a fight and he and Carlota are reconciled.[87]

The film was a huge undertaking. Fifteen hundred extras were hired to re-populate the town, and water was pumped in from four miles away. Paramount hired legendary gambler Scott "The Cherokee Kid" Turner to oversee the gambling sequences and after two weeks in the mountains the crew returned to film exteriors in Hollywood. The combination of Negri and "the wonderful direction of Paul Bern ... resulted in a picture well beyond anything she has ever done."[88] He was described as a director of "intellect, of subtlety, of strength, and beauty of dramatic theme"[89] and credited with producing it "sweepingly and gorgeously."[90]

Paul was still preaching that studios needed to continue the evolution of plots and themes to satisfy a market that he knew was smarter than perceived. He told a writer, "Sure-fire situations that supposedly [interest] the public are the greatest obstacles to movie progress. Unless we get away from the saving of mortgaged homes and ... aged mothers in distress, the screen will show little progress. Real dramatic punches lie in originality, in simple and human situations — not in time-worn hokum."[91]

He looked forward to the time when studios "ran out" of classic books and plays and "a new art form will be born; that of writing for the screen."[92] He believed writing for film was a talent separate from writing for books or stage and that scenarists had to be "neither playwright nor novelist...." To make his point, he suggested that the 1924 Adolph Zukor Award for writing awarded Rafael Sabatini for his book *Scaramouche* should be given to Willis Goldbeck, who adapted the book for the Metro film. Paul singled out Goldbeck, Frances Marion, Forrest Hasley, Agnes Christine Johnston and William A. Younger as masters of the art of screenwriting. All were young but eventually were recognized among the greatest of that generation.

Just before *Flower of Night* began, Paramount announced that Paul would direct *The Talk of the Town* at the Long Island facilities as the screen debut of Gilda Gray, a Shubert's Follies dancer known for her scandalous, sexually charged "shimmy." But on August 3, stories calling him "the successor to Cecil B. DeMille at Famous Players–Lasky" reported he was "leaving on the completion of one year's service at the finish of *The Night Flower*...."[93] A few weeks later it was confirmed "Paul Bern ... will transfer his megaphonic talents to the Metro-Goldwyn-Mayer studio."[94] Irving Thalberg hired him as his editor, running the story department and writing staff.

❧ FIVE ❧

Paul and Irving

MGM was born of a series of events involving Adolph Zukor and Marcus Loew dating back to 1919. Some were planned but most were due to fortuitous, blind luck. Zukor's Lasky-Paramount group needed bigger theaters and Loew's huge theater chain needed product, so in 1919 Loew took over Metro and with it, Louis B. Mayer's small production unit. For the next four years Metro churned out five movies a week but Loew hated running studios and was disappointed with his profits and made a last-ditch trip to L.A. in February 1924 with the idea of getting rid of it altogether.

He returned to New York impressed with Mayer's young assistant Irving Thalberg but still wanted to sell and a few weeks later at his Palm Beach estate mentioned his plan to Broadway impresario Lee Shubert, who unbeknownst to Loew owned a piece of Goldwyn Studios and suggested that Loew buy Goldwyn and merge the companies.[1] Shubert introduced Loew to Frank Godsol and Loew bought Goldwyn Studios to expand Metro's production for his theaters.[2]

Loew's, Inc., absorbed the Goldwyn and Louis B. Mayer Studios and became Metro-Goldwyn-Mayer, described by Thalberg biographer Roland Flamini as "the triple merger of a long-established but inefficient studio, a financially ailing one, and Mayer's smaller but thriving outfit."[3] The new MGM was a division of Loew's and would take over Goldwyn's Culver City lot, run by Mayer and Thalberg. MGM would produce films and Loew's would be the primary exhibitor through their 125 theaters and 150,000 seats, most in the heavily populated northeast.[4] MGM would also rent films to 25,000 non–Loew theaters. Mayer was paid $1,500 a week and Thalberg $650, but a side agreement paid Mayer 10 percent and Thalberg 5 percent of the profits.[5] Loew didn't think the two would make much money but the clause made both rich. MGM came into being on April 14, 1924.

Loew inherited several intellectual properties created by reporter turned Goldwyn publicity man Howard Dietz, who suggested the new MGM use

Goldwyn's "Leo the Lion" logo Dietz designed (Mayer wanted to use his eagle). Dietz also created the "Ars Gratia Artis" motto, based on the incorrect Latin translation "Art for Art's Sake," and would later coin MGM's "More Stars Than There Are in Heaven" nickname.[6]

During MGM's first year, Thalberg organized the studio with his small cadre of trusted advisors: Bernie Hyman, Arlie Lewin, and Harry Rapf. Paul was a member of the inner circle from the moment he arrived, recognized as Thalberg's creative man and No. 2.[7] Hyman was gregarious and funny with the face of a child; he wore nothing but plaid sport coats. Lewin had an encyclopedic knowledge of the written word, a Masters from Harvard and an unfinished doctoral dissertation from Columbia, and was Thalberg's source for intellectual advice. Rapf's large nose earned him monikers like "The Anteater" or "Thalberg's sundial" and was known for Rapf-isms like "This is the best apple pie I ever ate with my whole mouth" and for once telling Thalberg, "I woke up last night with a terrific idea for a movie, but I didn't like it."[8]

Just outside the circle were Kate Corbaloy and Hunt Stromberg. Thalberg found Corbaloy, his chief writing assistant, teaching screenwriting at the Palmer Institute of Authorship. Producer Stromberg was a handsome Kentucky-born sportswriter with a nervous tic who was the sloppiest dresser at MGM; Thalberg could tell what he had for lunch by looking at this tie. Thalberg valued their opinions and actively sought their counsel.

Getting into Thalberg's second-floor office was difficult. The reception area was larger than the office and crowded with people trying to get past secretaries Dorothy Howell and Vivian Newcomb. Even Mayer rarely got in on his first attempt. Director Victor Seastrom once sat outside for three days waiting to see his boss before leaving for two weeks in Sweden. When he returned, he ran into Vivian Newcomb, who told him, "Oh, Mr. Seastrom, I think Mr. Thalberg can see you now."[9] Paul and his secretary were down the hall from Thalberg, sharing a reception area with Rapf.

Paul's contract paid $675 a week (roughly $12,000 today) but he continued to live in his small Ambassador Hotel aerie. He was ambivalent toward possessions and did not believe in owning property, feeling that he was an instrument through which property should flow for good. He freely loaned money and expected no repayment. Carey Wilson helped him organize receipts for his accountant and was shocked to discover that almost 40 percent of Paul's income went out as "loans" that Wilson knew would never be repaid.[10] When writer Jim Tully was adamant that he wanted to repay a $100 loan in 1924, Paul finally agreed to accept the money on the condition that Tully name another writer who needed it.[11]

To Irving, Paul became a private transmitter of the atmosphere and culture of a world of sophisticates with which young Thalberg had little contact and which as a man he had come to enjoy deeply. Joan Crawford said of Paul, "He understood talent. He also understood the undisciplined uneducated girls who were unable to handle that talent. He certainly understood me.... [H]is impeccable taste guided me as it guided so many others ... in books, in art, in learning, he had a keen perspective on the business."[12] He joined the new studio in late October and Thalberg announced his first assignment was directing Charles Ray, Eleanor Boardman and Carmel Myers in *Paris*.[13]

Paul attended his friend Viola Dana's wedding to actor Maurice Flynn on June 20 in Hollywood. He escorted Dana to dozens of industry events and parties during the years since her then fiancé, stuntman Ormer Locklear, died in a 1920 plane crash filming *The Skywayman*.

While Paul's star was rising, those of two of his closest friends — Mabel Normand and Barbara La Marr — were plummeting. After seeing her brushed with scandal one too many times, the public had tired of Mabel's excessive lifestyle. Her connection to the Taylor murder and the Dines shooting led to calls for a ban on her films and when she was named a co-respondent in a divorce case a few months later her career was effectively over. Paul tried unsuccessfully to get her work but by the summer of 1925 she had no place to go so she left Hollywood for the New York stage (though the prospect terrified her).

On August 2 she hosted a farewell party at her new Beverly Hills house at 526 Camden Drive. The house (still standing today) was a lovely but unpretentious Moorish stucco bungalow with a large backyard garden filled with wicker furniture. The party was attended by 100 of the Hollywood elite like Pola Negri, Rod La Rocque, Bessie Love, Marie Prevost and Normand's ex-fiancé Mack Sennett. Paul served as unofficial co-host and the next morning the same group and 25 photographers saw Mabel off aboard the Sante Fe Limited in Glendale.[14]

At the same time, years of drug and alcohol abuse caught up with Barbara La Marr. Thalberg biographer Roland Flamini suggested that she convinced Paul to try heroin and his subsequent addiction forced Thalberg to put him into a sanitarium.[15] But that seems to be fiction; it never arose during research and interviews and if it were true, MGM would probably have used it after his death but did not.

By 1925 she was barely able to function as her health rapidly failed. During the previous year, even as her health and appearance deteriorated she made six films like *Thy Name Is Woman* and *Heart of a Siren*.[16] In January–February 1925 she managed to complete *The White Monkey* in New York but as soon as filming finished she collapsed and returned to Hollywood. Paul moved her father and her to a home at 1234 Boston Avenue in Altadena, a far-off

When Barbara La Marr made *The Heart of a Siren* she was on the verge of a total collapse.

town north of Burbank. Today the area is crowded with homes but in 1925 half the lots on the block were empty and the acreage between was farmed. It was a restful spot where Barbara spent the rest of 1925 unsuccessfully trying to regain her health.[17]

She had wasted millions of dollars on men, parties, and drugs and had no money left. Paul had been sending money to her for a year and now paid for a visiting nurse three days a week, for weekly doctor visits and for her other bills.[18] She told one reporter, "No one is really poor who can boast a friendship with Paul Bern. Dear Paul is the only man I have ever known who has permitted me to love him as a friend."[19]

Another close friend, actress ZaSu Pitts, took in La Marr's son Marvin. Only her closest friends knew that La Marr was dying. Several times a week Paul made the long trip from Hollywood to Altadena — in the pre-freeway days, it could take over an hour — to just sit with her. For months he sat for hours holding her hand, talking, or reading to her as he had done for little Lucille Ricksen a year before.

Paul delayed joining MGM until the fall because he was busy helping

La Marr. He gave her one final gift — an original scenario he sold to First National with the proviso she play the lead, but he refused credit so people wouldn't know she got the role through his intervention. He based *The Girl from Montmartre* on the Anthony Pryde novel *Spanish Sunlight*.[20] It was shot in October and November.

The Faneaux family lives on the island of Majorca, product of a wealthy but derelict English father and a Spanish mother. During World War I the Faneaux brothers fight for the Allies and sister Emilia (La Marr) dances in a Paris café to support the family. After the war she returns home where Jerome Hautrive (Lewis Stone), an aristocratic English officer and writer who knew her during the war, comes to court her. Her ne'er-do-well brother Rodney urges her to marry Ewing, a crooked but wealthy actor intent on swindling Hautrive, convincing her she can't marry Hautrive because of her status. She takes a job dancing in a dive to discourage Hautrive, but when Ewing abducts her, Hautrive rescues her and brings the Faneaux family back to his English estate.[21]

Critics lauded La Marr's performance and the "human touches" in Paul's script after the film's January 31, 1926 release.[22] But Barbara did not live to see the film. The shoot was physically taxing for her and she collapsed near the end of filming and retired to the Altadena bungalow.

Paul arrived at MGM in August and began working closely with Thalberg on the studio's newest project, a Swedish import named Greta Garbo, who would would arrive in September. Paul helped Thalberg — who retained producer credit for himself— prepare for *Torrent*, which would start after Thanksgiving. Thalberg often gets credit for Garbo's stardom but Paul either produced or co-produced every Garbo MGM film made in his lifetime. He was the primary caretaker of Garbo's film career; the final note typed onto her scripts was "SCRIPT OKAYED BY MR. BERN."

In October it was again announced "Paul Bern ... is a Metro-Goldwyn-Mayer director now. His first picture under this banner will be *Paris* in which Erte, the famous Parisian fashion creator, will work with him."[23] Charles Ray was to star "and Carmel Myers and Eleanor Boardman are the only other players cast so far."[24] Production was to start in the spring.

Paul arranged a role for Joan Crawford in *Paris*. Their relationship was probably mercenary; it's probably not coincidental that as the relationship blossomed she was more seriously groomed for stardom. Still, they appeared as a couple often during the spring and summer and she liked him; he provided her some much-needed culture along with the career support.

Garbo's *Torrent*, a Dorothy Farnum adaptation of a Vicente Blasco-Ibáñez novel, began filming in November. Garbo starred with Ricardo Cortez and Gertrude Olmstead in the Spanish love story of a mama's boy politician and a young diva of different classes. The female lead was originally offered to Norma Shearer, who declined the role.

Garbo's on-camera presence remains stunning. She turned a one-dimensional character into a sultry screen persona that has rarely been duplicated. Critics loved the film and said Garbo could look like "Carol Dempster, Norma Talmadge, ZaSu Pitts and Gloria Swanson in turn."[25] Paul and Thalberg would personally guide her every project at MGM.

When Paul arrived at MGM he was a prominent member of the movie colony but his reputation for helping people was already equally celebrated. The November, 1925 issue of *Photoplay* featured a story entitled "A Modern Samaritan" with the subhead "That's the Only Title That Quite Fits Paul Bern."[26] He was described as having an "age-old understanding and sympathy for human problems — the key to greatness." Studio publicity embellished his childhood: 18 Levy children now shared a "wretched and squalid" tenement with furniture made from boxes, he sold newspapers with holes in his shoes to support his family, his parents were "over sixty" and his father was said to have lost his fortune. It was all untrue but made for great pathos.

Jim Tully said Paul possessed "the elegance and poise and the manner of one with centuries of breeding" and was "a rare spectacle in Hollywood. In a city where ego floats to the surface like bubbles he remains in the background. His name is a byword of kindness and understanding. He is the most beloved citizen in the City of Make-Believe." Tully said "People come to Paul with all manner of troubles. He is the priest of Hollywood."

Writer Hedda Hopper

All Garbo scripts bore the label "Script Okayed by Mr. Bern." This is the MGM vault copy of *Susan Lenox: Her Fall and Rise.*

said, "Paul is for the downtrodden ... for the oppressed and for those in trouble, whether there are young or old, black or white, male or female. You hear of the sensational and exotic women he befriended (La Marr, Joan Crawford, Estelle Taylor, and Normand) ... but you never hear of the dozens of obscure and humble persons he befriends, gives money to, gives time to. Paul Bern is Hollywood's Father Confessor." Hopper also described Paul's habit of remembering important dates after they were mentioned; "If you just happen to mention casually, in his presence, that you have a fancy for yellow roses on some strange anniversary, you will *get* a crate of yellow roses on that day for the rest of your life!"[27]

Of his behind-the-scenes work at MGM, a fellow director described him as "more than a producer. He is the diplomat of the lot. It is Paul who Irving turns to smooth down ruffled temperaments and pour balm on injured feelings. It is Paul who pacifies an irate star when some cherished part is given to another. He is the producer of— Peace."[28]

Everyone seemingly loved this quiet, introspective, kindly man. He received invitations to almost every social event in Hollywood and attended many; he loved a party and being around people. He was among the most respected executives in the movies and the most beloved man in Hollywood.

Paul began 1926 working with Thalberg on Garbo's second film *The Temptress*. Filming was scheduled to begin in late March and was expected to take at least two months.

Back in November, 1925, papers had reported "Death Poised to Write Finis to Colorful Career of Girl Who was 'Too Beautiful.'"[29] By December, La Marr was barely able to speak, had wasted to less than 80 pounds and remained virtually bedridden through the holidays.

Almost every day for two months Paul had visited the woman who called him "the

Swedish import Greta Garbo at the time she arrived at MGM in 1925. With Thalberg, Paul took an active hand directing all aspects of her career.

understanding heart."[30] He tried to help her cope with the death they both knew was imminent. When she said to him, "I don't want to die, Paul. I'm too young," he told her, "You've lived seven lives, Barbara. You're not being cheated when you go."[31] She gave him her favorite beautiful black fan with a rosary tangled in its plumes.[32] A few days later on the sunny Wednesday afternoon of January 27, 1926, Paul coaxed her out of bed for a walk around the neighborhood, after which she retreated to bed. The following Sunday, the 30th, she died. She was only 29. Paul was alone with her, holding her hand when she died.

For his own reasons La Marr's father didn't want a funeral and arranged for a cremation without a service. Paul stepped in and stopped the cremation and organized for the elaborate funeral service that La Marr's fans expected, and insisted on an open casket. Papers noted, "Vampire of the Screen to Receive One Last Tribute in Death."[33]

For three days her casket lay on a gold velvet bier covered with flowers. In her hand was a single red rose, a gift from a young fan. A spray of orchids from Douglas Fairbanks and Mary Pickford lay across her waist. An estimated 40,000 people streamed past as several mini-riots broke out among the throngs waiting outside. Two dozen policemen were called to maintain order.[34]

On February 5, all of Hollywood attended the annual WAMPAS ball. The next morning a few close friends traded gowns for funeral suits. Paul led a contingent of John McCormack, Colleen Moore, ZaSu Pitts, Bessie Love, Gladys Brockwell, Marshall Neilan, Blanche Sweet, Milton Cohen, Gloria Swanson, and Claire Windsor. Paul was not a pallbearer, too upset to attend to that duty with Tom Gallery (ZaSu Pitts' husband), Bert Lytell, Henry Hathaway, Henry Victor, Alfred E. Green, and R.D. Knickerbocker. The simple service was presided over by a Christian Science reader after which La Marr was interred in a crypt at Hollywood Memorial Park, just down the aisle from Rudolph Valentino.[35] When La Marr's estate was probated it was worth less than $10,000.[36] Paul paid for the funeral and designed a marker saying simply: Barbara La Marr With God in the Joy and Beauty of Youth 1896–1926.

Just a few weeks after the funeral, papers reported that Tom Gallery and ZaSu Pitts had begun the process of adopting young Marvin La Marr. Interestingly, it was also reported that Paul was trying to adopt the child, for some reason called "Ivan" in period stories.[37]

It would make sense that Paul would want to adopt his son but equally reasonable he would allow Gallery and Pitts to do so. No records of any legal wrangling could be found so it appears Paul simply backed off and let the Gallery-Pitts adoption take place. Once their adoption was complete, Marvin was renamed Donald.

After La Marr's death, Paul returned to work on Garbo's *The Temptress*,

Barbara La Marr, as beautiful in death as she was in life.

like *Torrent* a Dorothy Farnum adaptation of a Vicente Blasco-Ibáñez novel. Gaetano Gaudio was assigned to film but Garbo demanded William Daniels; she was pleased with his results in *Torrent* and for the rest of her career would not accept a role unless Daniels was the cameraman. Filming began the end of March and lasted into July. It was the story of a married woman who follows her engineer lover to a construction project in Argentina while destroying every man she meets.[38] Thalberg was credited as producer but Paul was involved in everything from casting to suggesting that the original ending — the alcohol-muddled vamp in a seedy Parisian bar unable to recognize her former lover — be replaced with a happy ending where the engineer wins an award for the project, sees her in the crowd and calls her onstage and gives her credit. Exhibitors were given the choice of the original or a happy ending; the city theatergoers liked the original ending while the far-off viewers wanted the happy ending.

In the next four months, three of Paul's scenarios were produced by Robert T. Kane's unit at Cosmopolitan Pictures, William Randolph Hearst's company that produced films featuring Marion Davies. She was talented but suffered from Hearst's insistence she do lavish drama rather than comedy that better suited her. MGM inherited Cosmopolitan after an earlier 1924 deal between Hearst and Goldwyn; the studio distributed Cosmopolitan's films in exchange for publicity from Hearst's papers, a relationship that was one of the most important parts of the original Loew merger agreement.[39] Kane filmed at the Cosmopolitan lot at 127th and 2nd in New York.

In March and April, Kane made *The Wilderness Woman*, a romantic comedy starring Aileen Pringle, Chester Conklin and Lowell Sherman. The film has not been credited to Paul but papers credited "Paul Bern and Paul Schofield" for adapting the Arthur Stringer serial from the *Saturday Evening Post*.[40]

Alaskan miner Kodiak MacLean (Conklin) sells his gold strike for $1,000,000 and sets out for New York with his daughter Juneau (Pringle). On the train they meet con men The Colonel and Robert, who try to swindle the pair out of their bankroll. Their pet bear Skeemo creates a riot in the lobby of their plush hotel as the two innocents are met by Alan Burkett (Sherman), the engineer who appraised their mine. Juneau is entranced by Fifth Avenue fashions while the swindlers then try to steal Kodiak's money by getting him drunk; he drinks them under a table in a funny and cleverly crafted scene. When Robert makes a pass at Juneau — becoming more sophisticated as the film continues — she knocks him out as Burkett arrives and all ends happily.[41] The film was released to good reviews on May 6. The only writing credit that survived was Don Bartlett's titles.

Kane next made Paul's *The Great Deception*, starting on April 12. Based on the George Gibbs novel *The Yellow Dove*, it was an elaborate and expensive shoot; 35 sets were built including a replica German village on Long Island. Kane also filmed at a Tudor estate in Morristown, New Jersey, and arranged to film at Army bases at Fort Totten and Fort Slocum on Long Island and the Navy submarine base at New London, Connecticut. He also rented dozens of planes from Curtis Aviation, filmed complex aerial scenes at their airfield in Mineola, Long Island, and staged a complicated automobile chase on a New Jersey highway.[42]

Paul adapted Gibbs' spy thriller of pilot Cyril Mansfield (Ben Lyon), who grew up in Germany with a German mother and an English father and during World War I is a double agent, working for the German Secret Service but loyal to British intelligence. His love Lois (Aileen Pringle) is pursued by another double agent, Rizzio (Basil Rathbone), who suspects Cyril is betraying Germany. Cyril, his faithful mechanic Handy, and Lois fly his plane (the "Yellow Dove") to Germany to sell false information and when Lois is taken by Rizzio to headquarters in a U-boat she innocently betrays Cyril and they are both sentenced to death. Rizzio takes Lois on a diplomatic mission but Cyril and Handy escape, rescue her and flee to England in his plane.[43]

Director Howard Higgin's filming of 500 scenes lasted until June 12, cost over $250,000, and was plagued with delays; Lyon fell and wrenched his back, Pringle and Higgin fell ill, and a prop man died after falling and splitting his skull with the claw of his hammer.[44] It was finally released on July 25 with Paul's scenario earning plaudits as "possessing an element of mystery and suspense mindful of the yarns that come from authors like E. Phillips Oppenheim."[45]

Paul spent the spring shuttling between L.A. and New York during the *Wilderness* and *Deception* shoots but by then he would not visit Dorothy. For several years she had been living at the Algonquin like a recluse, rarely engaging people in conversation and leaving her room only to buy her newspaper, for meals, and infrequent wanderings talking to herself about religion and speaking with God. She always wore the same clothing; a long red coat and matching turban.[46] Ominously, she convinced herself she could be an actress in grand Biblical pictures and Paul could make it happen.

Henry Bern said the visits with the increasingly more delusional Dorothy made Paul physically ill. His newly hired secretary Irene Harrison began sending his monthly checks to Henry in New Rochelle rather than to Dorothy. Henry then gave Dorothy her money.

The Prince of Tempters was the third of Paul's scenarios produced by Robert Kane and was filmed in late June. The scenario was based on the novel *The Ex-Duke* by E. Phillips Oppenheim and was the American debut of German actress Lya De Putti and German director Lothar Mendes.[47]

The British Duke of Chatsfield secretly marries an Italian peasant girl and they have a son, Francis (Ben Lyon), but the couple dies and Francis is raised in a Roman monastery until an uncle learns of him and restores him to his position as duke. While he's gone, con man Mario Ambrosio pursues Francis' beautiful cousin Monica (Lois Moran) and hires his ex-mistress Dolores (De Putti) to go to London and ensnare Francis and keep him away. When Francis' romance with Monica is ruined after she learns of his dalliance with Dolores, he returns to London and a series of wild affairs (that gave title to the story). After learning that Monica was to marry Mario, he renounces his title and returns to the monastery but a chastened Dolores admits her duplicity to Monica, who travels to Italy to retrieve her lost "prince of tempters."[48]

Critics praised the film as "the most nearly perfect picture from an artistic point of view this year"[49] and noted the adaptation by Paul that artfully blended comedy and romantic drama so "that neither ever got in the way of the other."[50]

The daughter of a Hungarian baron, Lya De Putti trained in classical ballet and made her way from Hungarian vaudeville to German films. She resembled Colleen Moore and, working with F.W. Murnau and Fritz Lang, became a star known for vamp roles. After her 1925 German classic *Variete* (*Variety*) became a U.S. hit, Adolph Zukor imported her for D.W. Griffith's *The Sorrows of Satan*.

She met Paul during *Tempters* filming and was terrified of failing in America since she spoke no English and knew nothing of the life and customs. So Paul arranged for tutors, found her a place in New York, and helped with studio dealings.[51] They dated during the summer and fall of 1926 and years later papers noted whenever she had problems she "ran to Paul Bern for help."[52]

Paul was known as Thalberg's first assistant and as "Thalberg's strongest right arm," and responsible for all MGM story decisions.[53] It was his job to find vehicles for specific stars, suggest how a story might be adapted, and ensure writers created appropriate MGM product. Among his first 1926 suggestions to Irving was to buy rights to the Alexandre Dumas fils novel and play *La dame aux Camélias* which became the hit *Camille* with Norma Talmadge and Gilbert Roland.[54] He and Irving were also preparing for the late summer production of Garbo's next film, *Flesh and the Devil*.

In June, Irving came to Paul, panicked because John Barrymore was balking at returning to Hollywood to star in the lavish spectacle *The Beloved Rogue*. A month earlier Barrymore took part in a California-to-Honolulu race in his 93-foot gaff-rigged racing schooner *The Mariner* and intended to enter the Honolulu-to–San Francisco race the following month and was showing no disposition to leave for Hollywood any time soon. Irving sent Paul to Hawaii to bring him back.

Hungarian beauty Lya De Putti, who Paul dated during 1926.

Barrymore was an authority on *Rogue* lead character François Villon, one of France's greatest poets and lovers who lived a life Barrymore considered similar to his own. Oddly, when Barrymore was a struggling artist he drew the original theater poster of E. H. Sothern as Villon for the famous play.[55] He didn't believe a studio could produce a strong enough script about a nuanced character he described as having "a whimsical integrity ... [but] skipping, bounding, and crawling on his stomach through a Gothic dimension of a dying chivalry and a brutal and slightly sacerdotal materialism until ... he is forced, through the reality of his suffering ... to a different attitude, always, however, flecked with a pinch of gaiety."[56]

Paul and director Alan Crosland sailed from L.A. on June 18 — with Paul's script revision in hand — and spent two weeks carousing with Barrymore aboard his yacht (with his monkey Clementine, who sailed in a tiny sailor's cap made especially for her). They convinced him to return with them and Paul, Crosland, and Barrymore left Hawaii aboard the S.S. *City of Los Angeles* on the 30th. After a stopover in San Francisco on July 2, they arrived in L.A. the 4th.[57] During the voyage, Barrymore collaborated with Paul on the script and Paul let him add a role for a friend's pet duck.[58] In L.A. they were met by Bennie Ziedman, head of the Schenck production unit, who escorted Barrymore directly to a studio bungalow. After costuming, filming began on the 20th.

The Beloved Rogue was produced by Joseph Schenck's Art Cinema unit. Barrymore personally selected Conrad Veidt for the role of King Louis XI and wired him in Germany that he wouldn't make the film without him. The studio was surprised to learn that Veidt was 6' 3" and, knowing Louis XI was short and squat, concealed his height with long robes and made him walk in a stooped fashion.

William Cameron Menzies, acclaimed for his massive *Thief of Baghdad* sets, crafted incredibly detailed and lavish period sets described as "imaginatively grotesque." He created lavish royal dwellings at the Pickford-Fairbanks Studio on Santa Monica Boulevard, along with a slum neighborhood, and an entire city of intricately snow-covered roofs. The realism is stunning.

Villon lived an amazing life. His father was martyred (burned at the stake fighting for France in 1432) and as an adult Villon became Paris' best-known poet, passionately devoted to country but a notorious carouser not above criminal acts. (He was described in title cards as "poet, pickpocket, patriot — loving France earnestly, French women excessively, French wine exclusively.") Rather than earlier books and plays, Paul based his film version on Villon's wills, the Petit Testament and the Grand Testament. He wrote his wills in verse form and filled them with strange bequests because he considered them ironic jest since he was a pauper with nothing to leave but his words. Unpublished for 30 years after his death, they are considered poetic masterpieces.

Paul's scenario was a complex story with simultaneous plot lines centered on Villon, who lives among the city's poor. The king (Veidt) is timid and weak-minded, a "superstitious, crafty, cruel — slave of the stars" who relies on his astrologer Nigel, who advises that war with Charles, duke of Burgundy would be disastrous. The duke seeks the throne through subterfuge and when he asks the king to give his ward, Charlotte of Vauxcelles (Marceline Day), to his cousin Count Thibault d'Auvvigny, in marriage, the king accedes in spite of Charlotte's protests.

Holiday revelers honor Villon by choosing him King of All Fool's Day and he accepts the title and allows himself to be made up as a clown and placed atop a horse statue in the town square. The duke arrives, but Villon knows of his intentions and insults him. The King's fear of the Duke leads him to banish Villon from Paris. While in exile, Villon steals the king's catapult and launches stolen food over the city walls for the poor but is himself accidentally catapulted through a window into an inn where Charlotte is waiting to leave for her wedding. She runs away with him and, in a wonderful scene, follows Villon across snow-covered rooftops to his mother's house, where he slides down a rooftop right into an open window and encourages Charlotte to follow. She is afraid but he urges, "Slide, gentle lady, slide — and I will catch you — without catching a glimpse," and she slides right into his arms.

Villon is captured and sentenced to death but he escapes to save Charlotte, who has been kidnapped by Burgundy's men, even though he has learned that "Charlotte of Vauxcelles may not marry a man without lands and a great name." Villon finally convinces the king of the schemes of the duke, and after another capture and death sentence and yet another escape, is rewarded with Charlotte's hand in marriage.[59]

Filming and retakes lasted until February 14 and the movie was released March 12, 1927, but the artful piece strayed over the heads of viewers and critics. *The New York Times'* Mordaunt Hall criticized Crosland's lavish sets as "extravagancies" and "exaggerations" and Barrymore's performance as "a comic character in the Sunday [papers]."[60] Critics also disapproved of Paul straying from the novel: "It is obvious in *The Beloved Rogue*, which comes to the screen from Paul Bern's pen, every effort has been made to dodge Mr. McCarthy's novel and play."[61]

Audiences were also confused by Barrymore's straggly shoulder-length hair, pencil-thin moustache and wispy beard described by biographer Margot Peters as looking like "an aged Peter Pan." His athletic performance — sliding down banisters, leaping from buildings, and flying through the air — also reminded viewers of the film antics of Douglas Fairbanks; "[T]he

Fairbanksian style heartily adopted by Barrymore was so unexpected by his fans and so unanimously condemned by the critics that the film did not do well financially."[62] Barrymore himself hated the film and sat in the balcony at one of the first showings and startled the audience by shouting, "Call yourself an actor? My God, what a ham!"[63] He fled Hollywood for a month, sailing to South America aboard *The Mariner*.

Watching *The Beloved Rogue* today, one is at once enthralled by Barrymore's characterization of the complex character and stunned by the beauty of the filming. Paul's script effortlessly bounces between the different story lines on the back of Crosland's story-telling and the beautifully crafted sets.

In a fortuitous twist, the single surviving print of *The Beloved Rogue* was discovered secreted behind a wall in John Barrymore's former Tower Road estate in Beverly Hills by its then current occupant, Edgar Bergen, who donated it to the American Film Institute. The masterpiece was subsequently preserved by the Library of Congress.

After *The Temptress* and *Torrent*, it was apparent that Greta Garbo was at another level; Louise Brooks said, "From the moment *Torrent* went into production no contemporary actress was ever again to be quite happy with herself."[64] On August 8 she began her third film, *Flesh and the Devil*, the story of an unfaithful wife whose husband is killed in a duel caused by her affair. She then marries the man who shot her husband while carrying on another affair with *his* best friend. She starred opposite John Gilbert in the film which neither originally wanted to do.

A blazing on-screen chemistry was sparked during one of the first scenes filmed, the first horizontal love scene put on film. Gilbert's daughter later said, "You can actually see these two terribly attractive people falling in love with each other in the scene."[65] During filming she impetuously agreed to marry him.

On September 8 at Marion Davies' 1700 Lexington Road mansion, there was to have been a double wedding: director King Vidor to Eleanor Boardman and Gilbert to Garbo. As the morning dragged on, Gilbert realized Garbo was leaving him at the altar, retreated to a bathroom and encountered Louis B. Mayer, who slapped the weeping star on the back and laughed, "What's the matter with you, Gilbert? Why don't you just go on fucking her and forget about the wedding."[66] Gilbert grabbed Mayer by the throat and hurled him to the floor as Mayer screamed, "You're finished, Gilbert! I'll destroy you if it costs me a million dollars!"

For the next five years, Thalberg tried to protect Gilbert, as did Paul, but Mayer would make Gilbert suffer for the deed. Surprisingly, Gilbert forgave Garbo, and *Flesh and the Devil* filming continued to the 28th as if nothing happened. Within a month she was moved into his Tower Road estate. Their movie earned MGM almost $475,000.

There was another wedding surprise in September when Mabel Normand married Lew Cody on the 17th. Her exile to New York in 1925 was a miserable failure. Her incurable stage fright during *A Little Mouse* was met with resounding criticism; "We owe her thanks for added proof that ... there is a vast gulf between motion-picture work and acting."[67] She fled back to Hollywood in March but was only offered five shorts for Hal Roach, after which her contract was dropped.

During a drunken dinner on the 16th, Cody jokingly asked her to marry him and she agreed. They raced to Ventura and awoke a justice of the peace, were married and raced home. They seemed a good match, the "I Don't Care Girl" and the "Devil May Care Man."[68] Like Mabel, Cody enjoyed practical jokes and parties, and was even more famous than Mabel for his drinking. But the next morning she told Eddie Sutherland, "I don't feel like working. When one isn't happy, one doesn't like to work."[69]

Paul's weekend visits to see his son Donald became more important in the fall of 1926 after ZaSu Pitts' husband Tom Gallery essentially abandoned the family. His once-promising career was idling while the multi-talented Pitts' prospects were rising quickly. A veteran of over 200 films, she was a talented actress with a reputation as a scene-stealer who often overshadowed the star. Her scenes were often removed from the final print to keep the peace. Gallery couldn't handle the "Star Is Born" situation with his wife and walked out on the family that fall. Pitts filed for legal separation on November 25.[70]

On November 18 it was announced that "Corinne Griffith's next picture, following completion of *The Lady in Ermine*, will be *Purple and Fine Linen* from the story by May Eddington. Paul Bern will write the continuity and James Flood will direct."[71] Paul's script, re-titled *Three Hours*, was an adaptation of the Eddington story in the *Bedside Book of Famous British Stories*.[72] The film began production in New York in December.

Madeline Durkin (Griffith) is reduced to poverty after she divorces wealthy but ill-tempered Jonathan Durkin (Hobart Bosworth), who gains custody of their baby by making up an alleged affair. Receiving a letter from him allowing a visit as long as she arrives before 10:00 that evening, she realizes she is too poorly dressed to see her child. Businessman James Finlay (John Bowers) is about to give her money when he is distracted and she tries to steal his wallet but he finds her in a shop buying a dress and hails a cab to take her to the police. She begs for three hours' reprieve and he takes pity and buys her dinner as she tells her sad tale (shown in still-photo flashbacks). Finlay

Opposite: **John Gilbert on the porch of his Tower Road aerie, at the time of his tortured relationship with Garbo.**

Greta Garbo's screen presence was unmistakable as seen here with Antonio Moreno in *The Temptress*.

travels with her to Jonathan's apartment and when she breathlessly arrives she realizes he invited her only to see the baby's small white coffin. The baby had died the day before. Heartbroken, she finds consolation in Finlay's love.[73]

    Three Hours received decidedly mixed reviews. One review, entitled "A Gruesome Revenge," described it as "a distasteful affair that never by the wildest stretch of the imagination could be construed as entertainment."[74] But others praised the film as "pulling at the heartstrings..." and Griffith's acting as "the dramatic masterpiece of her career."[75] Paul—a "famous director and scenarist"—received praise for the melodramatic scenario.[76]

Paul took the Sante Fe Limited to New York on December 10 and spent three weeks there during filming, also looking for screenplays and meeting with authors like Zoe Akins and John Hunter Booth, a process he described as "buying a suit of clothes for a star."[77] He returned to L.A. on January 2, again without seeing Dorothy.

As MGM headed into 1927 there were ominous clouds gathering. Studios already concerned with declining attendance also worried about the growing popularity of radio and, simply, sound in general. Al Jolson's later 1927 film *The Jazz Singer* is widely recognized as the first sound film but as early as June, 1925, Warners partnered with Vitaphone and Western Electric to develop a system synchronizing phonograph records with running film and affecting a "talking picture."

On August 6, 1926, Warners offered a program of sound films: a short speech by Will Hays, the L.A. Philharmonic performing the Tannhauser overture and, after an intermission, John Barrymore's *Don Juan* with a musical soundtrack. Hays later said, "In the darkness I said to myself, 'A new miracle has been wrought and I have been part of it."[78] It was a new era, nothing short of a miraculous technology. *The New York Times* confirmed, "[N]o single word, however compounded, is quite adequate to suggest the amazing triumph which man has at last achieved in making pictures talk naturally...."[79]

Fox followed with its Movietone sound system used for early 1927's *What Price Glory?* and in May released film of Charles Lindbergh taking off in Paris and another of President Coolidge welcoming him to America.[80]

For all his brilliance, Thalberg moved MGM into sound slowly. While Warners was building three huge sound stages in February, MGM joined First National, Universal, and Producers Distributing, agreeing to take a year studying concepts before choosing one system. Thalberg was strangely uninterested in what he considered a novelty and Paul seemed to at least publicly agree. Whether he was toeing the party line or actually believed it is hard to decipher.

He understood movies were commerce, candid in his assessment that a movie must be great industry before it is great art. Production cost $20,000 a day so the business side must succeed first. He hated paying $40,000 or $50,000 for a property he knew would be changed—"hammering and beating [it] out of all recognition and changing its original meaning and purpose"[81]—and still believed the best scripts came from in-house writers tailoring scripts to available casts.

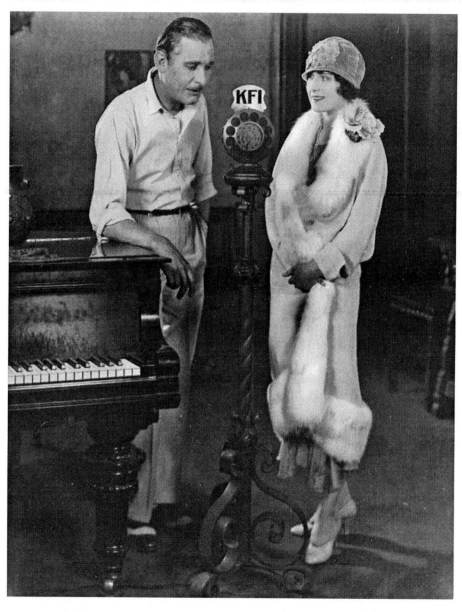

An early MGM sound test featuring Mabel Normand's husband Lew Cody and Norma Shearer.

He reiterated his belief that writers were still slowly evolving to writing for film rather than page, though "by slow and perhaps imperceptible degrees...." But he remained enthusiastic that so many stage people were finally over their belief that movies were beneath them. He still believed that the "big idea" film was the most likely to work and that film had a specialized ability to catch the imagination of the public. He offered an interesting lesson on the psychology of filmmaking:

> First there is the scenario writer, who receives the original story. Then there is the director with whom he works. They introduce into the screen effort a reflection of their personalities. The director and the writer are the sieve through which the idea filters, and while they are engaged on their work they may learn from the producer that they are putting in something that will offend the Mohammadans in India, or they may be told that they have something in the script that won't be acceptable to the Nebraska farmer. What novelist thinks of readers all over the world, as we have to?

Even beyond that, Paul realized a director's job was the most challenging since he must consider the personalities of everyone involved, from actors to cameramen. He retained an amazingly intuitive understanding of the process. It was easy to see why Thalberg put so much trust in Paul's opinions. The two were involved in almost every step of the process, which at MGM could be cumbersome according to writer Katherine Hilliker:

> You're told to write a set of titles for a picture, then instead of having them made up ... and fitting them into a picture, you have to take your title list to Mr. Rapf or Mr. Thalberg (or Paul) ... then the cutter, the continuity writer, a stray author or two ... are invited in and hullabaloo begins, every one of the assembled guests trying to outdo the other as your titles are read....[82]

Paul remained an open heart and wallet to friends from all levels. During February and March he made frequent visits to Santa Monica Hospital to visit Mabel, whose health was rapidly failing. Alcohol and drugs worsened already tubercular lungs and she spent a month near death before recovering and returning home to Camden Drive. Headlines like MABEL NORMAND NEAR DEATH and MABEL NORMAND DYING were common as she died "by inches."[83] From mid–1928 through 1929 the once-legendary comedian was absent from any mention in papers.

Friends and MGM employees beat a path to Paul's second-floor office for advice. Fredric March and Florence Eldridge were successful stage actors hesitant to move to film and after the 1927 theater season took a secret cross-country automobile trip to get Paul's advice first-hand.[84] They took his suggestion to try films and became among the best-known actors in Hollywood. Paul socialized with the couple often.

Joan Crawford continued to seek him out for career advice and that spring was reeling after the end of her relationship with meatpacking heir Michael Cudahy, who wanted to marry but couldn't overcome his mother's objections and broke if off. Paul nursed her through that period and the two again appeared to be a couple for six months or so. He also gave her the rosary-decorated fan he had been given by Barbara La Marr, saying, "I think Barbara would want you to have this."[85] Later that summer he helped arrange a studio loan so she could purchase her first house.

Paul's largesse sometimes hurt him. When writer Jim Tully arrived in Hollywood "in very straightened circumstances," Paul prevailed upon his friend Charlie Chaplin to hire Tully. After working for Chaplin for a year, Tully tired of studio life and wrote for movie magazines. Anxious to capitalize on his closeness to Chaplin, he wrote a serialized account of the comic's life and sold it to *The Pictorial Review*. When the magazine announced in early 1927 that it would publish Tully's stories and the "intimate anecdotes" of Chaplin's life, Chaplin sued Tully and the magazine for $50,000 to block publication.[86] Paul was dragged into the case, which was settled out of court.

On May 11, Paul attended a dinner at the Crystal Ballroom at the Biltmore Hotel for the official founding of the Academy of Motion Picture Arts and Sciences; he was one of three hundred industry heavyweights invited to become charter members. The organization was broken up into five segments: producers, actors, writers, directors and technicians. Paul wrote his check for $100 and listed himself as a director.

That spring Paul worked with Irving Thalberg on several major MGM films without credit but newspaper stories confirmed his involvement in the development and writing of *The Dove*, a Norma Talmadge vehicle based on the popular 1925 Willard Mack and Gerald Beaumont play. William Cameron Menzies earned an Academy Award for his stunning sets of old Mexico. Talmadge reported to the set the day after she completed the classic *Camille*.

The Mexican-themed film takes place in a café and gambling house just over the American border in the town of Costa Roja, where a fiery dance hall girl is caught between a young American and a Mexican gang chief. Dolores (Talmadge) — "The Dove" — is in love with gambler Johnny Powell (Gilbert Roland) but wealthy cattleman Don José Maria de Sandoval (Noah Beery)

Paul's studio portrait.

hires the café for the evening and becomes obsessed with her. To get rid of Powell he frames him on a murder charge. Dolores agrees to marry Don José if he releases Powell but on the eve of the marriage Powell returns to claim Dolores. Powell is arrested and both he and Dolores are to be shot when a mob inexplicably forces Don José to release them. Seeing his obsession isn't love, he says, "Dios, what a man I am," frees the couple and offers them his carriage in which to depart.[87]

Filming lasted from late spring into early summer but it was not released until December 31. Director Roland West, Mack and Wallace Smith were credited with the adaptation and Paul with the continuity, but Paul actually wrote the scenario; pre-filming stories noted, "Paul Bern [was] writing the adaptation of *The Dove* for United Artists...."[88] and "the scenario was written by Wallace Smith and Paul Bern."[89] Paul didn't care about receiving credits, allowing director West the writing credit for *The Dove*.

Thalberg was known as the creative force behind MGM but rarely made a production decision without Paul's input. Thalberg is usually credited with Garbo's rise but Paul was perhaps more responsible. He worked on all of her films, selecting half of them himself or having Irving buy vehicles for her, and put together her crews. His only credits were for *Romance*, *Susan Lenox: Her Fall and Rise*, and *Grand Hotel*. Even in those cases he was not publicly identified, however.

Garbo was still living with Jack Gilbert on Tower Road. To make her feel at home he built a mock Swedish cabin in a stand of pine trees behind the house and installed a remote-control stream stocked with trout. His weekly Sunday afternoon tennis gatherings attracted the cream of Hollywood but the core group was Paul, Carey Wilson, Thalberg, King Vidor, Eleanor Boardman, Edmund Lowe and Lilyan Tashman, Arthur Hornblow and Herman Mankiewicz.[90] This group was Paul's inner circle; he was particularly close to Wilson, Gilbert and Irving.

That spring, Irving and Paul were working on Garbo's next vehicle, *Love*, based on Leo Tolstoy's novel *Anna Karenina*. Ricardo Cortez was slated to co-star but after the public response to *Flesh and the Devil* he was replaced by John Gilbert on May 27. Lorna Moon and Frances Marion adapted the story about a woman who leaves her husband and son but soon realizes her tragic fate and the futility of her existence and commits suicide by throwing herself in front of a moving train.[91] Filming began on June 22.

The Gilbert-Garbo sexual chemistry hadn't cooled and as they had done with *The Temptress*, Thalberg and Paul offered an alternate happy ending to the Tolstoy version. Again, East and West Coast exhibitors preferred the tragedy and the middle of the country favored the Frances Marion reuniting of Vronsky and Anna. Even though it cost $488,000 (five times the original

$125,000 budget) it was Garbo's most profitable silent film, earning MGM $571,000. Gilbert and Garbo were "becoming the biggest box office team this country has yet known."[92]

In July, Paul made his first visit to the palatial San Simeon estate that William Randolph Hearst built for Marion Davies. Only Hollywood elite received the coveted invitation for a weekend at "Nuestra Encantada" (Enchanted Hill), the spectacular centerpiece of Hearst's 450,000-acre estate in California's Central Coast where Davies played host to notables like Charles Lindbergh, Winston Churchill, Calvin Coolidge and George Bernard Shaw.

The building of the Hearst Castle began shortly after he met the 14-year-old Davies dancing in New York. The construction work and their affair lasted until his 1951 death. Three ornate guest houses encircle "Casa Grande," a Spanish-Moorish cathedral visible five miles down the coast (52 miles of which Hearst owned). Hearst filled every one of the 165+ rooms with art and furniture purchased in cash-strapped European countries after World War I; every ceiling was a hand-carved masterpiece disassembled and rebuilt at the site. There are indoor and outdoor marble pools with gold-inlaid tile, tennis courts surrounded by dozens of statues, and 127 acres of pristine countryside. The world's largest private zoo was just below the hilltop with lions, panthers, tigers, leopards and chimpanzees.

Orson Welles' based the fictional "Xanadu" in his 1941 classic *Citizen Kane* on the Hearst estate but even Welles' extravagant copy still paled by comparison.[93]

Marion's weekends were organized to minute detail. Guests received invitations from Hearst's private secretary Bill Williams and gathered on a private train in Glendale. Several sleeping cars, a dining car and a bar car ferried 50 to 70 guests up the coast to San Luis Obispo where a fleet of cars met the travelers at three in the morning for the ninety-minute drive along the coast to San Simeon. Turning off the coast road, the caravan wound its way up a winding 17-mile road past herds of game animals roaming the property.[94] Buffalo, elk, zebra, camels, moose, yak, Barbary wild sheep, and goats roamed near signs warning **ANIMALS HAVE THE RIGHT OF WAY!**

Once they arrived, guests were free to swim, play tennis, or join Hearst on a ride on one of 100 horses. Some of the weekend was choreographed custom. Gourmet dinners were served in the 85-foot long Refectory but in keeping with Hearst's childhood remembrances of the family ranch, bottles of ketchup and mustard dotted the table. After dinner, guests retired to the 50-seat theater to watch first-run movies flown in to the private airfield down the hill. Sunday night everyone shared a big ice cream social. Hearst did not allow drinking but Marion instructed friends how to smuggle in liquor.[95]

Paul visited with an MGM group led by Garbo, Edmund Goulding,

Harry Rapf, Eddie Mannix, Nick Schenck, Norma Shearer, Irving, Eleanor Boardman and Jack Gilbert. Other invitees were Aileen Pringle, King Vidor, Beatrice Lillie, Richard Barthelmess, Buster Keaton, Hal Roach, Constance and Norma Talmadge (and their ever-present mother, Peg), and Frank Orsatti. A group photo taken beneath the massive front door to Casa Grande shows Paul seated on the ground next to Irving with Gilbert reclining on the ground and Keaton playing impishly with Norma Talmadge's hair. Paul had certainly arrived.[96]

Writer Frederica Sagor Maas described a different Paul at a different social setting in her autobiography *The Shocking Miss Pilgrim*. Maas arrived in 1925 and created an instant stir with Norma Shearer's *His Secretary* and Clara Bow's *The Plastic Age* but the headstrong Sagor Maas ran afoul of studio executives — Harry Rapf called her a "troublemaker"— because she didn't like her ideas being stolen without credit. She left Hollywood after 1928's *The Farmer's Daughter*.

In her memoirs, Sagor Maas described a bacchanalian orgy during which "undressed, tousled men chased naked women shrieking with laughter.

Paul (seated, second from right) on the front steps of Casa Grande at San Simeon with (lying in front) John Gilbert, (sitting, from left) Hal Roach, Nathalie Talmadge, Eddie Mannix, Norma Talmadge, Buster Keaton, Paul, and Irving Thalberg. Standing (in front, from left) are David O. Selznick, Frank Orsatti, Eddie Goulding, (Mother) Peg Talmadge, Greta Garbo, Nick Schenck, Eleanor Boardman, Harry Rapf, Constance Talmadge, unknown, and Norma Shearer. Paul's friend Carey Wilson is standing, rear left, with a white visor; the three persons center rear are unknown.

Included in the group was Ray Long, Mr. Hearst's representative; Harry Rapf
... even the immaculate Irving Thalberg — all drunk, drunk, drunk." She also
mentioned Paul's involvement.

Her story has to be taken with a grain of salt. By the time she wrote her
memoirs at 99 her bitterness with Hollywood was deep and she particularly
relished describing the bosses with whom she so frequently battled as amoral
debauchers. That is not to say that such things didn't go on — they certainly
did and 1920s-era MGM Friday Christmas parties were indeed virtual orgies.
But it's difficult to imagine Paul engaging in such antics and it would be
anathema to Thalberg. When his friends visited Madame Francis' famous
Hollywood brothel, he sat in the lobby reading the trade papers. The ax Sagor
Maas so clearly grinds shades her memoirs.

On August 27, Paul received his passport for a trip to Europe, arranged
by Mayer's secretary Ida Koverman, who took care of those types of details.
The well-connected Koverman had been a secretary for Herbert Hoover.[97]
On September 7, Paul left L.A. for New York, and from there he sailed to
Germany. Unlike his first ocean voyage, he didn't travel aboard a cramped
mail ship; he traveled First Class aboard the luxurious liner *Berlin*.

Paul spent three weeks in Germany, visiting Hamburg and spending ten
days in Berlin looking for stories and meeting with German filmmakers. It
had become customary for studio executives to return from the continent
with European directors, writers or actors to work for their studio. These
imports added mystery to the product whether or not they worked well. Paul
returned empty-handed; not surprising since he though domestic films were
better than European and German films.[98] He sailed from Hamburg on October 1 and after stopping in Southampton, England, on the 2nd arrived in
New York on October 10 and returned to L.A. on the 12th by train.

His travels coincided with filming of Garbo's *The Divine Woman*, her
only film he did not produce or co-produce. He also missed a September 29
gathering in the garden at Irving's rented 9401 Sunset Boulevard estate when
he married Norma Shearer. Thalberg had doggedly but unsuccessfully pursued Constance Talmadge but settled for Norma when Talmadge would not
marry him. The relentlessly ambitious Shearer, who called herself "Lotta'
Miles, Irving's spare tire,"[99] welcomed the marriage and what it could do for
her career.

The small wedding was attended by Irene and Edie Mayer, Bessie Love,
Marion Davies, Sylvia Thalberg, Howard Hawks, and the rest of Irving's
inner circle. Norma's brother Douglas traveled from Canada for the wedding
and surprised guests at the reception dinner by predicting that talking pictures were the coming thing, but nobody paid much attention. He stayed in
L.A. and got a job tending the Warners studio animal kennels.

The marriage was more arrangement than love story. Irving held a story conference with Laurence Stallings as he got dressed and when the couple returned from a honeymoon in Monterey his mother Henriette still sat at the head of the dinner table. The couple slept in separate bedrooms at opposite ends of the massive mansion in rooms assigned by Henriette, who still tucked her son into bed.

Norma's career took the expected jump. If Irving mentioned, "Norma wants it," the role was given to her. Joan Crawford explained all when she said, "What chance do I have now? Norma sleeps with the boss."[100] Paul served as matchmaker for Crawford on October 17, though taking her to the Vine Street Playhouse to see his friend Douglas Fairbanks, Jr.'s play *Young Woodley*. Afterwards he brought Joan backstage to introduce his friends and on New Year's Eve, Fairbanks proposed to Joan at a Long Beach pier.

Most meetings at MGM that fall concerned sound. On November 8, Paul met with Thalberg and Mayer to discuss how quickly their stages could be converted and at what cost. Thalberg maintained his wait-and-see attitude but it was obvious to all that something would be done. On the 11th, Paul was given a new contract, raising his salary to $1,000 a week. He was making the equivalent today of $1,250,000 a year.[101]

❧ SIX ☙

Sound

Warners' *The Jazz Singer* premiered in New York on October 6 but didn't arrive in Hollywood until the last week of December.[1] Only 15 percent of the 89-minute film had sound, just five songs and a few lines of dialogue. When he recorded Gus Kahn's "Toot Toot Tootsie Goodbye," Al Jolson got so excited he blurted out, "Wait a minute. Wait a minute. You ain't heard nothin' yet. Wait a minute, I tell ya.' You ain't heard nothin.'"[2] His ad-libbed lines drove audiences wild.

Paul attended the L.A. opening with Irving and Norma. The ride home was quiet; Irving told his wife that "sound is a passing fancy. It won't last,"[3] and later told his team, "It was a good gimmick, but that's all it was."[4] Hearst writer Louella Parsons wrote, "I have no fear that the screeching ... sound film will ever disturb our peaceful theaters,"[5] but the crowds foretold otherwise. For weeks there were lines around the block, forcing Warners to start showings at 9:00 A.M. and run past midnight.

Thalberg wasn't alone in his indifference. Other executives agreed at least publicly, but it was probably economics more than naiveté. Sound presented huge challenges. Almost none of the 20,000 movie theaters in the U.S. were equipped and it cost $15,000 apiece to do so.[6] Thalberg was among the first to note also the impact on foreign distribution, wondering aloud to Mayer and Mannix if European audiences wanted to hear English dialogue.

Production was also more complex; in silents, verbal instructions were given as cameras rolled so there were fewer retakes. Recording was challenging since microphones only heard from one direction and controlling sound level was impossible. Actors had to stand still near bulky microphones hidden in potted plants, flowers, lights, even in extras' costumes. Sam Marx said, "Suddenly the movies stopped moving." Jack Holt stood up from a chair, hit his head on a 10-pound microphone and was knocked out cold. Noisy cameras were encased in soundproof contraptions nick-named "Iron Mikes" because they were so hot. Noisy air conditioners banned so sound stages sweltered.

The impact on actors was swift. After the *Jazz Singer* premiere, Sam Goldwyn's wife Francis looked around at the hundreds of assembled stars and saw "terror in all their faces."[7] Thalberg himself knew intuitively that "audiences have formed their own idea of how each star sounds. They've heard the voices in their head in picture after picture, and what they hear may be disappointing. It's very risky."[8] Joan Crawford had a simpler assessment: "Panic!"

Sound was a blessing to some, a curse to many, a threat to all. Hearing his voice for the first time, William Powell ran out of the room. Stutterer Marion Davies, driving home from the premiere, told Hubert Voight, "M ... M ... M ... Mister V ... Voight ... I ... I ... I ... ha ... ha ... have ... a problem." Fortunately for her, the affliction disappeared if she recited memorized words. Gloria Swanson hired Broadway star Laura Hope Crews as a private diction coach, paying her $1,000 a week to help lose her New York accent. Hundreds of Broadway actors flooded L.A. to work as speech coaches.

Careers ended overnight. Vilma Banky's Hungarian accent was heavy and just three months after her lavish wedding to Rod La Rocque she retired to a Beverly Hills mansion they shared for the next 40 years. New Yorkers were almost all unsuitable. The Brooklyn accent of sisters Constance, Norma, and Natalie Talmadge was a death knell. Constance said, "Leave them while you're looking good and thank God for the trust funds mom set up."[9] The first time Clara Bow heard her own nasal Brooklyn-ese she screamed in anguish.[10] Alla Nazimova didn't even take the test. She simply retired to the apartment hotel she built around her Sunset Boulevard mansion. Karl Dane, who appeared in the silent blockbusters *The Big Parade* (1925) and *The Son of the Sheik* (1926), was earning $5,000 a week and kept 13 servents at his 622 Oakhurst Drive mansion and 5 Rolls Royces. But he could not speak English. By 1933 he was selling hot dogs outside the studio gates and on April 15, 1934, shot himself in the head in his tiny apartment.[11]

Heading into 1928, Thalberg remained unconvinced and Paul stood behind him. On February 15, Paul joined an MGM contingent with Mayer and Jack Gilbert to see Irving and Norma off at the train station for their delayed three-month honeymoon to Europe. Before Thalberg's departure, Eddie Mannix was charged with overseeing the sound conversion at MGM. Remembering Douglas Shearer's comment about sound at Thalberg's wedding reception, he entrusted the young man with the job of organizing the new department.[12]

While Thalberg traveled, Mannix paid college professor Vern Knudsen $2,500 for 10 days work, nearly twice his yearly teaching salary, to design sound stages. By April, Mannix was building two massive buildings, each 100' × 150' and seven stories tall, with 10-inch concrete walls and soundproof camera booths connected to recorders in a separate building. Paul argued that the rigid walls of the bunker-like stages would make sound lifeless (no reverberation), a theory that would eventually be proven correct.[13]

At the same time, MGM actors were still taking the dreaded test amid debate as to whether stage performers or film actors were more likely to test better. Paul said that the best screen voice he had heard belonged to child actor Junior Coghlan.[14]

Paul spent a lot of time searching for stories for Irving and managing the day-to-day production of dozens of films, usually without credit. One was *Beau Broadway*, a domestic comedy featuring Lew Cody and Aileen Pringle; it was similar to the later *Thin Man* films.

Jim Lambert (Cody) is a boxing manager and gambler who grants boxer Gunner O'Brien (former world boxing champion James Jeffries) his dying wish and agrees to care for Gunner's granddaughter Mona (Sue Carol). He is shocked when she turns out to be a beautiful young woman. He changes his nefarious ways as he falls in love with her while battling temptations from former flames and keeping his boxers away. After a confusing mélange of scenes, he and Mona end up together.[15]

Broadway was described as a "terrible muddle" that "trips over itself" though newcomer Sue Carol was described as "one of the most delectable young ladies ever to step in front of a camera."[16] She married Alan Ladd in 1942.

On May 28, Irving returned from his honeymoon with a European trophy, beautiful 16-year-old Viennese dancer Eva von Plentzner. He intended to transform her as he had Garbo. Irving renamed her Eva von Berne in honor of Paul and immediately cast her with John Gilbert in *The Masks of the Devil*. Unfortunately she was a complete failure as an actress and after that role was not given any work. After her initial six-month contract ended, she was unceremoniously returned to Europe.

On June 17, Paul was named a producer "in charge of stories" at MGM, along with Eddie Mannix, "sort of general executive utility man." Both headed five production units. Thalberg now had five men at this level: Paul, Mannix, Rapf, Hyman, and Stromberg.[17] At the time Paul was working with Irving readying several Garbo films, *A Woman of Affairs* to start in July and *Wild Orchids* in October.

Thalberg thought they needed the best writers available to create scripts for sound films but didn't believe they were in Hollywood. So Paul's first assignment was a trip to New York to look for plays and playwrights. On the 18th he flew east aboard a U.S. mail plane, making the trip sitting atop mail sacks in an open-cockpit bi-plane that made ten stops. But he was in New York in 36 hours. Thalberg followed by train.[18]

For his first sound project, Douglas Shearer spent a month in a small

New Jersey studio adding sound to W.S. Van Dyke's island film *White Shadows of the South Seas*, which opened on July 31 in New York. Shearer added a little music, the sound of clapping hands and a man moaning over the death of his child; and in the midst of a view of the ocean hitting the beach, Monte Blue is heard whistling like a bird and saying "Hello." But viewers most liked the opening, Shearer's recording of a roaring lion synched with Leo's growl during the MGM credit. The minor film earned MGM over $450,000 and forced Thalberg to accept sound as more than a novelty.

In early August, Cecil B. DeMille came to MGM in partnership with Mayer in a deal arranged by Nick Schenck. Cecil B. DeMille Pictures was absorbed by the Pathé Exchange and DeMille signed a three-picture deal with MGM. Paul was in charge of all Pathé (and DeMille) production at the studio, the "first major change at Pathé following the decision of Cecil B. DeMille to go with MGM ... when Paul Bern becomes producer in charge of entire Pathé production. Bern leaves MGM, where for two years he has been story chief and aid to Irving Thalberg."[19]

Technically Paul's work for Pathé came under the MGM brand and a Paul Bern Productions entity was structured for other projects like *Noisy Neighbors*, *Square Shoulders*, *The Flying Fool*, *Listen, Baby* and *The Getaway*. When he went to Pathé he brought his assistant Erwin Gelsey, whom he had hired a year earlier. The Pathé promotion meant Paul's work was limited on Garbo's *A Woman of Affairs* and *Wild Orchids*.

His first Pathé assignment was to add dialogue sequences to DeMille's *The Godless Girl*.[20] He worked with Barney Glazer and Jack Jevne though none received writing credit, which was given to DeMille's long-time assistant-mistress Jeanie Macpherson. Paul also added a synchronized soundtrack with background noises like alarm bells, traffic, and marching feet and added several scenes that were all shot during a single Saturday.

Godless Girl was a strangely symbolic romantic drama set in a high school embroiled in a battle between the Atheist Society and a group of "religionists." DeMille put together a talented production crew, with art direction by Mitchell Leisen and costumes by Adrian.[21]

Atheist Judith Craig (Lina Basquette) forms a club called the Godless Society at her high school battling Bob Hathaway's (George Duryea) Christian religionists. Her group disrupts an atheist meeting and somehow a girl falls out a third-floor window and is killed. Bob, Judith and Bozo Johnson are sent to a youth reformatory where they are tortured by the brutal head guard (Noah Beery). Bob steals a grocery delivery wagon and escapes with Judith but they are quickly captured and returned to their cells, where a fire breaks out. Bob rescues Judith and the guard and because of his bravery he and Judith are freed, with a renewed faith in God.[22]

On June 18, 1928, Paul boarded an open biplane full of mail for a cold and bumpy flight to New York (courtesy Paul H. Bern).

Critics roundly panned the film and Macpherson's typical dark imagery. The religious undertones were lost on viewers who found it difficult to believe high school students would be overcome with such zealotry. Her overdone story was "punctured with vapid, religious admonitions and strange, heavenly warnings in the form of crosses burnt into the palms of the heroine." Critics also criticized the added scenes that "served no appreciable purpose."[23] The result reinforced the difficulty of adding sound to completed films.

Working on *Godless Girl*, Paul was involved in an interesting but ultimately sad upheaval at MGM. DeMille originally gave the lead to an unknown he was told was Russian actress Sonia Karlov but was actually ex–Follies dancer Jeanne Williams, who dyed her hair black and invented the Karlov persona to get work. At a lavish studio luncheon in her honor, DeMille tabbed Karlov to star in *Godless Girl*, saying, "I bring you the next great star of the screen, Sonia Karlov." Lina Basquette, who was originally given the coveted role, stood up and said, "She isn't Sonia Karlov. Her name is Jeanne Williams and I knew her from the Follies!"

The luncheon erupted into frenzy as DeMille ordered Williams-Karlov escorted directly out the studio gates and gave the role to Basquette. Paul went to DeMille on Williams' behalf even though he didn't know her, imploring, "She was right for the role before. Why is she changed now?" But DeMille was adamant and Williams retreated to her tiny apartment, broke and unemployed. That night she received a telephone call and a male voice said, "You don't know me but my name's Paul Bern and I work at DeMille studio. I wonder if you are in need of a friend." The two had dinner in Hollywood and Paul told her the sad stories of Barbara La Marr and another woman he vaguely referred to as "the great love of my life" and a "secret tragedy." He offered money for her bills and a train ticket back to New York and then drove her home where by way of offering thanks she asked him to spend the night. He told her, "My dear, if we have an affair it will change everything and take away the enjoyment I get just by helping you."[24] She never heard from him again, though she received an envelope the next day stuffed with cash.[25]

It was an inopportune time for DeMille's arrival at MGM. His forte was historic spectacles and he had problems making the transition to sound. He showed promise with his first film, *Dynamite* (late 1929) but could not repeat even modest success with his next two, *Madam Satan* (September, 1930) and a remake of *The Squaw Man* (September, 1931). His contract with MGM was not renewed after his three films.[26] Paul worked on *Dynamite* and *Madam Satan* but was not linked to *Squaw Man*.

Cecil B. DeMille's first sound films made at MGM were supervised by Paul.

During the fall, Paul supervised production of two Eddie Quillan comedies, first the Melville Brown–directed *Geraldine* and then Charles Reisner's *Noisy Neighbors*. In November he began production on *Square Shoulders* and was in writing meetings on *Listen, Baby*. To ensure that the *Geraldine* crew was "keyed up to an 'emotional understanding' of the next day's scenes, [Paul] held mandatory story conferences every night during shooting."[27]

In *Geraldine*, Quillan was the opportunistic Eddie Able, hired by businessman Cyrus Wygate to teach his daughter

Geraldine (Marian Nixon) how to win a man. He has her discard her horn-rimmed glasses, learn to dance, and buy more fashionable clothes, but while she pursues dapper lawyer Bellsworthy Cameron, Eddie falls in love with her. They both end up in jail after a café raid and Eddie saves her from being arrested by taking the blame for her. That's when she — and her father — realize he is the one for her.[28]

The *L.A. Times* review "Paul Bern Film Scores Success" noted his "first production for Pathé, *Geraldine* ... has won unusual audience reactions because of the human quality invested in the production by Bern..." and credited his daily story meetings for overcoming a weak script.

Paul was never formally credited with *Noisy Neighbors*. His Paul Bern Productions was, and newspapers noted he was the supervising producer. *Neighbors* is the story of the Van Revels, a family of struggling vaudevillians who inherit a southern mansion from a distant relative. When they arrive at their ancestral home, they discover they are involved in a 60-year feud with the Carstair family that began over a game of croquet. Of course feisty young Eddie (Quillan) falls in love with a Carstair daughter (Vaughn), reigniting tensions. When mountain cousins led by Colonel Carstair (Theodore Roberts) ride in to shoot up Eddie and his family, love wins out and the feud ends.[29]

Geraldine and *Neighbors* were released on January 20, 1929 to good reviews and were modest financial successes. In late November, Paul's production company began *Square Shoulders* which featured Louis Wolheim, Junior Coghlan, Philippe De Lacy, Anita Louise, and a group of child actors.[30] War hero Slag (Wolheim) lives as a drunken hobo surviving by his wits and petty theft. When he and two fellow thieves return to his hometown (where he is thought dead), he learns his wife died leaving no one to care for his son Tad (Coghlan), "the sturdy little leader of the gas house gang" made up of boys playing soldier (De Lacy, Louise, and others). A guilt-ridden Slag does not tell Tad they are related and steals enough money to send him to military school, taking a job there as a stable boy to be near him. He teaches Tad to ride a horse, blow the bugle and fit in at the school but his former partners in crime arrive and force him to rob the academy by threatening to reveal his identity. When Tad walks in as they divide the money, Slag is killed by a bullet meant for his son before the commandant arrives and shoots the two men. Tad later plays taps over Slag's grave in a potter's field, never learning his true identity.[31]

Shoulders received good reviews after its March 10, 1929 premiere (a "dialogue and sound picture ... packed with action and drama" that "takes the audience through every phase of human emotion"). Paul added a touching childhood love story between Coghlan, De Lacy, and Louise, and scenes between Wolheim and Coghlan were ranked "with the finest bits of sentiment that the screen has ever offered."[32] All three of Paul's late 1928 films featured the same theme: young men living by their wits, *Geraldine*'s slag, *Noisy Neighbors'* Eddie and *Square Shoulders'* Tad.

Paul filmed *Shoulders* at the Urban Military Academy, an L.A.-area school for boys. In addition to sons of Erich von Stroheim and Charles Reisner (who directed *Noisy Neighbors*), the cadets were played by sons of some of Hollywood's most notable actors like Claire Windsor, Joe E. Brown, Earle Foxe, Hal Roach, Al Green, Frank Tinney, Daphne Pollard, directors E. Mason Hopper and Lonnie D'Orsa, and studio writers Ernest Vajda and Bess Meredyth.

On December 12 Paul traveled to New York for his annual scouting trip looking for scripts and actors for Pathé and MGM. He also stopped at Cornell University in Ithaca, New York, and gave several lectures on filmmaking to photoplay classes.[33]

MGM picked up the pace on the move to sound as 1928 drew to a close. The dreaded voice tests were completed in a whirlwind during which "One half [of Hollywood was] contemplating vistas of a brave new world and the other half—suicide."[34] Music and sound effects were added to almost all MGM movies and during the conversion the studio turned out some of its finest work; among the transitional efforts were Garbo's *Wild Orchids* and *Woman of Affairs* and Crawford's *Our Dancing Daughters,* both of which Paul worked on without credit.

Small bits of sound were added to silent films already in progress. Street noises and ringing phones were inserted into William Haines' *Excess Baggage* and Mannix rented a Paramount sound stage for dialogue additions to the Haines–Lionel Barrymore vehicle *Alias Jimmy Valentine.* During the climactic scene where reformed safecracker Valentine frees a trapped child from a safe, the child's moans were mixed with a brief set of dialogue between Haines and Barrymore. Audiences loved it and a minor film costing $208,000 grossed over $1,100,000.

MGM's first full sound movie was scheduled for October production: Bessie Love and Anita Page starring in *The Broadway Melody,* just the second full-length screen musical. Another sound film, Norma Shearer's *The Trial of Mary Dugan,* began on December 17 but only half of the studio's films were sound.

As the year came to a close, Barbara La Marr was back in the news when her last husband Jack Dougherty picked a fight and stabbed a man during a raucous Christmas Eve party at Lottie Pickford's Taft Avenue home.[35] He stabbed 32-year-old Dantel Jaeger several times in the hands, fleeing before police arrived. No charges were filed; it was rumored that Jaeger was delivering drugs to the hard-partying Pickford.

On Christmas morning Paul drove to the top of Angelo Drive to visit Enchanted Hill, the estate of western star Fred Thomson and MGM writer

Frances Marion, both close friends. The lavish estate boasted a 30-room mansion and a mahogany-floored stable for Thomson's horses. Thomson had been in Queen of Angels Hospital since the 14th fighting kidney infections; Paul visited every other day, but he worsened on Christmas Eve and died Christmas morning. On the 28th Paul joined Mayer, Thalberg, and most of MGM at the beloved actor's funeral. Douglas Fairbanks, Tom Mix, and Buster Keaton openly sobbed during the lengthy service.

The morning after Christmas, Kansas City beauty Harlean Carpenter signed a contract with Hal Roach Studios in Culver City. Roach's casting director saw her walk-on in her second film, *Moran of the Marines*, and convinced Roach to give her a five-year contract. She would "be professionally known as Jean Harlow" but signed the document "Harlean McGrew II." Just below, "C.F. McGrew II" signed as "Husband of the Second Party approving the terms of the contract." The next day Roach sent a one-page addendum stipulating, among other things, that should travel be required, expenses for Harlean and a chaperone — "which it is understood will be your mother whenever possible" — would be paid by the studio.[36] A few days later she reported to the set of the Laurel & Hardy short *Liberty*.

Initial results for MGM sound films were promising. *The Broadway Melody* cost $275,000 and grossed $4,000,000 after its early 1929 release and won the studio its first Best Picture Academy Award. The studio showcased their stars' voices in *The Hollywood Revue of 1929*, a vaudeville-like presentation with sketch comedy and song and dance numbers by the likes of Gilbert, Shearer, Keaton, and Marie Dressler.

Pathé was equally hesitant, filling their first all-talkie, *Strange Cargo*, with a dozen experienced stage actors. In February, Paul began the *Strange Cargo* script with Pathé writer John W. Krafft, basing their script on the play *The Missing Man*. It was filmed for both silent and sound presentation with Benjamin (Barney) Glazer directing the silent and Arthur Gregor the sound version.[37] Writing credits went to Glazer and Horace Jackson; Paul went uncredited and Krafft was credited only with titles.

Cargo is a murder mystery set aboard a yacht sailing from India to England. As the passengers gather in the lounge after dinner the light mysteriously go out, and when they flash back on, the ship's owner is found murdered. Since nobody in the lounge left or could enter, the killer must be among the group. The captain investigates an eclectic mix of suspects: a hot-blooded Spaniard who hated the captain, a psychic Yogi (Frank Reicher), the first mate, a thieving steward, and Hungerfold (Russell Gleason), angry with the dead man's intentions towards his fiancée (Lee Patrick). After several abductions and deaths, the killer is discovered to have been the psychic Yogi, who claimed to have been in a trance at the time of the murder.[38]

Strange Cargo made its L.A. premiere at the United Artists Theater on February 20 to very good reviews. The studio used the RCA Photophone sound recording process that was subject to glitches like poor background noise recording and synchronization problems but critics liked the film, calling the writing of Paul and Krafft "exceptionally good, and is a deliberate appeal to the intelligence rather than a play for laugh or thrills." It was a nod to Paul's writing strategy.[39]

One of Paul's first assignments at Pathé was *Listen, Baby*, adapted from an Elsie Janis–Gene Markey magazine story. Casey Robinson was originally assigned to direct, then it was given to James Gleason, but after Paul was assigned to produce he gave it back to Robinson and hired William Conselman to supervise. Conselman jumbled the writing process by demanding to lead the writing team with W. Scott Darling. Darling then wrote a theme song and contracted with Irving Berlin's production company to sell it. The only casting already confirmed was Eddie Quillan and Dorothy Appleby, an Elsie Janis protégé from the New York stage. When the various production snafus continued into early March, Paul postponed production until May. In the midst of the upheaval, Paul left the DeMille-Pathé assignment to return to MGM but continued to work on the Pathé films *The Flying Fool* and *Dynamite*.[40]

Much has been made over the years about Paul's alleged failures with women, a reputation that is positively false. He was also described as an eccentric Hollywood loner, which is also absolutely untrue. To the contrary, he loved people and parties. Jean Harlow later said, "He loved ... the color and gaiety of crowded rooms, music, laughter and conversation," a description confirmed by Henry Bern's daughter-in-law.[41] The fictional studio-crafted stories live on even as the real Paul had a large circle of intimate friends at all stations, was universally beloved, and received daily invitations to every conceivable industry function or private party. He was an active participant in Hollywood society and his outings — and girlfriends — made weekly note in columns like Myra Nye's *L.A. Times* "Society of Cinemaland" column and Elizabeth Yeaman's "Society in Filmland" columns. His early 1929 schedule is an example.

On March 3 he attended a performance by the Chicago Civic Opera Company at the Philharmonic and was mentioned in society columns along with the likes of the Lou Angers, the Edgar Rice Burroughses, and members of the Huntington family.[42]

He was also a sought-after speaker and frequent guest lecturer at classes at the University of Southern California's prestigious film school, speaking on composition of motion picture scenario writing, film architecture and art, etc.[43] From the program's 1927 founding through the early 1930s, Paul spoke dozens of times. On March 6 he discussed an analysis of silent filming history in Europe and America and the changes in plot development as audiences matured. He reiterated a common Paul theme, that a "happy ending explains the commercial success of the motion picture" and that it was important to have "the winter of conflict represented on screen" but that a happy ending offered at least a "temporarily successful solution to many of their own problems." Thalberg and Paul agreed on this; Anita Loos said that Thalberg believed every film had to be a love story.[44]

He also said the great virtue of the cinema was its universal appeal and that if studios tried to limit the presentation of a particular class, that such appeal would be lost. Tellingly, he said, "Every story represents every man's search for happiness." He said censorship itself didn't limit sexual themes in film as much as social norms and prejudice, and he thought producers ran afoul of audiences when they challenged "the limitations of taboo," that audiences wanted suspicions confirmed and "not ... eradicated."[45] Overall he believed censorship actually benefited movies artistically though at the cost of commercial success.

On March 24 Paul spoke at USC with Barney Glazer on "The Theory of Silent Photoplay"[46] and on April 15 he and Thalberg were invited to speak at a symposium sponsored by the Academy of Motion Pictures Arts and Sciences at another movie production class. Other speakers included J. Stuart Blackton, Frank Woods and Douglas Fairbanks.

Thalberg was finally grasping the importance of talkies, telling the students, "Talking pictures can and very well may create a universal language. [It is] the first truly universal medium to reach all races and people equally, the first medium which has a real chance to bring about an eventual Brotherhood of Man." Paul added, "The future of the art will depend largely on the manner in which its now unwritten technique is passed on through properly prepared text to the coming generation."[47]

On March 25, Paul attended a going-away party for Ona Wilson Brown at Ruth Collier's Sunset Boulevard mansion along with Irving Willat and Billie Dove, Lucien Littlefield, Al Christie, Lili Damita, Lilyan Tashman, William Seiter and Laura LaPlante, and Norman Kerry. Every week, he was somewhere in the society pages, movie columns or gossip rags. He was extremely social, nothing like the quiet loner portrayed in later fictions.

In mid–April, Paul began *The Flying Fool*, a Pathé assignment. Arthur Miller was in charge of filming intricate and dangerous flying sequences. It is a World War I love story set amid the world of pilots. Bill Taylor (William Boyd) is a good-natured fighter ace known as "The Flying Fool" who tries to keep nightclub singer Pat (Marie Prevost) away from his younger brother Jimmy (Russell Gleason) but falls in love with her himself when he discovers she is really just a small town girl. The brothers stage a flying contest to determine who gets the girl and after a dangerous air battle that ends with Tom's plane crashing, Pat decides she loves Bill while Jimmy meets another girl who steals his heart.[48]

Critics hailed the flying sequences, particularly a realistic dogfight between Bill and a German pilot that ends with the German plane spiraling to the ground in flames. Audiences were thrilled with the action and the two songs, "If I Had My Way" and "I'm That Way About Baby" by George Green and George Waggner.[49]

Next came *Dynamite*, DeMille's first talkie, a Jeanie Macpherson scenario suggested by the 1928 jailhouse wedding of condemned murderer Salvatore Merra at the New Jersey State Prison just two hours before his execution.[50] To fulfill the terms of her wealthy grandfather's will, society girl Cynthia Crothers (Kay Johnson) marries Hagon Derk (Charles Bickford), a coal miner sentenced to hang for murder, instead of her lover Roger. They marry in his cell seven hours before he is to die but he is found innocent at the last minute. Cynthia will lose her fortune unless she remains married for six months so she reluctantly moves to a remote mining town and lives as a miner's wife and slowly realizes the shallowness of her former life. A mine explosion threatens to take both Hagon and Roger away from her but Roger is killed helping them escape and Cynthia finds happiness with her husband.[51]

Critics panned *Dynamite* for Macpherson's typical complexity and the length. For what should have been a straightforward story, DeMille filmed scenes everywhere from a New York skyscraper to a country club to a lavish mansion and boudoir to a miner's shack and a mineshaft a mile underground. His two-hour film only permitted theaters two showings a night instead of three or four, which displeased exhibitors. DeMille's first MGM talkie was a failure.[52]

On May 19, Paul attended the Academy Awards at the Blossom Room at the Hollywood Roosevelt Hotel with a large MGM contingent led by Mayer and Thalberg. Douglas Fairbanks and William de Mille hosted the event and Fairbanks handed out the awards.[53]

On June 3, Paul's close friends Doug Fairbanks, Jr., and Joan Crawford were married in New York. Interestingly, they spent their first few married days at the Algonquin Hotel a few floors below Dorothy Millette. When they returned to L.A., Paul hosted a dinner for them at the Ambassador.

His next project, also previously uncredited, was *It's a Great Life*, written for the Duncan Sisters, Rosetta and Vivian. They were among the top acts in vaudeville and their play *Topsy and Eva*, loosely based on "Uncle Tom's Cabin," sold out theaters from 1923 to 1927 with Rosetta as a black-faced

Topsy and Vivian the angelic Eva. Rosetta was described as "a female Charlie Chaplin" and the sisters came to Hollywood in 1927 to bring their play to
film for United Artists.[54]

The moderate success of the United Artists film convinced Thalberg to
bring the Duncan sisters to MGM and he signed them on May 14 for *Cotton
and Silk*, released to preview as *Imperfect Ladies* and eventually released as *It's
a Great Life*.[55] Paul wrote the script with Joseph F. Poland though the writing credits went to Byron Morgan and Alfred Block. Production didn't begin
until September 4th and lasted the month.

Sisters Babe (Vivian) and Casey Hogan (Rosetta) work in the sheet music
section of a department store where they sing and dance for customers. But
this gets them fired so they take vaudeville jobs in a tiny theater. Babe falls
in love with their piano player Jimmy Dean (Lawrence Gray) and the sisters
split up when Babe marries but are reunited and resume their act, which by
then has become famous.[56]

It's a Great Life debuted to tepid reviews; the sister's singing and dancing talents didn't come across as well on screen as on vaudeville stages. After
a few more forgettable films, they both retired from the screen.

In June, young actor Lew Ayres, just released from Pathé after two films,
desperately approached Paul for work. Paul became a mentor to Ayres and
had Arlie Lewin give him a role in a Garbo film, *The Kiss*, that he was producing and would film in July. That favor led to work at Universal in *All Quiet
on the Western Front* (1930) and a 60-year career and over 150 films.

Just before starting *It's a Great Life*, Paul surprised friends when he arrived
at a mid–August party given by producer David O. Selznick at his new 910
Benedict Canyon estate. Selznick and his fiancée Irene Mayer were perhaps
Paul's closest friends. Paul and David worked together in the mid–1920s when
David was a script reader at Metro and Paul later helped him get established
at Paramount and helped bring him to MGM in late 1926 as head of the Scenario Department.

Irene loved Paul and of him later wrote he was "special in so many ways.
He was the only person I ever knew who cherished people he loved as much
for their frailties as for their virtues. He had compassion, erudition and great
generosity."[57] Louis B. Mayer was furious when Irene began dating Selznick;
he had feuded with David's father Lewis back to 1911 and regularly used
"Selznick" as an epithet. Even so, Paul remained close to the couple and,
according to Irene, "adopted them."

Paul earlier told Irene he was coming to the party and wanted to surprise her with his date. She was shocked when he arrived with Harlean Carpenter on his arm. Irene knew Harlean! When Irene first arrived in Hollywood,
she attended the Hollywood School for Girls. One of her classmates was a

beautiful blonde Kansas City heiress who was picked up every Friday by her "mother's lover ... a mysterious dark man...."[58] Harlean was Paul's date.

It's not certain how Paul and Jean were introduced since studio-crafted stories can't be believed. He undoubtedly saw her on the MGM lot when she worked on a half dozen Laurel & Hardy shorts in early 1929. Even bit parts got her known around the studio. Jean later offered Jimmie Fidler a believable scenario:

> We first met when I visited the Metro-Goldwyn-Mayer studios for a part in a picture Mr. Bern was supervising. He stared at me, but he didn't give me the part, because he said I was not suited to it. The next evening, he telephoned me. He secured my number from Leatrice Joy, a mutual friend. He was most gentlemanly, and when he asked my mother if she would grant her permission to take me out, I adored him.[59]

Paul arrived at the Selznick party with the stunning 18-year-old starlet. A struggling actress on a studio executive's arm would not surprise but Jean was clearly different. She was genuinely uninterested in fame and not impressed at all by movie people. And she was spectacularly pretty. People used almost ethereal terms in talking about the 5'2", 105-pound beauty. Her hair was described as almost "champagne or platinum blonde" and she had "the bluest eyes, which turn midnight blue when she gets excited.... [H]er eyelashes are the length of little girls that make delicate fan-shaped shadows on her cheeks. Her skin is the texture of a gardenia petal. Her teeth are all very even and very white. Her figure is one of those delicately turned-out pieces of porcelain." On her left ankle she always wore a very thin platinum ankle bracelet clustered with diamonds.[60]

Harlean Carpenter was born on March 3, 1911, into the family of wealthy Kansas City dentist Skip Harlow. Mont and Jean Harlow Carpenter (Skip's daughter) lived in Skip's large home, and Jean became obsessed with her daughter literally before birth, saying during her pregnancy that her baby would be "spiritual, mental, and physical perfection," christening herself "Mama Jean" and saying, "There is nothing else in my life worth talking about. My life began with her."[61] For the rest of her life she called Harlean "The Baby" or "Bunny" and shed her husband soon after Harlean's birth.

She grew up shielded by wealth; grandfather Skip gave her an ermine bedspread for her fifth birthday. Mama Jean wanted to be a movie star so in the summer of 1923 when Harlean was 11, she drove to California and enrolled Harlean in the Hollywood School for Girls. Harlean often visited the DeMille girls at their Laughlin Park estate and even at a young age her personality showed; classmates were shocked by her short skirts and boyfriends and loved her unpretentious manner.[62] She was the prettiest girl there but totally without conceit. She loved California but Mama Jean's experiment ended in failure and after two years they returned home to Kansas City.

During a 1926 visit to Chicago, Mama Jean met Marino Bello, a swarthy Italian gold digger and a thoroughly unlikable character. He was managing his wife's restaurant at the Sherman Hotel but began sleeping with Mama Jean within days of their meeting. Mama Jean sent Harlean to the Ferry Hall in Lake Forest, north of Chicago, so she'd have an excuse to see Bello, and he married his Kansas City meal ticket on January 18, 1927. Harlean hated him; he apparently regularly molested her.[63]

To get away from Bello, she accepted a four-carat diamond and eloped at 16 with wealthy 20-year-old Charles McGrew II on September 21, 1927.[64] The newlyweds cruised to Havana and through the Panama Canal to L.A. McGrew got so drunk he had to be helped to bed every night. To distance themselves from the Bellos they moved to a Spanish bungalow at 618 Linden Drive in Beverly Hills. Neither worked; their diversions were drinking, picnicking, and spending McGrew's $10,000 annual stipend.[65] Three months later, Mama Jean and Bello followed, renting a small bungalow on the south side of Beverly Hills below Wilshire.

Harlow's studio discovery is the stuff of Hollywood legend. In the spring of 1928 she gave her friend Rosalie Roy[66] a ride to a Fox audition where casting director Joe Egli saw her in the parking lot leaning on her roadster waiting for Rosalie, stunning in her tight clothes, *sans* underwear. Egli offered an introduction letter to Dave Allen at Central Casting which she put in her pocket and ignored until an evening bridge game when a friend told her, "I'll bet you $250 you haven't the nerve to go see Dave Allen." She replied, "I'll bet you $250 that's a bet you're going to lose," and the next morning went to Fox and then to Central Casting, signing in as "Jean Harlow" and winning her bet.[67] Allen later remembered, "I couldn't believe my eyes. I knew the instant I saw her that here was the material stars were made of."[68]

Casting people called daily but she ignored them until Mama Jean found out and forced her to take her first role, a walk-on in the prison drama *Honor Bound* where she earned $10 a day for two days' work. She made a splash on every movie set she walked onto. *Why Be Good?* director William Seiter said to Colleen Moore, "Look, you've never seen anything like it."[69] When Clara Bow saw her on the set of *The Saturday Night Kid* in a black-crocheted dress with nothing underneath, she demanded the director get rid of her, moaning, "Who's gonna see me in a scene with *her*?"[70] Jean was still barely 17.

Working for Hal Roach in the Laurel & Hardy short *Double Whoopee*, Jean exited a taxi and Stan Laurel closed the car door so her dress stayed in the door and tore away as she walked off in a see-through slip. Filming the first take, Harlow — as usual without underwear — walked across the set essentially naked after her dress fell away. In seconds there was chaos. But she didn't cause commotion for attention. She was genuinely unaware, perfectly at ease with her body (and didn't like the feel of underwear).

Jean had no inhibitions, no inner monologue suggesting decorum for the sake of people around her. Photographer George Hurrell said she had "no shame or inhibition about her body" at all.[71] She was totally unconcerned that not wearing underwear meant her pubic hair showed through her dresses and that her nipples were chronically erect (her mother later iced them before scenes, much to the disgust of friends). Her ease was so obviously natural that her actions rarely evoked jealousy or anger; studio people just knew that was Jean.[72] Her crews universally loved her. She was typically the most popular actress at any studio she worked at.

Just a few months before the Selznick party, Mama Jean convinced her to divorce McGrew and abort his child. His family was furious when he offered her a $200,000 trust fund and $375 monthly support, leading to a divorce that dragged on over a year.[73] She said of the divorce, "I am not planning to marry again ... soon. I'm too interested in my work. It wouldn't be fair. [T]hen

Jean Harlow with Stan Laurel and Oliver Hardy in *Double Whoopee*, just before her dress became caught in the car door (from the Darrell Rooney collection).

when I do marry I want to be sure I'm right … this time. I'm very happy making my home with my mother and stepfather. No one would believe me when I say I spend far more time in the society of my family than I do in night clubs or cafes."[74]

A *Modern Screen* story noted that the day McGrew returned to Chicago, Jean found herself with the house, a car, two servants, six diamond rings, four bracelets and a bar pin, $3,000 in debts, and $11 in cash. So she had a party. Jean's life was far from glamorous; she moved to the Bellos' small, green-roofed, gray stucco bungalow at 300 South Maple and then to another tiny house at 152 South Peck Drive, both on the wrong side of 1920s Beverly Hills. The family was in constant financial straits.

When Paul and Jean arrived at the Selznick party and Irene recognized her old schoolmate and welcomed her with, "Hello, Harlean," Jean gave her a toss of the head and indignantly responded, "Jean Harlow, if you please." Paul was greatly embarrassed. Irene and David were surprised at the coupling and David later claimed to Irene, "This dame keeps dragging me into the bushes!"[75] It would not have been totally out of character for Jean to do that. The date with Paul was probably platonic but David told several conflicting versions of the same story, so the truth is in doubt. Jean got over her initial anger at Irene; by the end of the party she bid her a very affectionate goodbye.

According to Irene, during the following months Paul and Jean rarely if ever appeared together in public and or even at small functions among their circle of friends. Everyone assumed she and Paul had other commitments but it is worthwhile noting that it wasn't a studio-choreographed date. Those evenings always took place in public venues.

During the summer she acquired an agent, Arthur Landau, whom she called "Pops." His father William A. Landau was the oldest film exhibitor in New York and his (Arthur's) clients included Lionel Barrymore, Basil Rathbone, William Farnum, Ben Lyon, directors Charles Brabin and Tod Browning and writers Dalton Trumbo and John Monk Saunders. He also listed Paul as a client in the 1930s but that is unlikely.[76]

The relationship between Landau and Jean was like father and daughter (though later Landau claimed he had sex with Jean) and he took credit for getting Jean the role that would springboard her to fame. He claimed to have introduced Jean to producer Howard Hughes, leading to her role in his spectacle *Hell's Angels* but the introduction actually was made by her ex-lover James Hall, one of the film's stars.[77]

The *Hell's Angels* juggernaut had been ongoing since 1927, the story of pilot brothers (Hall and Ben Lyon) in love with the same woman (Greta Nissen). Hughes' excesses are legend. He filmed for almost two years and spent almost $4,000,000, over $2,000,000 on aerial sequences alone. He assembled the largest private air force in the world and built an airfield near Van Nuys to house 87 vintage World War I aircraft, a German Gotha bomber, a Zeppelin and 137 pilots. A German airfield was built in Chatsworth and an English aerodrome near the site of present-day LAX.

Four stuntmen died during filming and several others were nearly killed; veteran pilot Al Wilson nearly died *twice*, once when he bailed out of his Fokker D.VII in a fog over Hollywood and landed on a house (the plane crashed just feet from Joe Schenck's Hollywood Boulevard house) and once parachuting from a second crash that killed a young prop man on board.

Hughes used 26 aerial cameramen and hired writers literally by the dozen, prompting Charlie MacArthur to ask, "What is this, a contest?"[78] Incredibly, after two years Hughes decided to add sound to aerial scenes and re–shoot the rest of the film. Unfortunately Nissen's heavy Norwegian accent made her unsuitable and Hughes went looking for a replacement. After a six-month search and 100+ screen tests, Hall mentioned Jean to Hughes and a test was scheduled, but Hughes was at first dismissive and said she sounded like "a Missouri barmaid screaming for a keg" before walking out of the room.[79]

But director James Whale recognized her obvious erotic appeal and helped her through another test and a now desperate Hughes signed her to a Caddo Productions contract on October 24. Lincoln Quarberg later recalled her contract was $100 a week with a six-week minimum but Caddo memoranda suggest she was paid $1,500, the lowest fee allowed by the Screen Actors Guild.[80] That same day, the entire Wall Street world came crumbling down and the country spiraled into the Great Depression.

Neither Bello nor Mama Jean worked and the family was in constant financial disarray, so Landau lent Jean $500 to pay bills and buy food when she signed with Hughes. Bello was "three months overdue with rent, the phone was about to be shut down, the gas bill was overdue and so was everything else." Mama Jean actively "helped" Landau manage Jean's career and signed her letters "Big Jean" or "Mother Jean."[81] It was amidst this maelstrom that Jean went to the Selznick party with Paul.

About that time, Jean literally burst into prominence. The previous summer, the then 17-year-old posed for photographer Edwin Bower Hesser, notorious for his Hesser's Art Photos, pictures of naked women sold as art rather than pornography and even so often removed from stores by police. Hesser's photos were typically described as "naughty nude photographs," but Jean's photos differ from the thousands of other Hesser shoots.[82] She is not nude. In her photos, taken in Fern Dell in Griffith Park, she is covered with a diaphanous scarf that, though it leaves little to the imagination, does cover her.

Three or four of the Hesser images from Griffith Park have become rec-

Above and opposite: Jean's natural beauty was displayed in a series of photos taken by Edwin Hesser at Griffith Park (from the Darrell Rooney collection).

ognizable over the years, Jean either standing or lying on a large rock out-cropping over a stream wrapped in her flowing scarf. But Harlow researcher Darrell Rooney has collected almost 75 different shots taken that afternoon. The other images, particularly a series of a nymph-like Jean standing among lily pads in a small pond, are spectacular. Her lack of inhibition is evident in

the relaxed posing but more striking is the vibrant sexuality that pours from the teenager.

On September 18, Paul was among MGM executives invited to a luncheon when William Randolph Hearst brought William Churchill and his son Randolph to the studio. Mayer, Mannix, and Thalberg's production team joined 150 actors including Marion Davies, Joan Crawford, Colleen Moore, Ramon Novarro, and Douglas Fairbanks, Jr. During lunch, an orchestra played and the biggest MGM stars strode onto a large stage at the end of the room and performed for the prime minister. Paul later joined a smaller group of 50 at a party for Churchill at Davies' Santa Monica beach house that included Charlie Chaplin, Harold Lloyd, and John Barrymore.

On the 24th he attended the opening dinner dance of the Mayfair Club, an annual event that signaled the start of the very important holiday movie season that was attended by everyone in Hollywood. Paul was a guest of Willis Goldbeck, along with Joan Bennett, King Vidor, Carey Wilson, Carmelita Geraghty, Fredric March and Florence Eldridge, and Lilyan Tashman.[83] Paul's date was Mary Duncan, a beautiful Virginia-born Broadway sensation brought to Hollywood by Fox for *Very Confidential* in 1927.[84]

The Mayers and Thalbergs hosted a star-studded midnight dinner on October 29 in the Blossom Room at the Roosevelt in honor of Sir Jagatiit Singh, the maharajah of Kapurhala.[85] MGM art directors transformed the dining room into an exotic version of old India, and filled it with beautiful dancing girls and veiled women serving food and drink. Paul and Mary Duncan joined the DeMilles, Eddie Mannix, Sid Grauman, King Vidor, Thalberg's team and several dozen other guests.

In the fall, Paul assisted Albert H. Kelley and Robert Ober directing *The Woman Racket*, the sound debut for Tom Moore and Blanche Sweet. He has not received credit although period newspapers identified him as one of three directors. Albert Shelby Le Vino and Fred Niblo, Jr. wrote the scenario from the Philip and Francis Dunning novel *The Night Hostess*.[86]

During a raid on a New York speakeasy, Irish cop Tom Hayes (Moore) meets singer Julia Barnes (Sweet) and instead of arresting her, takes her out to dinner. They fall in love and marry but Julia tires of life in a Bronx apartment and yearns for her former café life and deserts her husband for her old job. She is pursued by café owner Chris Miller but when she sees a gang murder a millionaire gambler, Tom saves her life (and in an amusing scene receives an award from real-life Mayor Jimmy Walker) and they are reconciled.[87]

Woman Racket was released January 24. A realistic police raid was filmed using New York policemen and a recently raided uptown speakeasy.[88]

Paul next supervised production of Lawrence Tibbett's musical *The Rogue Song*. Paul had a lot riding on MGM's first opera film since he'd been pushing Thalberg to adapt operatic vehicles for a year. Interviewed just after *Rogue Song* was finished, Paul said, "Grand opera will prove popular with motion picture audiences. [These films] will succeed, providing we do not attempt to do things audiences know are not done, such as having sing [*sic*] ordinary conversations." He also suggested that audiences had greater appreciation for music than ordinary grand opera audiences but didn't attend because "of the high prices and the lack of evening clothes."[89]

On the challenge of finding opera singers for movies, he said, "In the last 25 years of opera you will not find more than five or six stars who could [succeed] on screen. The camera demands more than voice; it needs personality, appearance and acting ability."[90] He thought the only two potential stars from all of opera were Tibbett and Grace Moore, both already at MGM.

In overseeing *Rogue Song*, Paul also had to monitor Lionel Barrymore, who was proving a disaster as a director, chronically late and usually hung over. *The Rogue Song* was Tibbett's first speaking and singing film.

Tibbett plays tribal chieftain Yegor, leading a group of bandits in Russia's Caucasus Mountains as something of a Robin Hood, who falls in love with Princess Vera (Catherine Dale Owen). She is attracted by his singing during an elaborate party at his camp featuring a ballet by 100 dancers (choreographed by Albertina Rasch). But when he learns his sister Nadja has been betrayed by Vera's brother Prince Serge, he kidnaps Vera to his mountain fortress intent on revenge. When she causes Yegor's capture, he sings to her as he is being flogged and she realizes his love and orders him released. In a strange ending, the lovers part hoping they will meet again.[91]

Critics applauded *Rogue Song* for magnificent mountain scenery, Technicolor filming, and the music. Cedric Gibbons designed spectacular castles with beautiful gardens and colorful gypsy camps. Tibbett sang eight songs from arias to love ballads, and fellow opera star Elsa Alsen offered another song. In one scene an entire chorus sang atop galloping horses. It was described as "the most elaborate picture of the year ... [that] changed motion picture history."[92] Thalberg also realized the potential for operatic translations when Tibbett received an Academy Award nomination for his performance.

¶ SEVEN ☙

Garbo

By that fall the only MGM star not to have done a talkie was Greta Garbo, and Paul was assigned to supervise her first, *Anna Christie*, based on the Eugene O'Neill play. Paul received no credit but was mentioned as the producer in newspaper stories. Garbo worried MGM, refusing to take a voice test and at first rejecting the role because she thought the characters sullied Swedes. But she reported on the first day of filming, October 9, saying "I've learned my lines."[1]

Garbo plays Anna, whose sailor father Chris returns to the sea and leaves her with abusive relatives on a faraway farm. When she finally escapes, she drifts into prostitution and later travels to New York and finds her father in a grimy waterfront bar keeping company with drunken barfly Marthy (Marie Dressler). Anna moves onto the barge, reconciles with her father and befriends Marthy. During a trip up the coast, they rescue young sailor Matt, who falls in love with Anna. But she has grown to hate men and her feelings for Matt leave her conflicted, so she confesses her past life to Matt and her father. At first Matt leaves in disgust but returns and in a powerful scene Anna swears on his mother's crucifix that she loves only him and they are reunited. Anna is then content marrying Matt and caring for her father.[2]

The reaction to Garbo speaking, even just a few lines, was spectacular. Headlines simply said **GARBO SPEAKS!**[3] Her momentous scene was actually simple; she walked into a saloon, sat down and said to the waiter, "Gimme a whiskey, ginger ale on the side. And don't be stingy. Baby." The film, which cost $325,000, grossed over $1,000,000 as the larger metropolitan theaters ran it five times daily instead of four.[4] Cedric Gibbons' cleverly crafted sets included the exterior and interior of a coal barge, a seaside saloon, and a Coney Island–like amusement park.

Anna Christie made a splash for MGM but 1929 offered dozens of other memorable films. The German newspaper *Der Deutsche* quizzed hundreds of famous people around the world as to their most memorable film of 1929:

people like King Don Alfonso of Spain (he chose the "sound film made of me by the Fox Company"), Benito Mussolini (*La Grazia*), President Portis Gil of Mexico (*The Singing Fool*), and writer Thomas Mann (*The Passion of Joan of Arc*). Paul was among several dozen Hollywood executives and stars queried and he joined Thalberg, Ernst Lubitsch, Lothar Mendes, and Fred Niblo in choosing *Hallelujah*, the first all-black film.[5]

That summer, Paul convinced Thalberg to buy the rights to the Ursula Parrott novel *Ex-Wife* and spent months working with writers John Meehan, Nick Grinde, and Zelda Sears crafting the story of a disillusioned divorcee going through a string of men. Thalberg originally tabbed Joan Crawford for the lead even though Norma Shearer dearly wanted the role. Paul wanted Shearer but Thalberg didn't think she was believable as a sensual, provocative woman so she secretly arranged a private photo shoot with George Hurrell, who created a stunning photograph of Shearer reclining in a chair, shirt half open. The sexually charged photo earned her the role over Crawford in the renamed *The Divorcée*.

After three years of happiness, newspaperman Ted (Chester Morris) enters into an affair which his wife Jerry (Shearer) learns of. When he's away on business she has a fling with his best friend Don but Ted refuses to accept her affair and they divorce. Jerry goes through a string of flings and serious affairs before reuniting with old friend Paul (Conrad Nagel), who loved her before she married Ted. Even though Paul is married, Jerry vacations on his yacht and decides to sail with him to Japan until she overhears his wife Helen pleading to save her marriage. Jerry flees to Paris, where, on New Year's Eve, she is reconciled with Ted.[6]

Divorcée reaffirmed Thalberg's faith in Paul, grossing over $1,200,000 on a $350,000 budget after its April 1930 release, Shearer earned her first Academy Award for Best Actress and the film was also nominated for Best Director (Robert Z. Leonard) and Best Production. Paul did not request producer credit for the film even after it was nominated and Thalberg tabbed him to produce Shearer's next film, *Let Us Be Gay*. He also bought another sexually charged Parrott novel which became another Shearer vehicle, *Strangers May Kiss*.

During the summer and fall of 1929, Paul dated a number of women but was most often seen with Mary Duncan, Virginia Valli, and Jeanette Loff. Chicago-born Valli started in Milwaukee stock companies, entered movies in 1916 and by the mid–1920s was among Universal's biggest stars. Loff was a beautiful Midwestern actress introduced to him by Douglas Fairbanks, Jr., her costar in *Party Girl* at Tiffany.[7] Paul dated all three women through the summer of 1930.

Paul's romantic attachments were regularly mentioned in papers and movie magazines. On November 5, wealthy real estate developer and yachts-

man Otto Wildey hosted a Hal-
loween party at his 224 North
Rossmore mansion with music by
the Paul Whiteman Orchestra.
Paul and Mary Duncan joined 50
guests including H.B. Warner,
King Vidor, Robert Z. Leonard,
Clara Bow, Polly Moran, Ruth
Collyer, and William Haines.[8]
The lead singer for the Whiteman
Orchestra couldn't appear because
he was serving 20 days in jail for
drunk driving. His name was
Bing Crosby.

In November, Paul was
invited to become a founding
member of the Embassy Club, a
private dinner club at the Biltmore Hotel opened so members
could entertain away from the
press. The luxurious facility was
the brainchild of Rupert Hughes,

**Actress Mary Duncan, one of three women
Paul juggled during the summer and fall of
1929.**

Charlie Chaplin, and Antonio Moreno and the founding members included
Paul, Jack Gilbert, King Vidor, Tod Browning, Cecil B. DeMille, Bebe
Daniels and Gloria Swanson. When the Club held its grand opening on
December 13, he wasn't with either Mary Duncan, Virginia Valli or Jeanette
Loff. Jean Harlow was on his arm. Gorgeous in her tight white gown, she was
a sensation. Friends said to Paul, "Paul you certainly can pick 'em" and asked,
"Who is this gorgeous creature?" He glowed.[9]

Just before Christmas he attended an engagement party for Bessie Love
and William Hawks at Blanche Sweet's Chateau Elysee apartment. Most of
his studio pals were there including Carmel Myers and Ralph Blum, Larry
Weingarten and Sylvia Thalberg, Jack Gilbert, Edmund Goulding, Jack Mul-
hall, and Lila Lee. Among the interesting guests was golf champion Walter
Hagen.[10]

On Christmas Day, Paul hosted a party with Loff at her Casa Granada
apartment at 1336 Harper in Hollywood. *L.A. Times* gossip writer Grace
Gingsley noted, "Paul Bern is making hay ... with Jeanette Loff, taking her
about and paying to her all those lovely attentions that only Paul knows how
to pay."[11] On New Year's Eve, he hosted 25 friends at the Embassy including
Douglas Fairbanks, Jr., and Joan Crawford, Irene Mayer and David O. Selznick,

Carey Wilson, Lilyan Tashman and Edmund Lowe, and Jack Gilbert and Ina Claire. Paul's date was Virginia Valli.[12]

Effects of the Wall Street crash that forced Garbo to do *Anna Christie* shook America to its core. Vast fortunes disappeared overnight. Hollywood wasn't immune. Thalberg, heavily invested in stocks, lost a fortune. Mayer, a real estate investor, lost little. The movie industry survived. Carl Laemmle boasted it would be "last to feel the pinch and the first to get over it"[13] since the bleakness of American life made movies a perfect escape.

The Depression changed the way Americans saw their lives. From 1929 to 1932, average family incomes would fall 40 percent to $1,500. America's bedrock virtues were in doubt as people doubted capitalism, democracy, indeed their way of life. Movies offered an escape and even as the economy tumbled, 100,000,000 people flocked to theaters monthly from a population of 130,000,000.

Laemmle was right to a point. MGM, with 6,000 employees, was the

most profitable studio, making $12,000,000 in 1929 and $15,000,000 in 1930, and was the only one to pay dividends. RKO had to reorganize, Universal and Paramount almost went under, Fox merged with 20th Century to survive and United Artists simply stopped making movies.

Paul spent early 1930 getting Shearer's *Let Us Be Gay* ready for May production, attending the L.A. stage premiere on March 2 with Joan Crawford and Douglas Fairbanks, Jr.[14] Thalberg often waited to see how the public reacted to a play before starting the filming.

"One of Hollywood's most gorgeous blondes," Jeanette Loff, was Paul's most frequent escort for a year beginning in mid–1929 (courtesy Tammy Matz).

At the same time, Garbo's *Romance* was filming. Again Paul has not been credited but newspaper articles confirmed him as supervising producer. Filming began on January 25.

Romance was a lesson about love told in a New Year's Eve conversation between a dying old man who lost the love of his life advising his grandson Harry (Elliott Nugent) not to do the same. He describes a party at the mansion of Cornelius Van Tuyl (Lewis Stone) where he, son of an aristocratic family and the rector of his church, met famous Italian opera star Rita Cavallini (Garbo). He fell in love with her and persisted despite his family's disapproval but by the next New Year's Eve it was apparent their differing stations would prevent their love and they agreed to part. The bishop tells Tom that even though he married a woman more acceptable to his family, he never got over the pain and he instructs his grandson to marry the woman he truly loves regardless of the consequences.[15]

Critics raved about the film after its August 22 premiere and both director Clarence Brown and Garbo received Academy Award nominations (coincidently, they had also received matching nominations for their work on the earlier *Anna Christie*).

There was no break in Paul's social schedule in early 1930. On January 12, he and Virginia Valli attended a performance by famed Spanish dancer La Argentina in a small Hollywood theater. The evening was noted in papers because sitting with Paul and Irving, in "utter oblivion to the stares," was the reclusive Garbo, who almost never appeared in public. On the 16th he and Valli attended the *Rogue Song* premiere with an MGM group including the Mayers, the Thalbergs, Cecil B. DeMille (who brought his daughter *and* one of his two mistresses, Julia Faye), Douglas Shearer, Edmund Goulding, and Eddie Mannix. The group gathered at a party at co-star Catherine Dale Owen's apartment at the Chateau Elysee and after the film at a private party at the Ambassador.[16]

On January 25 he and Jeanette Loff joined Erich von Stroheim's private party at a Mayfair Club ball at the Biltmore. Von Stroheim's was the lead table, hosting guest of honor Will Hays and including Buster Keaton, Ralph Forbes and Ruth Chatterton, Charles Brabin and Theda Bara, Lila Lee, Carmelita Geraghty and Carey Wilson. Other groups were hosted by Jack Warner, Irving, Harold Lloyd, B.P. Schulberg, and Mervyn LeRoy.

On February 8 he and Virginia Valli joined a large group at a dinner dance given by Lila Lee at the Embassy Club that included William Hawks and Bessie Love, Lydell Peck and Janet Gaynor, Erich von Stroheim, Louella Parsons, Bebe Daniels, Edith and Irene Mayer, Dolores Del Rio, Billie Dove, Howard Hughes and Ben Lyon.

On the 16th he joined Lawrence Tibbett's wife and a small group watching her husband's performance at the Philharmonic and for a dinner at their estate. Paul and Valli joined Basil Rathbone, Milton Sills, Ramon Novarro, Will Hays, Erich von Stroheim, Irving, Lloyd Wright, and Charles Farrell.[17]

He was still in demand as a speaker and on the 21st joined Ryllis Hemington, head of public relations for Fox, speaking to a meeting hosted by the California Women of the Golden West. Hemington spoke about "Talkies and the Theater" and Paul about "Problems of Motion Pictures from the Producer's Standpoint."[18]

In addition to work and social obligations, Paul was maintaining yet another deathbed vigil, this for Mabel Normand. After her career imploded amid various scandals and her stage failure in New York, Mabel's health steadily declined to the point that she was virtually absent from papers during 1929. She was in and out of hospitals all year with respiratory ailments worsened by drug and alcohol abuse and on August 28 was moved to Pottenger's Sanitarium in the hills above Altadena. Headlines told the world what Paul already knew: MABEL NORMAND SINKING.[19] He paid for the stay at Pottenger's.

For six months Paul drove to Altadena every week to visit his dying friend and sent her flowers and letters, signing "Pinkus ben rabbi Juano" and joking he wanted to visit but "somewhere in the offing is a doctor who will raise hell and kick me right out on-the-place-where-I-usually-sit."[20] By February 2 she was too sick to be told that her father had died and she could no longer visit with her beloved Chow.

For the last month Paul came to Altadena every other day, sitting quietly with Mabel, holding her hand and reassuring her, as he had with Lucille Ricksen and Barbara La Marr.[21] On February 22 she received the last rites of the Catholic Church and early on the 23rd she placed her hands across her chest, mouthed a prayer along

Paul's MGM portrait, ca. 1929.

with her long-time caretaker, and quietly ended one of the most riotous lives in Hollywood. Finally, MABEL NORMAND [was] AT PEACE.[22]

People crowded her wake at Cunningham & O'Connor Funeral Home in L.A. and massive crowds attended her February 29 funeral. Paul was an honorary pallbearer with Charlie Chaplin, Mack Sennett, Sid Grauman, Samuel Goldwyn, Roscoe Arbuckle, Ford Sterling, and Eugene Pallette. Thalberg, King Vidor, and Eddie Mannix came from MGM joining Mary Pickford, Douglas Fairbanks, Marion Davies, Mickey Neilan, Ben Turpin and hundreds of Mabel's studio pals.

It was an interesting comment on the changing industry as headlines noted FILM FOLKS OF OLD DAYS BURY MABEL NORMAND and an article mentioned that the "new Hollywood of microphones and music and dancing chorus girls was scarcely represented at Mabel Normand's funeral except by those few of the old days who survived in the new."[23]

In March, Paul began building a home for himself in Benedict Canyon, surprising after a lifetime living mostly in apartments and for the last five years in his attic room at the Ambassador. In late 1928 he contracted for a property near the Beverly Hills flats but the deal fell through and he wound up suing the real estate agent for $1,500 in lost fees.[24] He then paid $15,000 for a 3⅓-acre property in Benedict Canyon, at the top of winding Easton Drive, and started construction on a Bavarian-style lodge.[25]

In 1930, the property at 9820 Easton Drive was even more remote than it is today. At the bottom of the street, Benedict Canyon Drive wound from Beverly Hills over the mountain into the San Fernando Valley but pavement ended almost a mile south of Easton and it was a gravel road on through the Valley. Easton is steep and narrow and snakes almost a mile up the hill. Today it continues up past Paul's property but when he bought the land, the street ended at the entrance to his property, down Easton below the gated entrance used today. There were only a half dozen houses on the entire street and none up near Paul's gate. Today the lower reaches of Paul's property contain almost a dozen homes.

Ron and Maggie Hale have owned the Easton estate since 1970. Ron fell in love with it after first seeing it as a UCLA med student and bought the property from Jay Sebring's family after Sebring's 1969 murder at Sharon Tate's nearby home. The rubble of Sebring's life (papers and photographs of Christmas gatherings and pool parties attended by the likes of Steve McQueen) lay scattered about, unclaimed in drawers. In the 1970s the estate became a beacon for hippies and Charles Manson and Tate murder aficionados; one morning as he retrieved his morning paper, Ron came upon a couple having sex on his car in the driveway. Now the secluded property is only accessible via a large gate and long drive and is not visible from the road.

Sebring had painted walls purple, the master bedroom black, ceilings mint green and the beautiful interior woodwork white. The plaster between the beams was covered with brightly colored wallpaper. The Hales have spent 30 years working to restore the home to its original state.

Locals told Ron the house was started by John Barrymore and that Paul as a studio executive prevailed upon him to give up the house so that he himself could live there. That's untrue. It wasn't Paul's personality to make such a demand, Barrymore was a major star, and the design isn't Barrymore. He preferred the Spanish style. But somebody may have started a house there; Irene Selznick mentioned in her memoirs that Paul purchased "a half-finished place far up in a canyon."[26]

When Paul built there, the top of Easton ended at a gated entrance to a short driveway up an incline to a small circular motor court bordered by a wooden fence. Next to the turnaround was a small stucco bungalow and three-car garage where Paul's gardener Clifton Earl Davis lived. The original entrance below the house fell into disuse and was replaced by another entrance up the hill in the 1960s. The servants' house is now a private home.

To reach the main house from the parking area, guests walked up a path several hundred feet through a manicured lawn filled with trees. The house sits up against the south canyon wall that soars several hundred feet above the rooftop. Below the house is a 50-foot wide kidney-shaped pool surrounded by a patio butting up against the house. The patio was originally large flat stones separated by grass but has since been replaced with concrete. The entire pool area sits atop a curving 100-foot

In 1930, Paul built himself a gorgeous Bavarian chateau high up in Benedict Canyon.

Left: Some of the intricately made terraces, fireplaces and walkways covering the hillside below Paul's house. *Right:* The path from below led to the entry stairs, built into a massive retaining wall below the pool.

Left: The carved image of Carey Wilson, one of Paul's "four friends," still looking down on the pool. *Right:* The only face Paul never identified bears a striking resemblance to Dorothy Millette.

long, 20-foot tall, handmade stone retaining wall visible from the parking area below.

Intricate hand-crafted stonework is everywhere. The entire hillside from the driveway up to the house — nearly 100 feet in elevation and 200 feet in length — is a maze of terraced walls, walkways, patios, fireplaces, secluded grottos and gardens, everything intricately hand-crafted in stone. The magnificent stonework literally covers the hill. Patios and grottos were filled with wicker and wooden furniture and logs stacked next to large hearths. The site still evokes images of the Bavarian hunting lodges in Paul's native Germany.

The entrance path that wound up through the lawn was lined by a row of copper lamps hung from arched wooden beams that still stand. To the left of the path was a 60-foot waterfall cascading down through a series of boulders into a large pond. To the right was the wall of stone terraces. The effect remains spectacular; walking amidst what remains of two years of masonry work is awe-inspiring.

The pathway leads up the hill to a stairwell built into the massive retaining wall supporting the pool. Two huge stone flower pots frame the entrance to the stairwell that curves up along the wall underneath a large copper lamp suspended from a cedar post. Below the soft glow of the lamp, the face of a carved cherub set into the wall still smiles down on the peaceful scene. At the landing at the top of the stairs, the pool patio is to the left and up another small set of stairs the original front door is tucked into the side of the house next to a three-story stone turret that Paul originally topped with red tile. Still further up another half-dozen steps (hidden behind the turret) is the kitchen door and servants' entrance.

The stucco and beam house was built on four levels designed as a kind of split-level inside. The lowest level next to the pool contained a small changing room and shower in a space perhaps ten feet square. Above the entrance to the changing room at the end of four large beams protruding from the house are four visages gazing down like gargoyles. MGM story editor Sam Marx remembered the faces that Paul had studio craftsmen carve as representing the four winds, and others have identified them as everyone from Douglas Fairbanks and Mary Pickford to John Barrymore, Valentino, or Richard Barthelmess.[27] But Paul told intimates they were the faces of the four people who were closest to him in life, naming three: Barbara La Marr, Douglas Fairbanks, Jr., and Carey Wilson, but never identifying the fourth, a beautiful young woman.[28] The face is remarkably similar to photos of Dorothy Millette. The gorgeous creations still stare down onto the quiet patio.

Paul hired ex-girlfriend Jetta Goudal to decorate the house. After Mayer fired her in 1927 she sued MGM and won, effectively ending her career and leaving her in dire financial straits by 1930. She turned to interior decorating but, just after starting Easton, in April she suffered a nervous breakdown and would spend two months in Chase Sanitarium. Paul asked MGM designer Harold Grieve to help her; after her hospital stay, the matchmaking led to a romance and marriage that lasted 55 years.[29]

The main entrance opens into a small foyer on the second level in front of two staircases. To the left, several steps lead down to a large great room-living room. Hand-carved beams and exposed roof boards make the vaulted ceiling appear even higher than it is. The dark-stained walls and stairwell were hand-carved as were the matching bookcases at either end of the room. Facing the middle of the room is a five-foot-square fireplace with a wide hearth made of large stones and crowned with a hand-crafted copper awning. The fireplace is encased by the same gorgeous wood panels as the rest of the room and the floors covered with several large oriental rugs.

Just past the fireplace, a small bar is hidden behind a built-in bookcase, accessible by a hidden switch that opens the hinged case like a door. Behind the bar and yet another hidden panel is a small wine cellar. Remember, it was built in the Prohibition era. A five-foot wide chandelier constructed of elk antlers above the room cast a warm light over an array of large couches and over-stuffed chairs scattered about. Shelves and tables were filled with Paul's extensive and varied book collection. The room was relaxing and comfortable. Several intricate German clocks and small European landscape paintings graced the walls. At the end of the room, another door leads to a large patio above the pool and above the end of the room is a large balcony off the master bedroom.

The other stairwell at the foyer winds up to the third level, the main living area in the house. At the far end was Paul's master bedroom and near the stairs the kitchen that opened into a circular dining room inside the turret. Paul did not have a full kitchen in the house, preferring to have food prepared in the servants' house and carted up the hill. He did not want kitchen smells invading the house while guests were there. In the kitchen Paul had only a stove for coffee, a toaster, and a small refrigerator. The dining room looks out over the hillside through three windows around the turret. Paul had a circular table crafted of mahogany to fit the space.

From the kitchen, a small hallway to the left leads to a balcony overlooking the living room. Straight ahead is a hall toward the entrance to the master bedroom. Just inside the door was Paul's bathroom, which also had an entrance from the hall by the door. The left side of the large bedroom was a sitting area with a couch, several chairs, and a desk in a corner surrounded by a bank of large corner windows overlooking the pool. The windows kept the room bright and sunny, and constant canyon breezes kept it cool.

Paul's bed, several chairs and a few tables were on the other side of the room closest to the canyon behind the house. At the other end of the room was a large walk-in closet and changing area that was originally inside a short extension visible in 1930s photos. The closet has since been enlarged and is now a sunroom.

A narrow, winding staircase — so steep it's necessary to hold the walls to navigate — leads from the kitchen entryway up to the fourth level which contains a small bedroom and bath. The smallish room is tucked under the peak of the roof. There are windows at each end and two tiny gabled windows at the top of the house in that bedroom and bath. In a corner of the linen closet, a hidden door leads to a passageway into a small room at the top of the turret.[30]

Easton was obviously a bachelor house, spartan but comfortable. It was lovely, private, and quiet, so secluded he put a sign down on Benedict Canyon with an arrow pointing up Easton Drive that read THIS WAY TO PAUL BERN'S HOUSE. The gorgeous estate was described correctly as "a bewitching place of winding paths and sharply sloping hillsides in a magical setting."[31]

Paul remained at the Ambassador during construction and continued his hectic work and social schedules. On March 12 he attended a Thalberg-hosted party at the French Room at the Ambassador for Irene Mayer's sister Edith and her fiancé Bill Goetz. He was with Jeanette Loff and joined most of the top MGM names like the Mayers, Fred Niblo and Enid Bennett, Douglas Fairbanks and Mary Pickford, Joan Crawford, Leatrice Joy, John Gilbert, Edmund Lowe and a dozen others for the evening.[32] On the 19th he and Loff joined the same group for the Goetz-Mayer wedding, also at the Biltmore.

On the 16th he attended the wedding of Lowell Sherman and Helene Costello at the Beverly Wilshire with pals Jack Gilbert and Ina Claire, Mae Murray, and Estelle Taylor (married to boxer Jack Dempsey and also a close friend). Also there were Douglas Fairbanks and Mary Pickford, Allan Dwan and John and Lionel Barrymore.[33]

Paul also attended almost every major Hollywood premiere, movie or stage. On April 1 he attended the premiere of the Gilbert Emery play *The Hero*, sitting with *New York Times* executive Louis Wiley and Louis Mann. With Paul were Douglas Fairbanks and Mary Pickford, Catherine Dale Owen, Louis Wolheim, Julia Faye, and Clive Brook.[34]

The next weekend he was invited to the lavish home of composer Dimitri Tiomkin and his choreographer wife Albertina Rasch at 1445 North Fairfax for their first Hollywood party (they met on the *Rogue Song* set). Paul attended the housewarming with Adolphe Menjou and Catherine Carver, Sid Grauman, Arlie Lewin, Hunt Stromberg, Marie Dressler, and Douglas Shearer.[35]

In May, Norma Shearer's *Let Us Be Gay* went into production, based on

Rachel Crothers' play about a lonely divorcee who goes to Paris in search of happiness. Robert Z. Leonard was tabbed to direct because he finished her *The Divorcée* in 21 days and she was six months pregnant when *Let Us Be Gay* began. Cameraman Norbert Brodine hid Shearer's growing stomach behind plants, high chairs, and balustrades and Leonard completed the film in 23 days, after which Shearer retreated to Santa Monica to await the birth of the first Thalberg child.

During production, MGM casting director Fred Datig brought Jean to see Paul, who was in pre-production and casting for the next Garbo film, *Inspiration*. Datig and Jean realized Paul didn't think Jean right for the part of a prostitute but as they prepared to leave, Paul asked, "Is it all right, Fred, if we spend a little time discussing this charming lady's career?" Jean chirped, "Sure!" and sat back down and Paul said he didn't see her playing a prostitute. She told him, "I could do that. Easy." But Paul told her it wasn't her acting ability he was worried about but her American look and suggested she was "very much of today. You should never be in a period story."[36] According to Datig, Paul walked Jean out to her car where she suddenly invited him to escort her to the *Hell's Angels* premiere at the end of May.

On April 18 he joined Basil Rathbone and Ouida Bergère for an anniversary party at their 527 Crescent Drive estate in Beverly Hills. He and Virginia Valli joined Douglas Fairbanks, Jr., and Joan Crawford, Edmund Lowe and Lilyan Tashman, Fredric March and Florence Eldridge, the DeMilles, the Barrymore brothers, and Edmund Goulding.[37]

Paul attended the biggest premiere of the year on the 21st with Jeanette Loff at the Fox Carthay Circle: Universal's *All Quiet on the Western Front*. He was invited to the industry's most exclusive pre-movie event, a private dinner hosted by Carl Laemmle at the Embassy Club. He joined Fairbanks and Pickford, Ernst Lubitsch, *All Quiet* director Lewis Milestone, Harry Rapf, Cecil B. DeMille, Clara Bow, Joan Bennett, Bebe Daniels, Ben Lyon, Al Jolson, D.W. Griffith, Charles Chaplin, Howard Hughes, and Erich von Stroheim.[38] After the movie, Laemmle entertained a larger group of about 250; Paul attended that party also.

The next evening, he and Loff were invited to a masked costume ball for Irene Mayer at Ralph Blum and Carmel Myers' 621 Arden Drive hacienda. Among the 150 guests were the Mayers, Thalberg, Jack Warner, Harry Rapf, Billie Dove, Claudette Colbert, Douglas Fairbanks, Jr., and Joan Crawford, and Howard Hughes.[39] On the 30th he attended a small party given for Jean by Pasadena businessman Crane Gartz at George Olsen's Supper Club in Hollywood with Joe Saunders, Ona Brown, Hack Hartfield, and Ona Wilson.[40]

On April 29th he was a groomsman at Irene Mayer's wedding to David O. Selznick at her father's Santa Monica beach house at 625 Palisades Road.[41]

Jeanette Loff, here in a still from *The Boudoir Diplomat*, was Paul's most frequent companion during the spring of 1930 (courtesy Tammy Matz).

The other ushers were Myron Selznick, writer Oliver H.P. Garrett, William Goetz and B.P. Schulberg.[42] Paul's Easton house was nearing completion (though stonework went on for another year) and just before the wedding Paul offered the house to the couple as a wedding present, asking them to "bless his house" by living in it for two years. He told them he would stay at the Ambassador and would feel better about the house knowing his friends had lived in it. When Irene protested, he tried to convince them to take it for one year, to no avail.[43]

On May 21 Paul and Irene joined a small group of Colleen Moore, Warner Baxter and Ivan Lebedeff for dinner at the Coconut Grove before attending the premiere of the Maurice Chevalier film, *The Big Pond*.[44] On the 30th he attended the premiere of Marion Davies' *The Floradora Girl* with Jeanette Loff, joining a large MGM contingent including Joan Crawford, Dolores Del Rio, and Norma Shearer.

On June 7, the most spectacular movie premiere in the history of Hollywood took place at Grauman's Chinese on Hollywood Boulevard. Only Howard Hughes and four others had seen the finished *Hell's Angels* but it had already become a public legend.[45] Hughes' excesses continued to the last minute when he added a 20-second scene of American soldiers marching at the end of the war, spending $250,000 and hiring 1,750 extras.[46] It seemed that all of America was waiting breathlessly for the film.

The scene outside Grauman's approached pandemonium. More than 500 policemen and 250 Marines tried to control the 25,000 people crammed onto the sidewalks and streets (some claimed 50,000 to 250,000). The few hundred that got in paid $11 for tickets ($250 today). For a mile down Hollywood Boulevard, hundreds of half-size planes hung from light poles and 200 multi-colored searchlights (rented for $25,000) lit a squadron of bombers flying overhead in formation. They dropped 250 parachute flares that floated down over the crowd and spewed 3,000 gallons of liquid smoke that filled the night sky with red, white and blue smoke screens through which several dozen smaller planes dove, whirled, and performed stunts and dogfights.[47]

Among the 2,500 stars walking the gauntlet of fans and 200 photographers were the Thalbergs, Mary Pickford, Jack Gilbert, Marion Davies, Charles Chaplin, James Hall, Bebe Daniels, Ina Claire, Flo Ziegfeld, Bessie Love, Dolores Del Rio, Lupe Velez, Lionel Barrymore, Eddie Cantor, Joan Crawford, Buster Keaton, and Harold Lloyd.

Hughes and Billie Dove led the *Hell's Angels* contingent that arrived in a string of rented Dusenbergs. A month earlier Hughes paid Dove's husband Irving Willat $325,000 to quietly divorce her and paid Warners $250,000 to buy her contract so she could spend time with him. Ben Lyon, James Hall, John Darrow and Jean followed in their Dusenbergs. Most of the large crowd

Paul and Jean prepare to leave for the premiere of the blockbuster _Hell's Angels_.

had never seen Jean in person but during the six months it took to edit the film, Hughes launched a clever publicity campaign exploiting Jean's sexually charged role. For two years _Hell's Angels'_ stories were about dogfights and Zeppelin raids. Now they were about sex. And the new blonde.

Details of her performance and provocative photos leaked by Hughes created a huge buzz. Almost two hours after the scheduled start there was a roar when she exited her Dusenberg in a skin-tight white satin evening dress and large white orchid corsage. Paul followed with the Bellos, dapper in his black tuxedo and white tie. He was the better-known of the two, their arrival described as "this unknown girl with the well-known, much-loved Paul Bern."[48] His friends were surprised to see him with Jean. He had rarely been with her since Irene Mayer's party the previous August. But there they were.

With Paul standing behind, Jean spoke to a nationwide radio audience, saying, "Thank you. I would like to use this occasion to publicly thank Mr. Hughes for the opportunity he gave to me." She smiled and they walked into the theater beneath a 20 foot tall wooden cutout of Jean in her tight strapless gown, caressing her costar Ben Lyon.

Because of the crowds, the film didn't start until 11:00. The most-awaited scene was Jean arriving home with Lyon and removing her coat to reveal a flimsy décolleté gown — as usual, without underwear — and asking, "Would you be shocked if I put on something more comfortable?" The theater erupted in pandemonium and laughter. At that moment Paul reassuringly took Jean's hand in his and Arlie Lewin said to Sam Marx, "Good old Paul is at it again, he's found someone else to make over and fall in love with."[49]

When Hughes' spectacle ended, the crowd leapt to its feet and cheered for a full twenty minutes. It was a hit around the world but Hughes' reckless spending meant it could never recoup the cost. But it made Jean an overnight star, to her surprise. While some critics correctly described her as "just plain awful,"[50] others saw through the amateurish work and recognized her potential. *Variety* hit it on the head: "It doesn't make much difference what degree of talent she possesses for this girl is the most sensuous figure to get in front of a camera in some time."[51] *Time* wrote, "The climax of *Hell's Angels* was reached, not in the million dollar uproar of ninety planes but when Jean Harlow appeared in that evening dress and said, 'Do you mind if I slip into something more comfortable?'"

She was remarkably self-aware, later philosophically telling Thalberg, "People have been laughing at me my whole life,"[52] and of *Hell's Angels* said "[T]he planes get better reviews than me."[53] She knew the roles she was destined for, saying, "I'm not crazy about my wild-women roles on the screen, but then I know what I have to sell. I have never been fooled about myself."[54] She was soon receiving 5,000 letters a week and Hughes wanted her to star in *The Front Page* but director Lewis Milestone refused her take her so she was sent on a cross-country publicity trip starting in Seattle. Hughes assigned his top pilot J.B. Alexander to fly Jean but he wouldn't pay for Mama Jean; she followed Jean across the country on trains.[55]

Despite their public appearance at several *Hell's Angels* events, the relationship between Paul and Jean was far from better. She dated several men including Vic Orsatti, Howard Strickling, Cy Bartlett and, according to Arthur Landau, "myself" (hard to believe judging by surviving correspondence between the two, however).[56]

Paul dated Jeanette Loff, Virginia Valli, Mary Duncan and Olive Borden that summer. He'd know Borden since *Dressmaker from Paris*; she was considered one of the most beautiful actresses of the silent era. She was a Mack Sennett Bathing Beauty at 15 and by 19 earned $1,500 weekly and owned a Beverly Hills mansion. She and Paul were often mentioned as a couple in papers and movie magazines. She also offered advice on the Easton project, advice he followed faithfully.[57]

Paul tried to help resurrect her career, which crashed in 1928 when Fox reduced her contract and she walked out and moved to a tiny cottage in Malibu. She had not worked in almost two years and he helped get her a few roles. The Bern-Borden relationship was not studio-crafted. They spent more time away from cameras at private functions.

The afternoon before the *Hell's Angels* premier, Douglas Shearer's wife Marion, who had been despondent over his numerous affairs, walked up to a Venice Pier amusement park shooting gallery, grabbed a loaded .22-caliber pistol off the table and shot herself between the eyes in front of hundreds of horrified onlookers. MGM publicity blamed the suicide on undiagnosed depression but friends knew why she killed herself. The studio blamed the dead woman. It would not be the last time. Paul was among the small group at Marion's memorial service. On the 7th Jean left on the *Hell's Angels* trip, criss-crossing the country to New York and back.

On the 14th he and Jean attended the wedding of *Hell's Angels* co-star Ben Lyon and Bebe Daniels at the Beverly Wilshire. Jean was flown back to L.A. for the event, which attracted big names like Lila Lee, the Talmadge sisters with Gilbert Roland and Buster Keaton, George Fitzmaurice, Bessie Love, Billy Haines, Howard Hughes, Buster Collier, the DeMilles, Louella Parsons, and Paul's circle: Douglas Fairbanks, Jr., and Joan Crawford, Ina Claire and John Gilbert, and Carmelita Geraghty and Carey Wilson.[58]

A few days later Paul was invited to the opening of a Spanish café on Olivera Street owned by writer friend James Warner Bellah. He joined Harry Langdon, Marceline Day, Felix Hughes, Belle Bennett, Monte Blue, Frank Capra, and Rosetta and Vivian Duncan.

Jean returned to her *Hell's Angeles* trip, a grind she detested. She forced herself through the thrice-daily speeches before the film and charmed record crowds everywhere she went. The real Jean showed through when she spoke and fans loved that Jean. When she flew into Seattle, pilot Alexander was forced to land in a farm field five miles east of downtown. Alexander, Jean and her press agent walked through a plowed field to a country road and flagged down a local farmer taking a load of wood to town in a wagon. She clambered up and sat beside him and chatted about the country, farming conditions, crops, and the weather. He never knew who she was. Meantime, 2,000 people waited at the airport.[59]

During the summer, Paul began pre-production on *New Moon*, *The Southerner*, and *Paid*, all starting in August or September. It appears from newspapers that he was still helping Pathé and Cecil B. DeMille's three-picture MGM contract as he was credited as a production supervisor on DeMille's second MGM film, *Madam Satan*.

Thalberg and Paul committed some of MGM's most talented people to *Satan*, which starred Kay Johnson as wealthy socialite Angela Brooks. She

Jean's arrival caused a stir among the thousands gathered outside Grauman's Chinese Theater. Many in the crowd didn't recognize her escort.

suspects husband Bob's (Reginald Denny) affair with wild showgirl Trixie (Lillian Roth) but he tells her Trixie is his best friend Jimmy's girlfriend. To follow him, Angela poses as the mysterious "Madam Satan" and goes to Trixie's apartment and somehow is not recognized by either Bob or Jimmy, who invites her to a lavish costume party aboard a dirigible. During the party, "Madam Satan" catches Bob's eye as they participate in a spectacular electric ballet in which characters simulate everything from sparkplugs to lightning bolts. The dirigible is struck by lightning and the guests must para-chute to the ground. After Angela gives her parachute to the terrified Trixie, Bob sees it is his wife, gives her his parachute and dives from the ship. Some-how he survives after landing in the Central Park reservoir and the couple is reunited.[60]

DeMille's second sound effort suffered from another bizarre Jeanie Macpherson script and DeMille aiming for spectacle when simple would have been better. Like his earlier *Dynamite*, this film was too long and had dozens of superfluous scenes that confused viewers. The bizarre costumes were also perplexing: Theodore Kosloff paraded about as "Electricity" with metallic lightning bolts jutting from his head and hands, wearing leather straps lined with electric bulbs.[61]

On July 8, Paul attended a performance by Ann Pennington at the Blos-som Room at the Roosevelt. The party was for Jack Gilbert's ex-wife Leatrice Joy, and Paul attended with Ruth Roland, Theda Bara, Carmel Myers, Agnes de Mille, Lew Cody, Roscoe Arbuckle, and Leon Errol.[62] On the 13th he joined a small group at a party for Ruth Chatterton at the home of Leslie Carter with Katherine Cornell, Lowell Sherman and Helene Costello, Ralph Forbes, Herbert Brenon, and Eileen Percy.[63]

On the 17th he attended a party for composer and actor Gus Arnheim at the Coconut Grove with Beatrice Lillie, Catherine Dale Owen, Arthur Lake, Lillian Roth, Jeanie Macpherson, Sue Carol, Sid Grauman, Joan Ben-nett and Carmen Pantages. On the 23rd he was back at the Blossom Room for a small dinner hosted by Mexican diplomat E. de Iturbide, with Dolores Del Rio, Constance Bennett, Cedric Gibbons, and Billy Joy.[64]

The day of the de Iturbide party, Paul began production of the Jack Conway-directed *New Moon*, which starred Lawrence Tibbett and fellow Metropolitan Opera star Grace Moore. Irving's sister Sylvia wrote the script (based on the Oscar Hammerstein operetta *New Moon*) with Frank Butler and Cyril Hume.[65] It is a love story about an Army officer (Tibbett as Lt. Michael Petroff) and a princess (Moore as Tanya Strogoff) who meet during a voyage aboard the liner *New Moon*. Walking the deck six hours before the ship is to dock in Krasnov, Tanya comes upon Michael singing a sailor's song and a shipboard romance begins with a moonlight duet. Tanya's parents want her to marry the local governor, Boris Brusiloff, and after a drunken encounter Brusiloff sends Petroff to a dangerous Caucasus outpost where previous commanders have been killed by their own soldiers. Michael restores order before Tanya pays a surprise visit and admits she loves him just as the fort comes under attack by the rival Turks. They marry after he sur-vives a suicide mission to the Turk camp, joining Tanya in song upon his return.[66]

After its October 17 release, the film received mixed reviews; one called it a "sweeping and colorful narrative ... in which tense drama vies with a delicate love story..."[67] but another admonished that other than Tibbett, "the film would not make any studio proud."[68]

During the summer, Paul still visited ZaSu Pitts' house on Sunday afternoons to spend time with his son Donald. He was by now very close to the Thalbergs and socialized with them often, including weekend trips to San Diego and the Coronado Hotel via private planes. A surviving photo shows a group boarding their private tri-motor plane that summer; Paul stands amid Irving and Norma, her sister Athole and husband Howard Hawks, and Virginia (Mrs. Jack) Conway.[69]

On August 2 he joined a group of friends for a concert at the Hollywood Bowl and then a party at the Dimitri Tiomkin–Albertina Rasch estate. The estate was decorated as the Russian steppes with two orchestras playing Russian music. Paul attended with Mary Duncan, joining Basil Rathbone, Irving Berlin, Humphrey Bogart, William de Mille, Irene Mayer and David O. Selznick, Samuel Goldwyn, Edmund Lowe, King Vidor, Maurice Chevalier, Colleen Moore, Carmelita Geraghty, Constance Bennett, Ernst Lubitsch, and old friend Carey Wilson. Three nights later he joined Edmund Lowe and Lillian Tashman, Jack Dempsey and Estelle Taylor, and Douglas Fairbanks, Jr., and Joan Crawford at the Carthay Circle premiere of the Ann Harding film *Holiday*.[70]

On the 25th he and Mary Duncan visited the Thalbergs' Santa Monica house where Norma Shearer was resting after giving birth to a son, Irving, Jr., the day before. From there he and Duncan attended an intimate dinner party at Lawrence Tibbett's new 1005 North Rexford mansion with Lydell Peck and Janet Gaynor, Paul's ex-girlfriend Virginia Valli and her new fiancé Charlie Farrell.

At the studio, Joan Crawford was bitterly disappointed at losing the lead in *The Divorcée* to Norma Shearer so Paul gave her the lead in *Within the Law*, which he was producing and began filming in August. Sam Wood directed the Lucien Hubbard and Charles MacArthur adaptation of the Bayard Veiller play.[71] Crawford played a young shopgirl, unfairly convicted for a crime she didn't commit, who returns with three cellmates (Robert Armstrong, Marie Prevost, and George Cooper) to take revenge on the businessman who had her jailed. To gain revenge on her former employer she marries his son, but instead of ruining him falls in love with him and stays to expose her father-in-law's machinations.

The film was previewed as *Within the Law* but released as *Paid*. Crawford took Paul's advice and filmed her prison scenes with no makeup and unkempt hair and was lauded by reviewers: "Just wait until you see Joan

Crawford in this powerful romantic role. The story is absorbing and Joan is simply grand."[72] *Paid* netted almost $450,000 over its relatively low $385,000 cost.

On August 26, Paul's good friend Lon Chaney succumbed to throat cancer. He was only 47 and it was long believed his cancer was caused by a piece of artificial crushed gypsum snow that lodged in his throat during the 1926 filming of *Thunder* (Chaney biographer Michael Blake suggests a more likely cause was lifelong heavy smoking). He was intensely private and hated Hollywood life, lived quietly with wife Hazel and often hid out at his secluded Sierra Nevadas cabin, saying, "Between pictures there is no Lon Chaney." Chaney and Paul had much in common. Chaney's first wife Cleva Creighton was mentally unstable and tried to kill herself backstage during one of his performances by drinking mercury. She survived her horrific injuries and they divorced but her act tortured Chaney. And while Paul was building Easton, Chaney was building a magnificent mansion at 804 Whittier. Unfortunately, Chaney died as it was being completed.

Chaney's wake and funeral were devoid of the typical Hollywood histrionics. Thousands of ordinary citizens, many deaf like Chaney's parents, filed past the plain silver bronze casket atop the same bier where Mabel Normand's lay. A few feet away a battered World War I veteran in his aged uniform, medals across his chest, stood at attention for the entire three-day viewing. Chaney met retired Sgt. Frank McClouskey in 1923 and quietly paid for an operation to cure the paralysis caused by wartime wounds.[73]

Every Hollywood studio and every MGM office worldwide shut down for two minutes as the funeral began the morning of the 28th. Paul was a pallbearer along with Mayer, Irving, Hunt Stromberg, Tod Browning, Harry Carey, William Haines, Lew Cody, Wallace Beery, George Hill and Edgar Selwyn. Chaney was buried next to his father at Forest Lawn.

Chaney's death cast a somber shadow over Paul's move to Easton, which was completed the day of the funeral. Just before he moved in, Paul hired John and Winifred Carmichael as his valet and cook. They were from Texas; 29-year-old John and 25-year-old Winifred were working for stockbroker Thomas Balie and living at Balie's 336 South Las Palmas mansion when Paul hired them.[74]

At Easton, Winifred prepared meals at the servants' house that were then carried up to the main house. Winifred had worked at the famed Russian Eagle Café and made Paul his favorite meals — pancakes with caviar and beet soup, which took 48 hours to prepare.[75]

Paul had a house-warming party on September 12. Mentioning his offer to Irene Mayer and David Selznick to live in the house, he told her that day would have been a perfect day if it they were moving in.[76] With Mary Duncan at his side, Paul greeted several hundred friends including Jack Gilbert and Ina Claire, the Thalbergs, Carey Wilson, Cedric Gibbons and Dolores Del Rio, and Douglas Fairbanks, Jr., and Joan Crawford. Louella Parsons described the estate as "charming, different and very artistic."[77]

William and Friederike Marcus and their son Sig, who moved to L.A. and were living in the Hollywood Hills at 2141 Canyon Drive, also spent the day at Easton. Sig was the office manager for Paul's agent, Paul Kohner, and Paul (Bern) helped the family with expenses and Friederike's medical bills.

A few days later, Paul attended a party at the Blossom Room welcoming Julanne Johnston back to Hollywood after an extended absence. Paul and Mary Duncan joined Joan Bennett, June Collyer, Blanche Sweet, Rita Flynn, Bobbie Arnst, Carey Wilson, Clarence Brown, Ivan St. Johns, and William Bakewell.[78]

After *New Moon*, Paul supervised another Lawrence Tibbett musical, initially titled *The Southerner* but renamed *The Prodigal*. After five years riding the rails as a hobo, Jeffry Farraday (Tibbett) returns to his aristocratic family plantation where the extended Farraday family lives: brother Rodman and his unhappy wife Antonia (Esther Ralston), sister Christine and her husband George and their children Peter and Elsbeth. The only person Jeffry gets along with is fellow free spirit Antonia, whom he stops from leaving with another man, saying "a man can be a tramp, but a woman can't." He loves Antonia and decides to leave rather than betray his brother but his mother intervenes and, knowing Jeffry to be the more worthy of her two sons, allows Antonia and Rodman to divorce so that Antonia can marry Jeffry.[79]

The film contains remnants of director Harry Pollard's abandoned 1930 film *Great Day*, including the song "Without a Song." Like *New Moon*, *Prodigal* was beautifully filmed and had wonderful music but suffered from the unduly convoluted plot that is difficult to follow. The reviews were mixed. *Film Daily* called it "so meaningless that it doesn't look like an MGM film"[80] while *The Hollywood Reporter* praised the "unique and daring" theme with "not a foot of film to spare ... every moment of it holds you."[81]

Paul's opinions about music were evolving; he supported the musical genre but thought music was being over-used, that it was too intrusive and used with no "logic or balance" and that audiences were "fed up [with all the music]." For that reason, *Prodigal* had "no 75-piece orchestras suddenly chiming in from nowhere. Accompaniment is not always necessary. It's perfectly natural for a man to sing without an orchestra, which Tibbett (somewhat surprisingly) does." He didn't want the music to disrupt the viewers' ability "for a couple of hours, to lose itself in the story and characters."[82]

Paul (right) walking the MGM lot with one of his closest friends, Jack Gilbert.

Paul had a reputation for intuitively recognizing problems — script, acting, or direction — and solving them without ruffling feathers. He had no ego and accepted advice as freely as it was offered, without prejudice. After finishing *The Prodigal*, Roland Young was asked, "Why have a supervisor?" He replied, "I'm not sure I know. But I know that Paul Bern is at the head of that list. There is a man who knows the picture business. He knows every phase of the business and is an asset to the profession. His suggestions are nearly always helpful, and he, himself, is always open to suggestion."[83]

In early October, Paul began filming Garbo's *Inspiration*, based on Alphonse Daudet's mildly scandalous 1884 novel *Sappho*.[84] Garbo is Yvonne, a renowned Parisian artist's model who leaves a trail of destroyed men in her wake, telling her mentor Delval (Lewis Stone), "You're all alike, you men. You only want the satisfaction of being through with us first, that's all. So far, I have the good fortune of beating you to it — so I am heartless." She takes up with young student André (Robert Montgomery) but after another woman tells André about Yvonne's past and he leaves, she is plunged into despair and a destitute life on the streets. After a chance meeting with André and several suicides caused by Delval, André pleads with her to marry so she can avoid that fate. She accepts but, realizing he is marrying her out of sympathy, she writes him a farewell letter telling him to forget her and marry the right woman before walking away.

Inspiration was Garbo's third talkie, similar in character and theme to her earlier *Romance*. In both, Garbo shone above mediocre (in the case of *Inspiration,* awful) scripts and unimaginative Clarence Brown direction. Audiences didn't seem to notice the films, but they noticed Garbo, who got raves everywhere.[85]

Paul's social whirl continued without break into the fall. On September 28 he was mentioned among studio notables purchasing private boxes at the Belasco Theater to see Pauline Frederick's *The Crimson Hour*. Paul and Jeanette Loff were joined by Irene Rich, Ruth Roland, Richard Barthelmess, Lionel Barrymore, Ann Harding, and John Dillon.

On October 8, Paul and Mary Duncan hosted a wedding party at Easton for producer B.P. Fineman and his new wife Margaret de Mille (daughter of William C. and neice of Cecil). Guests included David and Irene Selznick, Edmund Lowe and Lilyan Tashman, Robert Montgomery, Hunt Stromberg, Rosetta Duncan, Kay Francis, Hedda Hopper, Eddie Sutherland, Gene Markey, Harold Grieve and Jetta Goudal, Willis Goldbeck, Herman Mankiewicz, and Gilbert Adrian. A summons to Easton, so different from other Beverly Hills estates, was a sought-after movie colony invitation.

On the 10th he and Duncan hosted a dinner at her 911 Beverly Drive mansion for Edmund Lowe and Lilyan Tashman, David and Irene Selznick, Charles Rogers, Arthur Hornblow, Aileen Pringle, Winfield Sheehan, Mack Sennett, Walter Wanger, Mervyn LeRoy, and Willis Goldbeck. He then joined most of MGM on the 15th for the wedding of studio staffers Richard Wade and Mildred Kelly at the Church of St. Augustine by the Sea in Santa Monica and a reception at the Miramar Hotel. Paul attended with Thalberg,

Mayer, Mannix, Rapf, George Hill, Bernie Hyman, Douglas Shearer, Bess Meredyth, and William Haines.[86]

In November, Paul was assigned to supervise *It's a Wise Child* for MGM's Cosmopolitan unit and Marion Davies. Paul has not received credit for this film but period records and Davies interviews confirmed the assignment.[87] Filming had been delayed several times; Paul was brought in after months of problems, settling on a leading man acceptable to Davies and more importantly, the ever-jealous William Randolph Hearst.

Paul spent much of 1930 lobbying Thalberg to get Jean to MGM since Hughes was not using her and she wanted out of her contract. She had spent a year on exhausting *Hell's Angels* publicity trips and no film assignments were forthcoming. She and Hughes were openly feuding. Paul wanted Jean for *The Secret Six*, filming in January. He first approached Hughes and somehow convinced him to loan Jean to MGM. He then convinced Thalberg — Mayer disagreed, thinking her floozy image was wrong for MGM — to pay Hughes' loan-out fee. Thalberg was still adamant they would not buy out her contract, but it was a start. She would be at MGM in a month.

Whether it was a small luncheon hosted by John Stahl for Carey Wilson, Erwin Gelsey and Edwin Knopf or the lavish Armistice Night military ball at the Ambassador at the Hunt Stromberg table with the Thalbergs, Mayers, Schencks, Selznicks, Mannix and Sid Grauman, Paul got an invitation.[88] His comings and goings were regularly reported in the society pages.

Irene Harrison was in charge of keeping Paul's complex calendar organized, and for sending Dorothy's twice-monthly checks to Henry Bern. Dorothy sometimes called Irene to thank Paul for her money. Paul never spoke to her but she would often stay on the phone with Irene "talking and talking about nothing in particular."[89]

On the 16th, Paul and Mary Duncan joined the Hunt Stromberg party at the Ambassador.[90] On the 21st he and Duncan attended the premiere of the Wallace Beery-Marie Dressler film *Min and Bill* at the Carthay Circle.

By the end of the month Duncan had disappeared from Paul's arm, replaced by Jean.[91] It was a rare gossip column that did *not* mention Paul and his date of the moment. On November 29, Hatton Kane noted his arrival at a Hollywood premier "brought cheers from the crowd. The principal reason being Jean Harlow. Paul's motto must be variety. Last week Mary Duncan was his choice."[92]

In December, Paul was preparing for *It's a Wise Child* and finishing post-production for *The Prodigal* (still called *The Southerner*). Several Tibbett scenes had to be re-done, requiring a trip to New York with a sound crew, normally overseen by the director. But instead of Henry Pollard, just after New Year's, Thalberg sent Paul.[93]

Paul had social commitments almost every night during December. He started the holiday season at Joan Crawford's birthday party for Douglas Fairbanks, Jr., on December 9 at the Biltmore, with Irving and Norma, Fredric March and Florence Eldridge, Leslie Howard, and Constance Bennett and her husband, the Marquis James Henri de la Falais de la Coudraye. Most of Paul's appearances made the papers, including a Christmas party at the Fairbanks-Crawford estate in Brentwood on the 18th and a small party at Bebe Daniels' house on the 20th with Douglas Fairbanks, Mary Pickford, George Fitzmaurice, Ralph Blum and Joseph Schenck.[94]

Jean and Paul attended several New Year's parties, the first at the sprawling 204 Rossmore mansion of Felix Hughes, uncle of Howard, founder of the Cleveland Orchestra and celebrated movie voice coach. Hughes' massive Chinese buffet supper was attended by an interesting mix of writers, stage actors, composers and performers like Hobart Bosworth, the Barrymore brothers, H.B. Warner, Paul Franklin, Earl Moss, Loren Melville, John Flynn, and Rupert Hughes. Marino Bello tagged along with Paul and Jean.[95]

That same night they joined 400 of Hollywood's big names at the Biltmore for the annual Mayfair Ball, mingling with hundreds of out-of-towners visiting L.A. for the next day's Rose Bowl. Arriving late with Douglas Fairbanks and Mary Pickford after attending four parties, they shared a table with Alan Hale, William Powell and Carole Lombard.[96]

At midnight they were at the Coconut Grove with Willis Goldbeck, Myron Selznick and his brother David and Irene Mayer. The Selznick table got pretty rowdy and when a waiter and another reveler said something to Myron, he and the other man got into a fight. Jean and Paul were in the middle of the fracas.[97]

The New Year was shaping up to be a big one for Paul, and Jean. He had risen to the top of the studio ladder, was arguably the most respected producer in Hollywood, and had finally arranged to bring Jean into the MGM fold. For Jean's part, she was on the verge of stardom. And Paul was there to help.

EIGHT

Platinum Blonde

Paul had a half dozen projects in the works as 1931 began, including producing Marion Davies' *Wise Child*, Jean's MGM assignment *The Secret Six*, and Garbo's *Susan Lenox: Her Fall and Rise*. He was also trying to make something out of DeMille's final MGM film, *The Squaw Man*. *Wise Child* and *The Secret Six* both filmed in January and February.

Wise Child had been delayed from the previous fall due to casting issues but Paul finally selected James Gleason and Sidney Blackmer in December and production finally began on January 15.[1] The film was a confusing mélange of family relationships that was hard to follow: A small-town farmer's daughter (Marion Davies) tries to save the family farm by marrying the local bank president even though she loves the new bank clerk, while the family lawyer loves *her*. From that point the film is basically a dozen interwoven comedy sequences following her attempts to rid herself of a fiancé and the advances of another man while realizing she really loves the lawyer. Everyone's involved: brothers, sisters, parents, cousins, neighbors and friends.

Shooting wrapped on February 5 and film debuted in L.A. on March 21 to generally favorable reviews. Davies was a wonderful comedienne but Hearst — who pulled the strings on everything Davies-related — believed comedy beneath her and forced her to do drama for which she was less well-suited. Hearst's "career guidance" prevented Davies from becoming the star she could have been, along the lines of a Carole Lombard.

Amid the various productions, Paul and Jean were equally busy off the lot. On January 10 they attended a small party at the home of B. P. Fineman and Margaret de Mille with David Selznick, Willis Goldbeck, Edmund Lowe, Lawrence Weingarten, Kay Francis, and, interestingly, Mary Duncan.[2] On the 24th they attended a party for George Gershwin at Leonard Sillman's 418 Orange Drive estate with Laura LaPlante, Ramon Novarro, Lola Lane, Patsy Ruth Miller, Cyril Hume, Carmel Myers, and John Murray Anderson.[3] On the 28th Jimmy Starr noted that Paul was at the *Once in a Lifetime* premiere, "still escorting the seductive Jean Harlow about...." And on February 14 Paul and Jean attended the wedding of good friend Charlie Farrell and Paul's ex-girlfriend Virginia Valli.

Thalberg is credited with producing Jean's *The Secret Six* but period papers and studio records confirm Paul as the producer. Jean was fourth-billed. Seventh-billed was another newcomer, Clark Gable, who Thalberg did not originally want to sign. But Mayer's secretary Ida Koverman — MGM's unofficial talent arbiter — convinced Mayer of Gable's "animal grace," and he was signed to a $650 a week contract.[4] He had a few small roles before *Secret Six* and his role was originally much smaller but writer Frances Marion was so certain he'd be a star she added to his part during every script revision.

After four months of casting, the group of players included Wallace Beery, Lewis Stone, Johnny Mack Brown, and Marjorie Rambeau.[5] Stockyard worker Louis Scorpio (Beery) is recruited by bootleggers and ends up in the middle of a gang war when a mob boss's brother is mistakenly killed. He is left to take the rap but escapes from the police, leaving his molls Peaches (Rambeaux) and Anne Courtland (Jean) to cover his tracks. Reporters Carl (Gable) and Hank (Brown) go after the story and court Anne not knowing Scorpio hired her to keep them off his trail. After Scorpio rigs the local mayoral election and starts another crime wave, the task force "Secret Six" is organized to catch him. Anne tries to save the reporters from a Scorpio killer but Hank is killed and eventually Scorpio winds up on death row.[6]

Jean and Clark Gable became fast friends during filming, a friendship that lasted the rest of her life. She had numerous scenes with her fellow newcomer who later said, "Neither of us knew much about the business. At the end of every scene, she'd ask me, 'How am I doing?' And I would ask her the same." At the time she said, "I know I'm the worst actress that was ever in pictures, but I can learn, and I will." After their first day on the set, Gable said to Jean, "You're not at all the kind of girl I imagined."[7]

As usual the entire cast and crew fell in love with Jean, with the exception of Beery, an ill-tempered alcoholic who disliked anyone who stole attention from him, particularly on camera.[8] He made her life miserable by roundly criticizing her but she took solace in the companionship of Gable. There were rumors of an affair but he was already involved in one extra-marital fling with Joan Crawford. It's doubtful Jean and Gable had a physical relationship. He always referred to her as his "kid sister."[9]

Secret Six opened on April 18 and critics were generally complimentary but (following the gangster masterpiece *The Big House*) critics said it was "an excellent film [that] didn't have the punch and force [of *Big House*]."[10] Jean was described as "the one noticeable female in the film"[11] and "Hollywood's latest gift to the gangster pictures."[12]

Production on Garbo's *Susan Lenox: Her Fall and Rise* began in May as a bitter disappointment to Jack Gilbert, who was promised the lead by Thalberg nine months earlier but was replaced by Gable. The Wanda Tuchock script was based on a novel by David Graham Phillips about an orphan farm girl who escapes a forced marriage, joins a carnival, and eventually finds love with a spirited engineer.[13] King Vidor was originally to direct but Paul replaced him with Robert Z. Leonard, who specialized in romances.

Gable and Garbo was such a mismatched pair that they clicked on-screen. A *Photoplay* review said, "If you were mad about her before, just wait until you see her teamed up with this manifesta-

For most of 1930 and early 1931 Jean was on an exhausting publicity tour for Howard Hughes, promoting *Hell's Angels.*

tion of masculine ... Clark Gable."[14] But the shoot itself was a nightmare for Paul. During production, 22 writers worked on the script and even after a 49-day shoot — during which Garbo walked off the set seven times — a disastrous press preview led to "extended retakes and revisions" for two weeks in August.[15] Like all Garbo films it made money, $364,000 over its $580,000 cost.

The on-screen chemistry between Garbo and Gable was so obvious that Thalberg immediately decided to pair them again in an upcoming romantic drama, *Red Dust.*

Paul was also working on DeMille's final Pathé film for MGM, *The Squaw Man.* DeMille's first two Pathé-MGM efforts — *Dynamite* and *Madam Satan* — were not the blockbusters expected but neither studio expected his problems adjusting to sound. Loew's president Nick Schenck and some at Culver City argued for canceling *The Squaw Man* altogether but DeMille countered it would cost as much to cancel as to finish the film so the project went forward. Paul put together an excellent crew for the early February production and quietly assigned Earl Haley and Mitchell Leisen, one of his favorite and most trusted directors, to assist DeMille.[16]

Even with the strong crew and a cast led by Warner Baxter, Lupe Velez, and Eleanor Boardman, the film lost over $150,000 after its September release. There was little anyone at MGM could do about the disappointing DeMille experiment, he himself later saying, "I do not know whether MGM or I was more relieved that my contract had come to an end." After *Squaw Man*, DeMille left on an extended European vacation and seriously considered moving there permanently.

Paul and Irving were planning an innovative film at the time. Most movies featured two or three main characters and one main story line but their film would be based on interactions between a dozen, each with their own plot-line. The first ensemble film was a huge gamble but Paul still held that audiences were smart and wanted to be challenged *and* entertained.

The film was based on Vicki Baum's play *Menschen im Hotel* that Thalberg had first seen in Berlin a year earlier. Paul suggested that Thalberg buy the rights with Garbo in mind and, after waiting for the Broadway version *Grand Hotel* to become popular, Thalberg paid $35,000 for the rights in late 1930 and began development with Paul. Story conferences commenced that winter and took place almost *every day* for over a year while Paul assembled the cast with Benny Thau.

Paul tried to give Jack Gilbert one of the leads but by late 1930 his feud with Mayer was an open secret and friends at the studio deserted him in droves lest it got back to Mayer they were chummy with him. Only a few — Cedric Gibbons, Thalberg and Paul — had the courage to stand up to Mayer. Paul was vocal about trying to keep Jack working but eventually agreed with Thalberg on the *Grand Hotel* decision. Paul next championed another underdog for director. Edmund Goulding was also on the outs at MGM after two flops and Thalberg did not want to hand him the plum project but Paul said, "People around here treat failure like it's a form of leprosy. You and I know that isn't right."[17] Goulding got the assignment.

On March 6 Paul hosted a 20th birthday party for Jean at Easton with several dozen friends. Douglas Fairbanks, Jr., and Joan Crawford, B.P. Fineman and Agnes de Mille, David O. Selznick and Irene Mayer, Carey Wilson and Carmelita Geraghty, Jack Gilbert and Clark Gable all came for the afternoon.

The Bern-Harlow relationship was still not exclusive even though papers noted that "Jean Harlow [is] being squired about by noted director Paul Bern." He was still seeing Jeanette Loff and Jean dated singer Harry Richman and wealthy local stockbroker Ernest Torgler that spring.[18] Louella Parsons mentioned, "The little platinum blonde, Jean Harlow, is one of the most popular young women in Hollywood. I used to see her about with Paul Bern at this and that party. Lately she has been seen with other masculine friends, dividing her time as it were. Good company, with a sense of humor, is the way she is described by those who know her."[19]

On March 22 Paul had a party at Easton attended by Gary Cooper and Lupe Velez, Jack Gilbert and Carey Wilson. In the green Moroccan-leather guestbook Paul left near the front door for guests to sign, Cooper drew a caricature of him as a caballero and signed and dated the page. On the opposite page Velez wrote, "Con mi cariño y Afecto," meaning "with my love and affection."[20]

Paul was seemingly invited to every party in Hollywood. On April 7 he was invited to Lawrence Tibbett's Rexford Drive estate to hear the London String Quartet with Charles Brabin, King Vidor, John Monk Saunders, James Gleason, Arlie Lewin, Leslie Howard, P.G. Wodehouse, Marie Dressler, Ina Claire, and Ramon Novarro.[21] The next evening he was at Edmund Lowe and Lilyan Tashman's home with Raoul Walsh, Ralph Forbes and Ruth Chatterton, Sam Goldwyn, Harold Grieve and Jetta Goudal, Cedric Gibbons and Dolores Del Rio, Carmelita Geraghty and Carey Wilson, Gloria Swanson, Billie Dove, William Haines and Jimmy Shields, Humphrey Bogart, and Howard Hughes.[22]

On the 20th he attended a party for Irving and Norma at Marion Davies' Ocean House in Santa Monica. William Randolph Hearst wanted her to have the most opulent beach house on the West Coast to visit with her film friends deemed unworthy of an invitation to San Simeon. Started in 1922, the 110-room Georgian manse dwarfed the nearby mansions of Thalberg and Mayer and cost $7,000,000. There were 55 bedroom suites each with a bathroom, a ballroom from a 17th-century Italian palazzo, and 60-foot-long living and dining rooms from Irish castles. There was a British tavern from 1560 that seated 50, crystal chandeliers from Tiffany's and 20 18th-century fireplaces. There were also 2,800 lockers for guests using the marble-lined 110-foot pool on the beach behind the house.

By 1926, Marion lived there full time and gave lavish theme parties attended by 300 to 400 (2,000 came to one holiday gathering). The Thalbergs were leaving on another European vacation so Marion invited 500 to a bon voyage party and papers noted that "[z]illions of guests were there, including Paul Bern, Joan Crawford, Cedric Gibbons, and Virginia Cherrill."[23]

He attended the opening night of the play *The Shanghai Gesture* on the 21st with the DeMilles, Norma Talmadge, Richard Barthelmess and King Vidor, and on the 29th was back at the beach at a day-long party hosted by Ralph Blum and Carmel Myers along with Herman Mankiewicz, Phil Berg and Leila Hyams, Groucho, Harpo and Zeppo Marx, Richard Rodgers, Rouben Mamoulian, Eddie Sutherland, Josef von Sternberg, William Haines and Jimmy Shields, and Elissa Landi. The party began with breakfast and lasted until early the next morning.[24]

Jean was slowly becoming a phenomenon. After *Secret Six*, Hughes loaned her to Universal for the boxing film *The Iron Man* and then to Warners for *The Public Enemy*. He also shoved her into an unbilled cameo in his own gangster epic *Scarface* and loaned her to Fox for the forgettable *Goldie* in April. He received $1,250 a week for the loan-outs; Jean received her $250 salary.[25]

With the exception of *Public Enemy* the films were only moderately successful but the public loved everything about the sexually charged newcomer. She was even slowly improving as an actor, standing out in the mediocre *Iron Man* where critics noted she "played convincingly the cat of a wife."[26] Hughes was dreadfully mishandling her career, a point Paul kept reiterating to Irving.

In May, Hughes sent Jean on a Midwestern publicity tour and during her visit to Chicago's Oriental Theater, gangsters Al Capone and Abner Zwillman were invited backstage to meet her by Marino Bello. Bello fancied himself a rogue but real gangsters knew him as a "zero" living off Jean.[27] During a golf game, mobster Eddie Nealis later told Eddie Mannix that Bello mentioned "trading" Jean to Zwillman for a piece of the New York liquor business and start-up money for a speakeasy there.

"Longy" Zwillman was a New Jersey mobster and murderer working for Lucky Luciano and Louis Buchalter, described by the F.B.I. as "the established boss of the New Jersey underworld."[28] Zwillman became obsessed with Jean, herself invigorated by an illicit relationship with a gangster. Interestingly though, he helped her professionally, first convincing Harry Cohn to pay Hughes $5,000 for a two-picture loan-out, twice the normal rate. Cohn owed the mob money and knew Zwillman and his pals wanted to wrest control of the IATSE stagehands union, but as added incentive Zwillman loaned Cohn $500,000 interest-free. Hughes refused to increase her $250 salary so Zwillman raised it to $1,000 and paid the difference from his own pocket.

During the summer they dated, Zwillman gave Jean extravagant gifts like jewelry and a red Cadillac according to her long-time maid Blanche Williams. His salary stipend allowed her to move from the Bellos' dingy Peck Drive bungalow into a lovely English-style house on a hilltop at 1353 Club View Drive, overlooking Wilshire Country Club south of Wilshire.

Club View sits unchanged atop a tiered lawn dissected by a stairwell from a street-level garage. A wing containing a large living room extends from the right of the entrance landing, fronted by a large picture window. The room is several steps down from the main foyer and is warm and inviting, with a pitched roof and exposed beams and large fireplace making it look bigger than it is. Just off the foyer is a tiny library and to the rear of the first floor the kitchen and maid's quarters.

On the other side of the foyer is a dining room and sun-room overlooking the front patio and hillside front yard. In 1930 the view was a sweeping vista over the golf course past Wilshire, South Mapleton and Sunset Boulevard to Benedict Canyon hills dotted with mansions several miles distant. There were three good-sized bedrooms on the second floor, not elaborate except for Jean's blue-green rose and cream-colored room in front with a specially built perfume cabinet for her extensive collection (she favored the expensive French perfume, Brise Ambrée).[29]

Behind the house, a lovely pool fed by a tiled fountain was built into the hillside. It was a home fit for a movie star. Another star lived across the street: Warners' top actor, Rin Tin Tin.

The Zwillman-Harlow affair was the talk of Hollywood but was kept from the press. The local buzz grew loud when it was learned that during a meeting of L.A. mobsters at the Ambassador he opened a false back to his pocket watch and removed several strands of pubic hair he identified as Jean's.[30]

That summer, Paul spearheaded a drive to fund a P.T.A. school lunch program for needy children in L.A., sending letters to every actor, director and crew member in every guild in Hollywood trying to raise $2,000 a week for ten weeks (totaling perhaps $500,000 today). He almost pleaded:

Left: **Present-day view of the entrance to Jean's home at 1353 Club View Drive.**
Right: **Another current view of the front façade at Club View.**

Ten thousand children in Los Angeles are now going without the one meal a day which was being supplied them by the Parent-Teacher Association. Ten thousand children in this city are therefore actually hungry, for only those were being fed who really needed it.

The idea of this tragic condition while we are living on in accustomed prosperity is horrible. The people of the motion picture industry, never deaf to the cry of suffering, cannot let this be. They have determined to raise $2,000 per week for the next ten weeks.

Will you be one of the group to supply not less than $5 and not more than $50 per week, the exact sum to be left to your generosity, for the next ten weeks? If you will help these children, please advise me at once to what extent, at the same time enclosing your first check.

Gratefully yours,
PAUL BERN

The need is immediate and dreadfully urgent.[31]

Paul quietly donated $500 himself and during the first weeks after his appeal over $6,000 was donated by studio personnel. His efforts earned almost $30,000 and helped salvage the lunch program.[32]

On June 11 he attended a small gathering hosted by Janet Gaynor and Lydell Peck at the Coconut Grove in honor of two visiting Hawaiian princesses. Among the guests were ex-girlfriend Virginia Valli and Charlie Farrell, and George O'Brien, who had been briefly engaged to Olive Borden before Paul began his lengthy relationship with her.[33] Paul's relationships rarely ended on poor terms or with rancor. He seemed to stay friendly with all of his ex-girlfriends.

On the 17th he attended an anniversary party for writer Richard Schayer and his wife at their 323 S. Peck Drive home with an MGM group including Thalberg, Sam Marx, and Harry Rapf, with Ephraim Asher, Sol Lesser, Milton Bren, and Richard Arlen.[34] The next evening he attended the premiere of Douglas Fairbanks, Jr.'s play *The Man in Possession* escorting Joan Crawford and Marlene Dietrich, and on the 20th attended a small party at writer Joseph Jackson's home in honor of Rupert Hughes with a small group including Anna May Wong and Dean Sullivan.[35]

Every Sunday afternoon he motored out to the Pitts house in Brentwood at 241 Rockingham to spend the day with Donald. During the summer of 1931 he brought Jean along for the first time. Since La Marr's 1926 death, Paul rarely missed his Sunday visit, always bringing presents and taking the boy and his sister on outings. Jean loved children so it's not surprising that Donald remembered Jean as sweet and friendly to him and his sister. During that summer, Paul and Jean also took the children on a weekend trip to Catalina Island, where they stayed at the Avalon Hotel, swam, and hiked among the island's wild animal herds.[36]

Jean in front of Club View in 1933; at the time the neighborhood was uncrowded and quiet.

After his Brentwood visit, Paul usually continued to the Thalbergs' Cedric Gibbons–designed French Provincial mansion at 707 Ocean Front on Santa Monica Beach. Norma hosted Sunday afternoon teas for an inner circle that included Paul, King Vidor, Jack Conway, Jack Gilbert, David Selznick and Irene Mayer, Carey Wilson and Carmelita Geraghty, and Henry Hawks (married to Norma's sister Athole). The lovely home remains unchanged today.[37]

At the studios, Jean was on another Hughes' loan-out preparing to start Paramount's *Gallagher*, which would catapult her to even greater stardom and define her image for the rest of her life. Paul was still involved in script development and working with Benny Thau on the casting for *Grand Hotel*.

In early July, Paul began work on a film that seemed an odd assignment given the major projects he was working on, the forgettable *West of Broadway*, a B-movie and a bad one. It was poorly written, director Harry Beaumont didn't want to make it, co-star Lois Moran was making her final appearance before retiring, and the cast was made up of obscure character actors or studio newcomers.

But Paul actually commandeered production responsibility for the low-budget effort because it was forced on Jack Gilbert as another below-grade assignment from Mayer and Paul wanted to at least try to salvage the film for his friend after he lost *Susan Lenox* to Clark Gable. The first thing he did was bring Gene Markey in to polish up the script but Markey realized it was hopeless:

> Jack had a good friend in Paul Bern. He was intent on getting a good vehicle for Jack, and so was I. But a story came along [*West of Broadway*] and I was given the insurmountable task of trying to make it come alive. It was written by a couple of actors who decided they wanted to be screenwriters too [Ralph Graves was one; the other is unknown]. It was a flimsy story. I never believed in it, but I did the best I could. It was not the vehicle Jack should have had, but the studio chief cockroaches thought it would be good to give Jack a change of pace. The damn thing had no pace at all. It was poorly directed, and I must confess that my script was no great shakes. That's what happened to what could have been an opportunity for Jack to have a galloping, romantic picture.[38]

Paul tried everything he could to make something of the mess. He brought Bess Meredyth in to work with Markey on the script and assembled a great crew. But Paul could do nothing about a bad story, and less about Gilbert's weak cast, led by Moran, and El Brendel.

Gilbert plays an alcoholic World War I veteran who returns to his fiancée to find her engaged to someone else. When he sees her at a party he drunkenly tells her he's engaged to the closest girl to him, pretty but poor Dot (Moran), whom he marries that night. He sobers up in the morning and demands a divorce but she won't take his money so he tells her he has six months to live. She still refuses his money and stays with him as he tries to "dry out" at his family's Arizona ranch. She ignores his scorn, bouts of delirium tremens, and the arrival of his old fiancée, and wins his heart.[39]

In addition to the awful script, filming was difficult. The western scenes were filmed in the Mojave Desert in temperatures of 120 degrees. Against Mayer's wishes, Paul ordered retakes costing $60,000 trying to fix glaring problems and according to *Variety*, "sweeten up John Gilbert's part" but it was still an unmitigated disaster.[40] Critics were merciless. The *L.A. Herald* wrote, "It is was the purpose of MGM to lead John Gilbert to the guillotine and end the waning popularity of one of the most popular stars the silver screen has ever known, then *West of Broadway* is a great success. Unless this was the purpose, the picture may be the most monumental piece of cinematic stupidity on record."[41]

Actor Ralph Bellamy (*West of Broadway* was his third film; he worked steadily for over 70 years) later said Gilbert knew MGM assigned him the "mediocre" film hoping he'd refuse it so they could break his contract but

Gilbert wouldn't buckle under to Mayer and said, "I'll clean the spittoons if those bastards tell me so, until this contract is up."[42]

In mid–July, Paul received a troublesome letter from Dorothy, telling him she still wanted to come to California and was counting on his help to get her started in films. He had been politely trying to prevent her trip west, and to this latest request replied:

> So far as work out here is concerned I think the present time is a horrible difficult one. Naturally, with the financial conditions of the country as bad as they are, we too have suffered. There are great numbers of people out of work, and it will not help to add to their numbers. Consequently, I don't think that you should come out here right now.
>
> Love, regards and best wishes, always,
> Paul[43]

He was doing everything he could to keep her from coming west but had to be worried she would come anyway. There were certainly discussions between Paul and Irving, Eddie Mannix and Howard Strickling concerning the Dorothy problem.

He enjoyed his quiet life at the top of Easton, joining the Benedict Canyon Volunteer Fire Department as an active (versus honorary) volunteer. He was also planning his first real vacation, a four-month trip from New York through the Panama Canal to the Orient scheduled for the spring.[44] He and Jean were often in public together but the relationship was not exclusive. She was still with Longy Zwillman and Paul was seen with a half dozen actresses.

During the summer of 1931 he dated Mary Brian and Ona Munson, who he took to a small dinner party on July 10 at Ernst Lubitsch's Santa Monica beach house with Lady June Inverclyde and Reginald Tash before attending the premiere of *The Smiling Lieutenant*.[45]

But his most frequent companion was beautiful Estelle Taylor, who had only recently separated from her husband, boxer Jack Dempsey. Taylor's rise from typist to star was a movie itself: The Wilmington, Delaware teenager married at 14, divorced at 18, worked as a model and chorus girl and entered films with Vitagraph in 1919. By the mid–1920s she was starring in films like DeMille's *The Ten Commandments* (1923) and Mary Pickford's *Dorothy Vernon of Haddon Hall* (1925). The popular vamp was adored by fans.

In 1925 she married Dempsey but his profligate womanizing led to her divorce filing in early 1931 and during the bitter feud that summer she dated Paul.[46] When an invitation came to a party to which Estelle, rather publicly, had not been invited, he replied she was his guest for the evening and unless she was included he would not go. Taylor was a good match for Paul; she was beautiful, independent, and extremely smart.

On August 2, Paul and Taylor hosted a Sunday afternoon pool party at

Estelle Taylor, ex-wife of boxer Jack Dempsey and Paul's frequent companion during 1931.

Easton with Lawrence Tibbett, Lupe Velez, Marie Prevost, Douglas Fairbanks, Jr., and Joan Crawford, Jack Gilbert and his new girlfriend Marjorie King, Carey Wilson and Carmelita Geraghty, Colleen Moore, and Swedish stage star Astrid Allwyn. As the group relaxed around the pool, Taylor's brother-in-law Joe Dempsey crept to the parking area below and sped off down Easton in Taylor's $8,000 Rolls Royce limousine with her chauffeur Frank Buford in pursuit. The return of her car became part of the eventual divorce settlement.[47]

Just two days later, Paul was in the middle of another divorce, this time that of Ina Claire and John Gilbert. Both asked him to speak at a hearing where he was the only witness. He said Jack had been temperamental of late, often "suddenly turning away and leaving the room ... Jack was very distressed with his stock market losses, and dissatisfied with his pictures. He said he regarded his wife with respect and affection, but wanted to be alone."[48]

Paul was friendly with both; he traveled directly from the hearing to the Ambassador, where he hosted a Russian-themed luncheon for Jack and his new girlfriend Marjorie King.[49] A few weeks later he escorted Claire to a party at director William K. Howard's Brentwood estate with Lionel Barrymore, Carmel Myers and Ralph Blum, Myron and David O. Selznick, Spencer Tracy and John Ford.[50]

Grand Hotel script and casting meetings continued and Paul was sadly aware MGM would not gamble on Gilbert, whose role was given to John Barrymore. He lived on a Tower Road knoll next to Gilbert and one night after Gilbert lost the role Barrymore heard gunshots from the direction of Gilbert's house. He was convinced that Gilbert was targeting him but the next day learned that Gilbert was drunkenly shooting at a young couple parked below his house. *Hotel* casting rumors merited daily mention in trade papers. *The Hollywood Reporter* incorrectly tabbed Clark Gable, Jimmy Durante, George E. Stone, Buster Keaton, Kathryn Crawford, Anita Page, and Ruth Selwyn as receiving roles. Paul was also in pre-production for Garbo's next, *Mata Hari*, based on the life of the legendary Dutch spy.

Howard Hughes continued using Jean for loan-outs instead of featuring her on film, and that spring she was the only actress in Hollywood with three films in release: *The Secret Six*, *The Iron Man*, and *The Public Enemy*. Hal Roach also used her in the Laurel & Hardy short *Beau Hunks* as their love interest but instead of paying her loan-out fee he simply used a *photograph* of Jean! He later said it cost him $3 to use Jean as his leading lady.[51]

But it was her Zwillman-brokered Columbia film that had people taking even more notice. *Gallagher*, the story of a reporter (Robert Williams) who marries a wealthy but snobby socialite (Jean) before returning to his true love (Loretta Young), began filming August 3. Director Frank Capra later admitted he added Jean strictly "for sex" and she was terrified of the role, still self-conscious about her skills.[52] Cameraman Joseph Walker later recalled, "[H]er reserved demeanor came from outright awe and fright at being in the company of such seasoned performers and an important director like Capra."[53] Everyone was impressed with Jean's effort portraying a society girl, a role for which she was woefully ill-prepared though she was born into wealth.

Hughes took an active role in *Gallagher* production and promotion, perhaps to maximize Jean's loan-out value. It was his suggestion the name be changed to *Platinum Blonde* and he who organized the massive publicity campaign run by his publicity director Lincoln Quarberg. It is a common misconception that Quarberg invented the "platinum blonde" moniker which was linked to Jean for the rest of her life. Hughes had indeed asked Quarberg for a nickname but Jean had been described as the "platinum blonde actress" as early as *Hell's Angels* and called that in *Goldie* reviews. Quarberg did not coin the phrase but he did market it.

He organized 3,000 Platinum Blonde Clubs and offered $10,000 to anyone replicating the coloring formula. His created a fiction ("How Error by Coiffeur Made Harlow a Star"), saying, "Because of a careless hairdresser, a perky young towhead rose to movie stardom.... Her hair was light, almost an ash blonde. A beauty parlor operator ... suggested a peroxide rinse to lighten it [but carelessly used the wrong formula and] when her hair had dried, Miss Harlow looked in the mirror. Her hands flew to her cheeks and she burst into tears. Her ash blond coiffure had become a silver gray. It was shocking."[54]

There was no real secret to Jean's hair color. She visited Jim's Beauty Parlor on Sunset Boulevard, always on Sunday, and Mama Jean brought lunch

for everybody and she'd spend the morning there. The formula for the platinum coloring was: a cup of peroxide, 10 drops of ammonia, and enough
white henna (powdered magnesium) to thicken the mixture, which was
applied as a paste and allowed to stand for 30 to 45 minutes.[55]

Critics were mixed on Jean's *Platinum Blonde* performance. In *The New
York Times* she was "spectacular rather than competent..." and the *Hartford
Courant*, though pleased that "for the first time she is not required to appear
as a half clad vamp," felt that the "results are mediocre. Miss Harlow's round
face and cotton-colored hair stand out prominently...." But the public didn't
care that she was still (slowly) learning to act. They loved her. Tragically, just
after the film opened her co-star Robert Williams died of complications aris-
ing from a burst appendix on November 3.[56]

During filming, her drawn-out divorce from Charles McGrew was finally
completed. She did in fact relinquish her $200,000 trust fund but received
the Linden house (she sold it) and $375 monthly in support. She told
reporters, "I gave him back the money. If $200,000 would make Mr. McGrew
any better friend of mine in the future with no money payments standing
between us, I prefer to have it that way. The money doesn't mean as much to
me as it does to him. So I gave it back."[57]

She was still dating mobster Longy Zwillman. In September, *New York
Times* columnist Mark Barron described the scene at a local nightclub in his
Lights of New York: "A dozen people are sitting in several tables jammed up
close to one another in a night club. One is a gangster not long ago tried for
murder. With him is a platinum blonde girl with blinding platinum blonde
hair and a couple of bodyguards." Nearby were Sylvia Sidney, Grant Withers, Helen Morgan, and coincidentally, Jean's ex-boyfriend Harry Richman.[58]

In October, Paul started filming *Arsène Lupin*, a detective thriller starring the Barrymore brothers, both of whom were battling demons. Lionel
worked completely numbed by drugs to combat worsening arthritis pain and
John had been fired by Warners because of his drinking and ego problems.
He needed money so took a $25,000 pay cut to come to MGM. (Paul had
tried to get the lead for Jack Gilbert.) It was the first of four films in which
brothers appeared together in the 1930s.[59]

John Barrymore plays the wealthy Duke of Charmerace, who is also the
notorious jewel thief Arsène Lupin, pursued by detective Guerchard (Lionel).
Guerchard tracks Lupin to a lavish country estate where Lupin empties a bur-
glar-proof safe and escapes with Guerchard's beautiful spy (Karen Morley) to
Paris, where he steals "the Mona Lisa" from the Louvre. As Guerchard closes
in, Lupin discovers that kidnappers have taken Guerchard's daughter and,
though it costs him his freedom, he obtains her release. Taking Lupin to jail,
Guerchard tells him he once lost a prisoner who leapt into the Seine, which

Platinum Blonde **made Jean internationally famous, the reasons evident in this European publicity photo.**

Lupin does. The film ends with Lupin and Sonia shopping for rings, Lupin jokingly saying, "Wouldn't old Guerchard love to see me *buying* jewelry?"[60]

Arsène Lupin received mixed reviews ("not particularly exciting") but Paul's work was noted: "[F]ew films if any have been better produced and directed."[61] Just after filming ended, Paul convinced Irving to purchase the controversial Katherine Bush novel *Red-Headed Woman* which had been serialized in *The Saturday Evening Post* that August and September. Irving hired F. Scott Fitzgerald to turn it into a script and wanted Garbo, but Paul thought Jean would be perfect as Lil Andrews, a small-town girl who sleeps her way to the top. Joan Crawford was rumored a front-runner but papers rightly noted, "MGM prefers to use free-lancers in unsympathetic roles."[62] Clara Bow bowed out when MGM required a long-term contract in exchange for the role.

Paul was still regularly featured in gossip and society pages, dating Karen Morley that fall. On September 21 he hosted 100 at the premiere of the Dickson Morgan play *Precedent* at the Music Box Theater in L.A. His guests included Rupert Hughes, Lionel Barrymore, Fredric March and Florence Eldridge, P.G. Wodehouse, Cedric Gibbons, Lili Damita, Jack Gilbert, Carey Wilson and Carmelita Geraghty, Harry Rapf, B.P. Fineman, B.P. Schulberg, Ralph Graves, and William de Mille.[63] The cast was headed by Robert Warwick and John Ince and, coincidently, Paul's American Academy classmate Mary Alden.

A few days earlier the *L.A. Times* ran the article "Cinema Maiden All Forlorn Has Friend in Bern — Lends Helping Hand at Break in Career": "There is one man in Hollywood who deserves an official title and decoration of some sort, and that is Paul Bern, film executive. [The title should be]

Chief Consoler and Aid to Lovely Women in Distress."[64] The story described Paul's help to friends like Mabel Normand, Barbara La Marr, Estelle Taylor, Jetta Goudal, Mary Duncan, and Ina Claire.

On October 11, Paul appeared in the political arena, speaking with Douglas Fairbanks, Jr., at a San Francisco rally in front of 10,000 people demanding a pardon for Tom Mooney, imprisoned for a 1916 San Francisco parade bombing that killed ten. Mooney and another man were convicted with false evidence paid for by corrupt detective Walter Swanson. Paul joined the Mooney cause in 1930 with a diverse committee including writers Rupert Hughes and Lincoln Steffens, Sacco and Vanzetti defense counsel Fred Moore, and Judge Franklin Griffith, who presided over Mooney's trial.[65] Mooney received his pardon, but not until 1939.

On November 8, Paul and Morley joined Douglas Fairbanks, Jr., and Joan Crawford hosting a large group at the annual fall Mayfair Ball at the Biltmore. Paul's guests included Carey Wilson and Carmelita Geraghty, Jack Gilbert, Cedric Gibbons and Dolores Del Rio, Rupert Hughes, and the Thalbergs. For the next two months there were almost nightly mandatory functions to attend.

On the 11th, Paul and Morley joined the Fairbankses and a host of movie people at the Hollywood Playhouse to watch Edward Everett Horton in the play *Private Lives*. MGM had recently produced a film version with Norma Shearer.[66] On the 14th, Mayer, Thalberg and Paul each hosted a large group at the Coconut Grove before the premiere of MGM's Wallace Beery feature *The Champ*. Paul's party included Douglas Fairbanks, Jr., and Joan Crawford, Russell Gleason and Marguerite Churchill, Clark Gable, Marie Dressler, Mary Brian and several others.[67]

Red-Headed Woman casting discussions were becoming heated, at least publicly. Columnists weighed in daily on who would get the coveted role. On the 20th Louella Parsons wrote, "Paul Bern is at his wits' end to get the right girl for *The Red-Headed Woman*..." and opined that Clara Bow would be the choice.[68] Others "confirmed" for the role were stage star Lillian Roth, Barbara Stanwyck, Nancy Carroll and Garbo. Paul initially suggested Jean for the role and she was always said to have been a last-minute casting decision, but Anita Loos claimed that Thalberg decided to cast her almost from the moment he bought the story. It would seem clear that Paul influenced Irving, Loos writing that though Jean's reviews had been unimpressive, Thalberg wanted her and instructed the publicity department to "play up the search." He later said she had "outlived more bad roles than any woman on the screen."[69] Jean just had to prove to him that she could do comedy.

With everything else going on, Paul still found time to quietly help when he could. Director Theodore Wharton was confined to his 1433 North Cherokee bungalow in Hollywood fighting a losing battle against thyroid ailments. "Pops" Wharton wrote, directed, or produced 100+ films from 1910 to 1920 including Pearl White's first films. His health forced his 1920 retirement and he had been long forgotten. When Paul learned Wharton was near death, he sent him the *Grand Hotel* script and told the dying man he had been chosen to direct the film. Several days later, on November 28, Wharton died believing he was to direct a great masterpiece.[70]

On another afternoon, his office was full of people waiting for their moment with him. He told Irene Harrison he couldn't see anyone, to send them away, but then stopped a moment and told her, "No, wait. Who am I to send people away who have been waiting so long to see me?" And he stayed until all had been seen.[71]

The *Grand Hotel* juggernaut lurched into the fall in its 18th month of daily script or story conferences. Paul and Irving were flying in the face of conventional studio wisdom with their risky film. Rarely were more than two stars featured; this ensemble had seven. And two die during the film. It was also expensive at a time when Depression-era attendance was down. As soon as script and casting were organized, Irving handed over production supervision to Paul.[72] Thalberg was forced to intervene in disagreements between Paul and director Edmund Goulding and one Mayer biographer inferred that Thalberg fired Paul and took over production himself, but that's not been confirmed and makes little sense. It was Paul who got close friend Goulding the assignment.

The cast was as grand as the production, led by Garbo, the Barrymore brothers, Wallace Beery, Joan Crawford, Lewis Stone and Jean Hersholt. *Hotel* was a glimpse into the failures of a group of people visiting a hotel. Garbo was Grusinskaya, a prima ballerina at the end of her career. John Barrymore was hotel thief Baron von Geigern, Grusinskaya's love interest. Lionel was Otto Kringelein, a terminally ill retired bookkeeper at the hotel for a last visit that's interrupted by former boss Preysing (Beery), whose business is failing. Crawford was Flaemmchen, a secretary who used sex to advance her station. Stone was hotel doctor Otternschlag and Hersholt was Senf, the everpresent porter.

Stone begins and ends the movie somberly intoning, "Life at the Grand Hotel is always the same. People come. People go. Nothing ever happens." The film used the underlying conflicts in each character's life to reinforce that, as Thalberg said during a writers meeting, "[N]o matter how much they fight against the certainties of life, in the end they have to succumb to it, and they do."[73]

Beautiful but aging dancer Grusinskaya believes her life has become "threadbare" but is buoyed after meeting Baron Felix Benvenuto Frihern Von

Gaigern, a charming thief with eyes on her jewelry. Ailing Otto Kringelein wants to spend his final days in style but his plan is derailed by the arrival of Preysing, his former employer. Preysing's secretary Flaemmchen is to meet Gaigern for dinner but when he first breaks into Grusinskaya's room to rob her and finds her suicidal he stops her by professing love and offering to take her to Vienna. He stands up Flaemmchen while making love to Grusinskaya, so Flaemmchen begins an affair with the slimy Preysing.

The next day Gaigern joins a card game to win money to leave with Grusinskaya, with whom he's fallen in love, but loses everything to Kringelein, who passes out drunk. Rather than stealing the unconscious man's money, Gaigern tries to steal Preysing's wallet and Preysing kills him just as a lovestruck Grusinskaya phones his room, ready to leave. Kringelein turns his old boss in for the killing and Flaemmchen accepts his offer to travel to another Grand Hotel, not knowing he's dying. Grusinskaya's loyal maid shields her from the news of Gaigern's death and she leaves for the train station assuming her new love will be there. The film opened in L.A. in April, 1932.

Even though Jean's movies did well — some like *The Public Enemy* and *Platinum Blonde* were hits — studios were still reluctant to take a chance on her still-developing skills. Paul remained convinced she could be a great star (particularly in comedy) but was unable to convince Thalberg or Mayer to sign her at MGM even though *The Secret Six* was a moderate success. Hughes wasn't making any films and apparently interest from other studios was waning, so Paul searched for a loan-out.

One MGM role that was available was in Tod Browning's bizarre circus film *Freaks*. Jean absolutely refused to take the role of an amoral trapeze artist who marries a midget for his money and, after trying to kill him, is tortured by his friends, a menagerie of legless and armless geeks, "pinheads" and dwarfs who turn her into a monster with a human head and a chicken's body.[74] She begged Paul to find her something else and he got her a role in the police thriller *The Beast of the City*, which began filming November 4 at Cosmopolitan.

After *Beast* filming ended in late November, Marino Bello booked Jean on a six-week East Coast publicity tour. She agreed because it paid $3,550, well above her $250 weekly Hughes salary. She left after Thanksgiving.

Paul was the best man at Edmund Goulding's November 28 wedding to dancer Marjorie Moss at Laura Hope Crews' 729 Bedford Drive mansion. (Jack Gilbert was supposed to be best man but didn't show up.) Only eight close friends were at the ceremony, including Paul, Ramon Novarro, and Ivor Novello. Papers said Paul and Novarro, "the town's most enthusiastic bachelors, were the most enthusiastic at the wedding." Goulding hosted a large reception at his own house the next day, inviting guests for "a cup of tea" without telling them it was a wedding reception.[75] Coincidentally, next to the

Goulding wedding story in one paper was a short obituary for director Theodore Wharton.

On December 6, Paul was invited to B.P. Fineman's estate for a holiday party for his (Fineman's) sister-in-law Agnes de Mille. Most of MGM was there: the Mayers, Thalbergs, Rapfs, Bernie Hyman, Cedric Gibbons, Eddie Mannix, Edmund Goulding, King Vidor and several dozen stars. Paul attended with his buddies Jack Gilbert and Ramon Novarro.[76] On the 21st he attended the premiere of good friend Bebe Daniels' stage comedy *The Last of Mrs. Cheyney* at the El Capitan Theater with the Thalbergs and Lionel Barrymore and then a party hosted by Ben Lyon at the Embassy Club.

Jean's grueling publicity trip had been poorly planned by Bello. Beginning in Kansas City she was booked for six sold-out shows a day, six days a week. To save money, Bello hired no writers so the terrified Jean laid eggs everywhere she went, frightened, visibly shaking and mumbling almost inaudibly without the script she so desperately needed. Reaching Pittsburgh in late December, she was tired and finally collapsed with intestinal flu, dehydration and exhaustion. Incredibly, Mama Jean and Bello defied doctors and convinced her to continue and for several days Bello had to physically carry her on stage for her performances.[77]

When Paul heard about the problems, he sent writer Nils Thor Granlund to Philadelphia to help.[78] Granlund — who found Jean to be "as naïve and guileless as a child" — forced Bello to hire writers who created a show-stopping opening with Jean atop a backlit staircase in a white satin gown and white sandals piped in gold, before a black velvet curtain. The emcee opened with, "Take my word for it, she doesn't steal husbands like they make out in the movies. And just between us, she's scared to death, because her whole future depends on what you think of her. Here she is, the adorable lady herself, Jean Harlow!"

Audiences went wild. The first show earned two curtain calls. Within a week she needed police escorts to leave her hotel. At every stop, people lined up before dawn. At Loew's New York City, 1,500 people stood outside the theater waiting for her without tickets. Paul also arranged for MGM to send her five white satin gowns. The original six-week deal lasted 4½ months and she visited 25 cities.[79]

During her Newark visit she spent the weekend with Longy Zwillman instead of accepting Florenz Ziegfeld's offer to perform with his *Follies*. She wowed crowds from Cleveland and Columbus to Indianapolis and Chicago. By this time Jean was writing Paul every day (Zwillman notwithstanding).

Back in Hollywood, studios were still dealing with attendance problems. MGM was more profitable than any studio, so Mayer and Thalberg kept a tight grip on payroll as salary squabbles became common. At one point

Marino Bello, although incompetent, thought himself Jean's manager and badly mishandled her 1931 publicity tour before Paul and the studio came to her rescue.

both Gable and Crawford walked off the same picture (Marion Davies' *Polly of the Circus*) over salary. Even Jean became involved. MGM called her back to L.A. for *Beast of the City* retakes but she refused, citing her Warners appearance contract (which was paying her significantly more than filming). When Mayer threatened to blacklist her, she returned just before Christmas for a week.[80]

Paul celebrated New Year's at a birthday party at Lew Ayres' Hollyridge Drive house with about 35 friends including Russell Gleason, Woody Van Dyke, John Miljan and Carl Laemmle, Jr.[81] But during the holiday season, Paul received a troublesome letter from Frank Case, the manager of the Algonquin. Dorothy's behavior had changed from mildly eccentric to obsessive and bizarre. Paul's friend Henry Hathaway saw the letter and told Sam Marx it basically said, "I'm concerned, the lady who's on the top floor is acting very strange. Her room is filled with movie magazines, she sits there all day reading them and has an obsession about going to Hollywood and you will star her in a biblical epic. She hardly ever goes outdoors. I think you should look into it."[82]

Paul asked Hathaway if he would check in on Dorothy during an upcoming trip to New York but the trip was canceled. Luckily, another friend, Jim Tully, was going there to work on some scripts and agreed to visit her. Tully found Dorothy no longer wearing her brightly colored clothes, her long red coat and matching turban replaced with black. Dress, hat, coat — all black. She still rambled about God and religion and the voices. But she also told him she was going to California after the holidays.

Attendance problems led to shake-ups at almost every studio except MGM. One newspaper described Thalberg's circle — Paul, Rapf, Mannix, Stromberg, Weingarten, Hyman, Fineman, and Lewin — as MGM's "old guard" and Paul as "one of the intellectuals of the colony."[83] Much of the credit for MGM's success was rightly given to this group.

Paul began the year with Jean (back in L.A. for *Beast of the City* retakes) at Louis B. Mayer's fourth annual New Year's Day brunch at his Santa Monica beach house, a few doors from Thalberg's. MGM's elite were there: Douglas Fairbanks, Jr., and Joan Crawford, Clark Gable, Eddie Mannix, Howard Strickling, Thalberg and his inner circle, etc. According to Mayer biographer Charles Higham, actor Chester Morris spent the afternoon openly flirting with Jean.[84] A few days later, Jean returned to the Warners East Coast tour.

Heading into 1932, the rift between Thalberg and Mayer was widening. What had begun as an ego-driven turf war degenerated into a schoolyard power struggle with loud arguments, reconciliations, and typical Mayer histrionics. Irving's value to MGM was unquestioned; Nick Schenck paid him $6,000 a week and his 1932 contract boosted his profit percentage to 36½

percent, equal to Mayer's.[85] Mayer's resentment led to artful second-guess-
ing almost all Thalberg decisions but he rarely offered credit when due. He
was appalled when Thalberg went ahead with Browning's *Freaks*, didn't like
Red-Headed Woman's amoral lead character that openly violated the Motion
Picture Code ban on the film, and didn't agree with casting Norma Shearer
in *Strange Interlude*.

Paul and Irving were both fascinated by *Strange Interlude*, Eugene
O'Neill's study of female sexuality that was something out of Freud with a
subplot of inherited family madness. They championed the film which
appealed to the interests of both. Irving had an interest in people's sexual pro-
clivities (he and Norma often exchanged clothes, cross-dressing for dinner,
with him in full makeup) and Paul's interest in the psychological aspects of
people's lives is well-known. Paul has never been credited with the film but was
involved with Irving in pre-production and script development. It only makes
sense that Paul would work on a film touching on areas of lifelong interest.

The lead (Norma) grows up with a romantic fixation on her father,
escapes into a dreary marriage (to Alexander Kirkland) and motherhood,

Paul at his desk at MGM; in early 1932 he had dozens of projects and was trying to convince Thalberg to hire Jean.

engages in a torrid affair (with Clark Gable) and ends up in a bizarre, almost Oedipal situation with her son. It was a challenge to transfer a five-hour play into a two-hour film and the result is a somewhat rushed presentation made more unappealing by the unconvincing 40-year aging process of Norma done by the makeup department.

It received lukewarm reviews and lost money, exacerbating the animosity between Mayer and Thalberg. Mayer was disgusted by the story from the beginning (he was obsessed with his own mother and motherhood in general) and thought Joan Crawford would have been better for Norma's role.[86]

Mayer also openly washed his hands of *Red-Headed Woman*; the play was long-banned by the Hays Commission.[87] If it failed, Thalberg would take all the blame. That Paul pushed so hard for *Red-Headed Woman* had more to do with Jean than the film. He was "one of the great thinkers of the movies" and said that in times of hardship, people were *less* interested in humor and more interested in serious subjects, that seeing people worse off was an anesthetic to their own pain.[88] Pushing a sex comedy during the Depression seems to contradict his ideals but the reality was, he wanted it for Jean. He fought for it, and in the end insisted.[89] Louella Parsons wrote that even though she couldn't imagine Jean as a redhead, "the only time I ever saw the gentle Paul Bern angry was fighting for this role.... [N]o knight had fought harder for his lady than Paul Bern battled to get that role for Jeanie...."[90]

On January 20, Paul attended the premiere of Douglas Fairbanks, Jr.'s *Union Depot*. (First, however, he was a guest of Fairbanks and Crawford at a dinner with Doug's father and Mary Pickford.)[91] It would be the last time he would socialize without Jean.

Among his assignments, Paul was readying production of the next Garbo film, *As You Desire Me*, the filmization of a Luigi Pirandello play about an amnesiac cabaret singer from Budapest. She is rescued from a sadistic novelist by an Italian count who may or may not be her lost husband but who takes her to Florence to regain her memory. Paul cast the film by early January except for the disturbed writer. Garbo wanted Erich von Stroheim but he and Thalberg hated each other since clashing over his absurd spending on *Foolish Wives* in 1923 and then Thalberg cutting 32 of von Stroheim's 42 reels from his orgiastic *Greed* a year later. And Mayer hated him too, once physically tossing him out of his office for saying, "All women are whores."[92]

At first Thalberg adamantly refused to allow von Stroheim to even come onto the MGM lot but when Paul and Garbo conspired to threaten that she would go on strike otherwise, Thalberg bit his lip and relented. He would not have given in but Garbo's MGM contract was expiring in June and it was not yet certain she would return. Paul managed the production to ensure *As You Desire Me* was completed before June.

The 42-day shoot was a nightmare. Paul acted as referee, smoothing over ruffled feathers and battered egos. The entire crew was fuming at the relationship between von Stroheim and Garbo, who sat at his feet and chatted between scenes while ignoring everyone else. And director George Fitzmaurice, making his second Garbo film, chafed at von Stroheim's habit of offering unsolicited advice about script, camera, and directing, and was incensed that he refused to memorize his lines.

As You Desire Me was released on June 2 and was a typical Garbo hit, netting $450,000 over the $469,000 cost. *The New York Times* claimed it would be Garbo's final film and she would leave MGM, but on July 8, 1932, MGM and Garbo agreed to a lavish two-picture deal worth $250,000 per film that granted her director and co-star approval. The pending contract was kept secret to deepen the public Garbo myth.

Starting in late February, Paul was in meetings — most of which lasted all day — editing and readying *Grand Hotel* for March previews. They began early in Thalberg's office and after lunch moved to his private projection room, where scene retakes or additions were hashed out. After an initial preview in San Bernardino, Thalberg let Paul and Edmund Goulding manage retakes and final editing for a March 17 preview in Monterey.[93]

Like *Grand Hotel*, *Red-Headed Woman* had become something of a juggernaut after almost a year of script and casting work. As of February 1932, the coveted lead was still not assigned. Dozens of actresses were tested in the event that Jean couldn't be funny. As late as February 29, one scribe noted that "some time or other the question of who will play the title role in *The Red Headed Woman* will probably be settled."[94]

Jean was known as "The Platinum Blonde" the world over but her career was faltering from Hughes' mismanagement even as she filled theaters six times a day across the country. Paul finally succeeded in getting her to MGM in late February due to some fortuitous help from Longy Zwillman and Nick Schenck. Jean appeared at Loew's theaters while her film *Beast of the City* was showing and the success of the film and public response to Jean prompted Schenck to suggest to Mayer that he sign her. Mayer still disliked Jean's image and at first refused but Paul's lobbying and Thalberg's intuition paid off; Thalberg and Schenck overruled Mayer. Coincidently at that moment, Zwillman was holding up Hughes for more money so Hughes discarded his problem by selling Jean's contract for $30,000.[95]

Paul got her $1,250 a week, up from $250 (Paul was earning $1,750). Interestingly, RKO approached Hughes at the same time to borrow Jean for a horror-adventure film. They wanted a blonde but Jean didn't want the role. Fay Wray took the lead in *King Kong*.

Paul and Irving called Jean on March 3 — her 21st birthday — to give her the news. Jean was in Baltimore and exhausted after five shows. She was leaving her hotel for the train station and initially she and Mama Jean ignored the call but Jean said, "We'd better answer it. Even if it's just one more person calling to tell me goodbye, I want to speak to them because I am so grateful for all the kindness the people of Baltimore have shown me."[96] When she answered, Irving told her, "Jean, I have a wonderful birthday gift for you. MGM wants you to sign a five-year contract. And someone who loves you very dearly is right here and wants to speak to you." Paul got on and told her how proud he was of her, that she would be a great star at MGM and greatly beloved. Mayer got on the line to get her verbal agreement that she would sign the contract when she returned to L.A. She was then sent to MGM's New York office on March 19 for a *Red-Headed Woman* test.

During Jean's prolonged tour, her feelings for Paul deepend and turned to love. She later told Jimmy Fidler, "For three years ... we never spoke of love. We were simply satisfied, each with the other. I know now that I was in love with him all the time."[97] By late 1931 she was writing him daily, according to Irene Harrison "bombarding my boss with letters" and telegrams, all bearing the same closing: "Love, Love, Love."[98] He told close friends like Irene Mayer that he was in love with her and often stopped at Irene's house on his way home — she was pregnant with her first child and Paul was one of few allowed to visit — saying, "I've had a letter from Jean."[99] He shared them with Irene and asked, "What would you think if I married her?" She responded tongue in cheek, "I think you'd blow your brains out."

Thalberg was mystified after watching Jean's film test, unsure whether she was good or bad and telling Paul, "Well, you know, that girl's so bad she might be good."[100] Jean was sent to Irving and she won him over when he asked her if she could make an audience laugh and she said, "With me, or at me?" When he replied, "*At* you," she told him, "Why not? People have been laughing at me my whole life." He told Anita Loos and Paul, "I don't think we need to worry about [her] sense of humor," and announced publicly on May 6 that she had the role.[101] She initially didn't want it; writers had warned "whoever played would be ruined."

Actresses often pretend to hate their image; Jean actually did. Her first picture in the *L.A. Times* labeled her as "sexquisite" and MGM ads said she was an "alabaster outlaw, beautiful, heartless and irresistible, the new kind of gotcha' girl."[102] She abhorred that she was packaged as a sex symbol, that audiences back to *Hell's Angels* attributed her characters' amorality to her personally. Hughes sold her sexuality; "she was presented as a trollop and remained that in the public consciousness."[103]

She was blamed for marriages ending and linked wrongly with dozens of men. If men spoke to her or they danced together, the movie colony assumed some torrid affair. During a weekend visit to Aqua Caliente, Mexico, one woman screamed at her, "If my husband doesn't stop staring at you, I'm going to slap you in the face!"[104] When Jean and Paul walked into a post–*Hell's Angels* party at Colleen Moore's Bel Air estate, Adela Rogers St. Johns said, "We all looked to see where our husbands were."

Paul and their friends knew she was not a siren, not a temptress, *not* anything like the women she so-convincingly portrayed. As poor an actress as she believed she was, audiences were convinced she was the character she played but those closest knew she was a sweet, simple, unsophisticated Kansas girl.[105] They echoed Gable's first comment to her that she was "not at all the kind of girl I had imagined."

Her crews knew the real Jean. Her maid Blanche Williams served donuts and coffee to them every morning. When producer J.J. Cohn banned coffee breaks, she refused to work until they were reinstated. She was nice. She was regular. And she understood who and what she was, saying, "I'm not crazy about my wild-women roles on the screen, but then I know what I have to sell. I have never been fooled about myself."[106]

Jean's self-awareness was surprising for a woman so young. Chester Morris said of her, "I don't think anybody holds fewer illusions about Jean Harlow as an actress than Jean herself. She is the frankest and most honest girl ... I have ever met." She understood herself and how and why people reacted to her, as Anita Loos described: "If men were stupid they'd fall for her, if they had good sense they'd laugh her off."[107] She understood men and didn't need one by her side for fulfillment, saying, "I'm satisfied as I am. I like my work, I like my life, and I love my freedom. I'm sufficient to myself ... and shall be quite content if I never marry again. I hope I'll stay single. I think I'm happier that way."[108]

Jean was indeed beautiful but not in the classic Hollywood manner of a Barbara La Marr, Billie Dove or Estelle Taylor. Of her own looks she said, "I never thought I was beautiful. I think I create the illusion of beauty because I'm different-looking than other girls."[109] But people were still drawn to her because she was the embodiment of what one writer described as "dangerously interesting unnaturalness...."[110] A 1931 article titled "Perfect Beauty Not Universal With Film Stars — It's Personality That Draws in Shekels" mentioned Jean as one of four actresses confirming Cecil B. DeMille's belief that classic beauty and talent don't usually go hand in hand. It noted that her "profile leaves a lot to be desired and [she] has a [unglamorous] nose with crinkled brow but when it comes to this and that Miss Harlow has the appeal."[111] Still today, Jean is at her most beautiful in candid photos.

She had flawless skin — soundman Bill Edmondson said, "My God, it's a shame to put makeup on that face"[112] — and a perfect body that was rarely hidden given her distaste for underwear. But she was curiously aloof about her physical beauty and totally comfortable with her body, probably because she had no vanity. When Jack Conway told her to take her jacket off during *Red-Headed Woman* filming, she did so even though she was nude to the waist. She told the shocked crew, "I'm sorry, nobody gave the order to cut."[113] Filming *Public Enemy,* James Cagney was so enthralled by her erect nipples he asked, "How do you make those things stand up?" She replied without the slightest embarrassment, "I ice 'em." Friends knew it was actually Mama Jean who handled that chore.

What made her so interesting was not just that she was different from her image, but that she was *so* different.

Jean during her first days at MGM. She was perhaps most beautiful when she wasn't in costume (from the Darrell Rooney collection).

She answered her own phone and her idea of a fun evening was to have a few friends over for dinner. She preferred sitting on the floor; conversation was her greatest stimulus and joy.[114] She rarely partied in clubs, preferring to get as much sleep as possible every night.

She was close to both her maid Blanche Williams and her secretary Barbara Brown. Williams, who called her "Miss Jean," was more than a maid; she was a friend, companion, and worried mother. Nancy Barbara Brown was a friend from Ferry Hall (and reportedly a cousin) who wanted to work in movies, studied stenography and came to Hollywood where Jean hired her to take care of her mail. They were inseparable.

In an era of demanding starlets, she was a conscientious worker, in bed

Jean during a golf-themed photo shoot at the Riviera Country Club just after joining MGM.

by 9:30 during filming and never once late for a call. She rarely went out when she was working, only venturing out once during *Red-Headed Woman* filming for the *Grand Hotel* premiere.[115]

She was equally comfortable hanging out with women or men. She loved cars and knew about them. In the years she knew Paul, she owned a 1929 L29

Cord Cabriolet, a Bugatti Type 57, and a 1931 Cord Cabriolet. She bought a 1932 Packard Phaeton in 1933 and kept it until she died, never once putting the top up.

She was surprisingly smart and read voraciously. When asked her favorite books she quickly replied from memory: Wasserman's *The World Illusion*, Galsworthy's *The Forsyte Saga*, and Sigrid Undset's *Kristin Lavransdatter* and *Jean Christophe*.[116] But she was insecure and self-effacing about her brains, saying, "I have to study so hard in order to do anything. The things that come easily to other people I have to struggle with."[117]

Actresses disliked the studio publicity process but Jean dutifully fulfilled those obligations without complaint. Strickling's publicity people posed her for golf photos at Riviera Country Club, stunning in a striped skirt with little makeup and golf clubs in her hand. At the actual shoot, she lost more than a dozen balls playing six holes and when she finished, like Tommy Bolt once had done, she threw her clubs into the bushes and walked to her car.[118]

She cared nothing about clothes. Blanche Williams picked out her outfits (and doled out her Brise Ambrée perfume so she wouldn't use too much). She liked wearing elegant silk pajamas everywhere so Blanche hid them to force her into dresses.[119] During the tour, she attended a presidential ball at the White House and stopped at Bullocks because she "only [had] two evening dresses and one of them is three years old." After visiting her at home, a publicity secretary told Gladys Hall, "I was at Jean's house and I have as many dresses as she does!"[120]

She loved dogs and always had a menagerie. She owned a Great Dane she named "Bleak" because she bought him on a rainy day, a six-year-old Pomeranian "Oscar," a St. Bernard "Nudger," and a Dachshund "Flying Dutchman." She tried to walk them every day and when she did, she walked two or three miles. It was not unusual to find one or more of her dogs curled up on one of Jean's expensive gowns.

It wasn't surprising she disliked the Lil Andrews character, "a redheaded ... despicable little thing," but Paul convinced her she could make Lil appealing and she trusted Paul without question. She later said he was the "only one man in all Hollywood [with] confidence in my ability to play another sort of girl. Only one man understood my ambitions to go forward rather than to die a screen death."[121] He made Jean understand she needed to "play her [Lil] so that the audience likes her in spite of herself."[122] Filming would start in April.

NINE

Red-Headed Women

For over a decade, Paul had been sending twice-monthly checks to Dorothy, first to Blythewood Sanitarium, then for seven or eight years to the Algonquin, then to Henry. Every two weeks Henry received a check for $175 (about $3,500 today) that he passed to Dorothy. Paul did not include personal notes and only occasionally signed the cover letters, always written in formal business tone on blue MGM stationery. They were addressed "Dear Miss Millette" and most signed, "Sincerely Yours, Irene Harrison, Secretary to Paul Bern."[1]

Dorothy's eccentric behavior became more bizarre as 1932 unfolded and by early spring she was insisting to Henry she was better and wanted to see Paul.[2] She told Henry she wanted to move to San Francisco because she thought the climate would be better for her, but he knew it was a ruse to get to Paul. But he "did not disturb her mentally by opposing her suggestion."[3]

It was now clear that Paul could no longer prevent her from coming to California — and San Francisco would keep her 400 miles away, at least temporarily. He remained outwardly gracious, evidenced in one of the few surviving letters between the two, a March 29, 1932, note sent to the Algonquin:

Dear Dorothy,

I was very happy to get your letter of March 17th.

I read with great interest that you are contemplating a trip to San Francisco. Of course I cannot give you any advice because you yourself can be the only person to know what is best. If you do go I hope that it will be a happy change.

I understand that the Plaza Hotel is a fairly reasonable and attractive one.

If you do change to any other place we will find some way of supplying you with funds in a manner convenient for you.

My love and best wishes always,
Paul.[4]

It had been at least six or seven years since Paul visited Dorothy face to face but it was clear she would be in California when he returned from his planned vacation in May and June.

In late March, writer Romney Scott approached Paul to write a story for *Picture Play* magazine about his (Paul's) good works. Paul refused to see him so Romney interviewed friends for "Tell It to Bern." Romney wrote, "The kindest man in Hollywood has helped all who need from Jim Tully to Jetta Goudal" and detailed Paul's relationships with friends like John Gilbert, Lucille Ricksen, La Marr, Goudal, Normand, and several others. Whenever anyone in Hollywood was in trouble, someone told them, "Get in touch with Paul Bern."[5]

Paul flew to Monterey with Irving and Edmund Goulding on March 17 for a final *Grand Hotel* preview and returned to Culver City to a letter from Dorothy confirming her trip to California. Paul replied with several suggestions for San Francisco hotels (including the Plaza and Clift Hotels), and Henry made her travel arrangements.

The April 29 premiere of *Grand Hotel* was reminiscent of the *Hell's Angels* event with tens of thousands of fans lining Hollywood Boulevard. After Mayer, Thalberg, Eddie Mannix, and Harry Rapf arrived, stars followed, led by Marlene Dietrich, Clark Gable and then Jean and Paul, who arrived with Douglas Fairbanks, Jr., and Joan Crawford.

A bellhop escorted couples from their limousines to the lobby where they signed an oversized guest book. On the page with Paul and Jean's signatures are those of Cecil B. DeMille, Crawford and Fairbanks, Marion Davies, and Constance and Joan Bennett. Paul's oldest friend Edward Bernays traveled from Washington, D.C. for the premiere; his signature is at the bottom of the page.

Jean laughingly asked photographers, "Do we need luggage?"[6] The film was a smash, MGM's biggest financial success of 1932, earning over $1,000,000 (it cost $750,000).[7] It was also an artistic success, voted Best Directed, Best Written and Best Acted picture of the year by a *Hollywood Reporter* poll of national film critics, and Best Picture by the *Reporter* and *Film Daily*. It also won the 1932 Academy Award for Best Picture. That award was presented to Irving with no mention of Paul.

The innovative plot device designed by Irving and Paul — mingling a large number of unrelated people in one setting — was so effective it was reused repeatedly and became known as "the *Grand Hotel* formula." The film is also remembered for Garbo's famous line, "I want to be alone." At the end of the evening, Paul brought Jean for her first visit to Easton, where they sat beneath the lanterns — and the faces of his four friends — sharing a bottle of sherry by the pool.

Red-Headed Woman began filming on April 27. Thalberg rejected F. Scott Fitzgerald's uninspired script (and six internal versions) and assigned Anita Loos to fix it.[8] She produced a playful but slightly naughty script about impoverished Lil Andrews, who sleeps her way to the top. Director Jack Conway told Loos, "You can't make jokes about a girl who deliberately sets out to wreck a family." She replied, "Why not? They deserve to be broken up."[9]

William Legendre (Lewis Stone) and his son Bill Jr. (Chester Morris) control the company town of Renwood, where Bill's secretary Lil "Red" Andrews (Jean) goes after her boss even though he's married to his childhood sweetheart Irene (Leila Hyams). Lil wears Bill's picture on her garter and after working late at Bill's house shows him the garter when he tells her she's "too darn pretty." After Irene catches the two several times in compromising positions, she divorces Bill and he marries Lil but she learns her marriage won't get her accepted in Renwood (shown in a wonderful scene with Lil driving down Main Street in a Rolls Royce with a wolfhound at her side and the radio blaring a Sousa march). She decides to move to New York. Bill won't go so she seduces visiting tycoon Charles Gaerste and tells Bill she's going alone. Bill's father shows him Lil's handkerchief that was found in Gaerste's hotel room and Bill warns Lil he will divorce her if she gets into scandal.

Lil becomes Gaerste's mistress when she gets to New York and begins an affair with his chauffeur Albert (Charles Boyer). Bill shows Gaerste photos of Lil with Albert, says he is divorcing her, fires Albert, and tells him to take Lil with him. She and Albert return to Renwood. When the senior Legendre offers her $500 to leave, she chases after Bill and shoots him in his car but he recovers but refuses to prosecute. Two years later, Bill and Irene are at the races in Paris with Bill's father and see Lil, now the mistress of another millionaire and a Parisian society matron. They watch her leave in her limousine, chauffeured by Albert.

Shooting ended on May 27 and papers reported it would be in theaters in two weeks but the release was delayed after a June 2 preview in Glendale went poorly.[10] At the preview, Thalberg and Loos realized the audience couldn't decide if Lil was serious or funny so he crafted a comic set-up of three short prologues. First, Jean looks at the camera and asks, "So gentlemen prefer blondes, do they? Sez who?" The second has Lil asking a sales clerk if her dress is too tight and when the clerk answers, "I'm afraid it is," she replies "Perfect." In the third Lil puts Bill's picture onto her garter and says, "Well, it'll get me more there than it will hanging on a wall." A subsequent preview in Pasadena ended with thunderous applause.[11]

Adding comic elements was the first fix; removing some scenes the second. The Hays Office approved the film only after some suggestive dialogue and shots of Jean were removed. Several state and local censorship boards required even further eliminations.

On May 2, Dorothy checked out of the Algonquin, telling manager

An MGM publicity photo featuring the stars attending the gala premiere of
Grand Hotel, with Paul and Jean just below the upper right corner.

Frank Case she was going to California to "arrange some financial affairs."[12]
Henry Bern took her to Grand Central and put her on a train to San Francisco. On the 4th, just after Jean started *Red-Headed Woman*, Dorothy took
a cab from the San Francisco train station to the Plaza Hotel at Sutton and
Stockton. Dressed head to toe in dark blue, almost black, she arrived with

Paul is seen in the background of this photograph of Jean at the *Grand Hotel* premiere at Grauman's in Hollywood (from the Darrell Rooney collection).

two large green steamer trunks and signed the register "Miss D. Millette, New York City" instead of her usual "Mrs. Paul Bern."

The Plaza wasn't a luxury hotel like the impressive hotels a block away surrounding Union Square but it was nice and reasonably priced. For the next four months, "D. Millette, New York City" rarely left the hotel and was

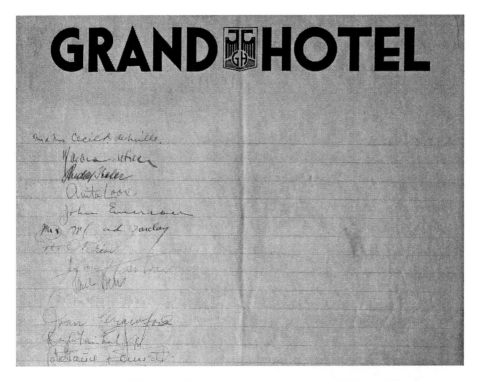

Jean and Paul signed the Grand Hotel register along with Cecil B. DeMille, Anita Loos, Pat O'Brien, Joan Crawford and Douglas Fairbanks, Jr. (from the Darrell Rooney collection).

never in the lobby longer than was necessary to pick up mail or her room key. She never spoke to anyone unless spoken to and paid no outward attention to other people.[13] Hotel manager Ray Maxwell remembered her as a "quiet, lonely little woman. Fairly attractive but not beautiful and an ideal guest. She always wore a dark blue suit and hid her auburn hair under a tight blue turban."[14]

On Sunday the 8th, Paul and Jean visited Colleen Moore's 345 St. Pierre Road estate for a combination housewarming and premiere gala for her play *The Church Mouse*. They joined the Mayers, the Thalbergs, Harold Grieve and Jetta Goudal, B.P. Fineman, Fredric March and Florence Eldridge, Hedda Hopper, Louella Parsons, Lilyan Tashman, Billie Dove, Mary Pickford, Estelle Taylor, and Gary Cooper.[15]

Hollywood took notice that they were a couple rather than studio pals, making headline in every gossip column and movie magazine. In San Francisco, the quiet redhead in dark blue picked up all the L.A. papers every morning in the lobby. She too knew that Jean Harlow was dating Paul Bern.

On May 16, Paul left Jean and *Red-Headed Woman* filming and left on his first real vacation, a month-long trip across the country and a cruise to Central America. Just before he left, Paul learned that Dorothy was at the Plaza in San Francisco.

He flew to Washington, D.C., traveled by train to Wilmington, Delaware, and boarded a ship for a two-week trip with stops at Cristobal, San Salvador, Balboa, Merida, the Yucatan peninsula and, finally, Vera Cruz. From Vera Cruz he took the train to Mexico City where he spent a week visiting theaters and the two large libraries (looking for stories, as always). He flew from Mexico City to Brownsville, Texas, and traveled by train to Fort Worth, then to Columbus, Ohio, and to New York. He visited MGM offices there and returned to L.A. on June 15. Every film-related columnist in L.A. announced his return. Louella Parsons and Jimmy Starr both led with the story.[16]

Paul scheduled his vacation to stay out of Jean's limelight, returning in time for the premiere on the 15th. When his train pulled into the Glendale station, Jean and Bello were waiting for him.[17] Being away helped prevent rumors he was responsible for her getting the role or whispers she was trading sex for stardom. They attended the premiere on the 15th at Loew's L.A. where she said, "I was scared to death but halfway through the picture I started to laugh at myself. For the first time since I have appeared in pictures I really enjoyed looking at myself."[18] She needn't have worried. The picture was a smash, playing to packed houses across the country and winning a *Vanity Fair* award for the Best Picture of the Year. The royal family kept a copy at Buckingham Palace for private viewings even thought the film was banned in England.

The *L.A. Times* said "JEAN HARLOW SURPRISES." It was called "as frankly honest, audacious and provocative a story of bad baby as ever hit the screen" and of Jean, "Miss Harlow is an actress. She is called upon to display only a few emotions ... but the assurance and aplomb of their display are enough to convince us that things have been happening to her in the business of learning to [act]."[19] *The Hollywood Reporter* said Jean's "[was] the sexiest performance since Clara Bow discovered 'It.'"[20] Still another reviewer said, "Hers is anything but a sympathetic role [but she] plays the part of a gold-digger par excellence. Unquestionably she looks the part but it is her convincing acting that evinces surprise, even from her harshest critics."[21]

More important the film grossed almost $750,000, twice its cost. She gave her all during filming; during a raucous fight scene with Chester Morris, he didn't pull his punch and she ended up with a bruised face.[22]

Paul and Jean spent time together every day. Since they were both working six days a week, they spent lunches and dinners together and what remained of weekends. Sundays began with lunch with the Bellos at Club View followed by a visit in Brentwood with Donald Gallery and then to the Thalberg house for dinner.

Free nights were usually spent at Easton sitting by the fireplace reading, or relaxing by the pool. Paul suggested books on philosophy and literature and introduced her to classical music. She told Carey Wilson, "All I want is to sit at his feet and learn the things he knows." When they did go out, it was usually a late-night supper at out-of-the-way places away from reporters. She once described herself as "the loneliest girl in Hollywood" and she enjoyed being treated as intelligent, even though some writers still called them the "bombshell and the egghead." She adored Paul, telling Howard Strickling, "Paul is the first guy who ever took me out who didn't reach inside my dress." He was living up to his reputation as "the little gentleman of MGM." She told Zwillman they had not made love and told Jack Conway and Strickling that Bern was nice to her and "explains things and lets me know I had a brain. He doesn't talk fuck, fuck, fuck all the time."[23]

A much more relaxed Jean made several *Red-Headed Woman* publicity appearances. On the 24th she visited the L.A. Loews and asked the audience whether they liked her as a redhead or a platinum blonde. People overwhelmingly wanted her blonde. She had an interesting take on that, too: "I suppose I ought to say that the red wig made me feel differently. You hear about brunettes with a blonde soul and all that, but honestly I didn't feel one bit changed. I even forgot I was wearing a wig. Women are fundamentally the same, no matter what color their hair is. After all, it isn't the color of your hair which changes a personality. It may have some effect, but not a great deal. Any change of character comes from within, not without. The girl I play in this part is really awfully amusing. She has such a definite reason for everything she does."[24]

With a single role, Jean went from casting afterthought with a middling career to one of the most recognizable actresses in the world, earning compliments for talent along the way. Much of the transformation was Paul's work helping her gain confidence in herself.

On the 18th they visited David Selznick and Irene Mayer at their Benedict Canyon house. Irene was pregnant and while she and Jean visited in the bedroom, Jean told Irene her greatest wish was to have a child (she had already aborted at least one) and asked if she could touch her swollen stomach. When they returned downstairs, Jean said to Paul, "You know, I may just marry you. I'd like a home like Irene."[25]

Leaving the Selznicks, Paul and Jean stopped for some dancing at the Cotton Club and then took a late-night drive through Malibu along the beach on Roosevelt Highway (now the Pacific Coast Highway) and than back to

Jean and Paul spent many quiet evenings relaxing and reading in Easton.

Easton. Paul later described what happened next: "I was sitting in the living room and Jean was sitting on my lap. I said to her, 'Jean, we can't go on like this much longer.' She said, 'What do you mean?' I asked, 'Do you think you'll ever marry me?' Jean replied, 'Do you want me to?' I said, 'You know I do,' and she said, 'Yes, then.'"[26]

They immediately drove over to Club View to tell Mama Jean and Bello, who said the wedding had to be "in a big church and lots of class." Paul quietly overruled them, saying that it would be wrong to have a lavish wedding during the Depression and when the Bellos argued, Jean shouted, "Stop it! Whatever Paul wants is what I want." Bello got drunk in celebration, prompting Jean to ask her mother, "Tell me, isn't there some way we can keep him from coming to the wedding? I'd pay to send him to Europe until my hair turns old and gray."[27]

Mama Jean was outwardly thrilled. She knew what Paul could do for Baby's career and genuinely liked him and knew he'd treat Jean well. She later wrote, "They were old souls, the Baby and Paul. There were drawn together by a profound, mutual respect, the one for the other; by admiration for the qualities of mind and spirit each found in the other. How often Paul said to me and to others, 'If Jean would be my wife for two days, two weeks, two months, I would die content.'" But Marcella Rabwin, David Selznick's assistant, later said Mama Jean worried about the marriage but kept quiet so as not to anger Jean.[28]

After informing Mama Jean and Bello, they called Strickling so Louella Parsons would know. To go public without first telling her would invite a lifetime of snarky reviews. Arthur Landau told Irving Shulman that he told Parsons and Strickling told Hedda Hopper but he wasn't involved (Hopper didn't even start her column until 1936).[29] The first thing Sunday morning, Paul called Irene Selznick wanting her to be the first to know of the engagement and thanking her for being responsible for his "incredible good fortune."

Writers invented their own proposal stories. Jimmy Fidler said the proposal took place during Sunday dinner at Club View, when Paul asked, "What do you say we get married?" and Jean responded, "Sounds elegant to me." That's an unlikely scenario; Paul would not have asked in front of Mama Jean and Bello.

The timing was fortuitous for the Bellos. On the 7th the First National Bank of Beverly Hills closed its doors, reportedly wiping out Garbo's $1,000,000 savings and costing Jean "all [her] money" in the bank.[30] Garbo may have lost a lot but it is doubtful Jean had much to lose.

On Monday morning the 20th, Paul sent an MGM limousine to pick Jean up at Club View and deliver her to his office (with Bello in tow). They went to the red-brick County Courthouse to file a three-day notice of intent to wed. Jean wore a hat and dark glasses but Marriage License Bureau manager Rosamond Rice recognized her when they entered. Paul listed Easton as his home and Jean listed Club View and signed "Harlean Carpenter McGrew."

She told Jimmy Fidler she was "a bit frightened, somewhat amazed, and tearfully happy. I'm terrible in love, and oh, so lucky; he is such a fine man."

Fidler wrote, "Of course, all people say such things, but it is a fact; Paul Bern is a fine man. He is one of the most respected, most beloved men in Hollywood. Jean Harlow *is* lucky."[31] She later reportedly said, "Paul asked me before to marry him many different times and I had never accepted until the other night." She'd had "one bad experience with marriage and [wanted] to be absolutely certain about my feelings before I make a second attempt."[32]

They wanted to get in and out of the courthouse quietly but just two floors above, a jury was hearing testimony in a $1,000,000 lawsuit filed by Alma Rubens' mother against James Quirk and *Photoplay*. When reporters learned Jean was in the Marriage License Bureau, there was literally a mad rush from the Rubens courtroom and minutes later Jean and Paul were surrounded by reporters, photographers and autograph seekers.[33] Bello muscled his way into staged photos of the couple signing their application.

The next morning Jean and Paul were on front pages everywhere. The license bureau photos were on front pages captioned, "The fateful step. Jean

With the ever-present Bello forcing his way to the front, Paul and Jean apply for their marriage license, June 20, 1932.

Harlow and Paul Bern are shown here signing away their rights to single blessedness ... while Miss Harlow's stepfather, Marino Bello, smiles approvingly."

The engagement was described as a complete surprise to the picture colony. Gladys Hall wrote, "The news that Jean Harlow ... and Paul Bern ... filed legal intention to wed had Hollywood gasping — the news was that unexpected. Not that Jean and Paul hadn't been seen places together. For three years, off and on, they have attended premieres and nightclubs in each other's company. But Paul has been following so many gorgeous stars down aisles and among tables in his Hollywood history, that no one had taken their companionship seriously."[34]

After leaving the courthouse they had dinner with Douglas Fairbanks, Jr., who was having marriage problems with Joan Crawford and came alone. In his memoirs, Fairbanks claimed Jean played "very active footsie with me under the table" during dinner, which seems unlikely. He told versions of that story several times, the location changing with the telling (one took place at the Selznick party when Paul first went out with Jean).[35] It's doubtful it ever happened and a wonder why Fairbanks felt the need to propagate the myth.

The couple themselves expressed surprise at the turn of romantic events. Jean had said, "Friendship, not love, is the finest thing in life ... loves seems such a cruel affair. I'm afraid of it. It does such strange and terrible things to people. I shall be quite content if I never marry again. I hope I'll stay single. I think I'm happier that way."[36] For his part, Paul had told Sam Marx, "I love solitude. I've always been self-sufficient. When a man isn't married by forty he isn't likely to be."[37] But there they were, engaged.

Jean said Paul "was my friend long long before he became my husband.... [H]is friendship, his sane wisdom, his understanding were the greatest influences in life."[38] To her, he was "the kindest, most genuinely *good* man I have ever met. He looks upon everybody as a human being to be loved and sympathized with. I can't get over being proud that I'm the girl he wanted to marry."[39]

She said "absence from Paul while away on my personal appearance tour ... helped me realize that Paul was more than a dear friend. I missed him horribly. Aside from loving him, which I do with all my heart, I respect and admire Paul as a man and as a friend more than anybody outside my family that I have ever known. He's so wonderful as a person, it's easy to love him as a sweetheart."[40]

She said of the engagement, "No one can be more surprised than I am with the news! I didn't expect it a week ago. We have often talked casually about the possibility of marriage. Then, suddenly, last Sunday he asked me to marry him. And, suddenly, I knew that he was what I wanted more than

One of the official MGM engagement photos, taken in front of Joan Crawford's studio bungalow (from the Darrell Rooney collection).

anything else in the world."[41] She waited to accept his proposal for so long because she "wanted to make good first. You know if I had married him before this happened [the success of *Red-Headed Woman*], people would have said that I did it to get some place on the screen. They can't say that now. If I can go on and improve and learn a great more than I know now in my work, it's going to make Paul happy. Now I can't let down, because I belong to Paul. I want him to be proud of me." She also said, "We want to have children. It's a pretty important thing in a girl's life, isn't it? Marrying the man you love, wanting a baby, having one, both of us interested in the same work. It's all like a very beautiful dream and it must not change."[42]

Of marriage she said, "My marriage is going to be an amazing responsibility. I've got to make Paul happy. He is the most wonderful man in the world and he has never done anything else except make other people happy. He has always done everything for his friends, even for people he scarcely knew. There isn't anyone I know who deserves happiness as much as Paul. I just can't fail at this. I didn't even want an engagement ring or wedding gift. I just wanted Paul. And my wedding ring is sweet, perfect. Just a hairline of platinum. I am so glad that everything has happened just the way it has."

Walking Jimmy Fidler to his car at Club View, she offered another reason to be happy about marriage, telling him, "I'm happy to be married [and] that Paul and I will move into a new house. I'm tired of climbing those damned stairs."[43]

Typical, Paul made few comments and deferred to Jean, except saying, "She is not at all like the characters she plays. She's a simple child at heart. She's good and sincere and honest. Of all the women I have known in Hollywood, I think my little Jean is the most completely honest." He said she "is a wonderful girl and has a great future ahead. Our plans are in her hands; but you must talk to her." Jean told writers that Jack Gilbert would be Paul's best man but she dispensed with bridesmaids because she didn't want any feuds or jealousies to erupt from her wedding.[44]

Inside the studios, people who didn't know the two assumed she was marrying Paul for money, studio prestige, or career advancement. Of Paul, it seemed incongruous that "the gentle sweet soul chose the most exotic flaming women as his companions" or why those women "seemed to like going with the quiet, unexciting Paul."[45] The truth was that Paul understood women. He didn't stalk them as most men did and never took advantage of them, typical behavior for men in his position. Quite simply, he was a charming man and a kind, devoted friend.

Movie magazines continued a decade of praising Paul, calling him "quiet, polished, one of the most charming and cultured men in the motion-picture business. He has never been married, although in years gone by his name was

Another version of the MGM engagement photographs taken at the Crawford bungalow.

connected with Barbara La Marr and other famous beauties."[46] Gladys Hall wrote, "[T]he red-headed woman has married the black-haired saint ... the man of whom Estelle Taylor said, 'Paul is the only individual in Hollywood about whom *no one* ever says an unkind thing.'"[47]

A most interesting comment came from Hedda Hopper: "If Jean Harlow doesn't make Paul happy, there are a thousand women right here in Hollywood who will cut her throat for her!"[48] She described Paul as "for the down-trodden ... for the oppressed and for those in trouble whether they are young or old, black or white, male or female. You hear of the sensational and exotic women he had befriended, the La Marrs and Crawfords and Taylors and Mabel Normand.... But you never hear of the dozens of obscure and humble persons he befriends, gives money to, give time to, gives *himself* to. You never hear of the homes that are saved, the hearts that are strengthened, the courage that is stiffened because of Paul."

Jean was booked for a week of appearances at Loew's State Theater at the end of July so the wedding was set for August 2, the day after that commitment ended. The ceremony would be at 8 P.M. at Club View, said to be "the home of Mr. and Mrs. Marino Bello, stepfather and mother of the bride-elect" even though Jean paid for it.[49] Invited were Jack Gilbert and his fiancée Virginia Bruce, the Thalbergs, the Mayers, David and Irene Selznick, Henry Bern, the Marcus family, Jean's cousin Don Roberson, Jedda Belle Chadsey (her beloved "Aunt Jetty"), the couple's lawyer Oscar Cummins and Jean's best friend Barbara Brown.[50]

As a wedding present Paul gave Easton to Jean, his "park-like estate [and] one of Beverly Hills' most beautifully landscaped homes."[51] He also hired 18-year-old MGM scenery artist Alexander Ignatieff to paint a mural above the living room, a medieval tableau of 18 people seated around a banquet table.[52] The 7' × 13' mural was angled to fit in a corner between large angled rafter beams above the windows and bookcases and was painted on a canvas frame built to fit the odd space. The dinner guests wear brightly colored Elizabethan garb and have the faces of the couple's friends.

Jean is the focal point at the center of the table, surrounded by some of MGM's most famous actors, writers, producers and directors. Paul's secretary Irene Harrison is seated with Gene Markey, Bebe Daniels, Lawrence Tibbett, Jack Gilbert, Carey Wilson, Irene Mayer, Jean, Irving, Joan Crawford, Norma Shearer, David Selznick, B.P. Fineman, Edmund Goulding, Ben Lyon, Willis Goldbeck and Douglas Fairbanks, Jr. The painting hung across from the master bedroom balcony. Jean was actually a little embarrassed by her prominence in the painting.

Paul re-decorated the interior for Jean's tastes, actually starting in April or May before she accepted his proposal.[53] Harold Grieve and Jetta Goudal transformed the interior top to bottom. The fourth floor bedroom would be Jean's sanctuary. The mansard was paneled in cedar and two large walk-in closets lined with mirrors were installed; a large mirror hung near the entry. A small closet was expanded into a linen closet and the bathroom upgraded and lined with blue and white tiles and voile curtains. The bed — just a day

A more candid MGM engagement photograph, apparently taken on the lower lawn at Easton (from the Darrell Rooney collection).

bed — was upholstered in blue chintz with matching curtains framing the two windows at either end and two small windows in the roof. The room was smallish; Grieve built shoe racks in behind the door, Jean's bed was pushed against a wall, and bookshelves were installed next to a small desk and lounge chair.[54]

The entrance to the small room above the turret, reached by climbing through the closet in Jean's room, was enlarged. Present owner Ron Hale was told she used the tiny space "to pout" if she and Paul had a disagreement.[55]

The master bedroom was totally redone. Paul's high-backed desk chairs were reupholstered in brown leather, his desk refinished, and antique maps hung above. A separate dressing area for Jean was built in behind the fireplace with a built-in mirror-topped dressing table and cabinet. The table was upholstered and dressing area outfitted with lighting matching studio makeup tables; white chiffon gauze curtains in the dressing area matched a skirt made for the dressing table, on which were two framed photos, one of Paul and the other of Marino Bello. Mama Jean's picture was prominently displayed on a table in the living room.[56]

White linen curtains with blue and white wool trim were hand-made and pads matching Paul's chairs made for the two large corner window seats. A large chaise lounge completed the room and more mirrors were installed for Jean. A floor-to-ceiling triple mirror was installed next to the closet, mirrors hung around a window to encircle her dressing table, and mirrors attached to the four bureaus. Paul's hunting lodge–style light fixtures were replaced with silk lampshades.

The master bathroom was redone with white and blue tiles matching Jean's upstairs bath and white voile curtains installed. Lastly, new beds were brought in and head- and footboards hand-upholstered.

Three other photos graced the bedroom and sitting room, all of Jean. On Paul's desk in the corner surrounding by windows was a large 11X14 of Jean with her hands clasped, head to one side, her expression described as "half-exotic, half sensual, that expression which made her such a favorite in the movie colony."[57]

In the living room, Grieve built a cabinet for Paul's music equipment and remodeled the bar with a corner cabinet made from a wine barrel. He brought in a large glass-topped coffee table, replaced a large dark rug with a peach-colored oriental and added copper mugs and small items to feminize the room. All the furniture was re-upholstered in brighter colors; Easton looked less like a hunting lodge and more like a relaxing mountain aerie.

According to Sam Marx, Jean was not thrilled with the remote location and that was a source of conflict. Later stories actually said Jean hated the secluded property, which is strange since she told her favorite Aunt Jetty after she was married, "I've found peace and happiness at last. I'm so happy here I don't care if I go on a honeymoon."[58]

Paul and Jean went back to work. Her week of appearances at Loew's State began on Friday the 24th, three shows daily at 1:00, 3:00 and 9:00. At the studio, Anita Loos was creating an original screenplay for Jean tentatively

The couple, from the same MGM photo shoot at Easton.

titled *The Ritz Bar*.[59] Paul had five features in progress and seven more slated to start within two weeks, including *Rasputin and the Empress, Smilin' Through, Tinfoil, The Mask of Fu Manchu, Lost,* and *Red Dust* with Clark Gable (another role taken from Jack Gilbert). He still managed to take a day and help Estelle Taylor move into her new Malibu colony cottage.[60]

Top: The mural commissioned by Paul as a wedding present for his new bride, hanging over the great room–living room at Easton. *Right:* In a close-up of part of the mural, Jean is seated between Joan Crawford (left) and Irene Mayer Selznick, with Irving Thalberg standing behind (courtesy Bill Lewis).

Thalberg brought Jean to MGM to fill a specific role: She was the studio's sex symbol. They had Garbo, Shearer, Crawford and to some extent Marion Davies, but *Red-Headed Woman* proved none had Jean's screen presence in that type of role. She was also given a role originally slated for Crawford in a Clark Gable–Wallace Beery vehicle tentatively titled *Soviet Russia*.[61]

On the 25th, Fredric March and Florence Eldridge hosted an engagement party for Jean and Paul at their 1026 Ridgedale estate.[62] The Thalbergs, the Mayers, Jack Gilbert and Virginia Bruce, David and Irene Selznick and over 100 other friends attended. Exhausted from work and travel, in the middle of the party Paul took a nap. When he came downstairs, Jean was leaning against the piano listening to New York socialite Cornelius Vanderbilt Whitney play and moving slowly to the music. Paul said to Irene, "Look at her. She's an angel from Heaven. No matter what happens, remember she's an angel from Heaven."[63]

In the days before and during the Loew's appearances, Jean scrambled with final plans. A few days after the engagement, she and writer pal Marcella Burke and best friend Barbara Brown shopped for a wedding dress. Earlier in the day, Mama Jean went to a Hollywood boutique and picked out a soft blue chiffon and satin dress that "made Jean's eyes look like sapphires." Jean hated it, saying it made her "look like she's graduating from a girl's seminary." As salesgirls scurried about bringing her dresses she saw a simple white dress, pulled it on and said, "I'll take it." The entire process took ten minutes.[64]

She insisted on writing hundreds of thank-you notes herself. The first wedding present arrived at Club View within days, a set of crystal glasses from Arthur Landau. On a light blue note-card emblazoned with her profile in silver, Jean wrote:

> Darling Mrs. Landau and Pops,
>
> Today I came home from the theater and found these exquisite goblets and sherberts [*sic*]. What precious friends you are to remember me in such a beautiful way. My Lord, Pops and Mrs. Landau, how can I write to you and express what is in my mind and heart. All I can say is that I love your expression of friendship for me and — yours was my *first* wedding gift.
>
> My love and heartfelt appreciation,
"Your Blond Child"[65]

Hundreds of lavish gifts flooded Club View, displayed in the small library which soon became a blaze of light. Silver, gold, crystal and cloisonné caught the rays from a lamp and turned them into a rainbow of color. A complete set of crystal arrived from David Selznick and Irene Mayer, another from John Barrymore and Dolores Costello, a set of silver vases from Bebe Daniels and Ben Lyon, a sterling coffee service from Josef von Sternberg, and a silver and enamel French telephone from Jack Conway. There was a sterling silver birdcage with a cut-glass parrot encrusted with gems perched on a silver swing that was a decanter. Jack Gilbert sent a bizarre clock, the base a bronze bonbon dish and inside the rim a bejeweled turtle, his tiny head and tail pointing toward the numbers. Paul's family sent a large, engraved sterling silver punchbowl.[66]

The couple received over 100 *dozen* crystal glasses of every size and shape and dozens of complete sets of china. But the gift that touched Jean the most was a set of sterling spoons that had been in Barbara Brown's family for generations. Mama Jean's gift was a picture of herself inscribed "Baby Mine, You have filled my life with such great happiness. No mother ever had the devotion, friendship. Or exquisite love such as I have had from you — My Baby — My Life — My Everything. Mommie."

On Thursday, Henry and Miriam Bern arrived from New Rochelle with their four children. Also in town were Jean's Aunt Jetty and cousin Don Roberson, staying at the Beverly Wilshire. Jean's last Loew's appearance was Thursday and the wedding was Saturday, July 2. It was a bright, hot day but clustered outside on the sidewalk, the front-yard terraces, and even the porch were several

Jean's beauty was striking at the time of her wedding to Paul.

hundred photographers and fans held back by a half dozen policemen and a squad of chauffeurs who delivered the 27 guests.

At the last minute, Jean decided to make one final appearance at Loew's, even though it was unscheduled and unannounced, to thank her fans for their support of her wedding. The enthusiastic response delayed the movie's start for an hour and she wasn't delivered back to Club View until mid-afternoon.

The photographers and reporters were allowed inside a few dozen at a time after Jean made a deal with them: They were given access to the wedding if they stayed away from the reception at Easton. About 15 minutes before the ceremony began, she came out to the top of the stairs and said, "Oh gee, boys, I'm scared stiff. I've had 16 glasses of bicarbonate of soda and I'm still scared. Do you mind if I stick in here with you until it starts?" She stayed with them until the ceremony began, still wearing Paul's cigar band on her ring finger; she hadn't wanted an engagement ring.

Hundreds of telegrams had arrived and the house was full of flowers — a huge bouquet of yellow roses from Paul and dozens of white and pink roses from the likes of Howard Hughes, the Mayers, and the Thalbergs. Paul and best man Jack Gilbert waited with the rest of the guests in a first floor literally filled with huge clusters of lilies [67] Mama Jean came upstairs with Judge Leon Yankwich, who would perform the ceremony, and Jean asked, "What do I have to say?" Yankwich grinned and told her, "All you have to answer is 'I do.' And when you have to do any repeating, I'll tell you."[68]

A few minutes later, Jean descended the staircase looking radiant in a shimmering, tight-fitted white crepe gown with a fringed shawl. She had no veil, carried no flowers and wore no jewelry. None of the flowers were put in the living room except for two enormous baskets of roses framing the couple facing Judge Yankwich. Jack stood next to Paul and both were visibly trembling. Jack fumbled for the platinum wedding ring, rifling through all his pockets before finding it in his jacket. After a simple ceremony and three clinging kisses, Jean Harlow became Mrs. Paul Bern.

Photographers swarmed down into the living room to pose the bridal party. While the photographers re-loaded their cameras, Jean and Paul exchanged long kisses. The wedding photo shows a happy group surrounding a beaming Jean and a smiling Paul next to Yankwich. To his left are Gilbert, Friederike, Barbara Brown, Virginia Bruce and the Selznicks. On the other side are Mama Jean and Bello, Arthur Landau, Henry Bern, Don Roberson, and the Thalbergs. Jean's Aunt Jetty is to the left of Thalberg.

John and Winifred Carmichael and Blanche Davis served small sandwiches, expensive caviar, champagne and coffee. A drunken Bello insisted on reading dozens of the telegrams from famous names around the world, greatly embarrassing Jean until Paul quietly told her that every wedding had to have a buffoon. Jean told him, "I can't help crying. I'm happy for us, for me, for knowing that we're married and that I'm going home with you. But I've got to leave Mama with him."[69]

When Jean cut the lavish three-tiered wedding cake set amid a huge ring of lilies, the first pieces went to Irving and Norma. Judge Yankwich left at 11:00 and the other guests soon followed. Jean and Paul escaped to the solitude at Easton after midnight.

Guests had been invited by "Mr. & Mrs. Marino Bello" to "the wedding reception of their daughter Jean Harlow and Mr. Paul Bern on Sunday, the third of July at three o'clock in the afternoon, Ninety-eight twenty Easton

Mr. and Mrs. Paul Bern in the living room at Club View Drive just after the wedding (from the Darrell Rooney collection).

Drive, Beverly Hills, California."[70] Circular tables and chairs were arrayed about the lower lawn and around the pool and Colleen Moore and Marian Nixon arrived early to help Jean get ready. The press honored their deal with Jean; the only photographers present were from MGM and only a few photos were taken.

Between 150 and 200 friends drank champagne and sampled finger sandwiches. Most of Hollywood was gone for the July Fourth weekend or writers estimated that 500 would have come.[71] Harrison Carroll wrote that the celebration "drew many of the stay-at-homers" over the weekend. The crowd overflowed into the gardens of Paul's home."[72]

Family members visited with the Thalbergs, the Mayers, the Selznicks, Jack Gilbert and Virginia Bruce, Douglas Fairbanks, Jr., and Joan Crawford, Clark Gable, Chester Morris, Louella Parsons, Spencer Tracy, Anita Page, Cedric Gibbons and Dolores Del Rio, Rouben Mamoulian, Carey Wilson and Carmelita Geraghty, and dozens of Jean's studio crew member pals. Sam Marx said the newlyweds spent the afternoon holding hands "like adolescents."[73]

Parsons told Paul, "You're the guardian of one of the world's most precious treasures. Protector of one of Hollywood's most glittering crown jewels," to which he replied, "I'm fully aware of it, dear lady."[74] It was Paul's habit to address women as "Dear lady" or "Dearest dear."

Marino Bello was conspicuous in his tuxedo, the only one in evidence, as he lorded over the proceedings as if the party were for him, speaking in

A wedding-day family photograph at Club View; from left, Jean's Aunt Jetty, Mama Jean, Miriam Bern, Friederike Marcus, Henry Bern behind, Paul, William Marcus behind, Jean, her cousin Don Roberson, and Bello.

his faux Italian accent and telling anyone who would listen the fiction, "I intend to continue managing my daughter's career." Guests came and went until midnight, and Bello took six bottles of champagne and a case of caviar with him when he left.[75]

There was a frenzy of press following the weekend festivities. *Photoplay* noted, "Hollywood's most exciting wedding of the month was that of platinum Jean Harlow and executive Paul Bern, for just when the town had it all doped out that Paul would continue being an eligible bachelor for the rest of his life and that nothing could tempt Jean to the altar a second time — the marriage ceremony was read. Congratulations, Paul! And worlds of happiness to you, Jean."[76] The *L.A. Times* highlighted the age difference between Paul and Jean, that the "wedding ... climaxed a romance in which Miss Harlow, now 21, took as her husband a man *considerably her senior* [italics in original article] and considered one of Hollywood's confirmed bachelors."[77]

Photoplay complimented Paul and hinted at a career boost for Jean from the wedding; "But then — filmtown's ladies may be a bit miffed. For Harlow has carried off their favorite bachelor and most dependable friend. Bern's kindness to young film aspirants are innumerable. Also — since *Red-Headed Woman*, Jean is ace, king, queen and jack of the Metro lot. Perhaps some of the old guard are burning up, burning up. Ah, mates, thorny indeed is the path of the sudden success in pictures — especially when she simultaneously annexes the town's most eligible bachelor."[78]

Of the weekend, Jean said, "I'm so happy since I married Paul Bern and this coming on the heels of my first real picture success makes my cup of happiness overflowing. I feel like a different person from the Jean of a year ago. I know I'm different. But marriage is apt to make any girl change. Before I got married I didn't dare say anything, do anything or feel anything. I seldom went out dancing."[79]

Jean settled in at Easton. Every morning Blanche bought breakfast to her: a glass of hot water with the juice of half a lemon, black coffee and toast, scrambled eggs and sausage. Blanche was a demanding mother to Jean, and Jean allowed her to take on the role. In addition to picking her clothes and rationing perfume, when Jean would buy dozens of pairs of silk stockings Blanche hid them and doled them out one pair at a time. She went to work with Jean almost every day, bringing coffee and donuts for Jean's crews and helping Jean with her lines. Blanche fiercely defended Jean until her (Blanche's) 1984 death.[80]

Barbara Brown came up to Easton every day to handle secretarial duties, but the two more often relaxed by the pool or on one of the patios like the two high school friends they were. They also sat through several dozen photo shoots at Easton in the months after the wedding.

Jean cuts her wedding cake with (from left) Irving Thalberg, Mama Jean (hidden), Norma Shearer, Bello, and Paul.

On the 14th it was announced that Jean would star with John Gilbert in the jungle romance *Red Dust*, originally purchased for him and Garbo. In addition to a demanding production schedule, Paul was trying to keep the peace during the biggest salary bloodbath in Hollywood history, one that impacted people at every level.[81] As the Depression kept millions out of theaters, the studios demanded concessions and across-the-board salary reductions and even though everyone had contracts they "voluntarily" agreed to help the studio.[82]

Thalberg asked Paul to help re-write *China Seas*, a pirate adventure that had been mired in script problems for over a year. The top role was originally assigned to Gilbert but Thalberg was thinking about a Gable-Harlow match-up.[83] He also asked Paul for a script based on the Sinclair Lewis story "The Willow Walk," which he worked on for the rest of the month. Paul submitted his nine-page *China Seas* revision on September 3.

Paul and Jean laid low at Easton for a week or so and then jumped back into the social scene. There were several *Strange Interlude* events the week of the 16th and on the 25th a dinner hosted by Cedric Gibbons for his wife Dolores Del Rio at the Coconut Grove before the preview of her *Bird of Paradise*. They joined Edmund Goulding and Lilyan Tashman, the Marquis Henri de la Falaise and Constance Bennett, and actors Dorothy Jordan and Donald Dillaway.[84]

On July 29, Paul met with his attorney Oscar Cummins to draw up a new will. The simple document read, "I give, devise and bequeath all of my property of whatever kind, real and personal, and wheresoever situated, after the payment of any just debts that may constitute a claim upon it at the time of my death, to my beloved wife, Harlean Bern. I do hereby name and appoint my beloved wife, Harlean Bern, the sole executrix and administratrix of my last will and testament, to act without bond." He signed the will and gave it to Irene Harrison, who put it in his safety deposit box at Bank of America in Culver City. On his way home from Cummins' office he stopped at May Department store and bought $11.95 worth of toys to bring to Donald on Sunday.[85]

According to Arthur Landau, at the same time Jean purchased a 1⅓-acre lot on South Mapleton below Sunset, across from prominent banker A.P. Giannini.[86] She already owned a lot on Beverly Glen

The official MGM portrait of Paul Bern and Jean Harlow Bern (from the Darrell Rooney collection).

where she was planning a home for the Bellos. Sam Marx said Jean didn't like the remoteness of Easton and she later said she and Paul were going to build a house in which they and the Bellos would occupy separate wings and use Easton as a "weekend retreat." Paul, she said, was "happy about this arrangement."[87]

On August 2, Jean made her first solo public appearance as Mrs. Paul Bern when she was the guest of honor at a luncheon given at the Assistance League tea-room in Hollywood.[88] On the 4th they both attended the premiere of *Back Street* at the Carthay Circle with Ben Lyon and Bebe Daniels, Colleen Moore, and Jack Gilbert. The commitment kept Paul from the hospital where Irene Mayer had given birth to a son earlier that day.

During Irene's pregnancy, Paul was the only non-family member the hospital admitted. Other visitors could see the baby through the nursery window but could not see Irene.[89] For some reason, Paul did not visit her, which was unusual. Jean did go on the 12th, bringing a baby plate and cup set and crystal goblets costing the equivalent of $2,000, but Irene remained deeply hurt.[90] Paul told her he was sorry, would explain everything later, and that she would understand. He was very distracted by something.

On August 8, Paul and Jean attended the Olympic games which began on July 30 with the Coliseum the main venue. Paul paid Cherry Ticket Agency $265 for his tickets (about $5,000 today).[91] Hollywood was very involved in the games, especially MGM. Mayer was the chairman of the industry's entertainment committee for athletes, and all employees were "encouraged" to attend.[92] On the 10th he hosted a lavish Ball of All Nations at the Coconut Grove attended by 5,000 people.

Paul took Jean and Anita Loos and joined 60,000 fans at the Coliseum for a demonstration football game between a West Coast team from Stanford, Cal-Berkeley, and U.S.C. and an East Coast team from Yale, Harvard and Princeton.[93] Paul made sure they had blankets, food and drinks and asked Jean if she wanted anything else. She laughed and told him, "Yes, Daddy, get me one of those," pointing at a group of the players. They all laughed but Loos and Adela Rogers St. Johns later exaggerated Jean's off-hand joke as an indictment that there was something wrong with the marriage. Jean was thrilled with the whole Olympic experience, watching events and meeting athletes. She displayed an Olympic license plate on the front bumper of her Cord roadster and later her Packard.

Among the dignitaries Jean and Paul befriended was Prince Ferdinand von Liechtenstein, who came to America for the games and to pursue actress Lili Damita, whom he had met in Europe.[94] Funding the nine-member Austrian team and acting as the *de facto* manager, the dashing nobleman was the darling of Hollywood and honored at the best parties from Pickfair to the studios.

Jean and her best friend and secretary Barbara Brown read fan mail next to the pool at Easton (from the Darrell Rooney collection).

Paul and Jean met Ferdinand at an Olympic party at Colleen Moore's Brentwood estate before the games. Jean followed protocol described by Paul, referring to the prince as "Your Serene Highness," but as the evening wore on he told her, "Please, Jean. No formalities. We're friends, aren't we?" Later they played poker and the prince laid down a full house and asked Jean what she had and she said, "Four queens, Tootsie-boy prince!"[95] The Prince roared his approval but (like the earlier football story) this innocent comment would also later be exaggerated by writer St. Johns.

She later claimed that Paul, furious at Jean's lack of decorum, grabbed her arm and dragged her out of the party. The ridiculous version is unlikely; Paul would never drag Jean anywhere by the arm, nor would she let him. Colleen Moore laughingly recalled the evening and never suggested there was an argument. But she did recall there was a pistol in Paul's pocket and when she asked, "What are you carrying, all my silver?" he responded, "We live up in a lonely canyon and somebody might try to hurt my darling."[96]

Moore didn't think anything of it; Hollywood was alive with paranoia after the Lindbergh kidnapping and an attempt to kidnap Marlene Dietrich's child. Seemingly everyone carried a gun. Paul owned several pistols he bought after moving to Easton, keeping one in his bedroom and the other in a locked compartment in the dashboard of his car. According to his chauffeur he "always carried a gun in the car."[97]

On Friday the 10th, one of Jean's close companions died. On September 15, 1918, Corporal Lee Duncan found a litter of five-day-old puppies in a bombed-out kennel in France. He named two Rintintin and Nenette after tiny French puppets given to U.S. troops for good luck and he brought them home (Nenette died during the voyage). A novice filmmaker saw Rin Tin Tin at an L.A. dog show and approached every studio selling his dog movie. Only nearly bankrupt Warners agreed and Rin Tin Tin's 26 films saved the studio.

Lee Duncan and the regal German Shepherd lived across from Jean on Club View and she brought her dogs over there regularly to play. She also arranged visits for Paul's son Donald and his sister. Rin Tin Tin was devoted to Jean and she to him, but on the afternoon of the 10th Mama Jean called her to tell her that the dog had unexpectedly taken ill and Duncan was not home. Jean rushed to Club View and spent the entire afternoon sitting under a tree in the front yard with the ailing dog's head in her lap, stroking it and softly crying. When he died late in the afternoon, Jean was distraught. He was originally buried next to the fence in the backyard but was interred in Paris some years later.[98]

The death of Rin Tin Tin kept Paul and Jean from attending Mayer's huge Ball of All Nations for the Olympic athletes, and Jack Gilbert's surprise marriage. At 6:00 P.M. that afternoon, Gilbert married a fourth time in a ceremony at his studio bungalow. He met Virginia Bruce filming *Downstairs*. Even though Irving replaced him in *China Seas* and it was rumored he was about to do the same in *Red Dust*, he was Gilbert's best man. Guests included Norma, Lupe Velez, the Donald Ogden Stewarts, Dolores Del Rio, the Lawrence Stallings, the Barney Glazers, and Charles Green.[99]

Paul would surely have attended had he been able. When Gilbert announced the marriage during *Downstairs* filming, Paul dropped everything and rushed to the soundstage to offer congratulations. It was the day after Paul and Jean had announced their wedding.

On the 12th, Thalberg formally announced that Gable, "instead of John Gilbert, will play the male lead in *Red Dust*."[100] It was the second time Gable replaced Gilbert, the first in Garbo's *Susan Lenox: Her Fall and Rise.* Also learning he lost *China Seas*, Gilbert knew he had no career left at MGM. Mayer would have fired him earlier but Nick Schenck had given Gilbert a multi-million dollar five-year contract in 1928 over Mayer's furious objections. Even so, Gilbert's slide had as much to do with his inability to go from silent film pantomime to emoting in sound. It's admittedly hard to conclude if he could have survived sound given the awful roles Mayer gave him but the work he *did* do was uneven. More important, by 1932 Thalberg had a new crop of actors (led by Gable and Robert Montgomery) to replace him.

The blame for Gilbert's decline has fallen on Mayer. He did hate Gilbert but Irving made casting decisions and, though a loyal friend, he knew Gable was better-suited for the roles. He was not unsympathetic — in every case he told Gilbert personally — but it was ultimately his decision. After his wedding, a dejected Gilbert embarked on an extended European honeymoon and quietly left the studio upon his return.[101]

Coincidently, Jean replaced Garbo in *Red Dust*. After the blazing on-screen performances of Garbo and Gable in *Susan Lenox*, Thalberg planned to pair them again in *Red Dust*. The casting had evolved from Garbo-Menjou to Garbo-Gilbert to Garbo-Gable to Harlow-Gable.[102]

On the 15th, Paul and Jean attended the *Strange Interlude* premiere at Grauman's.[103] It was a mob scene; thousands crowded Hollywood Boulevard and when a restraining rope snapped, 100 fans fell headlong into the gutter, injuring a dozen. Another man was pushed through a plate glass window by the crush and several more were hit by arriving limousines. Everyone was there, among them Mayer, Stromberg, Rapf, DeMille, Lasky, Zanuck, Jack Warner, Gable, Constance Bennett, Gary Cooper and Countess Dorothy Di Frasso, Marion Davies, Bebe Daniels and Ben Lyon, Sally Eilers and Hoot Gibson, and Douglas Fairbanks and Mary Pickford.

Arriving late with the Thalbergs, Jean received one of the biggest ovations of the night. She was relaxed and radiant in one of her form-fitting white silk dresses next to Paul in his tuxedo and white shirt and tie, photographed with Gable and Norma and with Columbia executive Harry Cohn. Jean invited Lee Duncan, still grieving over the death of his beloved Rin Tin Tin, who escorted Mama Jean.

Paul's circle of friends quickly embraced Jean. Carey Wilson and

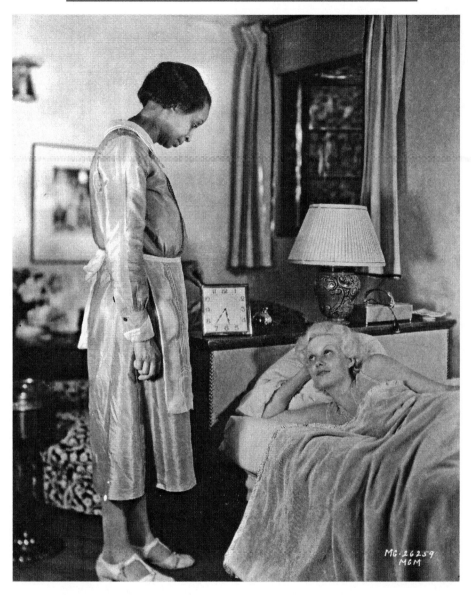

Jean's loyal friend and maid Blanche Williams, at Easton.

Carmelita Geraghty — Paul's oldest friends — became Jean's close companions as did the Selznicks. The Wilsons and Jean quietly and anonymously visited art galleries and museums together.

Paul's life seemed perfect but privately friends noticed him becoming more distracted as the summer wore on. Irene Selznick noticed it when he did not visit her at the hospital after her son's birth and later when he failed to show up for a visit to Santa Monica but he told her that, when she learned why, she would understand. Jean also thought he seemed preoccupied but unlike everyone else she knew why.

Dorothy, still secluded at the Plaza in San Francisco, rarely ventured out of her room except for meals. Her obsession had shifted from a movie career

An MGM publicity still taken in the entryway at Easton; the photographer stood in the living room (from the Darrell Rooney collection).

to Paul and Jean. Maid Lena Meredith later said, "She kept the door locked and all she did was read movie magazines. The room was full of them and I always saw her staring at articles about *Red-Headed Woman*. She had one of the magazines propped open to 'The Life of Beautiful Jean Harlow,' and others that showed pictures of the wedding."[104] Dorothy was probably less disappointed Paul would not get her into the movies and more betrayed that he married someone else.

Without doubt, Paul told Jean about Dorothy; he probably kept *no* secrets from her, even telling her about Donald, whom she embraced as her own. Mannix and Strickling obviously knew about Dorothy, who was making ever more strident demands as the summer wore on, to the point of blackmail. MGM did not want Dorothy coming to Hollywood, where the press could learn that in the eyes of the State of New York, she and Paul Bern were married, never divorced, thus making Paul Bern's marriage to MGM's most popular sex symbol bigamous.

MGM negotiated with Dorothy for months to keep her from Hollywood and had reached an agreement; Paul would continue to pay her bills — probably studio-subsidized — and she would quietly relocate to Mexico. A home was purchased and money agreed upon but at the last minute, "the woman Malett [*sic*] did not go to Mexico as agreed and she began to blackmail Bern."[105]

It appears that Paul and Jean tried to solve the Dorothy problem themselves in the days after the *Interlude* premier. On the 18th Jean and her mother flew to San Francisco and checked into the Mark Hopkins, a luxury Nob Hill hotel two blocks from the Plaza.[106] But just a few hours later she received an MGM telegram demanding she return to L.A.[107] She complied, but not before receiving a female guest dressed in dark clothes and making over a dozen telephone calls to two different L.A. law firms.

Hunt Stromberg later said the trip was a pre-planned four-day shopping excursion cut short by the start of *Red Dust* filming.[108] But it was well known not to be ready for filming; trade papers watching the status of the film mentioned almost daily that "the script of *Red Dust* is not yet ready for the cameras."[109] As it was, filming did not begin for yet another week. There was another reason MGM made her come home; they didn't want her there. With Dorothy.

Even more interesting, I discovered that Paul was in San Francisco *at the same time*. He had been there several days; Jean followed him there. A note buried in archives confirmed that an MGM limousine met Paul at the Glendale station at 8:30 A.M. Friday morning and took him directly to the studio. He arrived aboard "The Lark," a luxury overnight commuter train that arrived in L.A. every morning at 8:30. From San Francisco.[110]

In one of the last photographs taken of Paul and Jean, the couple sit above the entry stairwell at Easton. The pool is off to the right (from the Darrell Rooney collection).

Jean followed Paul to San Francisco. There is no record of his departure from L.A. but he was in San Francisco Thursday so left L.A. no later than Wednesday. The reason for his trip, and why Jean apparently followed him, would become obvious in a few weeks. As soon as he returned, Paul ordered a huge bouquet of flowers sent from Sada's Flowers to Jean's dressing room.[III]

A week later, Paul asked Carey Wilson to prepare a treatment for a movie
for Jean based on a Joseph Moncure March poem titled "The Wild Party."
Wilson didn't think the book could be made into a movie. It is an erotic story
of a vaudeville dancer at an all-night Greenwich Village party full of booz-
ing, fighting and indiscriminate sex that ends in murder. He later said, "Not
a single line could be placed literally on screen. I was amazed. But then I saw
Paul's point and the interesting character. Paul was overjoyed and told me,
'That's my point. That girl, a pagan little animal, would fit right in with the
character Jean has established on the screen.... I think it would be mar-
velous.'"[112]

Wilson said Paul made him work "like the devil" on the script and had
him revise the story so that Jean's character would not be killed but would
instead give *her* life to save her friends from scandal. Irving and, interestingly,
Jean, were both thrilled with the project, which was scheduled for production after *Red Dust*.

Jean arrived for *Red Dust* filming on Tuesday to a dressing room full of
flowers and gifts from Paul. Actual filming did not start until the 29th or 30th.
The film is set on an Indonesian rubber plantation owned by Gable's character Dennis, who falls in love with his newly arrived surveyor's wife Barbara
(Mary Astor) although local prostitute Vantine (Jean) is in love with him and
a better match. It was a difficult shoot; to create an Indonesian rain forest, a
soundstage was filled with dirt and water and huge lamps used to create trop-
ical heat. The set smelled awful and was insufferably hot but Jean endured
the shoot without complaint, showing her sense of humor during a scene
bathing naked in a rain barrel and talking to Gable. In the middle of the scene
she stood up, bared her breasts and said, "Something for the boys in the lab!"
Director Fleming destroyed the film the moment it was removed from the
camera.[113]

Other than the San Francisco trip, for Paul and Jean August had passed
like any other month at work and at home with nothing out of the ordinary.
They shopped for the normal things. Paul bought tickets to the Olympics,
paintings from artist Oscar Strobel for $150, a suit at the May Department
Store, two dozen handkerchiefs from Bullock's, nine ties from Alexander &
Oviatt, seven of his beloved records from Barker Brothers, and a dozen books
from the Dora Ingram Bookstore.[114]

Jean paid $821 for four dresses and some hats from I. Magnin, $95
for a red satin pocketbook and handkerchiefs from Bullock's. Between
Thursday the 1st and Saturday the 3rd Paul had the equivalent of $200 in
groceries delivered to Easton. It was a normal weekend during a normal
month.

The evening of the 31st, Paul and Jean attended a dinner party at Sam

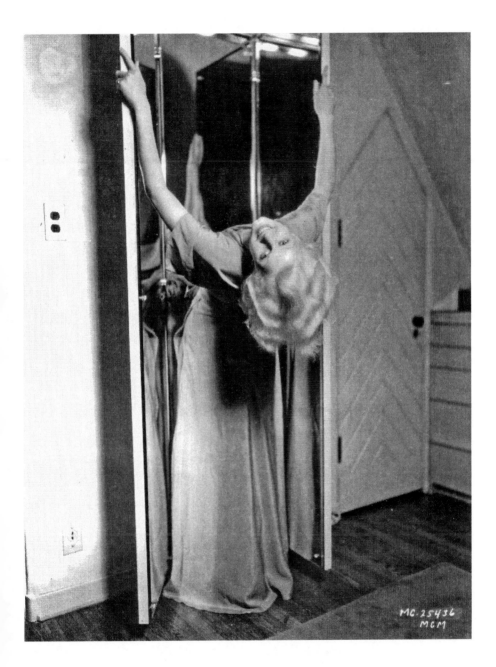

Jean in front of the triple mirror installed in her bedroom by Harold Grieve during the renovation of Easton prior to her arrival (from the Darrell Rooney collection).

Marx's Hollywood apartment with writer Sidney Skolsky and his wife. Marx recalled that Jean sat happily excited about her new stardom with Paul contentedly by her side. Paul told the group they had to leave because "my darling wife is due on the set at an ungodly hour." When Marie Marx gave Paul his expensive camel hair overcoat, she asked him why it was heavy. Paul told them he carried a pistol because "we live in a canyon, you know. It's to protect Jean."[115]

The next day, Thursday the 1st, Paul was visited at the studio by Dr. Harry Brandel for a physical required for an $85,000 life insurance policy purchased the week before (worth several million dollars today) that named Jean as beneficiary. Brandel found Paul "in the best of spirits and health" with "no medical deficiencies."[116] That night the couple went to the Miramar Hotel on the beach in Santa Monica, and happily danced until about 10:00.[117]

The next evening, Friday, they were joined at Easton for dinner by good friend Willis Goldbeck, who sat and chatted with Paul after Jean retired.

Saturday morning a letter addressed to Miss Dorothy Millette, from "Metro-Goldwyn-Mayer Studios, Culver City, California," arrived at the Plaza Hotel and was delivered to the quiet redhead who always dressed in dark blue, almost black. Inside was a check for $100. But she was not at her hotel. She was on her way to L.A.

❧ TEN ❧

Death and Disgrace

Monday

The comings and goings of Paul and Jean over the Labor Day weekend
are tangled in a mesh of conflicting stories, fictional studio accounts, outright
lies, and a little truth. We know Paul spent most of the weekend at Easton
while Jean was in and out of MGM and Club View. Not a soul close to
them—Blanche Williams, the Carmichaels, Clifton Davis, or any of their
friends—noticed any outward problems between the couple.

Paul worked Saturday and during the morning called Florence Eldridge
to beg off going to a birthday party she was having for Fredric March that
night, telling her he couldn't attend without Jean. Before leaving the studio,
he gave Irving his nine-page script revision for *China Seas*, which contained
a notable revision: In the final scene the hero dies in what is, in effect, a rit-
ual suicide.[1] The hero rescues his American girlfriend from Chinese pirateers
before admitting to his wayward life and returning to the Chinese clan from
which he had fled. In Paul's words:

> Within the house a different judgment is waiting for him. He has violated the
> Code—he has betrayed the secret of the Band. Stoically he goes back to the
> inner chamber where the others are gathered. He bares his arm ... submits to the
> torture—finally dying in [his Chinese girlfriend's] arms.

Paul's fade-out was an odd choice and not typical of him or MGM. Jean
was supposedly at the studio all day Saturday shooting *Red Dust*, though
Gable left that afternoon with Marino Bello to spend the weekend at a Mojave
Desert hideaway with two young women. They were engaged in a sport known
to studio men as "dove hunting." Jean told Paul her mother had asked her to
"keep her company" since Bello was gone and would stay at Club View.[2] As
he did every day, Paul stopped at the studio barber shop for a shave before

leaving. Bernie Hyman visited with him there and "Slickum" Garrison waited to drive Paul home.

Harold Allen Garrison was a fixture at MGM, a black man with a fourth-grade education who ran the studio shoeshine stand and chauffeured Irving and Paul. Paul often hired out from Tanner Limousine Service and when he did use Slickum he preferred being driven in his own black convertible coupe. At 7:10, Slickum drove him to the Ambassador where Paul was seen having drinks with a young woman before walking to one of the hotel's secluded bungalows, where they were joined by another man.

The man was his friend Hyman and the woman Hyman's mistress, actress Barbara Barondess. Paul was doing a favor helping Hyman facilitate his tryst with Barondess, and even put the charges for dinner, drinks, and the bungalow on his Ambassador charge (along with the telephone calls from the room).[3]

Paul left with Garrison at 9:30 and during the ride Paul said, "Well, Slickum, Mrs. Bern has to work tonight and I'm going to be lonesome. We were supposed to go to the Fredric March party but had to call it off." Slickum suggested going alone but Paul replied, "I wouldn't think of going without

Paul's Easton estate was beautiful, and quiet, that Labor Day Monday morning.

my darling wife." To Carey Wilson, who was supposed to attend the March party with Paul and Jean, he said, "You know Hollywood and its rumors. If I were to go and ... dance with an unattached girl, they'd have a triangle story out in no time."[4]

Arriving at Easton a little after 10:00, Paul told Garrison he had a lot of reading to do and said, "Slickum, it was a lovely ride. Be back at 9:30 tomorrow morning."[5]

Garrison was back Sunday morning but Paul was sleeping after a late night reading scripts, his habit on the weekends. Garrison waited in the shade of the turnaround for several hours, venturing up to the house a few times to get coffee or food from Winifred Carmichael and hearing Jean call several times. In the middle of the afternoon, Clifton Davis finally told him Paul wouldn't need him.

Paul arose in the afternoon as Jean returned from MGM. John Carmichael heard Paul puttering around upstairs and was in the house while Jean was there. She was returning to Club View for dinner and would stay there again; Paul said he had a headache and would try to join her there later.

It's difficult to know exactly what happened during the next 24 hours because everyone's stories kept changing. The Carmichaels, Blanche Williams, and Clifton Davis would all lie. During the next week, all four spoke to reporters and police and testified at a coroner's inquest, and then six months later testified before a grand jury looking into the events of the weekend. The discrepancies between the tales offer the real story of Labor Day at Easton; their contradictions tell us what actually took place.

The story begins with conflicting versions of Jean's departure from Easton on Sunday. On Monday the inner circle — the Carmichaels, Davis, and Blanche — told reporters the weekend was uneventful, ending with Jean going to Club View for dinner Sunday night. But by Tuesday afternoon they were describing a loud argument between Paul and Jean, after which she supposedly ran crying from the house on her way to Club View.

John Carmichael and Davis both claimed the argument arose from Jean's insistence that Bello be allowed to mortgage Easton for some treasure hunt, against Paul's wishes. Jean's ambivalence about the secluded estate may have been real but it wasn't an issue. It's also impossible to believe Jean siding with Bello — who she disliked for many legitimate reasons — in that situation. Blanche said a distraught Jean emerged and said, "He doesn't want me here" before leaving.

However, during interviews and later grand jury testimony, the Carmichaels said Jean left on good terms Sunday, telling Paul, "In case you don't come over, good night dear," and he replying, "Well, I will be seeing you, dear."[6] Bello also testified the couple never fought and he never mentioned hearing Jean's comment to Blanche. Those statements also contradict Blanche's story about Jean crying that Paul did not want her there.

Blanche also contradicted herself, later saying she overheard the Sunday fight while waiting at the car with the person who drove her to Easton, Marino Bello. Bello did drive to Easton, but not Sunday. He drove on Saturday. On Sunday he was in the desert with Clark Gable and had been since the day before. That's why Bello wouldn't remember Jean telling Blanche — who was allegedly standing with him — that Paul didn't "want me here." Lastly, on Saturday when Blanche *was* there with Bello, Paul *wasn't*. He was being driven to the Ambassador, so Blanche couldn't have heard a fight Saturday.

Most important, Paul didn't need an excuse to *force* Jean to leave Sunday; she was already going to spend the night at Club View anyway. Telling Blanche "he doesn't want me here" makes no sense. Jean wasn't staying at Easton anyway. There was no fight.

It quickly became impossible for the Carmichaels, Davis, and Blanche to keep their lies straight. They were simple people and were scared. They had never faced this type of pressure and were trying to follow orders from MGM. Jean's was the only story that never changed, not an iota.

John Carmichael's most blatant lie was that he took Jean from Eaton to Club View at 8:00 or 9:00 Sunday night. We know John took Jean to Club View and that Winifred remained at Easton preparing the Club View dinner and was taken there by Davis later, but John lied about the departure. It was closer to 5:00. Jean ate meals on a strict schedule and never ate late at night. Leaving at 9:00 means Winifred wouldn't be serving dinner at Club View until well after 10:00. Mama Jean said that Jean called Paul to see if he would join them (he declined, saying he had a headache). She wouldn't expect Paul for dinner at 10:30 or 11:00 and as an aside, if they had a fight, why invite him to dinner? Winifred later told the grand jury she left Easton a little after 5:00, forgetting her original story and contradicting her husband's.

So now we know John Carmichael and Jean were gone by about 5:00 on Sunday. Later inquest testimony confirmed that fact and pointed to *why* she was gone. Waiting to take Winifred to Club View, Davis was picking up the yard when a limousine pulled into the turnaround. Winifred came down the path from the main house after leaving a piece of Jean's favorite devil's food cake on the bed (with a note "from your staunchest admirer") and also saw the big car arrive. They both watched a smallish woman with big high heels exit the limousine dressed in black from head to toe and wearing a veil. They'd never seen her before.[7]

Why *did* Jean go to Club View again Sunday night? She left Easton because she knew Paul was expecting company. Dorothy was coming. For months and years Paul kept her at bay, ignoring her strident entreaties and

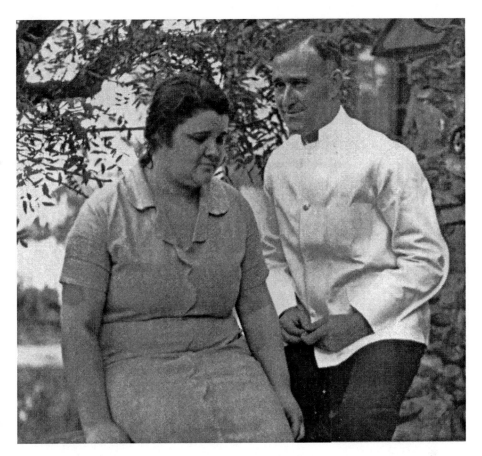

Winifred and John Carmichael, Paul's cook and butler, were both used by MGM to spread false stories about Paul's activities during Labor Day weekend.

threats, trying to prevent her from interrupting their lives. Paul and Jean, together or separately, made one final attempt to keep her away during their mysterious trips to San Francisco just two weeks earlier but those efforts were for naught. In a few hours, Dorothy would be there, so Jean left.

We'll probably never know exactly what happened at Easton on Sunday night. The surviving version was created during the next few days and went unquestioned for 40 years. But during the next 30 years that account has become increasingly less believable.

Monday morning was a beautiful California day, a sunny and warm Labor Day. The Carmichaels awoke early and began their normal duties. They would tell police they spent Sunday night at their West Hollywood apartment and came to Easton in the morning. Winifred walked up to the

The windows in the corner of Paul's bedroom let the cool canyon breezes in. They were all open when John Carmichael arrived for work Monday morning.

main house to start the coffee, passing the pool and entering through the back kitchen door behind the turret. From the kitchen she could not see down the hall into the still dark master bedroom.

John followed a few minutes later and let himself into the master bedroom. He said the house "seemed terribly quiet. I tiptoed into his bedroom. It was empty. Then I stepped into the dressing alcove to turn up the blind, and stumbled over his body."[8] Looking down, he saw something he later described as "quite pitiful."[9] In a large pool of coagulated blood, Paul was lying naked, crumpled in a heap on the floor facing the wall outside his dressing room. Part of the side of his head was missing and his hair was soaked and matted with dried blood. Large bloodstains and bits of brain dotted the wall and ceiling. An arched trail of blood on the wall traced the path of Paul's body as it fell to the floor. There was a hole in the wall near the ceiling with blood and bits of brain stuck to it. One of his two guns was in the middle of the floor, perhaps 12 feet from the body. Carmichael fainted dead away and fell to the floor next to Paul.

Hearing a thud, Winifred came into the bedroom and quickly retreated, running out the front door screaming for Clifton Davis to come up to the house. When he saw the two bodies he thought Carmichael was also dead. But John was moaning and Davis helped him away from the "gruesome" scene.[10]

Winifred called Mama Jean and managed to blurt out that Paul was dead. Without telling her daughter, Mama Jean called Mayer and woke him up at his Santa Monica house. Mayer's first thought was that Jean killed Paul but he put that aside and jump-started MGM's protection machinery. He called studio police chief Richard (Whitey) Hendry and publicity director Howard Strickling and they gathered a crew to keep whatever happened at Paul's house quiet and contained, at least for the moment. Mayer then got dressed and left for Easton, telling his wife to call the Thalbergs down the beach.

Hendry called Al Cohn, a writer who monitored police wires, and told him to call if there were any reports of Paul's death. Right away Cohn called his friend Sam Marx, who he knew was friendly with Paul, waking him up saying, "Just thought you'd like to know your friend Paul Bern has been found dead up in his house. Don't tell anyone where you heard it." He then abruptly hung up. Driving toward Benedict Canyon, Marx noticed the time. It was a little after 9:00.[11]

Strickling called Virgil Apger, a 28-year-old MGM still photographer who lived at the Shotwell Arms Apartments on La Salle near downtown, and told him to meet Hendry at the studio at once. Apger left without asking why and when he arrived at Culver City he and Hendry were driven to Easton by Slickum Garrison. Apger knew the place; he did several photo shoots of Paul and Jean there. They arrived the same time as Mayer and the three went inside.

Margaret Mayer called Thalberg, who became so upset by the news that Norma thought it might kill him. He called David Selznick, and Irene heard her husband cry in anguish, "Irving? My God! No! When? Oh, God, no!" She yelled out, "It's Paul. He's killed himself! I will kill her!" Like Mayer, she instinctively blamed Jean. The distraught Irene stayed in bed for a week.[12] Selznick joined Irving and Norma in the Thalberg limousine for the trip to Easton.

When the Thalbergs and Selznick arrived, Hendry and Mayer were inside with Strickling and Apger. He took several rolls of pictures of everything from Paul's body to detritus by the pool and gave them to Strickling, wondering why he was there instead of a police photographer. After he gave the film up, he never saw it again.[13] Selznick couldn't even get out of the limou-

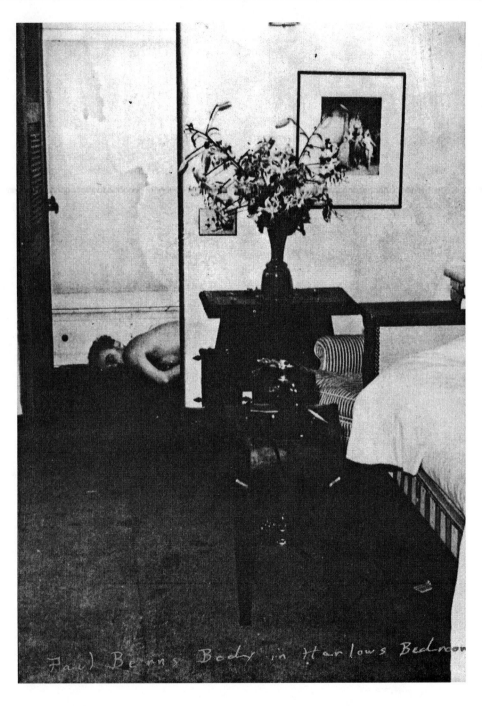

Carmichael tripped over Paul, lying on the floor just outside his closet in the changing room near his bed. He immediately fainted dead away.

sine, staying there with Norma. Thalberg went as far as the patio by the front door but couldn't bring himself to go inside and see Paul's body. He sat quietly on the stone fence, at the same spot where Jean sat on Paul's lap for a post-wedding photo by Apger just a few months before.

When Sam Marx arrived around 9:30, he noticed the limousines of Thalberg and Strickling in the turn-around among several smaller cars. Walking up the path, he found Thalberg sitting on the fence talking to Clifton Davis. Thalberg was surprised to see Marx and Marx surprised that Mayer was not there. Thalberg said he had gone to Club View to see Jean.[14]

A few minutes later, Slavko Vorkapich, who lived across from Paul's driveway and did special effects work at MGM, walked up the path and joined Thalberg, Marx, and Davis. Told of Paul's death, he sat down stunned next to Thalberg and told the men what he heard during the night. It was loud, a man and a woman alternately laughing and yelling, obviously having an ugly fight by the pool. He had earlier seen a woman arrive in a limousine, dressed in black and wearing a veil, and was awoken later by the car spewing gravel as it sped down the hill at "45 miles an hour and skidding 200 feet at the bottom of the hill. It was almost 3:00."[15] Thalberg took Vorkapich aside and the two chatted, after which Vorkapich walked back down the hill. Thalberg suggested that Marx also leave, which he did.

Inside, standing over Paul's body, Strickling, Mayer and Hendry faced a momentous decision. They knew several things. That Dorothy was at Easton the night before; the limousine that brought her there was hired through the MGM Transportation Department. That Paul and Dorothy were technically married and had never divorced, making his marriage to Jean bigamous. That Dorothy was pressuring Paul and blackmailing him. That Paul was murdered by Dorothy. And that the scandal would tarnish Jean, whether she was a murder suspect or had entered into a bigamous marriage, and that her career and millions of MGM dollars would be gone. What to do?

They had to make decisions quickly; the news was already leaking. Douglas Fairbanks, Jr., called the house asking if he should come but was told to stay away.[16] After combing the house, Strickling calmly detailed the potential problems facing MGM. Hendry, a former detective and Culver City police chief, recognized a murder immediately, telling a friend, "Hell, I knew it was a murder the minute I saw it. He was lying in the closet and the gun was on the floor halfway across the room. Whoever killed him threw it there. It didn't walk there!" Strickling had to separate Jean from the death and Hendry suggested they arrange the scene to look like a suicide. Mayer said, "Do what you have to do" and left to go to Jean.[17]

Mayer stumbled on the linchpin of a suicide narrative while absent-mindedly thumbing through Paul's green leather guestbook by the front door.

There were notes from Margaret de Mille, Gary Cooper, Lupe Velez, Carey Wilson and Carmelita Geraghty, Jack Gilbert, Selznick and even his (Mayer's) own daughter Irene.[18] The last entry was "Paul Carey," which may have been a note from Carey Wilson.[19] On the 13th page — not the last page but in the middle — he allegedly found a note that read:

> Dearest Dear,
>   Unfortuately [sic] this is the only way to make good the frightful wrong I have done you and wipe out my abject humiliation. I love you.
> Paul
>
>   You understand that last night was only a comedy

Mayer thought the note sounded damning, tore it from the book and put it in his pocket. He later mentioned it to Strickling, who realized its value supporting a plausible suicide story. He replaced it from where it had been torn and moved the book to Paul's bedroom.

Hendry and Strickling had several pressing needs. First they had to stage the scene to appear that Paul's death was a planned suicide, not spur of the moment. Second, Strickling had to direct the press reporting, an easy task with his long partnership with the press and the Hearst relationship. Lastly, Strickling and Hendry would use their contacts with police and D.A. Buron Fitts' office to ensure that neither ventured too close to the truth.

There was plenty to use in the bedroom: the confusing note, the gun, and a body. They turned Paul around to face away from the wall and Hendry wiped the gun clean of fingerprints and tried to place it in Paul's right hand. But the body was in advanced rigor mortis and the arm tucked under his chest, so Hendry could only jam it awkwardly into his palm. Surviving photos show the strange position of the gun. Paul's guestbook was placed on the bureau, conspicuously next to Paul's other pistol.[20]

They needed a reason for Jean to be at Club View so leaked a rumor that Paul forced her to leave by starting a fight. "Last night's comedy." They also needed Jean's cooperation in a campaign against Paul. Strickling, Mayer, and Thalberg all separately claimed they went to tell her. Strickling, the least prone to hyperbole, told Marx, "After Paul's suicide I went to Jean at her mother's house and said, 'Jean, tell me everything so I can help you.'"[21] That probably took place later; he spent all morning at Easton with Hendry.

When Marx first arrived, Irving told him Mayer already left to go to Jean. Mayer described Jean's hysterics upon hearing the news and of saving her from trying to "join Paul" by throwing herself off the balcony to "the rocky chasm below" her bedroom. Mayer's oft-repeated story could not have taken place. There *were* no balconies and no "rocky chasm," just the small court-yard 10 feet below her window.

We know Irving went to Club View with Norma, who again waited in the car (with Selznick). Irving wanted Jean to make sense of the note, which he took with him. Norma said she watched as he told Jean and said she saw a figure from the waist down "in a pale negligee and slippers" who "almost collapsed and was led back into the house."[22] But she couldn't have seen that; the limousine was below Club View on the street, making such a view impossible. Jean provided Irving no motive, no reason, and no understanding of the note. Overcome by shock and grief, she paced the living room and repeated over and over, "This is too terrible, too horrible." That was all she would say.

The cryptic comment found by Louis B. Mayer and identified as Paul's farewell even though there was no proof of such.

Jean offered nothing to help MGM with their media scourging of Paul, flatly refusing to have anything to do with it. She never spoke with them about Paul's death. Blanche Williams took charge and called Jean's doctor, Harold Barnard, who came and sedated both Jean and her mother, also close to a breakdown. A shaken Irving returned to Easton. They could now call police.

At 2:50 in the afternoon, Officer C.E. Childs took a call from Irving at the West L.A. police station reporting a suicide and asking to "please send someone and do it as quickly and quietly as possible." About 15 minutes later, detectives Joe Whitehead and Thomas Sketchley arrived at Easton, more than six hours after the MGM cabal first arrived. During that period, Strickling's press contacts had been busy. As police pulled up to Easton, papers were already running extra editions reporting Paul's "suicide."[23]

To the detectives, the scene appeared to be a straightforward suicide but they wondered about the crowd of MGM people at the house and how the large mob of reporters and photographers crowding Easton learned about the death. Whitehead found two .38-caliber handguns, a Colt automatic (no. 40739) in the dead man's hand, and a Colt pistol (no. 572972) on the bureau. Next to the second gun on the bureau was a "diary containing note." He did not notice the gun's strange position but was troubled by the conflicting sto-

ries from the MGM people, the Carmichaels, and Clifton Davis, who was
telling anyone who would listen about the big fight by the pool the night
before.

Only then was the pool area searched. Next to Paul's favorite lounge chair
near the house they found an empty bottle of champagne, a crystal champagne flute and, scattered among the flagstones, pieces of a second broken
glass. Winifred Carmichael had been snooping around and found a yellow
bathing suit hanging near Paul's body, still damp, and too large for Jean.
Clearly the dead man had a visitor and *something* happened by the pool.

At about 4:00, Whitehead released the body and attendants from Price-
Daniel Funeral Home carried it down the path on a stretcher and loaded it
into a hearse surrounded by a phalanx of photographers. The body was taken
to the mortuary on Sawtelle Avenue in Culver City. The crowd of reporters
remained all night at Easton and camped out in front of Club View, where
Slickum Garrison sat in a parked car with two friends, "negroes [who] looked
threateningly at newspapermen who continually watched the place."[24]

A heavily sedated Jean slept while her lawyer Oscar Cummins, MGM
lawyer Mendel Silberberg, and Howard Strickling kept vigil downstairs.

Paul's body is carried down the hill and placed in a waiting mortuary truck.

Strickling ordered Bello and Clark Gable back from their desert hideaway. Gable could not be seen socializing with Bello, who arrived at Club View late Monday afternoon.[25] He lied and said he had been deep-sea fishing.

By late Monday it was clear the police and the press needed a better story. There were too many nagging inconsistencies, and worse, Jean was whispered to be a killer hiding in silence at Club View. MGM faced a dilemma. It was one thing to stage a suicide but quite another to convince everyone it took place, and in this case that Jean had nothing to do with it. If she was tied to any of this, her earning power at MGM would dry up.

To address the multi-million dollar problem Mayer called a Monday night meeting at his office with Strickling, Mannix, Irving, and Irving's men Thau, Rapf, Stromberg, and Arlie Lewin. That afternoon, Mayer received a telegram from his personal physician Edward B. Jones, who cabled from Hawaii: **UNDERSTAND SUICIDE MOTIVE. WILL RETURN AT ONCE IF NEEDED TO TESTIFY.** During a 20-minute radiophone conversation, Jones volunteered that Paul might have had "a terrific mental depression" from a "lack of marital relations."[26] That became MGM's solution: Paul was impotent, sexually inadequate, and depressed because he couldn't have sex with his beautiful wife. Jean would be off the hook.

Thalberg wanted MGM to hire private investigators to find out what happened to Paul but Mayer told the group — some didn't know Dorothy was at Easton — that Paul had done the right thing by killing himself because they all *knew* he was homosexual and impotent. There were bitter disagreements. Arlie Lewin told Mayer he knew Paul was neither impotent nor homosexual and Irving, appalled at the repulsive lie, backed him up. Mayer became so out of control he threatened to kill Irving if he didn't go along, and finally wore down an exhausted Irving, who agreed. Like Jean, he went along only to the extent that Mayer's lies weren't exposed. Neither ever publicly supported the stories. That night, Strickling began the second murder of Paul Bern, now said to be sexually dysfunctional.

Before boarding the S.S. *Monterey* to return to L.A., Dr. Jones told reporters he "understood the motive" for the supposed suicide and said, "There isn't any doubt that Bern's death was suicide. I am all broken up over it, because he was one of the finest fellows I ever knew and there wasn't any reason for him to do it."[27]

Monday night, Henry Bern prepared to board a Transcontinental and Western Airlines plane in Newark, New Jersey, for a two-day trip to L.A., his first-ever airplane trip. He told reporters it was "utterly ridiculous" that Paul killed himself after a quarrel and the "Bern family is not satisfied with published explanations of the tragedy" and "wanted to hear first-hand the stories."[28] After a layover in Jean's family home of Kansas City, he would arrive Wednesday.

Tuesday

Tuesday morning the quiet woman in high heels (whom maids had noticed was gone all weekend) ventured to the lobby of the Plaza Hotel in San Francisco and bought a copy of every newspaper on the rack. Every front page was plastered with stories about Paul's death.

At MGM, the first order of business was that *Red Dust* production continued uninterrupted. Mayer actually approached Joan Crawford and asked her to take over Jean's role, but she refused because she thought it would be in poor taste. Shooting was rearranged and scenes were filmed that didn't require Jean. The studio hoped "production won't be held up appreciably before the little platinum blonde is able to return to work."[29]

Paul's death — THE STORY THAT ROCKED HOLLYWOOD! — was front-page news everywhere. At first the stories were fairly clinical, details of the scene and the bizarre note, Jean's grief and the obvious shock in the movie colony. There were photos of the couple, of Easton, and of Paul's bedroom with an "X" on the spot where the body laid.[30]

Most of the initial stories became testimonials to Paul. Edwin Schallert wrote, "The death of Paul Bern strikes deep into the heart of the motion-picture colony." But there were early signs of Strickling's burgeoning smear campaign. Hollywood writers were eager to trade coveted star interviews or photo shoots in exchange for running his fictions. In late Tuesday papers, Paul was described by "un-named" friends as morbidly suicidal, the "the sixth member of his immediate family to commit suicide" and "time and time again, he discussed the possibility of ... solving his problems with self-destruction." He was said to have an "unhappy viewpoint on life" from his allegedly poverty-ridden childhood; David Selznick described him as "a student of suicide."[31] There were also small mentions of a purported fight between Paul and Jean.

MGM released a John Gilbert allegation that he saved Paul from killing himself after Barbara La Marr died, but the "circumstances ... are too close to my heart for me to discuss them now.... Paul Bern was my best friend. And if he thought that this was the time for him to go, it is not for me to criticize him."[32]

Hundreds of Hearst newspapers said LOUELLA PARSONS SAYS DEATH OF PAUL BERN DUE TO SUICIDAL MANIA. She liked Paul and called him "the soul of kindness" and "one of the finest men in the industry" but still wrote that Jean married him out of "gratitude." Interestingly, MGM attorney Ralph Blum denied there had been any suicides in Paul's family.[33]

Magazine writer Marcella Burke offered a jealousy motive, saying Jean complained, "Paul is insanely jealous of me. It must stop."[34] Jones' UNDERSTAND MOTIVE telegram was leaked and he and "others blamed Bern's melancholia for his act."[35] These themes — depression, unhappy marriage, a long suicidal obsession, and a fight with Jean — would be amplified over the coming days to impugn Paul and keep attention away from Jean.

At 10:00 Tuesday morning at Price-Daniel, assistant autopsy surgeon Frank R. Webb and county coroner Frank A. Nance began the autopsy on Paul's body. Nance found a close-contact bullet wound to Paul's right temple two inches in front of the right ear — "a typical suicide wound" — with gunpowder residue around the entrance wound, inside the scalp and inside the skull. The bullet traveled slightly up and to the left and exited two inches above the left ear, leaving a large exit wound. The weapon was held close to the head. The only other physical attribute noted was that Paul had "underdeveloped" genitals for a 42-year-old man.

The nature of injury and cause of death was "gun shot [*sic*] wound of head" and the death ruled a suicide. Nance then released the body and filed the L.A. County Standard Certificate of Death.[36] The informant was not Jean but MGM business manager Martin Greenwood.

Paul's underdeveloped sexual organs became the smoking gun that tied MGM's story with a bow. Nance made no assertion whether size affected sexual activities, but a rumor was nonetheless planted that this "physical handicap" would "prevent a happy marriage," and that Paul was a "mental giant but a physical stripling."[37] MGM then suggested that Paul was impotent and that his marriage to Jean was "platonic," a fraud also perpetrated on her.

MGM got help from the autopsy but trouble was brewing with police and D.A. Buron Fitts. Chief of detectives Joseph Taylor said "he felt that discrepancies existed in versions of the apparent suicide and wanted to know why police were left out of the case for so long a period after discovery of the body."[38] His detectives were turned away when they attempted to see Jean at Club View Monday night and Tuesday morning.

Tuesday midday, Fitts told Mayer that Clifton Davis, Slickum Garrison and the Carmichaels were ready to admit they lied at MGM's direction, that he knew about Vorkapich and was aware that Dorothy was at Easton. Worse, he would indict Jean for murder. It was probably just the first step in a choreographed process of demanding bribes, a system in place for years. Mayer told Jean if she didn't support the story that Paul was impotent, she would be indicted but she still flatly refused, so Strickling, Hendry, Bello, and MGM lawyers Silberberg and Ralph Blum met in Mayer's office so Hendry could call his old friend Blaney Matthews, chief of Fitts' Investigative Division.[39]

Speaking a language clearly understood by the two, Hendry promised Matthews "full and complete cooperation on the part of MGM studio in any investigation into those recent matters of concern...." Saying "I knew I could count on you" and making a circle with his thumb and finger, everyone in the room knew Fitts had just been paid to stay away from Jean.

She was at Club View surrounded by hundreds of reporters massed on the terraced yard and on the sidewalks. Strickling visited at 1:00 P.M. and every half-hour a messenger brought a parcel with some of the 200 telegrams that arrived Tuesday. Bello enjoyed the spotlight and ventured out every hour or so to speak with reporters. Occasionally the furious barking of Jean's Great Dane "Bleak" stopped a reporter from sneaking into the backyard.

There was nothing too worrisome to MGM in the papers but things were starting to come apart at Easton. Reporters hounded Davis and the Carmichaels and heard from John Carmichael, "He loved his wife. Yes, I guess he loved her almost too much. And she loved him. There were presents, candy and flowers.... He brought them when he was late for dinner and he would always come in and kiss her, apologizing for being late." He also repeated that the couple parted on Sunday without rancor, that "she went to his room, where he was in bed, and said, 'Goodnight, dear, in case you don't come over.'... He said, 'Goodnight, dear,' and we left."[40]

Tuesday afternoon, Clifton Davis was at the *Photoplay* offices in Hollywood talking about the limousine and about a second note he claimed to have read, one taken by Thalberg and "more sensational than the 'abject humiliation' message."[41] Strickling had Bello call Davis and tell him, "You are talking too much. Move your wife and children over to the garage and keep your damned mouth shut."[42]

Strickling could shut up the Carmichaels and Davis but was powerless to stop Slavko Vorkapich and his wife from talking. She told reporters about the "large, expensive limousine [that] dashed away from the Bern home at three o'clock Monday morning." Tuesday afternoon papers announced AUTO NEAR JEAN HARLOW'S HOME ADDS TO MYSTERY, asking, "Who was in the car?"[43]

After lunch Tuesday, Dorothy left the Plaza briefly to pay $10.50 for a pair of shoes and an extra 50¢ to have lifts added to the heels. She returned to her room and spent the afternoon reading her newspapers. At 4:00 she appeared at the front desk in her usual dark blue dress, paid her $25.89 hotel bill with a personal check drawn on an L.A. bank and quietly checked out. Before leaving, she placed a wardrobe trunk and a large handbag in hotel storage. Inside the handbag was a packet of letters — all from Paul — neatly wrapped in a folded piece of blotter paper and tied with a ribbon. She left no forwarding address, nor did she make arrangements to recover her luggage.[44]

She took a taxi to Pier 3 and purchased a round-trip ticket to Sacramento on the *Delta King*, signing "Dorothy Millette."[45] Every night at 6:00 P.M. the 285-foot stern-wheel riverboat left for a 10-hour, 125-mile trip offering lively bars and jazz bands, gambling and gourmet dining. The ship had three levels: the topmost California Deck with large hotel stateroom suites, the Observation Deck's slightly smaller suites, and the Promenade Deck's staterooms.[46] Inside, the lower level and the uppermost Observation Deck were connected by a grand staircase made of hand-rubbed oak, mahogany, and teak.

Dorothy's California Deck stateroom #304 was toward the back of the ship and cost $3.50. At 6:30 the *Delta King* eased away from the pier and churned east across San Francisco Bay, passing below the Sausalito hills and through the San Pablo Bay to travel the Sacramento–San Joaquin River "Delta Route" to Sacramento via the Sacramento River. Dorothy didn't feel well; just before the *Delta King* left, she rang the bell for porter Paul Cantor and said she had a severe headache and was sick to her stomach so he gave her bromide headache powders.[47]

MGM could no longer prevent the police from seeing Jean after they obtained a subpoena to speak to her Tuesday.[48] Tuesday evening at 6:00, detectives David Davidson and Frank Condaffer and chief of detectives Joe Taylor were led to Jean's bedroom where she was surrounded by Mayer, Strick-

Dorothy boarded the *Delta King* in San Francisco, bound for Sacramento. Her cabin was just to the left of the top of the stairwell on the right, between the second and third decks.

ling, lawyer Silberberg, and her doctor Harold Barnard. Still heavily sedated
and almost incoherent, she alternately moaned and sobbed through the meeting.

She repeated her weekend chronology: After work Sunday she stopped
at Easton before going to Club View for a pre-arranged dinner but Paul stayed
home because he had a headache and told her during a later phone call that
he was still ill and would remain there and see her in the morning. She told
them, "I can't understand why this terrible thing should have happened," and
when pressed repeatedly for a motive she cried, "I don't know. I don't know."[49]

She continued her non-support of MGM's story, and about the alleged
suicide note said, "I have no idea what it means. This 'frightful wrong' Paul
thought he'd done to me is all a mystery. I can't imagine what it means." She
told them he never once mentioned suicide and "there was nothing between
us that I can think of that would have caused him to do this."[50] Reiterating
a final time that she last spoke to Paul on the phone Sunday evening, she burst
into uncontrollable tears as the interview ended.

By then the L.A. police were as harmless to MGM as the D.A. Whitehead photographed the two guns and said his camera was not strong enough
to identify fingerprints but somehow vouched that "he thought fingerprints on
both guns tallied with those of the dead executive."[51] They ignored the items
at the pool, the woman's bathing suit, and the mysterious limousine seen by
Davis and Slavko Vorkapich even though it had been mentioned in the papers.

As detectives were leaving from their visit with Jean, Henry Bern arrived
in Kansas City, where he would stay overnight before continuing to L.A.
Wednesday morning. Speaking with reporters at the Hotel Muehlebach, he
became livid when asked about Paul's rumored impotence. He denied it and
shocked those assembled by offering proof, saying that Paul "lived with a
woman once, a long time ago. She became deranged and he placed her in a
sanitarium where she was given the best of care. It was an open secret he never
tried to hide. Miss Harlow knew of it because Paul told her, as did many of
his friends. He concealed nothing, he lived openly. Nothing was misrepre-
sented when he married Miss Harlow; I know this," adding, "She is alive. I
will reveal her identity later."[52]

Henry's comments were a blow to MGM. Reporters pounced on his
mystery woman. By Wednesday morning, what Strickling and MGM had
known for years would be public: The woman was long-time Algonquin Hotel
resident Mrs. Paul Bern, who said her maiden name was Dorothy Millette
and who received twice-a-month checks from MGM.

MGM put off addressing Dorothy's existence, lawyer Blum saying they
would "announce something definite concerning Paul Bern's previous marriage status within 24 hours. We are beginning to investigate reports that Paul

Bern had provided for women said to be his wife."[53] They were planting a seed with a question. Could Paul have married other *women*?

At about 8:30 the *Delta King* was east of San Francisco after passing through the San Pablo Bay into the Suisan Bay and the Sacramento River. Dorothy appeared in the dining room and, after paying 75¢ for fruit cocktail, spaghetti, and ice cream and eating quickly, she returned to her room. Her waiter Lorenzo O'Hare said she appeared very nervous and ill. After returning to her cabin, she again rang for porter Paul Cantor and again asked for something for a bad headache. He gave her more bromide powder.[54] After 9:30 she was not seen again by any of the crew.

Steward John Lee checked the decks every hour and did not see her, even as the ship made its scheduled 2:00 A.M. stop at Rio Vista, about halfway up the Sacramento River to Sacramento. But as Walnut Grove lumberman Henry Karrick disembarked at 2:30 he looked up to the topmost Observation Deck and saw "a very beautiful woman [with] pretty hair and pretty eyes, who seemed to be quite nervous." The woman in the black dress walked "clear around the boat and didn't seem to notice anyone. She seemed to have her eyes off in the distance." She was fretfully pacing, wringing her hands, and running them through her hair.[55]

When Lee checked the area near the ship's stern at 4:45, he found a pair of shoes outside #304 and a black coat on the deck at the bottom of the stairwell leading to the deck below. The shoes were new, from a store in San Francisco, and had lifts in the heels. The clothes were not there when Lee checked that deck at 4:15 but he thought nothing of it; it was after all, a party boat, and "strange things happened during Prohibition."[56]

Wednesday

Wednesday morning, a letter arrived at the Plaza Hotel addressed to "Miss Dorothy Millette" bearing the logo of Metro-Goldwyn Mayer Studio in Culver City. Inside was a polite letter from "Irene Harrison, Secretary to Paul Bern," and a check for $160.

The *Delta King* arrived in Sacramento at 7:00 A.M. and the passengers disembarked. Remembering the clothing found on deck, the crew contacted Lawrence McKim, the River Lines' general passenger agent in Sacramento, to report that someone might have gone overboard during the night. The crew didn't know from which cabin the person might have come.

Sacramento police waited until the ship emptied to check cabins. Ship's Captain W.J. Atthog[57] showed detectives where the coat and shoes were found. They conjectured that a jumper would leap from the bottom, not the top, since the topmost deck was inset; jumping from there meant throwing yourself some 15 feet out from the rail. From the lower level there was only a low railing to prevent a 40-foot drop to the water.

Stateroom #304 was inspected at 9:30. "D. Millette" could have left the ship in Rio Vista or Sacramento but her belongings were scattered about the room. The bed was only slightly mussed and police found a traveling bag, a purse containing $38, some cosmetics and a key to the bag. Inside the bag were some expensive dresses with New York labels matching the coat found on deck and an empty yellow rubber bathing suit bag that seemed to be part of a matched set.

The crew and detectives paid little attention to the name "Dorothy Millette," unaware that she was the object of a frantic nationwide search. All they knew was that she probably jumped into the river between Rio Vista and Sacramento in the predawn darkness.

The MGM campaign against Paul was ratcheted up on Wednesday with more stories of recurring melancholia and unsubstantiated and anonymous comments that Paul "became a changed man since his recent marriage," that he was a "recluse ... and some burden apparently occupied his mind." Bello now said that Paul "suffered several nervous breakdowns recently [due to] overwork." For the first time it was mentioned that "the couple had quarreled last Sunday night...." Worse, now Paul was alleged to have "threatened his bride." And, incredibly, Slickum Garrison said Paul asked him two weeks earlier, "[If] you wanted to commit suicide, how would you do it?" He also supposedly said, "Would you shoot yourself?"[58]

Autopsy notes were leaked that the coroner noticed "certain subnormal physiological characteristics" on Paul's body, a point Mayer would use with Dr. Jones' bogus depression story to use impotence as a suicide motive. Tuesday, after detectives left Jean, he had argued vehemently she had to tell the press that her marriage wasn't consummated but she flatly refused and told him there was nothing wrong with their marriage. Jean wouldn't have anything to do with defaming Paul. Mayer and MGM would have to do it themselves.

Unrepentant liar Mayer made up stories every time he spoke to reporters, saying Paul often spoke of suicide, that "his demeanor during the week before he killed himself changed entirely," that he had been acting "strangely ... had a queerest look about his eyes ... had something preying on his mind."[59] The helpful Jones diagnosed "acute melancholia" due to a "physical condition" that made Paul "unfit for matrimony."[60]

Even more bizarre falsehoods arose. Paul was alleged to have soaked himself in Jean's favorite Brise Ambrée perfume before killing himself. The number of his family members who were suicide victims grew from one to as many as eight (siblings, aunts, uncles, cousins, or grandparents). He was alleged to have paid to change Henriette's death certificate from "suicide" to "accident," which wasn't possible for Paul at the time. Most egregious, he was said to be a sexual deviate who physically abused Jean.

MGM enlisted employees to malign Paul and suddenly actors and directors were offering psychoanalysis or said they "knew" he was impotent. John Gilbert, who supported the party line in a misguided effort to save his career, said of his best friend, "Paul once told me that ... 'I would not hesitate to snuff out the candle.'" David Selznick said that Paul "often showed me books he collected on the subject of suicide" and that Paul said, "A man should be ready to kill himself if he has outlived his usefulness." Lothar Mendes opined that Paul's "delicately balanced sense of life gave way."[61]

Blanche Williams was recruited to volunteer that Paul actually told her the morning after the wedding, "Baby's still a virgin."[62] It's ludicrous to think he would make that comment to the maid, particularly since he was certainly aware of Jean's abortions, boyfriends, and first marriage.

Opinions were solicited from people who barely knew Paul. From London, actress Lady June Inverclyde, who only saw Paul at a few parties, offered, "As charming as Paul was, one could not help noticing that he was morbidly inclined. He talked lengthily about suicide and discussed methods of killing oneself ... I looked upon him definitely as a dual personality."[63] Even anonymous people were quoted, one unnamed Malibu woman saying Paul told her, "'There are too many dead people walking around already. When life becomes futile, it should be ended.' That's the last thing I ever heard him say. Please don't quote me."[64]

Strickling's pal Adela Rogers St. Johns became the primary source of unfounded and malicious stories, leaking the coroner's observation about Paul's underdeveloped genitals and then creating and embellishing a half dozen fictions regarding Barbara La Marr. She first said the "deformity" was why La Marr never married Paul; that La Marr supposedly said, "Paul has no right to marry any woman...." To support her lies, she said Leatrice Joy said that Paul's penis was "smaller than my pinkie."[65]

Then she fabricated a ridiculous story that when La Marr married Jack Dougherty, Paul tried to kill himself by drowning himself in the toilet, saved only by the intervention of his housemates Jack Gilbert and Carey Wilson. She would later further embellish the yarn by saying a plumber had to come to remove Paul's head from the toilet seat. But she didn't know that Paul arranged the wedding, was there when they married, and planned the reception. Another problem is St. Johns' timing; when La Marr married Dougherty, Paul and his friends hadn't lived together for two years.

She then created another fiction, that Paul was so distraught about La Marr's wedding, he had a tantrum-breakdown at the Leatrice Joy-John Gilbert house, tearing apart a $15,000 emerald and diamond bracelet he bought for her and throwing it into a canyon. St. Johns said the guest spent hours searching the canyon for the gems. But like her other creations, this story is easily refuted. First, Paul wasn't at a party when La Marr married. He was with her. Second, Joy and Gilbert never lived anywhere near a canyon when they were together; they lived in Hollywood at Sweetzer and Fountain.

When St. Johns was questioned about the discrepancies, she later said the bracelet tantrum took place when Paul heard about Mabel Normand's wedding to Lew Cody, that he was waiting for Mabel at the Joy-Gilbert house with the bracelet. But this story is equally implausible; Paul's romantic relationship with Mabel ended two years earlier. And Joy and Gilbert had been divorced for two years when Normand married Cody (Gilbert was living on Tower Road with Garbo). And, nobody in Hollywood knew about Normand's wedding until the next day when Cody mentioned it during a luncheon speech.

St. Johns also took Paul to task about his guns, exaggerating sinister motives for owning the weapons. She named at least four people who allegedly discovered guns in Paul's coat pocket without ever offering the logical reason why he owned them: Hollywood lived in fear after the Lindbergh kidnapping and an attempt to kidnap Marlene Dietrich's child and seemingly everyone carried a gun.

St. Johns wrote dozens of inaccurate and inflammatory stories in the months after Paul's death but not a single one was based in fact or could be substantiated. She also claimed to have been a close friend of Jean when she was not; she always exaggerated her relationships with people she wrote about. Strangely, in later years she also contended Jean was at Easton when Paul died.

Wednesday headlines asked, WILL TRAGEDY END JEAN HARLOW'S FILM CAREER?, JEAN HARLOW FILM CAREER IS UNCERTAIN and SUICIDE OF HUSBAND MAY MAKE HER A "MYSTERY WOMAN" AND ALIENATE FANS. She was compared to Mary Miles Minter, Mabel Normand, and Edna Purviance, women whose careers ended after the Taylor and Dines scandals, and writers asked if she would "fade from the limelight" due to Paul's death. Worse, she was portrayed as benefiting from the McGrew divorce, that the "Chicago playboy gave her a Beverly Hills house worth $17,500 and an income of four hundred a month. And a car." It was also noted that "the Benedict Canyon home was put in her name ... as a gift." The story ended with the question, "Where does Jean Harlow go now?"[66]

For the first time the death was called a "supposed suicide" and the obvious discrepancies in the MGM timeline questioned under headlines like **PROBE FILM TRAGEDY FLAWS** and **POLICE HUNT SECOND NOTE.**[67]

Worst for MGM, non–Hearst papers openly questioned the studio *and* hinted at Jean's direct involvement, that she might be a killer or knew who was; "Jean Harlow knows perhaps why Bern shot himself. But she isn't talking. Maybe those who arrived in the Bern mansion hours before police were called know why the Metro-Goldwyn-Mayer producer shot himself. But they aren't talking either. The body of Bern was discovered by John Carmichael, his butler, at approximately 11:45 A.M. Authorities were not notified until 2½ hours later." If reporters knew the *actual* time that Paul's body was discovered, the story would have exploded. Questions about Jean led to the big question MGM didn't want to hear, mentioned in dozens of papers: "Was someone else present when Bern was shot?"[68]

Columnist Harry Carr pointed an accusing finger at Jean: "Unless she drops all the mystery and comes forward with a frank, straightforward story, I wouldn't give Miss Harlow 2 cents for what remains of her career. And I wouldn't give more than 3 cents anyhow. Paul was the beloved 'Little Father' of the screen colony. He was happy before he was married; committed suicide after a brief married life. It was the end of an unselfish, sensitive life."[69]

Another problem for MGM was the widening search for "Mrs. Paul Bern." In the 24 hours since Henry Bern mentioned Paul's "long ago" bride, reporters learned that she lived at the Algonquin Hotel for a decade, that she was receiving checks from Paul, that she'd lived with him "in Canada as his common-law wife," and that he visited her once a year. And that she left in May and had her belongings forwarded to San Francisco. The hunt for "Mrs. Paul Bern" moved to California.

Also Wednesday morning, coroner Nance announced an inquest into Paul's death to take place Thursday, over strenuous objections from MGM's Silberberg who said, "We can see no reason for conducting an inquest in view of the fact the police and everyone else is satisfied that Bern took his own life." Subpoenaed to testify were detectives Whitehead and Condaffer, Jean, Bello, Thalberg, MGM business manager Martin Greenwood, "Harold (Slickum) Garrison, Negro studio employee, who at times acted as chauffeur for Bern, John and Winifred Carmichael, domestics in the Bern household, Clifton Davis, Negro gardener at the Bern estate, and Blanche Williams, Negro maid employed by Miss Harlow."[70] Henry Bern was originally among the 11 witnesses on Nance's list but strangely was not called to testify about Dorothy.[71]

The three-day search for Paul's will by his lawyer Oscar Cummins and MGM lawyers Silberberg and Blum was interrupted by a late-afternoon telegram from the 521 Fifth Avenue offices of lawyer Henry Uttal, who'd known Paul and his "very pretty blonde" wife from 1912 to 1921.[72] Uttal said he prepared several wills for Paul that left most of his wealth to "my wife, Dorothy Millette," a woman he described as "beautiful and very intelligent"

who was "well known to all of Bern's associates and intimate friends" as "his
wife."

At the same time, Paul's L.A. insurance advisor George G. Clarken said
he was Paul's "friend for many years and about eleven years ago I wrote a rel-
atively small policy for him. He told me that he was married to a woman who
had suffered a derangement and that he still loved her and hoped, if she
regained her mental balance, to take up their marriage." Her name was
Dorothy Millette and he added incorrectly that she "is now a patient in a New
York sanitarium" and beneficiary of a large trust held by the New York Trust
Company to support his now "incompetent wife."[73] Dorothy's part was growing by the minute. She had quickly become the subject of a massive and frantic nationwide search.

At 8:00 Wednesday night, Henry Bern stepped from a Ford Tri-motor
airliner at the Grand Central Air Terminal in Glendale after a two-day trip
from New Jersey.[74] In a suit and tie and tan fedora, a visibly drained Henry
told reporters, "I am simply a man come to the funeral of his brother. I want
no secrecy veiling the matter of my brother's death. He would not have had
it that way...."[75] He did not answer questions about Dorothy.

Irene Harrison met Henry at the plane and after the two posed for pictures, he was whisked off to the Ambassador Hotel for dinner and then to
Club View at 10:30. Standing in front of the street-side garage, he confirmed
for reporters that Paul had a common-law wife who had recently moved to
San Francisco but he was still adamant that Paul could not have killed himself. Inside with Jean and the Bellos were Mayer, Silberberg, and Strickling.
Ida Koverman was there with her typewriter to transcribe the meeting.

During the sit-down, Henry was no doubt told Dorothy was at Easton
on Sunday and that she killed Paul. Jean's loud sobs could be heard as a shaken
and much less strident Henry left Club View and met with reporters at 1:00
A.M., adding to the mystery by saying, "Certain complications which have
come to my attention make it impossible for me to give out a statement.
Please don't ask me what these complications are. Let's just say that when they
have been straightened out I will tell all."[76] He returned to the Ambassador
where he placed a call to "Miss D. Millette" at the Plaza Hotel in San Francisco and was told she had already checked out.[77]

Thursday

Some of the far-off papers had yet to embrace the MGM version, run-
ning more accurate stories like HOLLYWOOD LOST GREAT FRIEND BY
TRAGIC DEATH OF PAUL BERN describing him as "Hollywood's Little
Confessor and one of the best-loved figures on the Hollywood scene."[78] But

while the hinterlands were still mourning a movie colony gentleman, the city papers were destroying Paul.

MGM papers and the Hearst press ran with Paul's phantom "wife" and Nance's autopsy note that BERN AUTOPSY BARES REASON FOR HIS SUICIDE.[79] Without directly describing Paul's under-developed sexual organs, vague references to "Paul Bern's secret," a "physical condition [that] was an all-important factor" that "might induce ... melancholia" made it clear that he killed himself because he was impotent. They also stated incorrectly that the condition "was one that would prevent a happy marriage."[80]

Paul being married carried its own momentum and by Thursday, papers heralded FIRST WIFE NAMED IN BERN WILL HERE and BERN ROMANCE WITH MYSTERY GIRL REVEALED and BERN MARRIED TO ANOTHER, SAYS FRIEND. The fact that he was secretly married was front and center, to the delight of MGM. Still known only as "Mrs. Paul Bern," Dorothy was described as a "gorgeous red-headed creature" and Paul was alleged to have admitted that he was "morally her husband." Hearst papers were the first to mention BERN NEVER DIVORCED FROM WOMAN PLACED IN SANITARIUM. There was now a mysterious "other woman."[81]

Strickling-created news items were easy to spot, adding brick by brick to the wall being built around Jean at Paul's expense. He was "an unhappy man of 41 who had never known a real romance." He spent his last few days reading and working on a script entitled *Violence* which climaxed in a sudden death.[82] Laurence Stallings — a Paramount writer who barely knew Paul — volunteered a story almost too ludicrous to believe, that Paul told him he carried a gun "because I often think of suicide, and when the right mood and the right moment come, I want to be ready."[83]

At the same time, Jean's role in Paul's death was being cleverly re-crafted with headlines like JEAN VICTIM OF LOVE TRAGEDY.[84] The "Jean as victim of Paul" theme became central to the MGM campaign.

By Thursday morning, reporters tracked Dorothy to the Plaza in San Francisco and descended on the hotel followed by police, only to learn she had gone. Hotel manager Ray Maxwell demanded a court order to open the trunk and bag that Dorothy had checked before leaving. She was then tracked to the *Delta King* but by then the ship was already in Sacramento and the passengers long gone. Reporters headed to Sacramento as afternoon papers first confirmed that "Mrs. Paul Bern" was Dorothy Millette.

At 10:00 Thursday morning there were 500 people milling around outside Price-Daniel's Sawtelle Avenue mortuary hoping to see Jean arrive for the inquest into Paul's death. But she remained in seclusion at Club View. Inside Price-Daniel, a dozen high-backed wicker chairs were arrayed in a hot, crowded ante-room. Coroner's Register no. 42753 listed the nine witnesses called, the details of Paul's death, the evidence collected by detective White-head, and Frank R. Webb's eventual verdict.[85]

Called were Marino Bello, John Herman Carmichael, Irving Grant Thalberg, Martin E. Greenwood, Clifton Earl Davis, Harold Allen Garrison, Blanche Williams, detectives Whitehead and Frank Condaffer and coroner Frank Nance. Surprisingly, Henry Bern was not called to discuss Dorothy and the Vorkapiches wouldn't describe the limousine and Paul's guest. Jean was subpoenaed but Dr. Robert Kennicott said "her appearance before the Grand Jury would gravely endanger her life."[86] She did not testify either.

The inquest was brief. The longest individual testimony lasted three minutes; the shortest 30 seconds. Bello testified Paul was fraught with "melancholia" and was "extremely nervous," and of course Bello lied about his whereabouts Monday, saying his "motorboat stalled in the middle of the channel returning home." John Carmichael lied about the time he and Jean left for Club View, where he stayed Sunday night, when he found Paul, and claimed Thalberg called police immediately. But he did say Paul was happy and there were no quarrels with Jean. Winifred was only asked if she knew any reason Paul might killed himself and answered, "None."

Thalberg, who arrived with an expressionless Mayer, of course lied about calling police, testifying he called "within a few minutes" of his arrival. He also said Paul was "nervous" sometimes. When asked why Paul might kill himself, he shrugged and said, "It's not up to me to decide. I don't know anything about it." When pressed by Nance, Thalberg would not explain what went on inside Easton from the time they arrived until police were called, even blaming police who were "a long time in coming."[87] Strangely, he said Mayer could better explain what went on.

Martin Greenwood said he was at Easton although he clearly was not but added he had no idea why Paul would kill himself nor had Paul ever discussed suicide. Clifton Davis said that there was never disharmony at the house and had no idea why Paul might kill himself but was not asked about the Sunday evening visitor he had heard to Easton.

Slickum Garrison was described as "the most loquacious of the three colored witnesses." He said Paul and Jean "was [sic] always huggin' and kissin'" and Paul often spoke of suicide and told him that his (Paul's) mother, father, grandparents and some cousins also killed themselves. He said there was never any disharmony between Paul and Jean and described taking Paul to the Ambassador on Saturday night. Blanche Williams offered nothing.

Dr. Webb put a dent in MGM's impotence-melancholia theme by testifying that Paul's under-sized (versus undeveloped) genitals did not indicate impotence nor would they necessarily cause nervousness or melancholia because the problem was "not to the extreme to suggest that." But the hand-written verdict in Coroner's Register No. 42753 was all MGM needed: "Gun shot [*sic*] wound of head, self inflicted by the deceased with suicidal intent at the home of the deceased, 9820 Easton Drive. West Los Angeles California. Motive: undetermined."[88]

The inquest helped MGM's evolving explanation for Paul's suicide. Afternoon editions dutifully mentioned "the latest theory — that Bern killed himself because some intimate physical condition made him a prey to melancholia during the last two months of his marriage to Miss Harlow."[89] It didn't take much for people to put the stories together.

Friday

Hearst and MGM-friendly papers contained attacks on two fronts: Paul was married to someone else and he fought with Jean the afternoon he died. It was mentioned that "piece by piece the strange career of Paul Bern has begun to fit together" while "friends dropped fragments of information forming a strange picture...." For the next two weeks, comments were attributed to friends, always unnamed and unknown.

The few "friends" who were identified barely knew Paul but nonetheless invented outrageous stories. New York stage producer Charles Erskine's secretary Jeanne Cohen said, "The night I met him, ten years ago, he seemed melancholy. I was told he tried to commit suicide the night before. Then last June, I had him over to tea. He told me if anything came between him and Miss Harlow he would kill himself." The second theme was that "Paul Bern was married to someone else when he took Jean Harlow ... as his bride."[90] Paul was now strange *and* a potential bigamist.

MGM also amplified the leaked argument story, Jean's reason for leaving Easton. Friday it was suggested that the note was directly "related to an outburst in which he threatened to kill Miss Harlow if she persisted in asking him to accompany her to her mother's home." Jean "fled in terror" after the "dramatic episode" during which Paul allegedly screamed, "Get out and let me alone — if you don't I'll kill you!" The ridiculous story was nonetheless quickly picked up by hundreds of non–Hearst papers.[91]

While MGM and Paul's friends and family readied for his afternoon funeral, morning dispatches from San Francisco first mentioned Other Woman's Suicide Feared! and PHANTOM BEAUTY MISSING FROM BOAT while those aligned with MGM screamed PAUL BERN MAY HAVE HAD MORE THAN ONE WIFE!!![92] It was confirmed that Dorothy had been aboard the *Delta King* and that her coat and shoes were found on the deck. San Francisco papers suggested a pair of stockings was also found, hinting perhaps that she "ended her life unclad, just as Bern shot himself standing nude before a mirror."[93]

Authorities dragged the Sacramento River near Courtland, 30 miles south of Sacramento, where the ship was thought to be at 4:30 A.M. When Henry Bern was told of Dorothy's probable suicide, he collapsed and was unable to attend Paul's funeral.

The funeral began at 2:00 at Grace Chapel at Inglewood Park Cemetery. Only about 35 invited guests were allowed past the 1,000 people gath-

Jean is helped down the steps at Club View by Bello (left) and Paul's close friend Willis Goldbeck, on her way to the funeral.

Jean exits her limousine at the side entrance at Grace Chapel and Inglewood Memorial Park.

Paul's casket was literally engulfed by hundreds of floral arrangements large and small from all over the world.

ered outside.[94] MGM publicist Dean Dorn said, "The place was swarming. The crowd, the press, the cameras. We could barely cope with it."[95] Inside the small chapel, Paul's bronze casket was smothered by a blanket of orchids the funeral director claimed cost $25,000. It rested on a bier surrounded by banks of flowers, almost 200 huge arrangements from the Thalbergs, Carey Wilson and Carmelita Geraghty, Bebe Daniels and Ben Lyon, Ralph and May Block, B.P. Schulberg, Clarence Brown, Jack Gilbert, Jack Warner, Roland Brown, Eddie Sutherland, Helen Chandler and Cyril Hume, Robert Montgomery, and dozens of smaller sprays from anonymous MGM employees.[96]

Jean arrived near collapse with the Bellos, Ida Koverman, and Willis Goldbeck, who helped her inside. Her black veil did little to hide her red, swollen eyes and she cried softly as she was led to a small alcove to the side of the bier where she sat weeping on the shoulder of Ida Koverman. Friederike, William and Sig Marcus sat in an alcove on the opposite side. Friederike collapsed outside and was carried in and as soon as she saw the casket startled the gathering crowd by screaming, "He's gone. Where have they taken him?"[97] Heavy purple curtains draped each archway, effectively shielding those inside the alcoves from view.

The invited guests sat in front of the casket and couldn't see Jean but could hear her low sobbing. A pale, weeping Irving sat with Norma in the first row next to Arlie Lewin, Hunt Stromberg, and Bernie Fineman. From the moment he sat down to the minute he left, Irving never took his eyes off Paul's casket, nor did he stop weeping. Mayer arrived with Strickling and Mannix, followed by Jack Gilbert, Clark Gable, Carey Wilson, George Fitzmaurice, Ralph Block, Jack Conway, John Considine, Jr., Edgar Selwyn, Jetta Goudal and Harold Grieve, Joan Bennett and Gene Markey, Ramon Novarro, and Ben Piazza, who had given Jean her first screen test in New York.

Two MGM musicians friendly with Paul softly played an organ and a muted violin (Saint-Saen's beautiful "Swan," and the "Evening Star" from Wagner's Tannhauser). "I shall lift up mine eyes to the mountains," began Rabbi Edgar Magnin, who gave a short prayer before Conrad Nagel walked up, stood behind the flower-bedecked casket and eulogized his friend:

> Hollywood is cruel and brutalizing to those seeking success. In no other place is the struggle for success so cruel. It is difficult not to bow down to one of Hollywood's false idols — the keenest and most dangerous being insincerity. Its cardinal and most devitalizing sin is insincerity. But Paul Bern was sincere.
>
> Paul bowed down to none. Paul was a creative artist. He translated life. We live not only our own lives in motion pictures, but a dozen other characters as well, the parts we play. This satiates us with life. It leaves us cruel and cynical. This did not affect Paul. He was as naive as a child; he was like a little child wandering around in a naughty world of grown-ups.

Near collapse, Jean is led from the chapel by Bello and Goldbeck.

Hollywood presents a series of strange contrasts. Nowhere else is success so great and failure so tragic. It is a sad commentary on our great industry.

But Paul never forgot those who did not attain success. He was always ready with money, always with his hand in his purse, ready to help.

He suffered a tinge of melancholia, so we must feel that Paul Bern was taken from us by an illness, a sickness, and not really by an act of self-destruction on his part. Had a strange noise interrupted his train of thought, had someone just knocked on his door, the illness would have passed over for the time being and Paul would not have done what he did.

Nagel paused as Mayer wiped away a tear and Thalberg sat deathly pale and sobbing ever more loudly. Jean's cries and Friederike's moans also broke the quiet. Gazing down at the casket, he finished:

> We'll just say to Paul: Paul, we want you to know that because we love you, we love her. In this hour of need, all your friends stand ready to extend to her all our help in her hour of grief. We bid you god-speed, Paul Bern, on your journey to a better place and in all reverence we say here in your own words you cheerfully said to us, "We'll be seeing you."

Rabbi Magnin offered the traditional Hebrew Kaddish prayer for the dead and gave a brief eulogy, saying Paul "was a great artist who lived in a gossamer world, but could not be understood by the man in the street."[98] The casket was then opened and a mechanical pulley attached to the casket slowly raised it to a more upright position, making it look like Paul was almost standing. Jean burst into louder tears, as did Thalberg. Gable scrambled out the door.[99]

The first to approach the coffin was the Marcus family cook, a large woman with work-worn hands and red-rimmed eyes who quietly cried as she kissed Paul's hands and cheek. Friederike Marcus, on the arm of her son Sig, stumbled from her seat up to the casket, gazed at Paul and loudly shrieked before she was led faltering out the door. Irene Harrison stood next to the bier weeping while everyone filed past.

Jack Gilbert, Joan Bennett, Gene Markey, John Considine, Jack Conway, and Hunt Stromberg all wept openly as they filed past. Mayer helped Jean to the coffin, shooting a glance at the man he was trying to destroy before handing Jean to Willis Goldbeck and walking out with Irving, who wouldn't approach Paul's body. Jean gazed down at Paul for several minutes while loudly crying before she was almost carried to her car by Goldbeck and Bello, loudly crying and staggering down the steps.

As she approached the limousine, the large crowd broke through the police lines and quickly engulfed the tiny grieving girl. Goldbeck and Bello wrestled her into the car amid hundreds of people yelling for autographs or shouting insults. She was crushed, later saying, "I was shocked. They seemed heartless. To them I was not a person ... I had no more personality than a corporation."[100]

When Jean was driven away, those outside were allowed in. MGM publicity man Dean Dorn sat to the side of the casket, where he remained until everyone had gone. He was instructed by Strickling that morning to go to

Price-Daniel and not to take his eyes off Paul's casket until it was sent for cremation. He was never given a reason but later said, "There was a lot going on with that whole Bern incident that I never understood."[101] MGM prop man Ray O'Brien was given the grisly assignment of witnessing the cremation, after which Paul's remains were placed in an urn for interment over the weekend.

After the funeral, MGM had Henry Bern address the Dorothy problem. He sat in Paul's office, in his brother's chair behind his desk, with Irene Harrison by his side. For two hours he answered reporters' questions about Dorothy, carefully following the party line. He reiterated the distilled Dorothy story, that they lived together as man and wife in New York and Canada and described her commitment at Blythewood and Paul's continued support.

He said Paul saw her at most four times over the years and not at all in San Francisco. Irene Harrison interrupted to admit she made all arrangements for Dorothy and that "there was no trouble with Miss Millette after Paul's marriage to Jean."[102] Henry also reiterated that Jean knew all about Dorothy and admitted he tried to call her Wednesday night.

When pressed about his meeting with Jean after arriving in L.A., the extent of his conversion was clear. He said, "I had just left the plane and was ill and exhausted from the trip. She was distraught. I can't remember, under the circumstances, what we talked about." Sadly for Paul, he also said, "There is no question in my mind but that it was suicide, but as to the motive that prompted it that's all hypothetical," and added "only Jean can offer a motive" for a suicide.[103] Henry said he met with Jean for "only about ten minutes" though he was inside Club View for over two hours. Dorothy's story was coming out, just the way MGM wanted it told.

Saturday

The SEARCH FOR BODY OF BERN'S "OTHER WIFE"!!! continued Saturday, as did the MGM drumbeat. Hearst papers said BERN FOUGHT AND THREATENED STAR NIGHT BEFORE DEATH and JEAN HARLOW FLED FOR LIFE.[104] The fight rhetoric was Strickling at his best; he began with a simple fight, than a fight from which Jean fled Easton, to a fight where Paul threatened Jean, and finally Jean fleeing in terror for her life. No matter that the fight never took place.

For her part, Jean still refused to take part in MGM's campaign and in her first comments since Paul's death revealed she did indeed know about Dorothy and that Paul supported her. Friederike Marcus also confirmed that the family knew her.[105] In response, MGM trotted out Henry Bern to confirm "there was no mystery about her" and he knew for a fact that "Miss Millette had nothing to do with" Paul's death. He also said that Paul "had many affairs."[106]

With no sign of Dorothy, San Francisco police obtained a search warrant for the trunks she checked at the Plaza. On the warrant, "Foul Play" was listed as a factor. Her large green wardrobe-steamer trunk contained perfumes from Paris, expensive dresses and lingerie from Fifth Avenue shops like I. Magnin, a luxurious pair of beaded slippers, a dozen pairs of shoes with lifts in the heels and, curiously, a book on shorthand. Papers carried photos of San Francisco detective Allen McGinn displaying the clothes and shoes atop the trunk.

Inside the handbag they found the bundle of letters and a writing pad. The notes were all from Paul's office, all typically impersonal, businesslike, and formal. A few were released to the press, one politely advising her not to come to Hollywood, another suggesting San Francisco hotels and another enclosing a check. Ominously, on the writing pad was a single word reversed as if made from blotting. When held up to a mirror it read, "JUSTIFICATION."[107]

MGM-allied papers jumped on the letters, hinting at ominous reasons in PROOF OF SOME FINANCIAL ARRANGEMENT. But they ignored the curious note on the writing pad.

Sacramento police went through the smaller trunk left in Dorothy's *Delta King* cabin and found more clothes (dresses, shoes and an expensive fur coat). Local detective Albert Barbayco was photographed among the items in a repeat of the San Francisco pictures.

Sunday

Even though there was no trace of Dorothy, MGM papers proclaimed her dead Sunday morning: **CURTAIN DRAWN ON BERN PAST, Dorothy Millette, Red Haired Common Law Wife of Film Head, Dead.**[108] Interestingly, a body *was* found over the weekend but it was a man about fifty wearing a blue suit, light shirt and a black tie and, coincidentally, carrying a *Delta King* key in his pocket. He'd been in the river for at least a month.

That morning, Paul's ashes were interred in a niche high on a wall in the Mausoleum of the Golden West in Inglewood Park. His plaque simply reads **PAUL BERN** and is near the top of a 12' wall in the Sanctuary of Faith.[109]

Longer Days

In the movies, a good story is a good story even if it's tragedy. On Monday, Harrison Carroll reported a script "suggested by the Paul Bern tragedy already is making the rounds of the scenario departments" with several studios bidding on the project. He was the first Hollywood writer, perhaps the only one, to publicly acknowledge the ongoing MGM-orchestrated attacks on Paul, writing, "Rather sickening the way Hollywood gossip is commencing to gnaw at the reputation of this kindly man. Not the things that are getting printed, but rumors of a vicious nature. Not a word of truth in them either."[110] But Carroll's was a voice in the wilderness. The MGM smear campaign only worsened.

On Monday morning, Jean returned to the *Red Dust* set, entering through a side gate accompanied by private nurse Adah Wilson and Bello.[111] Over the weekend she had called Thalberg and told him that she would go insane if he didn't let her come back to work. He instructed director Victor Fleming to ignore the shooting schedule and film a comedic scene with Jean bathing naked in a rain barrel and flirting with Clark Gable.

Always the producer, Thalberg figured splashing water would hide her red, swollen eyes but she was not at all ready and after several takes she had to be helped to her dressing room to rest. Fleming tried re-shooting the scene for three days without any usable results; he finally got some usable footage of Jean doing a café scene using long shots and low light. Between takes the normally boisterous Jean retreated to a corner of the soundstage and sat quietly in a char. When an acceptable take of the barrel scene was shot weeks later, Jean stood up and exposed her breasts to the camera. Gable was humbled by Jean's stoicism, saying, "She's got more guts then most men."[112]

Irene Harrison assumed that Paul's July 29 will was in his Bank of America safe deposit box in Culver City so MGM lawyer Silberberg requested it be opened, acting on Jean's behalf even though Oscar Cummins was her personal attorney. When deputy state inheritance tax collector Theodore Pettit opened the box, the July 29 will was not there but several earlier wills were.

The first, a six-page document written in New York on June 12, 1925, left Dorothy a $2,500 annual annuity but was not legally signed so had no standing in court. A second dated August 14, 1927, and also prepared in New York left Dorothy the $2,500 annuity and had small cash bequests to six actresses and some family members but this document wasn't notarized or witnessed by an attorney and was therefore also unusable. There was also a sealed letter addressed to Jean and written before their marriage. Nobody knows what that letter said.[113]

Monday papers included another Strickling gem, reports that Paul had a "mysterious supper" at the Ambassador the Saturday before he died. But they were chagrined to discover that the woman was actress Barbara Barondess, there to meet a married Bernie Hyman. She told writer Sidney Skolsky about the tryst and he called Strickling on the 8th and traded silence for later studio access.

A San Francisco detective goes through a steamer trunk Dorothy left at the Plaza Hotel. Inside the trunk was a bundle of letters wrapped in a piece of paper with the word "JUSTIFICATION" embedded within (from the Darrell Rooney collection).

Paul's crypt is near the top of the cluster of niches in the middle (courtesy Mark Masek).

Hearst papers described Paul's favor for Hyman as a "mysterious conference," a "suicide supper" where Paul "sought comfort to distract his tortured mind." MGM made sure Hyman and Barondess were never identified, leaving more mystery in the story. But Irene Harrison's perfunctory letters to Dorothy suddenly meant a "two-year relationship" strong enough that he sent "Love and Best Wishes to Dorothy Millette four months before he died."[114]

Early Wednesday morning the 14th, a Japanese fisherman and his son working the banks of the Georgiana Slough, a tributary of the Sacramento River just below Walnut Grove, came upon a woman's body next to the riverbank. Shoeless and wearing a black dress, the badly decomposed redhead was floating face down against the rocks, almost completely hidden by the branches of a willow tree overhanging the bank.

The fisherman called Sacramento police from Walnut Grove and coroner James Garlick and deputy sheriff Charles J. Ogle sped to the spot 30 miles down river. Plaza Hotel desk clerk Edward Sullivan was asked to meet the men there. It was seven miles from the area near Courtland that had been dragged and partially dredged looking for Dorothy. Normal currents made it unlikely for a body to float into the spot, which is why searchers had overlooked the location.

Coroner Garlick removed the body from the river, Sullivan identified it as Dorothy and it was removed to Sacramento. She wore a dark underskirt

Paul's sister Friederike was interred with Paul rather than with her husband William.

and black silk stockings; her black dress matched the black coat found on the *Delta King*; she wore no jewelry and carried no note. Garlick, Ogle, and Dorothy's body arrived at the morgue. Within minutes, Sheriff Don Cox said, "MGM people [rode] into town like a thundering herd" of lawyers and private police that took over the investigation.

Garlick's autopsy indicated Dorothy had drowned and on the 17th he signed her death certificate listing cause of death as "asphyxiation by drowning." Her death was ruled a suicide.[115] He said, "Unless some relative or friend takes charge of the body, we can only arrange to put her in a pauper's grave in Potter's Field." He wired Henry, who earlier had said, "If her body is found I shall certainly see that it is given proper care."[116] He never replied.

Thursday morning, two .38 caliber Colt pistols and one "diary containing note" were released by the West L.A. police property room to detective Joe Whitehead "for M. Silberberg, attorney for Jean Harlow." Mendel Silberberg was not Jean's attorney. He was MGM's attorney. The guns and the guestbook were never seen again.[117]

Also that morning, Mendel Silberberg called Garlick and offered to pay Dorothy's burial costs. Garlick owned the funeral home and arranged the burial, about which Silberberg directed, "[C]lients of my office wish Dorothy Millette buried in the best cemetery in Sacramento."[118]

One L.A. theater showing *Red-Headed Woman* plastered the lobby with over-sized headlines about Paul's death on Thursday but MGM demanded they be removed; one newspaper called the display "a new record in bad taste."[119]

On Saturday morning, September 17, as quietly as she had lived the last decade of her life, Dorothy Millette was buried at East Lawn Memorial Park in Sacramento. The Rev. J.J. Evans of the First Christian Church presided over a simple service at Garlick's funeral parlor and at the grave. A single large bouquet of gardenias and gladiolas sat atop her casket, sent by an unidentified local who signed herself only, "A Mother." A few reporters and five curious local women listened to the Rev. Evans, who said only, "No one living should judge the dead."[120]

On Saturday the 18th, Irene Harrison finally located Paul's July 29 will in, of all places, *her* safe deposit box. It was fortunate timing because Sacramento public administrator Herman Koch swooped in after Dorothy's funeral to wrest control of her estate — and the expected inheritance from Paul — if either New York will stood up. Silberberg and Cummins filed the July 29 will and it was accepted for probate on October 19.

On September 21, Sacramento county coroner Garlick held an inquest into Dorothy's death at the same funeral home where he performed his autopsy and then her funeral. He heard testimony from *Delta King* crew members who served Dorothy, from the local man who saw her nervously walking the ship

Just two days after Paul's funeral, Jean returned to the *Red Dust* set and tried to do this sexually charged scene with Clark Gable. She was unable to get through the shooting.

and from detectives who responded to the initial call when the body was found. Foreman J.J. Kearney declared "38-year-old Dorothy Millette came to her death on the 7th of September, 1932, by asphyxiation by drowning."[121]

Silberberg and MGM took charge of Paul's estate probate. Jean had no knowledge about anything concerning Paul's estate. Arthur Landau later said, "She never carried a dime with her and let Bello take care of her money." He also suggested that Bello "found something [money from Paul's estate] and told no one. He seemed to have money from some unknown sources after [Paul's death] and altho I accused him of it he would not give it up." [122]

Even before the probate began, Jean made her decision about Easton. She never returned, never set foot in the house or on the property again. Getting the house ready to sell, she instructed the painter-wallpaper hanger to remove the mural above the living room and dispose of it. When he asked if he could keep it, she said, "I don't care what you do with it, just get rid of the thing."[123]

Accompanied by Bello and lawyer Silberberg, on October 19, Jean — as the executrix of Paul's estate — had to appear at the L.A. courthouse for the probating of his will. Hundreds of people lined corridors for a glimpse as she walked past, and the courtroom itself was filled to capacity. Silberberg estimated the estate to be worth in excess of $100,000 ($37,000 from an insurance policy) but the final total was far less and a final discharge would not take place until February 20, 1937.[124]

Paul died with little cash; two bank accounts held a little over $500 and he was owed $1,194 salary from MGM. His cash holdings were the equivalent of $40,000, not insignificant but certainly less than might be expected. That was because during his adult life Paul gave away a good portion of his earnings to others. After his assets were inventoried and his Cord roadster auctioned, his estate was valued at $25,471.24 but after discarding some investment property in Beverly Hills and paying funeral bills and expenses, there was about $11,000 to pay creditors.

His debts were not out of line and confirm his less than extravagant lifestyle. The bills were typical: clothing for him and Jean from I. Magnin ($821) and Bullocks ($276.50), doctor bills, his supermarket ($21.71), gas station ($125.06), laundry service ($32.47), Olympics tickets ($265), flowers sent to Jean ($34), even milk delivered to Easton (in August he bought 21 quarts for 7¢ a quart). Creditor claims totaled $16,265, meaning the estate was insolvent to the tune of $5,300.

Papers reported that Easton was "not involved because that was an outright marital gift" to Jean but it was indeed.[125] Paul had taken out a $24,000 mortgage with Security First National Bank of Pasadena and the balance was $19,000. For some reason, instead of putting it on the market Jean allowed the property to be foreclosed upon. Bank filings indicated there was "clearly no equity" and after the dust settled, the bank obtained a judgment against the estate for $2,439,17.

There are some interesting items within the creditor claims. First was the Ambassador Hotel bill that included a bungalow, dinner, drinks and telephone calls the Saturday before he died; Bernie Hyman's expenses for his tryst with Barbara Barondess. Harold Grieve sued for the cost of remodeling Easton for Jean. The most interesting bill came from MGM.

MGM submitted an eight-page summary of expenses going back to March stating that, of the $1,136.99 charged to Paul they were still owed $198.32 up to his death and $330.10 for items after (the relative value of MGM's bills is over $10,000). Included are charges for everything from phone calls to rental furniture for the wedding reception. There are calls to people like Garbo, Fairbanks, Hearst, and March. Meals at the MGM commissary. Car charges to Grauman's, Easton, and the Ambassador. In May there were

Gable was humbled by the bravery and strength that Jean possessed, returning to work so soon after Paul's funeral as she did.

daily calls to Jean during her publicity trip just before their engagement; to "Harlow, N.Y.," "Harlow, Albuquerque," and "Harlow, Needles." On June 20, the day they were engaged, "Auto hire — pick up Miss Jean Harlow at 1353 Club View Dr., bring to Mr. Bern's office."

But there are dozens of eyebrow-raising listings. On March 23, Paul sent a $1.20 telegram to "Millette, N.Y." as she was getting ready to leave for San Francisco. On August 2 he allegedly charged a $1.92 "holster" to his studio account. And on September 10 was a $94.90 charge for "Transportation L.A. to San Francisco." The limousine seen by the Carmichaels, Davis, and Vorkapich.

The MGM limousine taking Dorothy to San Francisco stopped at Paul's favorite gas station — Boulevard Super Service not far from the studio — and filled up before and after the trip. Paul's personal account was charged.[126]

MGM showed no shame submitting expenses; the studio tried to bill the estate for watchmen posted at Easton after Paul's death, limousines taking Thalberg, Mayer, Strickling and Whitey Hendry to the funeral and coroner's inquest, even a final phone call to Henry Bern back in New Rochelle on September 22. None of these charges was approved; MGM got only the $198.32 for charges before Paul died.

The biggest claim against the estate was from the government, almost $9,500 in income and estate taxes. To settle the estate, Jean paid the outstanding tax bills in 1937 (she reportedly received $24,037.07 from insurance policies).

By September 18, the day Irene Harrison found Paul's will, questions about Paul's death were no longer discussed in newspapers. The discovery of Dorothy's body provided a perfect ending to MGM's campaign, tying everything up with a nice, neat bow. An impotent Paul was distressed because he could not have sex with his gorgeous movie star wife and tormented because of his other marriage, so he killed himself.

Dorothy's death removed MGM's final problem. MGM newspapers had hammered away at Paul's failures with women, sexual problems, and mistreatment of Jean, all untrue. Any lingering public doubt in Jean also vanished. The blame for Paul's death fell on Paul. Jean was the victim, carrying on bravely in the face of her impotent husband's massive betrayal. Paul's memory was tarnished to the point of black. MGM transformed the most beloved man in Hollywood into a mentally unbalanced, impotent wife-abuser.

By the end of November, the story was no longer in papers but people hadn't forgotten; even in December there was still a steady stream of cars inching up Easton so the curious could catch a glimpse of the house through the trees. They just didn't care any more if Paul was murdered.

❡ ELEVEN ☙

Who Killed Paul Bern?

In the months before Paul's death and in issues published after he died but written earlier, every movie magazine ran a feature article about him. *Motion Picture* said "Jean Harlow Marries Paul Bern: Groom is noted for his quiet benefactions to unlucky stars" and described him as "The Kindest Hearted Man in a Heartless Town," "The Good Samaritan of Hollywood," and "The Little Confessor of the stars." According to *Modern Screen*, Paul was "known as the best-loved man in Hollywood" with "the reputation of being the kindest and gentlest man in the studio world." *Screen Book Magazine* called him Hollywood's "most famous and beloved bachelor" and *Time* described his death as "a tragedy as bizarre and inscrutable as any in its bizarre and scandalous history. In a community founded upon the assumption that to be blatant is to be successful, Paul Bern was a curious exception. He lived quietly ... noted for his hypersensitive sympathy for the misfortunes of the unhappy...."[1]

An earlier essay said, "He has brought sympathy and helpfulness to more sorrowing souls than any other person I have ever known. He must sleep like a fireman with his boots by his bedside." A few days after Paul's death, a reporter spoke to MGM employees and then wrote, "In every discussion and among every group there was not a one that didn't say Paul Bern was the most charitable, the most gracious, the best liked and most respected man he had ever met."[2] How does such a man become so hated? The same *Time* obituary offered the answer asking, "Was Paul Bern ever married to Dorothy Millette? And was his marriage to Jean Harlow therefore bigamous? Grief-stricken Jean Harlow had cause to wonder whether her career in cinema would be destroyed."

All the evidence — physical evidence from Easton, psychological profiles of Paul and Jean at the time, circumstantial and testimonial evidence of Dorothy's presence at Easton, and actions of the MGM people involved — leads to an inescapable conclusion. Dorothy visited Paul on Sunday for reasons easy to assume but impossible to prove, and became angry and was deranged enough that she shot him with a gun she found in his bedroom. In desperation and knowing she would soon be found, she (thought) secretly killed herself two days later in the swirling, muddy Sacramento River.

The MGM story that is Paul's legacy is that he committed suicide because of a "physical handicap" leading to a "melancholia" that would "prevent a happy marriage." His depression was exacerbated by his legal marriage to Dorothy, whom he never divorced. MGM admitted Dorothy was present in his life but not at Easton. Paying attention to what people said (and *didn't* say), the building blocks for MGM's version tumble surprisingly easily when scrutinized.

MGM used an argument between Paul and Jean—"last night's comedy"—as Jean's reason for not being at Easton but no excuse was needed since she was staying at Club View anyway. At some point, Clifton Davis, John Carmichael, and Blanche Williams each described a fight but in later interviews and testimony under oath retracted that assertion. Carmichael said they "parted on the best of terms Sunday" and that Paul "was never harsh, nor was she." Even Marino Bello first said, "Paul was a wonderful, attentive husband, very attentive and devoted. I can assure you they never quarreled. They were extremely happy."[3] And Blanche wasn't even at Easton when she said Jean told her Paul wanted her out. Quite simply, there is no evidence at all of any fight.

The Carmichaels first said they stayed in West Hollywood on Sunday night and arrived at Easton in the morning, but later told the 1933 grand jury they actually stayed in the Easton servants' house after returning late from Club View. From there they had a front-row seat to most of Sunday evening's activities.

More contradictory were comments about the timing of Jean's exit. Carmichael first said she left at 8:00 or 9:00 but Davis later testified he and Winifred were there when the limousine and the veiled occupant arrived. She testified she left Easton for Club View around 5:00.

What did MGM know, and when? Papers reported that John Carmichael called MGM when he arrived late morning and the MGM contingent arrived at 11:45. But Winifred actually called Mama Jean while Clifton Davis was helping John after he fainted. Mama Jean probably called Strickling, who called Mayer, who called Whitey Hendry and Al Cohn, and then Thalberg, who called Selznick. Hendry called photographer Virgil Apger. And they learned much earlier. The Mayers were "awakened" by the first call and Sam Marx was awakened by Al Cohn and on his way to Easton by 8:45 A.M.[4]

Physical evidence from Easton clearly shows *someone* visited Paul Sunday night. A champagne bottle and two glasses—one broken—were found by the pool near Paul's favorite chaise. A damp yellow women's bathing suit—

too big for Jean — was found hanging in the bathroom near Paul's body, not far from his own. That suit matched a yellow rubber bathing suit bag found among Dorothy's belongings from the *Delta King* and a yellow bathing cap found in her checked hotel luggage. And someone ate the piece of chocolate cake Blanche left for Jean — and Paul hated chocolate.

The Carmichaels and Davis testified they saw the limousine with the veiled woman arrive late Sunday afternoon, and Davis and Slavko Vorkapich both claimed they heard loud discussions from the pool late Sunday night, alternately laughing or angrily yelling. Paul was heard to yell, "Get out of my life!" Vorkapich also witnessed the limousine's hasty exit. It was obviously the same MGM limousine that drove from L.A. to San Francisco after purchasing gasoline using Paul's account at the gas station near MGM. It was enough fuel to drive over 500 miles.

Then there's the note, which raises more questions than it answers. D.A. Buron Fitts' handwriting expert Clark Sellers said it was "unequivocably [*sic*] the ... handwriting of Paul Bern," but Fitts' bias is easy to impute.[5] To many, this writer included, there's some question as to whether Paul actually wrote it.

On the 12th, Irene Harrison said she didn't think it was Paul's handwriting. Too many letters were not Paul's style — she specifically mentioned his signature wasn't correct — but Strickling got to her quickly and she reversed herself a day later. In 1971, Strickling told writer Charles Higham *he* thought the note was a forgery and Arthur Landau told Higham the note didn't mean anything and was a "red herring."[6]

In the note, the misspelling of "unfortunately" as "unfortuately," arouses suspicion as errors in spelling are not found in any remaining samples of Paul's writing.

Comparing the note to several known samples of Paul's handwriting raises even more glaring questions. First, the spacing is much wider than any surviving sample; Paul wrote in a very tightly packed style while the note has unusually wide character spacing. Also, the letter sizing varies widely in the note while it is always stable in samples. The continuation between letters also doesn't match. For example, there are smooth upward lines between "t's" and following letters in the note; in the samples, the continuation upward was broken by a vertical segment before returning to the upward motion. That is missing from the note.

As to individual letters, it's very unusual to change basic letter shaping in a signature but the "P" is markedly different from samples; instead of a smooth upward curve to start the letter, it is jerky and broken. More telling, the end of the "P" tails to the side and slightly upward while in every single surviving signature the end tails *severely* downward. There are also versions of "f," "y," and "h" and commonly written words like "to" and "the" that are structured totally unlike those in samples.

This admittedly unscientific comparison doesn't conclusively prove Paul did not write the note but there are enough inconsistencies to raise the question. And given the emotional state of the weekend, certainly nervousness could have played a part but it's doubtful it would cause such marked differences in structure and style. But even assuming Paul did write the note, what does it mean?

It was clearly an apology for something, but what? If Paul did write it, I don't believe it had anything to do with Labor Day weekend. It was written some other time. Clifton Davis testified he went through the book often and saw the note "long before Mr. Bern died."[7] Paul usually included similar notes with the flowers he sent Jean almost every day. Also the salutation "Dearest Dear" was Paul's standard greeting to women. It seems odd he would use something so impersonal (to him) in a suicide note for his beloved Jean.

The imprecise text also raises doubt it was describing that weekend. The MGM fight reference doesn't fit; "you understand that last night was only a comedy." *Last night.* Not *tonight. Last* night. If Paul wrote the note just before killing himself Sunday night, it would seem to be "tonight," not "last night." And with Jean at Club View Sunday night, she wouldn't even be present for *last night's comedy.*

Where did the note come from? Mayer found the note on the 13th page of Paul's guest book on a table near the front door while leafing through self-portraits by Gary Cooper and intimate notes from friends like Lupe Velez. He didn't immediately assume it was a suicide note, didn't rush upstairs to Strickling. He tore it out and put it in his pocket because it sounded "bad" and only mentioned it to Strickling, who made it the linchpin of MGM's suicide story. Would anyone leave their last words on the 13th page of a closed guest book?

Genuine or not, I don't believe the note had anything to do with Paul's death. Maurice Rapf told this writer that people who knew Bern and Harlow knew his death was not a suicide, that the entire scene was staged by Strickling and Hendry. Asked for an opinion about this theory, Rapf said, "It makes more sense than what we were told. We all knew he didn't kill himself."[8]

Real note or not, was Paul suicidal? Was he prone to suicide from family influence? Did his interest in psychology and death equate to a melancholia that presumed suicidal leanings? It's impossible to confirm what Paul was thinking that weekend so we are left to deduce his frame of mind from the events during that period. Other than Mayer's disingenuous comment that

Paul was depressed in the weeks before his death, not a single person close to him echoed that sentiment. In fact, during the month before he died, Paul carried on as he always had, telling writer Marcella Burke he was "deliriously happy."[9]

On Wednesday he and Jean enjoyed a quiet dinner at the home of Sam Marx, leaving because "my darling wife is due on the set at an ungodly hour." On Thursday he took a physical for a new life insurance policy and the doctor pronounced him in "the best spirits and health" with "no medical deficiencies." Thursday night he and Jean were seen happily dancing at the Miramar Hotel. During the day Friday, Paul called Fredric March to beg out of going to his Saturday party, telling him what he later told Carey Wilson, that "I'd like to go" but would not because Jean couldn't go. He said the same thing to Slickum Garrison. Friday night he shared dinner and late-night poolside drinks with his close friend Willis Goldbeck and on Saturday met another good friend, Bernie Hyman, and Hyman's mistress Barbara Barondess, at the Ambassador. After drinks and dinner he was driven home by Slickum Garrison. Not a single person indicated that Paul was anything but his normal, cheerful self at any point that week.[10]

Even so, he was called moody, melancholy, or chronically depressed by biographers of Mayer, Jean, Thalberg, and others. Various reasons are offered: his mother's death, a family history of suicide, failures with women, his undersized penis, sexual inadequacy, even the deaths of friends. One writer said Paul was disconsolate after witnessing his friend, director Joe Jackson, drown off Laguna Beach in May. Paul wasn't even in the country when Jackson died.[11] None were true.

It was rumored he had an inferiority complex because he was underdeveloped sexually and reportedly impotent. He may indeed have been embarrassed by his size but it didn't prevent dozens of affairs and serious relationships. And remember that he lived with Dorothy for a decade. Director Henry Hathaway insisted that Paul "scored with women all the time." Louise Brooks said Paul "got into more beds with his 'culture' than any wolf in Hollywood" and dancer Sally Rand told film critic Kevin Thomas that she and Paul had a prolonged sexual affair.[12] Not one woman Paul was linked with ever mentioned sexual issues; the rumor surfaced after his death.

Perhaps the most convincing disclaimer grew up in Brentwood with ZaSu Pitts (after Tom Gallery abandoned the family in 1926). If Donald Gallery is indeed Paul's biological son and it appears circumstantially that he was, then Paul was certainly not impotent.

Ignored in all of the alleged confirmations is the fact that never — not once, ever — was Paul described as depressed or suicidal when he was alive. Was he prone to suicide? Carey Wilson said Paul lived his life with "one cardinal principal, to hurt no one." Suicide doesn't fit that credo although it admittedly also doesn't remove the possibility. There was no family history; MGM created that story. Henriette may have killed herself but even that simply can't be confirmed. According to Henry's son and daughter-in-law, there was not a single suicide anywhere in family history.[13]

Several Hollywood biographers imputed some death obsession from Paul's lifelong interest in psychiatry and psychoanalysis, an interest that predated Hollywood's 1920s–1930s fascination with the topics. Samuel Goldwyn tried to meet with Sigmund Freud during a 1924 trip to Europe; by the late 1920s, imported European writers and directors brought with them the influences of psychoanalytic discussion and debate then swirling around the German capital.[14]

Writers took particular note of several books Paul purchased from the Dora Ingram Book Shop in the months before he died: *The Worship of the Generative Powers* by Thomas Wright, an illustrated work with reproductions of the male organ; *A Discourse on the Worship of Priapus* by Richard Knight, similar to the Wright book; *The Biological Tragedy of Women* by A. Nemilov, a treatise on female sexuality, and *The Glands Relating to Personality* by Louis Berman, dealing with hormone problems that could impact sexuality.

The selections indicate an interest in male sexual activity but certainly don't confirm an obsession or sexual dysfunction. It is never mentioned that the same book order listed eight other books Paul bought, including *Origin and History of Hebrew Law*, Madeleine Ruthven's novel *Summer Denial*, and A.E. Kros' *The Talkies*.[15] Paul typically ordered a dozen books a month from Ingram's; to zero in on four to infer suicidal intent isn't logical.

The available evidence simply doesn't support Paul being suicidal. He certainly could have been but why would he buy life insurance just days before knowing it included a "suicide clause"? And why go swimming first? Much has been made of Paul being naked but his damp bathing suit was in the bathroom and a towel on the floor. He was drying off when he was shot.

The primary sources of Paul's false legacy were Adela Rogers St. Johns and later Irving Shulman. St. Johns was a Strickling mouthpiece who created most of the best-known falsehoods after Paul's murder, most importantly the various Barbara La Marr fictions. Later, she further embellished her stories by quoting a litany of dead witnesses and recalling encounters in which she never participated. Shulman picked up the baton in the 1960s after almost everyone involved was dead. Between the two, Paul's memory has been forever darkened.

Shulman's error-filled and vitriolic 1964 book *Harlow: An Intimate Biography* was based largely on the fantasies of Arthur Landau but has somehow become truth in the years since. It is full of unsubstantiated and patently false

SALLY RAND

Fan dancer Sally Rand disputed rumors of Paul's impotence, saying the two carried on a heated sexual affair.

stories and stunningly laughable claims. In his defense, Shulman was a novelist but he passed off his story as non-fiction, exaggerating MGM fiction to the point of absurdity by claiming that Paul was unable to perform sexually on their wedding night and became so enraged he beat Jean with a cane and inflicted injuries that caused her later death from kidney failure. The story has unfortunately become part of Jean Harlow and Paul Bern lore.

According to Shulman, Jean called Landau at 4:00 A.M. on her wedding night saying, "Come and get me. I'll be waiting outside. Come and get me and don't ask questions. He's liable to wake up."[16] He said he found Jean, eyes swollen and red, and took her to his home at 209 McCarty Drive where he found five ugly welts across her back between her shoulder blades and hips and a deep bite-mark just above her blood-matted pubic hair. Landau's storytelling — her nightgown "held Jean's breasts high so that their rounded fullness fell over the lace eyelet border of the neckline" — remains laughable.

Jean supposedly told him, "The little bastard's a maniac. A dirty rotten Goddamned sex fiend," that if he "wasn't so drunk he would've caught me across the head [with the cane], because that's where he aimed," and asking, "What's the most I could get if I killed him?" As Landau and his wife Beatrice treated Jean's wounds, "her bared breasts rose and fell in rhythmical movement." She also said the pain was worst near her kidneys.

At 5:30, Landau and Jean drove to Easton and hunted for Paul, finding him passed out, "naked, pot-bellied and hairless" on "the floor of the den." To awaken him, Landau threw water and slapped him with a towel while Jean yelled, "Sonofabitching little fairy! You have no right to be alive." She threatened to give him poison in his coffee and, in a scene out of slapstick, Landau supposedly slapped a crazed Jean across the face to keep her from getting past him to Paul while she screamed, "Let me at him! Let me at him! You're just a rotten awful fag with a dangle half the size of my pinkie. You stinking bastard, you did something to my kidney." The climax came with Jean stripping naked to show "what my so-called husband did to me!" Paul reportedly said, "Every man ... gets an ... erection just by talking about her ... didn't I have the right to think Jean could help me at least as much?"

Then, incredibly, the three planned the wedding reception during which Beatrice stayed by Jean's side and Landau by Paul's while Jean pretended everything was fine. Paul "was most charming, smiling sober and his usual self. Jean was gowned to perfection, sweet and gracious to all. She, too, performed as if nothing had happened. But Arthur knew different."[17] After the reception, he allegedly locked Paul in "the den" and Jean retreated to the master bedroom and braced a chair against the doorknob.

Landau said he told Paul to get rid of his mistresses and forced him to see MGM doctor Herman Sugarman, who told Landau that Paul purchased a $200 (perhaps $5,000 today) machine to increase the size of his penis but couldn't have sex due to a convoluted Peter Pan–type syndrome rooted in his under-developed organ and Jewish background.

The next day, Jean supposedly told him to "forget what happened and what he saw, she must find some way to make her marriage work — she really loves Paul for what he is, although no sex, he has much tenderness, warmth of personality, she can learn much from him and perhaps in time by medical help he can become a husband. Meanwhile she will do her utmost to make him a good, loyal wife, and a happy home."[18]

Landau's tales are ridiculous; among other things, he takes credit for discovering Jean, negotiating her *Hell's Angels* role, salvaging her Hughes screen test, and getting her an MGM contract (Paul did that). And he claimed Paul routinely slapped and beat Jean in public, in cabs and during dinner at the Bellos. Landau is an absolutely disreputable source and the stories fraught with errors and blatant lies that evidence themselves from the first pages. Several key scenes take place in Paul's den; there is no den at Easton. If he passed out in the living room, they would see him as soon as they came in the house, yet they had to "search" for him. The Carmichaels and Davis were at the servants' house and never mentioned either Jean leaving or Landau visiting when they would have been preparing breakfast. As for Jean's alleged injuries, Colleen Moore and Marian Nixon helped her dress for the reception; had she been covered with welts and bite marks they would have seen them. And Jean's transformation — in eight hours — from a bloody and beaten victim into a loving wife wanting to make her marriage work, defies logic.

Landau and Shulman branded Paul impotent even as Landau warned him to get rid of his many mistresses. Landau told Shulman that Paul had dozens of affairs, kept a concubine-mistress at MGM and had an affair with Irene Harrison, who was overcome with jealousy and hopelessly in love with him.[19]

Time magazine suggested that Shulman's book was "BETTER LEFT UNSAID," that the "thoroughly unpleasant book" was full of stories that are "clearly imaginary" and that whenever he and Landau didn't know something as fact, "between them, they improvised."[20] Shulman later sought a job as an English professor at California State College and during the vetting process the school's chancellor received dozens of letters from people opposing his hiring. One was from writers Dale and Katherine Eunson calling *Harlow* a "scatological piece of fiction masquerading as biography" and warning the school not to hire him, that the "thought of exposing students to him as a model and mentor fills [us] with horror."[21]

Little of Shulman's book survives scrutiny. Reviewing notes, correspondence, and research files at the AMPAS library that chronicled the collaboration with Landau, it is clear the recollections are tainted at best and fiction at worst. The tawdry book had impact, though. During the 1970s, people who knew Jean and Paul — by then elderly and with failing memory — created memoirs that included bits of Shulman's book as if by osmosis. Anita Loos was close to both Paul and Jean, socializing with them often and attending the Olympics together just before Paul's death. But by the time of her 1974 memoirs *Kiss Hollywood Good-by* she called him "that German psycho" and sensationalized Jean's joke about Paul getting her a football player into an indictment of their relationship.[22]

Irene Mayer, while clearly sympathetic to Paul, later includes David Selznick's dubious claim that Jean made a pass at a party. Douglas Fairbanks, Jr., made the same claim, that Jean grabbed his leg while she and Paul were telling him of their engagement (while describing her engagement ring; she never had one). For her part, St. Johns sauced up her own story in later writings, accusing Paul of trying to rape Jean with a strap-on appendage before the wedding-night beating.[23]

Paul's intimates and friends scoffed at Shulman. Colleen Moore attended the wedding reception and contradicted Shulman in her 1968 memoirs. She amusingly wrote that it more likely for Jean to beat up Paul than vice versa and said, "[I]f Jean were anything other than her normal self, she was happier."[24] Louise Brooks, perhaps the most honest chronicler of 1920s Hollywood, also defended Paul's sexual reputation.

As important as some of the awful things written and said by people like Shulman and St. Johns are the things that *weren't* said. Irving Thalberg refused to cooperate with Mayer and MGM defaming Paul. Jean also adamantly refused to even become a small part of the studio plan. She never spoke to anyone about Paul's death and denied the basic tenets of Mayer's stories.

Unlikely confirmation that Paul never harmed Jean came from Mama Jean, obtained more precisely from what she *didn't* say about him. Had Paul done anything to hurt Jean, physically or otherwise, it's hard to imagine the seismic impact of Mama Jean's response. But she never made a single disparaging remark about Paul and did not participate in the MGM flogging.

In a later *Modern Romance* story she wrote, "They were old souls, the Baby and Paul. There were drawn together by a profound, mutual respect, the one for the other; by admiration for the qualities of mind and spirit each found in the other. How often Paul said to me and to others, 'If Jean would be my wife for two days, two weeks, two months, I would die content....' The Baby's marriage to *poor Paul* [italics added by author] was over and finished in two months. She went through agony and suffering the depth and extent of which no-one will ever know ... She loved Paul very dearly and to love is, always, to understand and so, forgive."[25] In later correspondence with Arthur Landau and Irving Shulman, she repeatedly referred to him as "Poor Paul."

Had even a small portion of the Shulman-Landau story been true, Mama Jean would have been the first to confirm such. But to her, he remained "Poor Paul."

The question remains: Who killed Paul Bern? Did Paul Bern? A suicide narrative simply cannot withstand scrutiny. He certainly *could* have killed himself but there is nothing to support that conclusion. The only "proof" offered that Paul killed himself was that the gun that killed him belonged to him. But that really doesn't prove anything, particularly with all of the evidence to the contrary. So if Paul didn't kill himself, who did?

For some time it was whispered that Jean killed him after learning about Dorothy. Indeed, Louis B. Mayer and Irene Selznick both initially assumed she shot him, as did the D.A. Some believe Jean was at Easton when Paul was killed either by suicide or shot by Dorothy. She obviously could have been there for Dorothy's visit. She undoubtedly knew that Dorothy was coming Sunday night, but it doesn't seem like Jean to want to be there for that particular visit.

Still others suggest Jean witnessed some portion of the visit and left either before Millette killed Paul or was removed to Club View after the fact by Strickling. It's unlikely she was there; if Dorothy killed Paul, she would probably have killed Jean too. Also there were only two champagne glasses at the pool and Jean enjoyed drinking. If she were there, there would have been three glasses. It's doubtful Jean was there. She was at Club View to give Paul and Dorothy privacy.

Studio insiders considered Irene Harrison a suspect. Mousy but not unattractive, Irene worked for Paul for six years and was said to be in love with him. They were even rumored to have had an affair. Born in England, she emigrated with her parents and younger brother in 1911 and was 23 when Paul hired her. She lived in a bungalow at 4194 Lafayette Avenue with her parents and 22-year-old brother, whom Paul hired as a film editor.

Harrison was inconsolable during the weeks after he died, "the saddest figure on the lot ... who bravely tried to fight back tears, but it was impossible." Her only comment: "I just can't believe it."[26] Arthur Landau told Irving Shulman, "[T]he Irene Harrison girl, who was not of sound mind and much in love with Bern, somewhat revengfull [*sic*] and more so when she learned he was about to marry H. If you ever had met her you would soon realize she was up to some mischief. Her story about $45,000 being in a bank vault was a lie. She told me one time Bern was setting up a trust fund for her. He did not have enough money to buy cat food. Harrison was somewhat of a concubine to Bern and so was Barbara La Marr who was a concubine and a whipping boy for Paul. She had beauty and brains but Harrison was only being a 'spare.' If you remember rightly, Paul added $10.00 to her weekly studio pay. I called her a baby frightener. She never looked bathed to me, her clothes were drab and her hair stood up like the women on Figi Island. La Marr was fond of Bern and he loved her to a small degree until he met Jean."[27]

She was supposedly distraught but strangely, photos of her with Henry Bern after his arrival in Glendale on Wednesday evidence no such trauma. But it's a stretch to think an obsessed Irene Harrison killed Paul. In the end, it all comes down to Dorothy.

It seems clear Dorothy Millette killed Paul Bern. She was never cured of her mental problems. She was released from Blythewood Sanitarium because she was harmless, not cured. For years she lived reclusively and quietly at the Algonquin, supported by Paul. That arrangement was fine until 1931 or 1932 when she became more strident about seeing him. Who knows why; maybe she believed Paul could make her a star in biblical pictures or maybe she simply wanted him back. Whatever the motive, she forced her way to San Francisco in May and bombarded Paul with letters and telephone calls. These got more and more demanding after Paul's engagement was announced and he married.

Paul and Jean went to San Francisco in mid–August, I think to try to resolve the problem, but the trip was unsuccessful. Paul had been there at least one full day when Jean arrived and received a telegram from MGM ordering her back. Paul probably went to discuss the deal MGM brokered to solve the Dorothy problem. She was supposed to quietly relocate to Mexico and the arrangements were made but she reneged; "the woman Malett [*sic*] did not go to Mexico as agreed and she began to blackmail Bern." She was blackmailing him and MGM knew it; Landau told Irving Shulman, "The M.C.— the letters — the blackmail — gather them and keep" but the "Legal Department MGM won't allow them to be seen."[28] It was clear Dorothy would not go quietly into the night.

This is what happened Sunday night, September 5, 1932. I don't believe Paul, Jean, or even Dorothy expected her visit to turn violent. Paul knew she was coming and when she arrived between 5:00 and 6:00, John Carmichael and Jean were gone and Winifred Carmichael getting ready to leave with Clifton Davis, who was puttering around the grounds. Alone at Easton, they spent the evening visiting at the pool, swimming, drinking champagne and getting along fine until late that night.

Davis and Winifred Carmichael (having returned from Club View) heard the escalating noise; chatting and laughter turning to loud on-and-off arguing as the evening wore on. Winifred heard Paul yell, "Get out of my life!" Down the street, Slavko Vorkapich and his wife were awakened by the loud disagreement as well.

At 1:04 A.M. Paul called the MGM Transportation Department and ordered a car to take his visitor to San Francisco. When the car arrived at 2:00 he walked down the path and told the chauffeur — a popular Cockney driver nicknamed "Lymie"— that his passenger would be down in a little while.

Sometime after 2:30, Paul and Dorothy went from the pool into the house to change out of their wet bathing suits. Paul hung his wet suit on a hook in his closet-dressing room and began drying off. Just a few feet away from the closet door was a long, narrow table at the foot of Paul's bed near the window, strewn with letters, books, scripts he was reading, and his two pistols. There was always at least one there in case something happened at his secluded home.

As Paul dried himself off, Dorothy grabbed one of the guns, stepped into the large dressing area, put the gun to the side of his head and pulled the trigger. For some reason, she screamed as Paul fell to the floor. She stepped back and dropped the gun on the bedroom floor and quickly changed into dry clothes. Forgetting her wet bathing suit in the bathroom, she hurried down the hill to the limousine.

At the bottom of the hill, Winifred Carmichael was awakened by what she thought was a radio but as her head cleared she realized she "never heard a radio make sounds like that before. I was awakened by an unearthly scream."[29] She couldn't determine where they originated; sound carries in the canyons and is often muffled and these noises emanated from the back corner of the house in the dressing room. Winifred rose up to investigate and made her way to the pool, where she was examining the remnants of the visit when she looked down the path and saw the veiled woman running down the hill. Dorothy never noticed Winifred above and behind her at the pool when she ran down the steps. Stumbling down the path, she dropped one of her shoes with the extra lift in the heel.

When the later 1933 grand jury foreman W.W. Widenham asked Winifred why she never mentioned this earlier, she said simply, "I wasn't asked these things before and I didn't tell them." Shown a photo of Dorothy, she said, "This is the woman I saw. I'm sure of it."

When Dorothy reached the waiting MGM limousine she told Lymie to get out of there, fast. Slavko Vorkapich heard the limo careening down the hill just after 3:00. Lymie drove to the Plaza Hotel and told his boss, transportation manager Lou Kolb, that she never said a word during the eight-hour drive up Route 101, that "she didn't want to talk. Cripes, man, she just kept telling me to go faster."[30]

Perhaps the best evidence that Paul was murdered was Dorothy's own suicide the next night. When she picked up her newspapers at the Plaza newsstand Monday afternoon, she would have had the first inkling she was already being hunted. It would only be a matter of time before they learned her identity and where she was, so she fled. She checked two bags at the hotel, took some of her things in a single trunk and boarded the *Delta King* Monday evening. Early Tuesday morning she flung herself into the Sacramento River. Why would Dorothy kill herself if Paul, the man she loved and still wanted, was alive? She had no reason to kill herself unless she knew Paul was dead. And she would only know *that* if she had killed him.

There were three things important to Louis B. Mayer as he stood with Howard Strickling and Whitey Hendry gazing down on Paul's crumpled body that hot Labor Day morning. First was protecting MGM. Second was protecting Jean to safeguard an MGM investment. A distant third was Paul Bern. The memory of Paul Bern — charitable, sympathetic, generous, in love with his new bride, "a good, decent, honorable man" — was sacrificed by Mayer in his misguided attempt to protect his studio.[31]

Paul Bern was sacrificed for the sake of MGM, the studio he helped make the greatest in Hollywood. His legacy should be choosing, promoting, and crafting some of the greatest films in movie history, guiding the career of the biggest female star in MGM history, and for a lifetime of charity and good works. With the true story told, now it can be.

Epilogue — Shadows

The MGM fable went unquestioned for nearly 30 years until a 1960 magazine story by Ben Hecht reignited interest in Paul's death. Although he was a prolific screenwriter and Academy Award winner, Hecht "hated Hollywood for what it did to people," saying "a producer's job was to turn good writers into hacks, to guard against the unusual" and he called studio executives "the trusted loyalists of the cliché."[1]

Hecht suggested that he knew Paul was murdered by an unnamed woman and the suicide note a forgery and the investigation a "suicide whitewash." He said a suicide "would be less a black eye for their biggest movie making heroine. It might crimp her box office allure to have her blazoned as a wife who couldn't hold her husband."[2]

At first D.A. William B. McKesson said, "When a writer of Ben Hecht's stature puts in public print without qualification that a murder has been committed it is up to the district attorney to investigate the case...." But after concluding that Hecht's theories offered no actual proof, he reversed course and closed the investigation, saying, "When I ordered the record check I assumed Hecht was still a responsible reporter. It now appears ... that he apparently was peddling a wild and unconfirmed rumor as fact."[3]

Hecht and then Landau's 1964 book led to a resurgence of interest and resulted in two 1965 movies titled *Harlow*, one starring Carroll Baker and another featuring Carol Lynley. The Baker version was described as "gaudy, highly publicized valentine" with "Baker suitably bleached and lacquered as the Blonde Bombshell" and a script that "succumbed to silliness ... in the first reel."[4] The Lynley version didn't fare much better, described as a "rancid screen biography" featuring a "horribly miscast" Lynley.[5] In the years since, Jean's popularity has eclipsed even the level she achieved during her lifetime.

Easton remained empty for months. Jean never returned and over the years the property had several owners. Director Milo Frank and his actress wife Sally Forrest owned the property during the 1950s and 1960s, and during the late 1960s rented to Hollywood hairdresser Jay Sebring. Although he was chronically late with his rent, he somehow purchased the house in late 1968.[6] A frequent visitor was his close friend actress Sharon Tate.

Over the years, several urban legends have been attributed to the house. Allegedly at least four more people died there, a maid who hung herself, several men who drowned in the pool, and another alleged suicide. Tate told friends that while staying there alone (allegedly in 1965 though Sebring didn't live there at that time) she was so overwhelmed by unease lying in bed she kept the lights on, and looked up and saw an apparition of "a creepy little man" scurrying around the room ignoring her as he searched for something. Throwing on her robe, she fled down the stairs only to allegedly see a ghostly form tied to the posts with its throat cut, lying on the landing. After pouring herself a drink in the living room she surprisingly returned back upstairs past the still-visible figure on the floor and returned to sleep even though the little man was still pacing the bedroom.

Tate's is a famous ghost story but it should be remembered that during that era Tate and Sebring were allegedly serious drug abusers. Sebring was living at Easton when he was murdered in August 1969 at Tate's nearby estate by members of Charles Manson's "Family." For their part, current owners Ron and Maggie Hale — who have lived in the house for almost 40 years — report not a single such incident in all their time there.

The colorful mural above the living room — Paul's wedding gift to Jean — resurfaced in the 1990s, still in the family of the painter who removed it shortly after Paul's death and hanging in the dining room. It has been offered for sale for almost $200,000.

Paul's many girlfriends had varied career success after his death. Jeanette Loff appeared in small roles in a half-dozen forgettable films before marrying producer Bert Friedlob. She died after ingesting ammonia at their 9233 Doheny Road home in August, 1942, an incident never confirmed as suicide or accidental. Strangely, her family believed she was murdered.

Mary Duncan left the movies in 1933 after marrying Stephen "Laddie" Sanford, heir to the Bigelow-Sanford carpet fortune. She moved to Palm Beach, Florida, where she lived the rest of her life and became the grand dame of Palm Beach society living next door to her best friend Rose Kennedy. She died in 1993.

Virginia Valli retired from the movies and her 1931 marriage to Paul's friend Charlie Farrell lasted until his death in 1968. Long retired in Palm Springs and died in 1988.

In 1928, Lya De Putti left Hollywood for New York, disgusted at the thought of sound film that she believed was a fad. In late 1931 she was hospitalized for an operation to remove a chicken bone lodged in her esophagus but contracted pneumonia and died on November 27.

Olive Borden, who earned $1,500 a week in the mid–1920s, abruptly left Fox in 1928 and after another half dozen movies retired in 1938. She served in the WACs during World War II, after which she returned to Hollywood but was unable to revive her career. She died in 1947 from a stomach ailment — probably related to alcoholism — at the Sunshine Mission in L.A., a home for destitute women.

Paul's secretary and alleged former mistress Irene Harrison left MGM shortly after Paul's death and went to work for fan dancer Sally Rand, another ex-girlfriend. By the late 1930s she'd disappeared from Hollywood.

Most of Paul's male friends had long Hollywood careers with the exception of Jack Gilbert, whose career was undercut by the long feud with Louis B. Mayer. Carey Wilson was involved in over 200 films through the 1950s, producing classics like *The Postman Always Rings Twice* (1946), writing several Andy Hardy films like *Judge Hardy and Son* (1939), and acting in several dozen others including his popular 1940s series based on the writings of Nostradamus. His marriage to Carmelita Geraghty lasted over 30 years, until his 1962 death in L.A.

Willis Goldbeck, who shared one of Paul's last evenings at the pool at Easton the week preceding his death, wrote almost four dozen films during a career of over 30 years, including the popular 1940s *Dr. Kildare* series, the 1949 hit *Johnny Holiday* and his final film, 1962's *The Man Who Shot Liberty Valence*. He died in New York in 1979.

Irving Thalberg was deeply affected by Paul's death, probably moreso by the actions of Mayer and MGM. After the funeral he retreated to Santa Monica and would speak to no one; during the next week and a half the only call he took was from Jean asking to go back to work. For several months after he finally emerged, he was short-tempered and prone to fits of deep moodiness and despair. He no longer worked as hard as he had and for several months was determined to leave MGM for a year's sabbatical.

Nick Schenck responded by increasing his pay, which widened the gulf between Irving and Mayer. While Irving was hospitalized from a heart attack after the 1932 Christmas party, Mayer engineered a coup, replacing Thalberg's circle with a group led by David Selznick and Walter Wanger. Later, during his recuperative trip to Europe in March, Mayer delivered his death blow, offering Irving's men — Lewin, Stromberg, Hyman and Weingarten — their own production companies and removing the position of head of production. When he returned in August, Irving was at the same level as his former advisors.

But he remained at MGM and during the next few years produced the greatest MGM films of the 1930s, including *The Barretts of Wimpole Street*, *Mutiny on the Bounty*, *Camille*, and *Marie Antoinette*. Four years to the day after Paul's death, Irving and Norma were spending the weekend at the Del Monte Lodge in Monterey with Sam Wood, Jack and Virginia Conway and Chico and Helen Marx. Playing bridge on the porch, he got a chill which developed into a bad cold and by Saturday the 13th he was sick enough to miss the annual MGM studio picnic for the first time. By Monday he was in an oxygen tent at his Santa Monica house. He died Monday afternoon.

The day of his September 17 funeral, MGM closed for the day, the first and only time that ever occurred. During the last month of his life, Paul had written a full script based on the Sinclair Lewis short story "The Willow Walk" at Irving's request. Irving never put the film into production and kept the script in his desk until he died.

In late 1932, Mama Jean and Marino Bello moved with Jean into her new Beverly Hills mansion at 214 South Beverly Glen. Mama Jean finally divorced Bello on September 27, 1935, alleging that he wasted money and had "violent outbursts of temper."[7]

Bello sold oil investments and his dubious treasure hunts for 15 years after his divorce. Interestingly, in a November, 1938 F.B.I. interview, Longy Zwillman was questioned about his relationship with Bello.[8] He married twice more before suffering a heart attack on August 17, 1953, at his home at 4448 Cosgrove Avenue in L.A. He was buried at Forest Lawn.

Mama Jean opened an antique shop in Palm Springs before retiring to a small apartment on South Beverly Glen in L.A. On June 11, 1958, she died in an L.A. hospital from heart problems.

Paul's brother Henry lived the rest of his life in New Rochelle, New York, never speaking publicly about the circumstances of Paul's death or what he learned during his trip to L.A. He had a successful public relations and advertising career and he and Miriam had five children. His son Raymond survives, as does a granddaughter and a grandson, Paul Henry Bern. Henry died in 1971. Donald Gallery lives quietly in retirement in Mexico.

In the months after Paul's death, Jean was the defendant in a "trial being conducted on street cars, in restaurants, and on dance floors of the nation."[9] Everyone had an opinion but her refusal to buckle under to Mayer's demand that she directly or even tacitly support his version of Paul's life and death earned her the admiration of her close friends. Irene Selznick called her "truly a heroine" and Thalberg had called her braver than any man.[10] She never spoke of Paul's death nor did she allow it to be mentioned in her presence. The only thing she ever said was, "In the midst of my happiness came tragedy. Once again my house of dreams tumbled about my head with Paul's death. The only thing that saved me was my work."[11]

Red Dust began a four-year string of a dozen hits for Jean, including *Dinner at Eight* (1933), *Bombshell* (1933), *China Seas* (1935), and *Wife vs. Secretary* (1936). During those years she established her own screen persona: the tough-talking but kind-hearted dame who does not hide her sexuality. That character came through no matter the role, even playing a wealthy socialite in *Libeled Lady* (1936).[12] In the late spring of 1937 she began filming *Saratoga* with Clark Gable.

Her personal life was less successful. After an affair with boxer Max Baer she married cameraman Hal Rosson just a year after Paul's death. They divorced seven months later and she began a relationship with William Powell that lasted the rest of her life. She was madly in love with him and they were reportedly engaged several times but he would not commit to marriage or to the children Jean so desperately wanted. By mid–1937 she was an alcoholic, subject to violent mood swings brought on by the pressure of the Powell relationship. She was also dying and didn't know it.

On March 23 she had four teeth removed, almost dying during the operation and remaining hospitalized for 18 days. She never fully recovered and spent the spring in ill health while she filmed *Saratoga*. On May 27 she worked even though she was in dreadful pain but collapsed and had to leave the set. She spent the next week secluded at her 512 Palm Drive house drifting in and out of consciousness and coherence while Mama Jean refused entrance to her friends.

Her family physician diagnosed cholecystitis, a gall bladder infection, and she was given fluids, but he had in fact misdiagnosed Jean. She was actually suffering from nephritis, advanced kidney failure, and by the time she was rushed to the hospital on June 6 she had contracted uremia, an often-fatal product of kidney failure. The conditions were likely the long-term effects of a childhood bout with scarlet fever. On June 7 she died at Good Samaritan Hospital. She was just 26.

The entire studio went into deep mourning. So many calls flooded the MGM switchboard, the phone system shut down, and screenwriter Harry Risken said, "The day the Baby died there wasn't one sound in the MGM commissary for three hours. Not one goddamn sound."[13] Her funeral was a Hollywood spectacle attended by 250 invited guests including Gable, Mayer, Powell, Norma Shearer, the Barrymores, and the Marx Brothers. Hundreds of MGM grips, electricians and set workers waited quietly outside the small church at Forest Lawn in Glendale, unable to gain entrance.

Her $5,000 bronze and silver casket bore a silver nameplate inscribed with her signature and her birth and death dates, and it was covered with 1,500 lilies of the valley and 500 gardenias. She wore her pink mousseline de soie gown from *Saratoga* and was returned to her pre-illness beauty by her personal makeup artist Violet Denoyer. She held a single gardenia in her left hand with a note from William Powell saying, "Goodnight my dearest darling." Her crypt in Forest Lawn's great mausoleum is in the Sanctuary of Benediction, next to Irving Thalberg's.

Even hardened ex-mobster Eddie Mannix was touched by Jean's death, saying, "A sweet child has passed from us. She was not only a great artist, she was a wonderfully honest, sincere human being."

For many years after Jean's death, Mama Jean kept her clothes in storage at a Bekins warehouse in L.A. and once a month visited the locker to rearrange the dresses, smooth out a wrinkled sleeve, and chat with them as if they were alive. After Jean's death, Mama Jean rejected Christian Science and joined the Unity Church.[14] When she died, she was interred above Jean.

Since Jean's death, her films have been rightly recognized as among the greatest films of the 1930s and her popularity has soared. The value of Harlow memorabilia has also skyrocketed. Original George Hurrell photographs of Jean command over $10,000 and vintage studio photos sell for thousands. In 2006 a photo in her Kitty Packard costume from *Dinner at Eight* sold for over $2,800. Lobby cards for her minor films command over $1,000; a lobby insert poster for *Saratoga* sold for almost $7,000 in 2007. The original 1928 Roach contract she signed as "Harlean McGrew II" sold for $3,550 in 2006. What was allegedly the last bottle of Brise Ambreé perfume, owned by actress Ann Sothern, sold for over $5,000 in 2006.

For the rest of her life, Jean never spoke of Paul's death or of MGM's role destroying his legacy. Perhaps the last person to whom she spoke about

anything relating to Paul's death was Sacramento county coroner Jim Garlick. About a month after Dorothy Millette's death, Jean called Garlick, who
was understandably surprised that the star was calling from Hollywood. She
told him she read that his auction of Dorothy's belongings raised only $105,
far below the $350 needed for a headstone for her grave.

He told her, "You know, Miss Harlow, I got money from an MGM attorney, and I gave Miss Millette a beautiful funeral," but she interrupted him,
saying, "Mr. Silberberg was acting for me. I sent that money, and I appreci-
ate what you've done, but how much do we need to mark the grave?"

Garlick estimated $350 would be enough and Jean said, "You got it.
May I tell you how I'd like it to read?" After telling him, she said quietly,
"Make it pretty." Dorothy's headstone, etched with flowers, reads simply:
DOROTHY MILLETTE BERN 1886 – 1932.

Appendix I:
Handwriting Comparison

Left—Note sent to Mabel Normand and *above*—alleged suicide note found in Easton guestbook.

Appendix II:
Paul Bern's Will

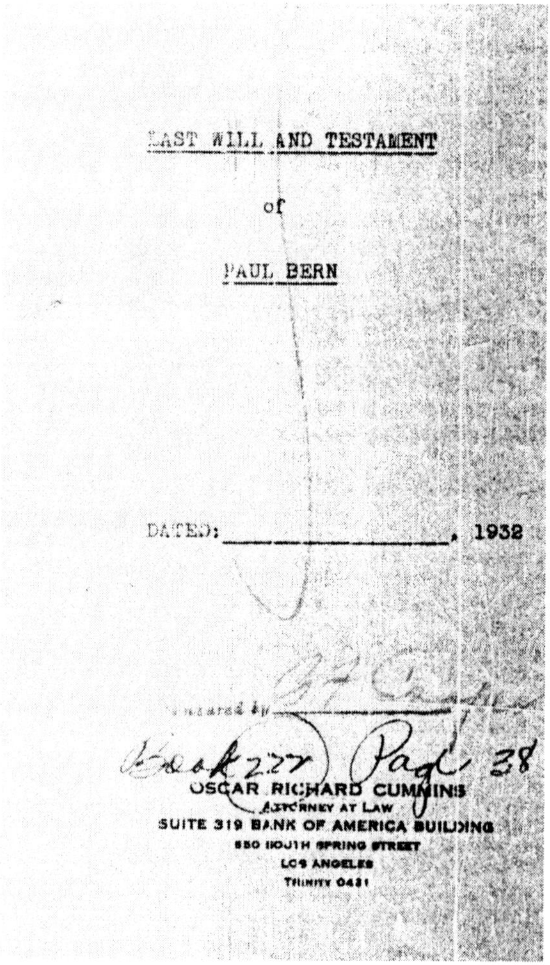

LAST WILL AND TESTAMENT

of

PAUL BERN

DATED: _____, 1932

Prepared by

Book 227 Page 38

OSCAR RICHARD CUMMINS
ATTORNEY AT LAW
SUITE 319 BANK OF AMERICA BUILDING
650 SOUTH SPRING STREET
LOS ANGELES
TRINITY 0431

LAST WILL AND TESTAMENT

of

PAUL BERN

FILED
SEP 28 1932
L. E. LAMPTON, County Clerk

I, PAUL BERN, of the City of Los Angeles,
County of Los Angeles, State of California, being
of sound and disposing mind, and in every respect
in full vigor of mind and body, do declare the
following to be my Last Will and Testament:

FIRST: I give, devise and bequeath all
my property of whatever kind, real and personal,
and wheresoever situate, after the payment of any
just debts that may constitute a claim upon it at
the time of my death, to my beloved wife, HARLEAN
BERN.

SECOND: I do hereby name and appoint my
beloved wife, HARLEAN BERN, the sole executrix and
administratrix of this, my Last Will and Testament,
to act without bond.

IN WITNESS WHEREOF, I have hereunto set my
hand and seal this 24ᵗʰ day of _July_____,
in the year of our Lord 1932, in the presence of
the witnesses whose signatures are hereunto subscribed.

_____
(PAUL BERN)

The foregoing instrument, consisting of
one (1) page, including the page signed by the
Testator, was, at the date hereof, by PAUL BERN,
the maker thereof, signed in our presence and in
the presence of each of us, and at the time of
his subscribing said instrument he declared that
it was his Will, and at his request and in his
presence, and in the presence of each other,
we have subscribed our names as witnesses thereto.

Oscar Richard Cummins

Residing at _5444 Red Oak Drive_

Los Angeles, Cal.

Harry S. Cogen

Residing at _115 N. Sweetzer_

Los Angeles, Calif.

Will admitted to probate this
19th day of _October_ 1932
Attest: L. E. Lampton County Clerk
By _H. H. McDonald_

Appendix III:
Paul Bern's Estate

In the matter of the estate of Bern No. 130814

Assets at time of death		
Cash in bank(s)	$ 1696.37	
First National Bank (360.86)		
Accrued Salary (1194.00)		
First National Bank (141.51)		
Accrued Interest	531.66	
Bank of America (94.70)		
Bank of America (436.96)		
Refund — Automobile Insurance	2.46	
1930 Cord Cabriolet no. fd-2856-A	725.00	
Real Estate		
Undeveloped lot at s/w corner		
Beverly Drive and Gregory Way	10500.00	
Promissory Note — Frank Orsatti	750.00	
Stocks & Bonds		
Ten (10) shares, preferred		
stock, Dr. Johann Strasska Labs.	365.70	
Five (5) shares, common Stock,		
Dr. Johann Strasska Labs.	0.00	
shares, Victor Huehaus Prods.	0.05	
Life Insurance		
John Hancock, no. 603-g	10000.00	
TOTAL ASSETS		**$24571.24**
Less Credits		
Real Estate (transferred)	10500.00	
Loss on Sale of Cord Automobile	275.00	

Loss on First National Bank

Account Collection	83.87
Expenses	612.25
Price-Daniel Funeral Home (450.00)	
Insurance — Automobile (6.15)	
Federal Tax Check (0.02)	
Tax Preparation (50.00)	
Silberberg, Atty. (106.08)	
Attorney's Fees	1639.30
Payment — Super Floral	25.00
Total Credits	**13635.42**

Cash Available for Payment of Claims   **$10935.82**

Claims Allowed

Dora Ingram Book Shop (books)	86.25
Edward B. Jones, M.D. (medical)	60.00
May Department Stores (merchandise)	27.95
Young's Market (groceries)	21.71
Super Floral Service (flowers)	25.00
I. Magnin (merchandise)	821.00
Bullock's Wilshire (merchandise)	276.50
Boulevard Super Service (gasoline)	125.06
Golden State Co., Inc. (milk delivery)	11.11
Cosmopolitan Laundry (laundry service)	32.47
Ambassador Hotel (meals)	136.85
Robert Kennicott, M.D. (medical services)	55.00
Tanner Motor Livery (auto hire)	87.25
Barker Brothers (merchandise)	7.00
Fidelity Deposit & Guaranty (insurance)	23.77
B.P. Fineman (note)	500.00
H.W. Grieve (merchandise)	1009.50
M. Cherry (tickets)	265.00
Alexander & Oviatt (merchandise)	410.25
Brock & Company (jewelry)	87.50
Caillet Pharmacy (prescription drugs)	6.50
Metro-Goldwyn-Mayer (miscellaneous)	198.32
L.C. Chandler, M.D. (medical services)	30.00
Security First National (judgement)	2439.17
Beverly Wilshire Hand Laundry (laundry)	17.94
Internal Revenue (income tax, 1931)	2873.56
Internal Revenue (income tax, 1932)	6580.85
Total Claims Allowed	**16256.80**

Net Estate   **($ 5295.98)**

Filmography

China Seas (MGM, 1935) PB not credited but he revised the script, specifically the ending, at Thalberg's request and submitted his revision the day before he died. Shooting days: 53. Length: 9 reels, 8,021 feet. New York premiere date: August 9, 1935. General release date: August 16, 1935. Producer: Irving Thalberg. Associate Producer: Albert Lewin. Director: Tay Garnett. Assistant Director: Joseph Newman. Scene Directors: William Wellman (pirate scenes), Harold Bucquet (mob scenes), James McKay (night water scenes). Writers: Paul Bern, Jules Furthman, James Kevin McGuinness, Paul Hervey Fox, John Lee Mahin. Photography: Ray June, Ray Ramsey, Emily Fredericks. Film Editor: William LeVanway. Art Direction: Cedric Gibbons. Associate Art Direction: James Havens, David Townsend, Edwin B. Willis, Elmer Sheeley. Costumes: Adrian. Music: Herbert Stothart. Sound: Douglas Shearer. Cast: Clark Gable, Jean Harlow, Wallace Beery, Lewis Stone, Rosalind Russell, Dudley Digges, C. Aubrey Smith, Robert Benchley, William Henry, Countess Live de Maigret, Lillian Bond, Edward Brophy, Soo Yong, Carol Ann Beery, Akim Tamiroff, Ivan Lebedeff, Hattie McDaniel, Donald Meek, Pat Flaherty, Charles Irwin, Willie Fung, Forrester Harvey, John Ince, Emily Fitzroy.

The Divorcee (MGM, 1930) PB not credited but he convinced Thalberg to purchase the original Ursula Parrott story and is mentioned in period newspaper stories as both producer and script consultant; confirmed by Sam Marx. Shooting days: 22. Length: 9 reels, 7,640 feet. Release date: April 19, 1930. Director: Robert Z. Leonard. Writers: John Meehan, Nick Grinde, Zelda Sears. Photography: Norbert Brodine. Film Editors: Hugh Wynn, Truman K. Wood. Art Direction: Cedric Gibbons. Costumes: Adrian. Sound: J.K. Brock, Douglas Shearer. Cast: Norma Shearer, Chester Morris, Conrad Nagel, Robert Montgomery, Florence Eldridge, Helene Millard, Robert Elliott, Mary Doran, Tyler Brooke, Zelda Sears, George Irving, Helen Johnson.

Strange Cargo (Pathé, 1929) PB not credited but newspaper reviews and production records confirm his work with John W. Krafft to adapt writer Benjamin Glazer's original script *Missing Man*, which was produced as a silent. Length: 7 reels, 7,045 feet. Preview date: February 20, 1929. General release date: March 31, 1929. Director: Benjamin Glazer. Writers: John W. Krafft, Paul Bern, Benjamin Glazer, Horace Jackson, Melchoir Lengyel. Photography: Arthur Miller. Film Editors: Paul

Weatherwax, Jack Ogilvie. Cast: Lee Patrick, June Nash, George Barraud, Cosmo Kyrle Bellew, Russell Gleason, Frank Reicher, Claude King, Ned Sparks, Josephine Brown, Charles Hamilton, André Beranger, Otto Matieson, Harry Allen, Warner Richmond.

It's a Great Life (MGM, 1929) PB not credited but newspaper reviews and production stories confirmed his work with writer Joseph F. Poland, who was brought to MGM to work with Paul on the film. Working titles: *Cotton and Silk* and *Imperfect Ladies*. Length: 8,575 feet. Premiere date: November 25, 1929. General release date: December 6, 1929. Director: Sam Wood. Writers: Paul Bern, Joseph F. Poland, Byron Morgan, Alfred Block, Al Boasberg, Willard Mack. Photography: Peverell Marley. Film Editor: Frank Sullivan. Art Direction: Cedric Gibbons. Costumes: David Cox. Sound: Douglas Shearer. Choreography: Sammy Lee. Cast: Rosetta Duncan, Vivian Duncan, Lawrence Gray, Jed Prouty, Benny Rubin.

The Godless Girl (Pathé, 1928) PB not credited but newspaper reviews, production stories and archival research confirm he was brought in to add dialogue and scenes to a previously completed silent film. C.B. DeMille Productions. Length: 12 reels, 9,328 feet. General release date: March 31, 1929. Director: Cecil B. DeMille. Assistant Directors: Frank Urson, Curt Rehfeld. Writers: Paul Bern, Jeanie Macpherson, Beulah Marie Dix. Photography: Peverell Marley, J.F. Westerberg, Franklin McBride. Film Editor: Anne Bauchens. Art Direction: Mitchell Leisen. Costumes: Adrian. Technical Engineer: Paul Sprunck. Cast: Lina Basquette, Marie Prevost, George Duryea, Noah Beery, Eddie Quillan, Mary Jane Irving, Clarence Burton, Dick Alexander, Kate Price, Hedwig Reicher, Julia Faye, Viola Louie, Emily Barrye, Jimmy Aldine, Vivian Bay, Elaine Bennett, Wade Boteler, Betty Boyd, Julia Brown, Archie Burke, Colin Chase, Cameron Coffey, Cecelia De Mille, Jacqueline Dryis, George Ellis, Anieka Elter, James Farley, Larry Fisher, Evelyn Francisco, May Giraci, Grace Gordon, Milton Holmes, William Humphrey, George Irving, Peaches Jackson, Dolores Jackson, Jane Keckley, Nora Kildare, Richard Lapan, Ida McKenzie, Don Marion, Edith May, Mary Mayberry, Collette Merton, Buddy Messinger, Pat Moore, Jack Murphy, Pat Palmer, Janice Peters, Hortense Petra, Gertrude Quality, Rae Randall, Billie Van Avery, Dorothy Wax.

Three Hours (First National, 1927) Corinne Griffith Productions. Length: 6 reels, 5,774 feet. General release date: March 5, 1927. Producer: Asher Small-Rogers, E.M. Asher. Director: James Flood. Writer: Paul Bern. Photography: Harry Jackson. Cast: Corinne Griffith, John Bowers, Hobart Bosworth, Paul Ellis, Anne Schaeffer, Mary Louise Miller.

The Beloved Rogue (United Artists, 1927) Feature Productions. Length: 10 reels, 9,264 feet, General release date: March 12, 1927. Director: Alan Crosland. Assistant Director: Gordon Hollingshead. Writers: Paul Bern, Walter Anthony. Photography: Joe August. Art Direction: William Cameron Menzies. Cast: John Barrymore, Conrad Veidt, Marceline Day, Henry Victor, Lawson Butt, Mack Swain, Slim Summerville, Otto Matieson, Rose Dione, Bertram Grassby, Lucy Beaumont, Angelo Rossitto, Jane Winton, Martha Franklin, Nigel De Brulier, Dick Sutherland.

The Dove (United Artists, 1927) Norma Talmadge Productions. Length: 9 reels, 9,100 feet. New York premiere date: December 31, 1926. General release date: January 7, 1927. Producer: Joseph M. Schenck. Director: Roland West. Writers: Paul Bern, Roland West, Willard Mack, Wallace Smith. Photography: Oliver Marsh. Film Editor: Hal Kern. Art Direction: William Cameron Menzies. Cast: Norma Talmadge, Noah Beery, Gilbert Roland, Eddie Borden, Harry Myers, Michael Vavitch, Brinsley Shaw, Kalla Pasha, Charles Darvas, Michael Dark, Walter Daniels.

The Prince of Tempters (First National, 1927) Robert Kane Productions. Length: 8 reels, 7,780 feet. General release date: October 17, 1926. Producer: Robert T. Kane. Director: Lothar Mendes. Writer: Paul Bern. Photography: Ernest Haller. Cast: Lois Moran, Ben Lyon, Lya De Putti, Ian Keith, Mary Brian, Olive Tell, Sam Hardy, Henry Vibart, Judith Vosselli, Frazer Coulter, J. Barney Sherry.

The Great Deception (First National, 1926) Robert Kane Productions. Length: 6 reels, 5,855 feet. General release date: July 25, 1926. Producer: Robert T. Kane. Director: Howard Higgin. Writer: Paul Bern. Photography: Ernest Haller. Cast: Ben Lyon, Aileen Pringle, Basil Rathbone, Sam Hardy, Charlotte Walker, Amelia Summerville, Hubert Wilke, Lucien Prival, Lucius Henderson, Mark Gonzales.

The Wilderness Woman (First National, 1926) PB is not credited; there are no writing credits for the film other than titles but period newspapers credit Paul as writer with Paul Schofield. Robert Kane Productions. Length: 8 reels, 7,533 feet. General release date: May 9, 1926. Producer: Robert T. Kane. Director: Howard Higgin. Writers: Paul Bern, Don Barlett, Paul Schofield. Photography: Ernest Haller. Film Editor: Paul F. Maschke. Art Direction: Robert M. Haas. Production Manager: Joseph C. Boyle. Cast: Aileen Pringle, Lowell Sherman, Chester Conklin, Herbert Vibart, Robert Cain, Harriet Sterling, Burr McIntosh.

The Girl from Montmartre (First National, 1926) PB is not credited but production records and period accounts indicate that he wrote this specifically for Barbara La Marr. Associated Holding Corporation. Length: 6 reels, 6,200 feet. General release date: January 31, 1926. Director: Alfred E. Green. Writers: Paul Bern, June Mathis, Eve Unsell, George Marion, Jr. Photography: Rudolph Berquist. Film Editor: Al Hall. Art Direction: E.J. Shulter. Cast: Barbara La Marr, Lewis Stone, Robert Ellis, William Eugene, E.H. Calvert, Mario Carillo, Mathilde Cormont, Edward Piel, Nicholas De Ruiz, Hector Sarno, Bobby Mack.

My Wife and I (Warner Brothers, 1925) PB is not credited but is listed in newspaper stories and studio production schedules as writer. Length: 7 reels, 7,134 feet. General release date: May 16, 1925. Director: Millard Webb. Writers: Paul Bern, Millard Webb, Julien Josephson. Cast: Irene Rich, Huntley Gordon, John Harron, John Roche, Constance Bennett, Tom Ricketts.

Vanity's Price (Film Booking Offices of America, 1924) Gothic Pictures. Length: 6 reels, 6,124 feet. General release date: September 7, 1924. Director: R. William Neill. Assistant Director: Josef von Sternberg. Writer: Paul Bern. Photography: Hal Mohr. Cast: Anna Q. Nilsson, Stuart Holmes, Wyndham Standing, Arthur Rankin, Lucille Rickson, Robert Bolder, Cissy Fitzgerald, Dot Farley, Charles Newton.

Forbidden Paradise (Paramount, 1924) PB is not credited but is listed in newspaper reviews and stories as writer. Famous Players–Lasky. Length: 8 reels, 7,543 feet.

New York premiere date: November 16, 1924. General release date: November 24, 1924. Producers: Adolph Zukor, Jesse L. Lasky. Director: Ernst Lubitsch. Writers: Paul Bern, Agnes Christine Johnston, Hans Kraly. Photography: Charles Van Enger. Set Decoration: Hans Dreier. Cast: Pola Negri, Rod La Rocque, Adolphe Menjou, Pauline Starke, Fred Malatesta, Nick De Ruiz, Madame Daumery, Clark Gable.

Lily of the Dust (Paramount, 1924) Famous Players–Lasky. Length: 7 reels, 6,811 feet. General release date: August 24, 1924. Producers: Adolph Zukor, Jesse L. Lasky. Director: Dimitri Buchowetzski. Writer: Paul Bern. Photography: Alvin Wyckoff. Cast: Pola Negri, Ben Lyon, Noah Beery, Raymond Griffith, Jeanette Daudet, William J. Kelly.

Men (Paramount, 1924) Famous Players–Lasky. Length: 7 reels, 6,634 feet. General release date: May 26, 1924. Producers: Adolph Zukor, Jesse L. Lasky. Director: Dimitri Buchowetzski. Writers: Paul Bern, Dimitri Buchowetzski. Photography: Alvin Wychoff. Cast: Pola Negri, Robert Frazer, Robert Edeson, Joseph Swickard, Monte Collins, Gino Corrado, Edgar Norton.

The Marriage Circle (Warner Brothers, 1924) Length: 8 reels, 8,200 feet. General release date: February 3, 1924. Directors: Ernst Lubitsch, James Flood, Henry Blanke. Writer: Paul Bern. Photography: Charles Van Enger. Cast: Florence Vidor, Monte Blue, Marie Prevost, Creighton Hale, Adolphe Menjou, Harry Myers, Dale Fuller, Esther Ralston.

Name the Man (Goldwyn-Cosmopolitan Distributing Company, 1924) Goldwyn Pictures. Length: 8 reels, 7,771 feet. General release date: January 27, 1924. Director: Victor Seastrom. Writers: Paul Bern, June Mathis. Script Supervisor: Albert Lewin. Photography: Charles Van Enger. Cast: Mae Busch, Conrad Nagel, Hobart Bosworth, Creighton Hale, Patsy Ruth Miller, Winter Hall, Aileen Pringle, DeWitt Jennings, Evelyn Selbie, Mark Fenton, Anna Hernandez, Mrs. Charles Craig, Cecil Holland, Lucien Littlefield, William Orlamond, Charles Mailes, Andrew Arbuckle.

The Wanters (Associated First National Pictures, 1923) Louis B. Mayer Productions. Length: 7 reels, 6,800 feet. Release date: November 26, 1923. Director: John M. Stahl. Writers: Paul Bern, J.G. Wells, Leila Burton Wells. Photography: Ernest G. Palmer. Cast: Marie Prevost, Robert Ellis, Norma Shearer, Gertrude Astor, Huntley Gordon, Lincoln Stedman, Lillian Langdon, Louise Fazenda, Hank Mann, Lydia Yeamans Titus, Vernon Steele, Harold Goodwin, William Buckley.

Lost and Found on a South Sea Island (1923) PB is not credited as but newspaper articles confirm his appointment as Production Supervisor and Film Editor in addition to a writing credit. Length: 7 reels, 6,334 feet. L.A. premiere date: February 25, 1923. General release date: March 11, 1923. Goldwyn Pictures Corporation. Director: Raoul Walsh. Writers: Paul Bern, Carey Wilson, Katherine Hilliker, H.H. Caldwell. Photography: Clyde De Vinna, Paul Kerschner. Film Editors: Paul Bern, Katherine Hilliker, H.H. Caldwell. Cast: House Peters, Pauline Starke, Antonio Moreno, Mary Jane Irving, Rosemary Theby, George Siegmann, William V. Mong, Carl Harbaugh, David Wing.

The Christian (Goldwyn Pictures Corporation, 1923) Director: Maurice Tourneur. Writer: Paul Bern. Titles: Samuel Goldwyn, Paul Bern. Assistant Directors: Cedric Gibbons, Charles Dorlan. Photography: Charles Van Enger. Film Editor: Paul Bern. Eight reels; 8,000 feet. General release date: January 14 or 20, 1923. Cast: Richard Dix, Mae Busch, Garet Hughes, Phyllis Haver, Cyril Chadwick, Mahlon Hamilton, Joseph Dowling, Claude Gillingwater, John Herdman, Beryl Mercer, Robert Bolder, Milla Davenport, Alice Hesse, Aileen Pringle, Harry Northrup, Eric Mayne, William Moran.

Suspicious Wives (World Film Corporation, 1921) Trojan Film Company. Director: John M. Stahl. Writer: Paul Bern. Story: Robert F. Roden. Titles: William B. Laub, Harry Chandlee. Photography: Harry Fischbeck. Length: 6 reels, 6,240 feet. General release date: August, 1921. Cast: H.J. Herbert, Mollie King, Ethel Grey Terry, Rod La Rocque, Gertrude Berkeley, Frank De Camp, Warren Cook.

Greater Than Love (Trojan Film Company, 1920) Director: John M. Stahl. Writer: Paul Bern. Story: Robert F. Roden. Length: 6 reels, approx. 5,400 feet. General release date: some newspapers note a May 1920 release date. Cast: Mollie King, Louise Glaum, Donald MacDonald.

Women Men Forget (United Picture Theatres of America, Inc., 1920) American Cinema Corporation. Producer: J.A. Berst. Director: John M. Stahl. Writer: Paul Bern. Photography: John K. Holbrook. Length: 5 reels, approx. 4,500 feet. General release date: March 21, 1920. Cast: Mollie King, Edward Langford, Frank Mills, Lucy Fox, Jane Jennings.

NOTE: In 1919, Paul was a writer at United Picture Theatres of America, Inc., the precursor to American Cinema Corporation. There's a good possibility that Paul assisted on the scenario for *Her Game* in an uncredited capacity. The only information concerning the script is that it was based on a story suggested by cameraman John K. Holbrook. No other writer's names are included among the confirmed credits, but Paul was one of only three or four writers at the company at that time. For that reason, they are included here.

Her Game (United Picture Theatres of America, Inc., 1919) Tribune Productions, Inc. Producer: A.J. Bimberg. Director: Frank H. Crane. Story: John K. Holbrook. Photography: John K. Holbrook. Length: 5 reels, approx. 4,600 feet. General release date: October 19, 1919. Cast: Florence Reed, Conway Tearle, Jed Prouty, Florence Billings, Mathilda Brundage.

NOTE: PB is not credited with Benjamin Chapin's Charter Features Corporation films but he worked for Chapin as a writer and director from mid–1916 until Chapin's death in 1918 so it can be assumed that in such a small company he would have been involved in the writing and directing process for the *Lincoln* series of two-reelers produced by Chapin during that time. For that reason, they are included here.

The Son of the Democracy (States Rights: Charter Features Corp., 1918) Also known as *The Lincoln Cycle*. Series included: *The Call to Arms, Humanity's Man* (1917), *Myself, The Lincoln Man* (1917), *My Father, The Physical Man* (1917), *My Mother, The Spirit Man* (1917), *My First Jury* (1918), *Down the River* (1918), *The Slave Auction* (1918), *A President's Answer* (1918), *Tender Memories* (1918), *Under the Stars* (1918). Producer: Benjamin Chapin. Director: John M. Stahl. Assistant Director: Benjamin Chapin. Writers: Benjamin Chapin, Paul Bern. Photography: J.

Roy Hunt, Walter Blakely, Harry A. Fischbeck, (unknown) Freyer. Cast: Benjamin Chapin, Charlie Jackson, Madeline Clare, John Stafford.

The Lincoln Cycle (States Rights: Charter Features Corp., 1917) Series included: *Myself, The Lincoln Man* (1917), *The Call to Arms, Humanity's Man* (1917), *My Father, The Physical Man* (1917) and *My Mother, The Spirit Man* (1917). Producer: Benjamin Chapin. Director: John M. Stahl. Assistant Director: Benjamin Chapin. Writers: Benjamin Chapin, Paul Bern. Photography: J. Roy Hunt, Walter Blakely, Harry A. Fischbeck, (unknown) Freyer. Cast: Benjamin Chapin, Charlie Jackson, Madeline Clare, John Stafford.

NOTE: Conness-Till Film Company releases are confirmed through period newspaper articles and stories in *The Moving Picture World* between March, 1915 and July, 1915. There are few specific references to cast and technical crew identities; however, at the time A.J. Edwards and Thomas McKnight were the two directors on staff, Louis W. Physioc was the technical director (with assistance from Bern), and one of the company's writer was Bern. It can be assumed with fair certainty that each was involved in all of the company releases during the short time the company was operating. The acting company included Marie Cummings, Dorothy Millette, Reina Carruthers, May Anderson, Margaret Jackson, Frank Crane, Eugene Frazier, Frank Preistland, H. Webb Chamberlain, and Claude Norrie.

The Faithful Servant (B.C. Feature Film Co., 1915) Conness-Till Film Company, Ltd. Director: A.J. Edwards. Assistant Director: Thomas McKnight. Technical Director: Louis W. Physioc. Writer: Paul Bern. Length: 2 reels, approx. 1,900 feet. General release date: April 24, 1915. Cast: Edward H. Robbins, Clara Whipple.

The Moreland Mystery (B.C. Feature Film Co., 1915) Conness-Till Film Company, Ltd. Director: A.J. Edwards. Assistant Director: Thomas McKnight. Technical Director: Louis W. Physioc. Writer: Paul Bern. Length: 2 reels, approx. 1,900 feet. General release date: April 16, 1915. Cast: Edward H. Robbins, Clara Whipple.

A Soul's Affinity (B.C. Feature Film Co., 1915) Conness-Till Film Company, Ltd. Director: A.J. Edwards. Assistant Director: Thomas McKnight. Technical Director: Louis W. Physioc. Writer: Paul Bern. Length: 2 reels, approx. 1,900 feet. General release date: April 15, 1915. Cast: Edward H. Robbins, Clara Whipple.

To Err Is Human (B.C. Feature Film Co., 1915) Conness-Till Film Company, Ltd. Director: A.J. Edwards. Assistant Director: Thomas McKnight. Technical Director: Louis W. Physioc. Writer: Paul Bern. Length: 2 reels, approx. 1,900 feet. General release date: April 7, 1915. Cast: Edward H. Robbins, Clara Whipple.

His Awakening (B.C. Feature Film Co., 1915) Conness-Till Film Company, Ltd. Director: A.J. Edwards. Assistant Director: Thomas McKnight. Technical Director: Louis W. Physioc. Writer: Paul Bern. Length: 2 reels, approx. 1,900 feet. General release date: March 31, 1915. Cast: Edward H. Robbins, Clara Whipple.

Motto on the Wall (B.C. Feature Film Co., 1915) Conness-Till Film Company, Ltd. Director: A.J. Edwards. Assistant Director: Thomas McKnight. Technical Director: Louis W. Physioc. Writer: Paul Bern. Length: 2 reels, approx. 1,900 feet. General release date: March, 1915. Cast: Edward H. Robbins, Clara Whipple.

The Better Man (B.C. Feature Film Co., 1915) Conness-Till Film Company, Ltd. Director: A.J. Edwards. Assistant Director: Thomas McKnight. Technical Director: Louis W. Physioc. Writer: Paul Bern. Length: 2 reels, approx. 1,900 feet. General release date: March, 1915. Cast: Edward H. Robbins, Clara Whipple.

Canada in Peace and War (B.C. Feature Film Co., 1915) Conness-Till Film Company, Ltd. Director: A.J. Edwards. Assistant Director: Thomas McKnight. Technical Director: Louis W. Physioc. Writer: Paul Bern. Length: 3 reels, approx. 2,700 feet. General release date: February, 1915. Cast: Edward H. Robbins, Clara Whipple, Gene Frazier.

On the King's Highway (B.C. Feature Film Co., 1915) Conness-Till Film Company, Ltd. Director: A.J. Edwards. Assistant Director: Thomas McKnight. Technical Director: Louis W. Physioc. Writer: Paul Bern. Length: 2 reels, approx. 1,900 feet. General release date: January, 1915. Cast: Edward H. Robbins, Clara Whipple.

Director

The Woman Racket (MGM, 1930) PB is not credited but newspaper reviews and production stories confirm that he was among the three directors. Length: 6 reels, 5,550 feet. General release date: January 24, 1930. Directors: Paul Bern, Albert H. Kelley, Robert Ober. Writers: Albert Shelby Le Vino, Fred Niblo, Jr. Photography: Peverell Marley. Film Editors: Basil Wrangell, Anson Stevenson. Sound: Douglas Shearer, Russell Franks. Art Direction: Cedric Gibbons. Cast: Tom Moore, Blanche Sweet, Sally Starr, Wilbur Mack, Bobby Agnew, John Miljan, Tenen Holtz, Lew Kelly, Tom London, Eugene Borden, John Byron, Nita Martin, Richard Travers.

Flower of Night (Paramount, 1925) Famous Players–Lasky. Length: 7 reels, 6,374 feet. Premiere date: New York, October 18, 1925. General release: November 2, 1925. European release: January 3, 1927. Producers: Adolph Zukor, Jesse L. Lasky. Director: Paul Bern. Writer: Willis Goldbeck. Photography: Bert Glennon. Gambling Advisor: Scott Turner. Cast: Pola Negri, Joseph Dowling, Youcca Troubetzkoy, Warner Oland, Edwin J. Brady, Eulalie Jensen, Cesare Gravina, Gustav von Seyffertitz, Helen Lee Worthing, Thais Valdemar, Manuel Acosta, Frankie Bailey.

Grounds for Divorce (Paramount, 1925) Famous Players–Lasky. Length: 6 reels, 5,692 feet. Premiere date: July 27, 1925. General release date: July 27, 1925. Producers: Adolph Zukor, Jesse L. Lasky. Director: Paul Bern. Writers: Violet Clark, Guy Bolton. Photography: Bert Glennon. Cast: Florence Vidor, Matt Moore, Harry Myers, Louise Fazenda, George André Beranger, Gustav von Seyffertitz, Edna Mae Cooper.

The Dressmaker from Paris (Paramount, 1925) Famous Players–Lasky. Length: 8 reels, 7,080 feet. General release date: March 30, 1925. Producers: Adolph Zukor, Jesse L. Lasky. Director: Paul Bern. Writers: Adelaide Heilbron, Howard Hawks. Cast: Leatrice Joy, Olive Borden, Ernest Torrence, Allan Forrest, Mildred Harris, Lawrence Gray, Charles Crockett, Rosemary Cooper, Spec O'Donnell.

Tomorrow's Love (Paramount, 1924) Famous Players–Lasky. Length: 6 reels, 5,842 feet. General release date: January 5, 1925. Producer: Adolph Zukor, Jesse L.

Lasky. Director: Paul Bern. Writer: Howard Higgin. Photography: Bert Glennon. Cast: Agnes Ayres, Pat O'Malley, Raymond Hatton, Jane Winton, Ruby Lafayette, Dale Fuller.

Worldly Goods (Paramount, 1924) Famous Players–Lasky. Length: 6 reels, 6,055 feet. Premiere date: New York, November 2, 1924, General release date: November 24, 1924. Producers: Adolph Zukor, Jesse L. Lasky. Director: Paul Bern. Writer: A.P. Younger. Photography: Bert Glennon. Cast: Agnes Ayres, Pat O'Malley, Victor Varconi, Edythe Chapman, Bert Woodruff, Maude George, Cecille Evans, Otto Lederer.

Open All Night (Paramount, 1924) Famous Players–Lasky. Length: 6 reels, 5,671 feet. General release date: October 13, 1924. Producers: Adolph Zukor, Jesse L. Lasky. Director: Paul Bern. Writer: Willis Goldbeck. Photography: Bert Glennon. Cast: Viola Dana, Jetta Goudal, Adolphe Menjou, Raymond Griffith, Maurice B. Flynn, Gale Henry, Jack Giddings, Charles Puffy.

Head Over Heels (Goldwyn Pictures Corporation, 1922) Length: 5 reels, 4,229 feet. General release date: April, 1922. Directors: Paul Bern, Victor Schertzinger. Writers: Julien Josephson, Gerald C. Duffy, Nalbro Isadorah Bartley. Photography: George F. Webber. Cast: Mabel Normand, Hugh Thompson, Russ Powell, Raymond Hatton, Adolphe Menjou, Lilyan Tashman, Lionel Belmore.

The Man with Two Mothers (Goldwyn Pictures Corporation, 1922) Length: 5 reels; 4,423 feet. General release date: February, 1922. Director: Paul Bern. Writers: Julien Josephson, Alice Duer Miller. Photography: Percy Hilburn. Cast: Cullen Landis, Mary Alden, Sylvia Breamer, Hallam Cooley, Fred Huntley, Laura La Varnie, Monte Collins, William Elmer.

NOTE: Paul is sometimes credited with a film entitled *The Adventures and Emotions of Edgar Pomeroy* which is given a 1920 release date. There was no such film; Paul was brought in to direct the final episode of a 13-film serial with the general title of *The Adventures and Emotions of Edgar Pomeroy.* The Edgar films were produced and released almost monthly between March, 1920 and April, 1921. They were directed by Mason N. Litson and E. Mason Hopper with the exception of Paul's chapter, the last in the series.

Edgar, the Detective (Goldwyn Pictures Corporation, 1921) 2 reels, approx. 1,900 feet. General release date: April 10, 1921. Producer: Samuel Goldwyn. Director: Paul Bern. Writer: Booth Tarkington. Photography: Max Fabian. Cast: Cordelia Callahan, Nick Cogley, John Cossar, Marie Dunn, Kenneth Earl, Lucretia Harris, Virginia Madison, Buddy Messinger, Frederick Moore, Lucille Ricksen.

The North Wind's Malice (Goldwyn Distributing Corporation, 1920) Eminent Author's Pictures, Inc. Length: 7 reels, 6,275 feet. General release date: August, 1920. Producers: Samuel Goldwyn, Rex Beach. Production Manager: Robert B. McIntyre. Directors: Carl Harbaugh, Paul Bern. Writer: Rex Beach. Photography: Lucien Tainguy, Oliver Marsh, George Peters, Roy Vaughan. Cast: Tom Santschi, Jane Thomas, Joe King, Henry West, William H. Strauss, Walter Abel, Vera Gordon, Edna Murphy, Dorothy Wheeler, Julia Stewart.

NOTE: PB is not credited with Benjamin Chapin's films but he worked for Chapin as a writer and director from mid–1916 until Chapin's death in 1918 so it can be assumed that in such a small company he would have been involved in the writing and directing process for the *Lincoln* series of two-reelers produced by Chapin during that time. For that reason they are included here. See the credits for *The Son of the Democracy* (1918) and *The Lincoln Cycle* (1917) on pages 315 and 316.

Producer and Production Supervisor

Strange Interlude (MGM, 1932) PB is not credited but newspaper reviews and production stories confirm his work on the script and pre-production. A Robert Z. Leonard Production. Length: 12 reels. Premiere date: August 15, 1932. General release date: December 30, 1932. Producer: Paul Bern. Director: Robert Z. Leonard. Assistant Director: Earl Taggert. Writers: Paul Bern, Bess Meredyth, C. Gardner Sullivan. Photography: Lee Garmes, Lester White, Warner Cruze. Film Editor: Margaret Booth. Art Direction: Cedric Gibbons. Costumes: Adrian. Sound: Douglas Shearer, Robert Shirley, Ralph Shugart. Still Photography: William Grimes. Cast: Norma Shearer, Clark Gable, Alexander Kirkland, Ralph Morgan, Robert Young, May Robson, Maureen O'Sullivan, Henry B. Walthall, Mary Alden, Tad Alexander.

Grand Hotel (MGM, 1932) Shooting days: 49. Length: 12 reels, 10,545 feet. New York premiere date: April 12, 1932. General release date: September 11, 1932. Producer: Paul Bern. Director: Edmund Goulding. Writers: William A. Drake, Vicki Baum. Photography: William Daniels, A.L. Lane, Charles W. Riley, Albert Scheving. Film Editor: Blanche Sewell. Art Direction: Cedric Gibbons. Costumes: Adrian. Sound: Douglas Shearer, Karl Zint, Anstruther MacDonald. Casting Director: Benjamin Thau. Still Photographer: Milton Brown. Cast: Greta Garbo, John Barrymore, Joan Crawford, Wallace Beery, Lionel Barrymore, Lewis Stone, Jean Hersholt, Robert McWade, Purnell B. Pratt, Ferdinand Gottschalk, Rafaela Ottiano, Morgan Wallace, Tully Marshall, Frank Conroy, Murray Kinnell, Edwin Maxwell, Greta Meyer, Rolfe Sedan, Sarah Padden, Charles Trowbridge, Mary Carlisle.

Red-Headed Woman (MGM, 1932) PB is not credited but newspaper reviews and production stories confirm his work as production supervisor during pre-production; identified as managing production during casting process, confirmed by studio records and Sam Marx. Length: 8 reels, 7,471 feet. General release date: June 25, 1932. Producers: Paul Bern, Albert Lewin. Director: Jack Conway. Assistant Director: Charles Dorian. Writers: Anita Loos, Bess Meredyth, C. Gardner Sullivan. Photography: Harold Rosson. Film Editor: Blanche Sewell. Art Direction: Cedric Gibbons. Costumes: Adrian. Sound: Douglas Shearer, James Brock. Music: Raymond B. Egan, Richard A. Whiting. Cast: Jean Harlow, Chester Morris, Lewis Stone, Leila Hyams, Una Merkel, Henry Stephenson, May Robson, Charles Boyer, Harvey Clark, Henry Armetta, William Pawley, Sidney Bracey, William Pawley, Lee Phelps, Sarah Padden.

As You Desire Me (MGM, 1932) PB is not credited but MGM records and Sam Marx indicated that Paul assisted in the production. George Fitzmaurice Production. Shooting days: 42. Length: 7 reels, 6,533 feet. General release date: May 28, 1932. Producer: Paul Bern. Director: George Fitzmaurice. Assistant Director: Cullen Tate.

Writer: Gene Markey. Photography: William Daniels. Film Editor: George Hively. Art Direction: Cedric Gibbons. Costumes: Adrian. Sound: Douglas Shearer, James Brock. Cast: Greta Garbo, Melvyn Douglas, Erich von Stroheim, Owen Moore, Hedda Hopper, Rafaela Ottiano, Warburton Gamble, Albert Conti, William Ricciardi, Roland Varno.

Arsène Lupin (MGM, 1932) PB is not credited but newspaper reviews and production stories confirm his work as production supervisor even during pre-production. Length: 9 reels. General release date: March 15, 1932. Producer: Paul Bern. Director: Jack Conway. Assistant Director: John Waters. Writers: Carey Wilson, Bayard Veiller, John Jackson, Lenore Coffee. Photography: Oliver T. Marsh. Film Editor: Hugh Wynn. Art Direction: Cedric Gibbons. Costumes: Adrian. Sound: Douglas Shearer, James Brock, Jack Gordon. Cast: John Barrymore, Lionel Barrymore, Karen Morley, John Miljan, Tully Marshall, Henry Armetta, George Davis, John Davidson, James Macy, Mary Jane Irving, Joe Sawyer, Mischa Auer.

Mata Hari (MGM, 1931) PB is not credited but he assisted Thalberg on all Garbo films for MGM for which Thalberg received producer credit or was responsible for producing himself; confirmed by MGM records and Sam Marx. A George Fitzmaurice Production. Length: 10 reels, 8,740 feet. General release date: December 31, 1931. Producers: Paul Bern, B.P. Fineman. Director: George Fitzmaurice. Assistant Director: Cullen Tate. Writers: Benjamin Glazer, Leo Birinski, Doris Anderson, Gilbert Emery. Photography: William Daniels, A.L. Lane, Charles W. Riley, Albert Scheving. Film Editor: Frank Sullivan. Art Direction: Cedric Gibbons. Costumes: Adrian. Sound: Douglas Shearer, Fred R. Morgan, Paul Neal, James Brock. Still Photography: Milton Brown. Cast: Greta Garbo, Ramon Novarro, Lionel Barrymore, Lewis Stone, C. Henry Gordon, Karen Morley, Alex B. Francis, Blanche Frederici, Edmund Breese, Helen Jerome Eddy, Frank Reicher, Lennox Pawle, Mischa Auer, Cecil Cunningham, Michael Visaroff, Sarah Padden, Harry Cording.

West of Broadway (MGM, 1931) PB is not credited but the film's writer Gene Markey and star John Gilbert's daughter confirmed that Paul produced the film. Length: 7 reels. General release date: November 21, 1931. Director: Harry Beaumont. Assistant Director: Sandy Roth. Writers: Bess Meredyth, Gene Markey, J.K. McGuinness. Photography: Merritt B. Gerstad. Film Editor: George Hively. Art Direction: Cedric Gibbons. Costumes: Vivian Baer. Sound: Douglas Shearer. Cast: John Gilbert, El Brendel, Lois Moran, Madge Evans, Ralph Bellamy, Frank Conroy, Gwen Lee, Hedda Hopper, Ruth Renick, Willie Fung, John Miljan.

Susan Lenox: Her Fall and Rise (MGM, 1931) PB is not credited but he assisted Thalberg on all Garbo films for MGM for which Thalberg received producer credit or was responsible for producing himself; confirmed by MGM records and Sam Marx. Shooting days: 49. Length: 8 reels, 7,143 feet. General release date: October 10, 1931. Producer: Paul Bern. Director: Robert Z. Leonard. Assistant Director: Hugh Boswell. Writers: Wanda Tuchock, Zelda Sears, Leon Gordon, Delmer Daves. Photography: William Daniels. Film Editor: Margaret Booth. Art Direction: Cedric Gibbons. Costumes: Adrian. Sound: Douglas Shearer, Charles Wallace. Cast: Greta Garbo, Clark Gable, Jean Hersholt, John Miljan, Alan Hale, Hale Hamilton, Hilda Vaughn, Russell Simpson, Cecil Cunningham, Ian Keith, Theodore Von Eltz.

The Squaw Man (MGM, 1931) PB is not credited, but Paul was producer in charge of all Pathe-DeMille productions during DeMille's brief stay at MGM (1929–1931). Length: 12 reels. General release date: September 5, 1931. Producers: Paul Bern, Cecil B. DeMille. Director: Cecil B. DeMille. Assistant Directors: Mitchell Leisen, Earl Haley. Writers: Lucien Hubbard, Lenore Coffee, Elsie Janis. Photography: Harold Rosson. Film Editor: Anne Bauchens. Art Direction: Mitchell Leisen. Music: Herbert Stothart. Sound: Douglas Shearer. Cast: Warner Baxter, Lupe Velez, Eleanor Boardman, Charles Bickford, Roland Young, Paul Cavanagh, Raymond Hatton, Julia Faye, DeWitt Jennings, J. Farrell MacDonald, Mitchell Lewis, Dickie Moore, Victor Potel, Frank Rice, Eva Dennison, Lillian Bond, Luke Cosgrave, Frank Hagney, Lawrence Grant, Harry Northrup, Ed Brady, Chris-Pin Martin, Desmond Roberts.

The Secret Six (MGM, 1931) PB is not credited but newspaper reviews and production stories confirm his work as production supervisor during pre-production. A George Hill–Cosmopolitan Production. Length: 9 reels. General release date: April 18, 1931. Producer: Irving Thalberg. Production Supervisor: Paul Bern. Director: George Hill. Assistant Director: Phil Ryan. Writer: Frances Marion. Photography: Harold Wenstrom. Film Editor: Blanche Sewell. Art Direction: Cedric Gibbons. Costumes: René Hubert. Sound: Douglas Shearer. Cast: Wallace Beery, Lewis Stone, Johnny Mack Brown, Jean Harlow, Marjorie Rambeau, Paul Hurst, Clark Gable, Ralph Bellamy, John Miljan, DeWitt Jennings, Murray Kinnell, Fletcher Norton, Louis Natheaux, Frank McGlynn, Theodore Von Eltz.

It's a Wise Child (MGM, 1931) PB is not credited but newspaper reviews and production stories confirm his work as production supervisor; confirmed in interviews with star Marion Davies. A Robert Z. Leonard–Marion Davies Production. Length: 9 reels, 6,580 feet. Preview release date: March 21, 1931. General release date: April 11, 1931. Production Supervisor: Paul Bern. Director: Robert Z. Leonard. Assistant Director: Hugh Boswell. Writer: Laurence E. Johnson. Photography: Oliver T. Marsh. Film Editor: Margaret Booth. Art Direction: Cedric Gibbons. Sound: Douglas Shearer, Paul Neal. Cast: Marion Davies, Sidney Blackmer, James Gleason, Polly Moran, Lester Vail, Marie Prevost, Clara Blandick, Robert McWade, Johnny Arthur, Hilda Vaughn, Ben Alexander, Emily Fitzroy.

The Prodigal (MGM, 1931) PB is not credited but newspaper reviews and production stories confirm his work as production supervisor during pre-production (it was titled *The Southerner* for its preview release and changed to *The Prodigal* for the general release). A Harry Pollard Production. Length: 10 reels. General release date: February 21, 1931. Production Supervisor: Paul Bern. Director: Harry Pollard. Writers: Bess Meredyth, Wells Root. Photography: Harold Rosson. Film Editor: Margaret Booth. Art Direction: Cedric Gibbons. Costumes: Adrian. Sound: Douglas Shearer. Cast: Lawrence Tibbett, Esther Ralston, Roland Young, Cliff Edwards, Purnell B. Pratt, Hedda Hopper, Emma Dunn, Stepin Fetchit, Louis John Bartels, Theodore Von Eltz, Wally Albright, Jr., Suzanne Ransom, Gertrude Howard, John Larkin, H.B. Warner.

Inspiration (MGM, 1931) PB is not credited but he assisted Thalberg on all Garbo films for MGM for which Thalberg received producer credit or was responsible for producing himself; confirmed by MGM records and Sam Marx. Clarence Brown Production. Length: 10 reels. General release date: January 31, 1931. Producer-Director: Clarence Brown. Production Supervisor: Paul Bern. Assistant Director: Charles Dorian. Writer: Gene Markey. Photography: William Daniels. Film Editor: Conrad A. Nervig. Art Direction: Cedric Gibbons. Costumes: Adrian. Sound: Douglas Shearer. Cast: Greta Garbo, Robert Montgomery, Lewis Stone, Marjorie Rambeau, Judith Voselli, Beryl Mercer, John Miljan, Edwin Maxwell, Oscar Apfel, Joan Marsh, Zelda Sears, Karen Morley, Gwen Lee, Paul McAllister, Arthur Hoyt, Richard Tucker.

New Moon (MGM, 1931) Length. 9 reels, 7,016 feet. Preview release date: October 17, 1930. General release date: January 21, 1931. Producer: Paul Bern. Director: Jack Conway. Assistant Director: Maude Howell. Writers: Sylvia Thalberg, Frank Butler, Cyril Hume. Photography: Oliver T. Marsh. Film Editor: Margaret Booth. Art Direction: Cedric Gibbons. Costumes: Adrian. Music: Sigmund Romberg. Sound: Douglas Shearer. Cast: Lawrence Tibbett, Grace Moore, Adolphe Menjou, Roland Young, Gus Shy, Emily Fitzroy, Nena Quartaro.

Paid (MGM, 1930) PB is not credited, but MGM records and Sam Marx indicated that Paul assisted in the production. Shooting days: 39. Length: 10 reels, 7,946 feet. Producer: Paul Bern. Director: Sam Wood. Writers: Lucien Hubbard, Charles MacArthur, Bayard Veiller. Photography: Charles Rosher. Film Editor: Hugh Wynn. Art Direction: Cedric Gibbons. Costumes: Adrian. Sound: Douglas Shearer. Joan Crawford, Robert Armstrong, Marie Prevost, Kent Douglass, John Miljan, Purnell B. Pratt, Hale Hamilton, Polly Moran, Robert Emmett O'Connor, Tyrell Davis, William Bakewell, George Cooper, Gwen Lee, Isabel Withers.

Madam Satan (MGM, 1930) PB is not credited but he was producer in charge of all Pathe-DeMille productions during DeMille's brief stay at MGM (1929–1931). Shooting days: 48. Length: 13 reels, 10,320 feet. General release date: September 20, 1930. Producers: Paul Bern, Cecil B. DeMille. Director: Cecil B. DeMille. Assistant Directors: Mitchell Leisen, Cullen Tate. Writers: Jeanie Macpherson, Gladys Unger, Elsie Janis. Photography: Harold Rosson. Film Editor: Anne Bauchens. Art Direction: Cedric Gibbons, Mitchell Leisen. Costumes: Adrian. Sound: J.K. Brock, Douglas Shearer. Choreography: LeRoy Prinz. Cast: Kay Johnson, Reginald Denny, Lillian Roth, Roland Young, Elsa Peterson, Boyd Irwin, Wallace MacDonald, Wilfred Lucas, Tyler Brooke, Lotus Thompson, Vera Marsh, Martha Sleeper, Doris McMahon, Marie Valli, Julianne Johnston, Albert Conti, Earl Askam, Betty Francisco, Ynez Seabury, Countess De Liquoro, Katherine Irving, Aileen Ransom, Theodore Kosloff, Jack King, Edward Prinz, Maine Geary, Allan Lane, Kenneth Gibson, Youcca Troubetzkoy, Henry Stockbridge, June Nash, Mary Carlisle, Mary McCallister, Dorothy Dehn, Louis Natheaux, Ella Hall, Edwards Davis, Kasha Haroldi, Katherine de Mille, Vera Gordon, Natalie Storm, Elvira Lucianti, Marquetta Swope, Dorothy Vernon, Lorimer Johnson, John Byron, Abe Lyman and His Band.

Romance (MGM, 1930) PB is not credited but he assisted Thalberg on all Garbo films for MGM for which Thalberg received producer credit or was responsible for producing himself. Length: 10 reels, 6,977 feet. General release date: August 26, 1930. Director: Clarence Brown. Writers: Bess Meredyth, Edwin Justus Mayer. Photography: William Daniels. Film Editor: Hugh Wynn. Art Direction: Cedric Gibbons. Costumes: Adrian. Sound: Ralph Shugart, Douglas Shearer. Cast: Greta Garbo, Lewis Stone, Gavin Gordon, Elliott Nugent, Florence Lake, Clara Blandick, Henry Armetta, Mathilde Comont, Countess De Liquoro.

Let Us Be Gay (MGM, 1930) PB is not credited but newspaper reviews, production stories and MGM records credit him as producer. Shooting days: 23. New York premiere date: July 11, 1930. General release date: August 9, 1930. Director: Robert Z. Leonard. Writers: Frances Marion, Lucille Newmark, Rachel Crothers. Photography: Norbert Brodine. Film Editor: Basil Wrangell. Art Direction: Cedric Gibbons. Costumes: Adrian. Sound: Karl E. Zint, Douglas Shearer. Cast: Norma Shearer, Rod La Rocque, Marie Dressler, Gilbert Emery, Hedda Hopper, Raymond Hackett, Sally Eilers, Tyrell Davis, Wilfred Noy, William O'Brien, Sybil Grove.

The Divorcee (MGM, 1930) See credits on page 311.

Anna Christie (MGM, 1930) PB is not credited but he assisted Thalberg on all Garbo films for MGM for which Thalberg received producer credit or was responsible for producing himself. Clarence Brown Production. Shooting days: 20. Length: 10 reels, 8,268 feet. General release date: February 21, 1930. Producers: Irving Thalberg, Paul Bern. Director: Clarence Brown. Writer: Frances Marion. Photography: William Daniels. Film Editor: Hugh Wynn. Art Direction: Cedric Gibbons. Costumes: Adrian. Sound: Douglas Shearer, G.A. Burns. Cast: Greta Garbo, Charles Bickford, George F. Marion, Marie Dressler, James T. Mack, Lee Phelps.

The Rogue Song (MGM, 1930) PB is not credited but newspaper reviews, interviews and production stories confirmed his work as producer. Length: 12 reels, 9,723 feet. Preview release date: January 16, 1930. New York premiere date: January 28, 1930. General release date: May 10, 1930. Producer: Paul Bern. Director: Lionel Barrymore. Assistant Director: Charles Dorian. Writers: Frances Marion, John Colton, Wells Roots. Photography: Percy Hilburn, C. Edgar Schoenbaum. Film Editor: Margaret Booth. Art Direction: Cedric Gibbons. Costumes: Adrian. Music: Dimitri Tiomkin, Franz Lehar, Herbert Stothart. Lyrics: Clifford Grey. Sound: Douglas Shearer, Paul Neal. Choreography: Madame Albertina Rausch. Cast: Lawrence Tibbett, Catherine Dale Owen, Nance O'Neil, Judith Voselli, Ullrich Haupt, Elsa Alsen, Florence Lake, Lionel Belmore, Wallace MacDonald, Kate Price, H.A. Morgan, Burr McIntosh, James Bradbury, Jr., Stan Laurel, Oliver Hardy.

Listen, Baby (1930) Production cancelled after pre-production; Paul was identified in newspaper stories and interviews as the producer. Assistant Production Supervisor: William Conselman. Writers: William Conselman, James Gleason, W. Scott Darling. Music: W. Scott Darling, George Green, George Waggner (Darling wrote the theme song, assisted by Green and Waggner).

Dynamite (MGM, 1929) PB is not credited but he was producer in charge of all Pathe-DeMille productions during Cecil B. DeMille's brief stay at MGM (1929–1931). Length: 11,584 feet. General release date: December 13, 1929. Producers: Cecil B. DeMille, Paul Bern. Director: Cecil B. DeMille. Assistant Director: Mitchell Leisen. Writers: Jeanie Macpherson, John Howard Lawson, Gladys Unger. Photography: Peverell Marley. Film Editor: Anne Bauchens. Art Direction: Cedric

Gibbons, Mitchell Leisen. Costumes: Adrian. Music: Herbert Stothart, J.K. Brock. Sound: Douglas Shearer, J.K. Brock. Cast: Conrad Nagel, Kay Johnson, Charles Bickford, Julia Faye, Joel McCrea, Muriel McCormac, Robert Edeson, William Holden, Henry Stockbridge, Leslie Fenton, Barton Hepburn, Tyler Brooke, Ernest Hilliard, June Nash, Nancy Dover, Neely Edwards, Jerry Zier, Rita LeRoy, Clarence Burton, James Farley, Robert T. Haines, Douglas Frazer Scott, Jane Keckley, Fred Walton, Ynez Seabury, Blanche Craig, Mary Gordon, Scott Kolk, Russ Columbo.

The Flying Fool (Pathé, 1929) PB is not credited but he was producer in charge of all Pathe-DeMille productions during Cecil B. DeMille's brief stay at MGM (1929–1931) and period newspaper stories identify Paul as the producer. Length: 7 reels, 6,720 feet. General release date: July, 1929. Producers: Paul Bern, William Sistrom. Director: Tay Garnett. Assistant Director: Leigh Smith. Writers: Elliott Clawson, Tay Garnett, James Gleason. Photography: Arthur Miller. Sound: Ben Winkler, Earl A. Wolcott. Production Manager: John Rohlfs. Prop Man: Allan Smiley. Cast: William Boyd, Marie Prevost, Russell Gleason, Tom O'Brien.

Square Shoulders (Pathé, 1929) PB is not credited but he was producer in charge of all Pathe-DeMille productions during Cecil B. DeMille's brief stay at MGM (1929–1931) and period newspaper stories identify Paul as the producer. Length: 7 reels, 5,438 feet. General release date: March 10, 1929. Director: E. Mason Hopper. Assistant Director: Lonnie D'Orsa. Writers: Peggy Prior, George Dromgold, Houston Branch, John Krafft. Photography: David Abel. Film Editor: Barbara Hunter. Production Managers: Richard A. Blaydon, Robert McCrellis. Cast: Louis Wolheim, Junior Coghlan, Phillippe De Lacy, Anita Louise, Montague Shaw, Johnny Morris, Kewpie Morgan, Clarence Geldert, Erich von Stroheim, Jr.

Noisy Neighbors (Pathé, 1929) PB is not credited but he was producer in charge of all Pathe-DeMille productions during Cecil B. DeMille's brief stay at MGM (1929–1931) and period newspaper stories identify Paul as the producer and the production company as Paul Bern Productions. Length: 6 reels, 5,735 feet. Premiere date: January 27, 1929. General release date: February 17, 1929. Assistant Production Supervisor: William Conselman. Director: Charles Reisner. Assistant Director: Lonnie D'Orsa. Writers: W. Scott Darling, F. Hugh Herbert, John Krafft. Photography: David Abel. Film Editor: Anne Bauchens. Production Manager: Richard Blaydon. Cast: Eddie Quillan, Alberta Vaughn, Quillan Family (Joseph Quillan, Sarah Owens Quillan, John Quillan, Marie Quillan, and several other siblings), Theodore Roberts, Ray Hallor, Russell Simpson, Robert Perry, Mike Donlin, Billy Gilbert.

The Getaway (1929) PB is not credited but he was producer in charge of all Pathe-DeMille productions during Cecil B. DeMille's brief stay at MGM (1929–1931) and period newspaper stories identify Paul as the producer and listed this production title. However, the title release remains unidentified.

Geraldine (Pathé Exchange, Inc., 1928) Length: 7 reels, 5,959 feet. General release date: January 20, 1929. Producer: Paul Bern. Director: Melville Brown. Assistant Director: Leigh Smith. Writers: Carey Wilson, George Dromgold, Peggy Prior, John Krafft. Photography: David Abel. Film Editor: Barbara Hunter. Production Manager: Richard A. Blaydon. Cast: Marian Nixon, Eddie Quillan, Albert Gran, Gaston Glass.

A Woman of Affairs (MGM, 1929) PB is not credited but he assisted Thalberg on all Garbo films for MGM for which Thalberg received producer credit or was responsible for producing himself. Length: 9 reels, 8,716 feet. General release date: January 19, 1929. Assistant Producer: Paul Bern. Director: Clarence Brown. Assistant Director: Charles Dorian. Writers: Bess Meredyth, Marion Ainslee. Photography: William Daniels. Art Direction: Cedric Gibbons. Film Editor: Hugh Wynn. Costumes: Adrian. Cast: Greta Garbo, John Gilbert, Lewis Stone, Johnny Mack Brown, Douglas Fairbanks, Jr., Hobart Bosworth, Dorothy Sebastian.

Beau Broadway (MGM, 1928) PB is not credited, but MGM records and Sam Marx indicated that Paul assisted in the production. Length: 7 reels, 6,037 feet. Preview date: August 15, 1928. General release date: September 28, 1928. Assistant Producer: Paul Bern. Director: Malcolm St. Clair. Writers: F. Hugh Herbert, Malcolm St. Clair, George O'Hara. Photography: André Barlatier. Art Direction: Cedric Gibbons. Film Editor: Harry Reynolds. Costumes: Gilbert Duck. Cast: Lew Cody, Aileen Pringle, Sue Carol, Hugh Trevor, Heinie Conklin, Kit Guard, Jack Herrick, James J. Jeffries.

Flesh and the Devil (MGM, 1927) PB is not credited but he assisted Thalberg on all Garbo films for MGM for which Thalberg received producer credit or was responsible for producing himself. Shooting days: 43. Length: 9 reels, 8,759 feet. Premiere date: December 25, 1926. General release date: January 9, 1927. Producer: Irving Thalberg. Assistant Producer: Paul Bern. Director: Clarence Brown. Assistant Director: Charles Dorian. Writers: Benjamin F. Glazer, Marian Ainslee. Photography: William Daniels. Film Editor: Lloyd Nosler. Set Decoration: Cedric Gibbons, Frederic Hope. Costumes: Andréani. Cast: John Gilbert, Greta Garbo, Lars Hanson, Barbara Kent, William Orlamond, George Fawcett, Eugenie Besserer, Marc MacDermott, Marcelle Corday.

The Temptress (MGM, 1926) PB is not credited but he assisted Thalberg on all Garbo films for MGM for which Thalberg received producer credit or was responsible for producing himself. Shooting days: 83. Length: 9 reels, 8,862 feet. General release date: February 26, 1926. Cosmopolitan Pictures. Producer: Irving Thalberg. Assistant Producer: Paul Bern. Director: Fred Niblo. Assistant Directors: Mauritz Stiller, Bruce Humberstone. Writers: Dorothy Farnum, Marian Ainslee. Photography: Gaetano Gaudio, William Daniels. Film Editor: Lloyd Nosler. Set Decoration: Cedric Gibbons, James Basevi. Costumes: André-ani, Max Ree. Cast: Greta Garbo, Antonio Moreno, Roy D'Arcy, Marc MacDermott, Lionel Barrymore, Virginia Brown Faire, Armand Kaliz, Alys Murrell, Robert Anderson, Francis McDonald, Hector V. Sarno, Inez Gomez, Steve Clemento, Roy Couison.

Torrent (MGM, 1926) PB is not credited but he assisted Thalberg on all Garbo films for MGM for which Thalberg received producer credit or was responsible for producing himself. Cosmopolitan Pictures. Shooting days: 23. Length: 7 reels, 6,679 feet. Premiere date: February 8, 1926. General release date: February 26, 1926. Producer: Irving Thalberg. Assistant Producer: Paul Bern. Director: Monta Bell. Writers: Dorothy Farnum, Katherine Hilliker, H.H. Caldwell. Photography: William Daniels. Film Editor: Frank Sullivan. Set Decoration: Cedric Gibbons, Merrill Pye. Costumes: Kathleen Kay, Maude Marsh, André-ani, Max Ree. Cast: Ricardo Cortez,

Greta Garbo, Gertrude Olmstead, Edward Connelly, Lucien Littlefield, Martha Mattox, Lucy Beaumont, Tully Marshall, Mack Swain, Arthur Edmund Carew, Lillian Leighton, Mario Carrillo.

Lost and Found on a South Sea Island (1923) See credits on page 314.

Film Editing and Post-Production

Lost and Found on a South Sea Island (1923) See credits on page 314.

The Christian (1923) See credits on page 314.

Broken Chains (Goldwyn Pictures Corporation, 1922) PB is not credited but newspaper reviews and production stories confirmed his work with Carey Wilson. Length: 7 reels, 6,190 feet. General release date: December 24, 1922. Director: Allen Holubar. Writers: Carey Wilson, Winifred Kimball. Photography: Byron Haskin. Film Editor: Paul Bern. Cast: Malcolm McGregor, Colleen Moore, Ernest Torrence, Claire Windsor, James Marcus, Beryl Mercer, William Orlamond, Gerald Pring, Edward Peil, Leo Willis.

Hungry Hearts (Goldwyn Pictures Corporation, 1922) PB is not credited but newspaper reviews and production stories confirm his work. Length: 7 reels, 6,540 feet. General release date: November 26, 1922. Director: E. Mason Hopper. Writers: Julien Josephson, Montague Glass. Photography: Robert Newhard. Film Editor: Paul Bern. Cast: Bryant Washburn, Helen Furgeson, E.A. Warren, Rosa Rosanova, George Siegmann, Otto Lederer, Millie Schottland, Bert Sprotte, A. Budin, Edwin B. Tilton.

On-Camera Appearance

Screen Snapshots (Columbia Pictures Corporation, 1926) General Release date: August 1, 1926. Cast: Paul Bern, Pauline Garon, Lowell Sherman, Billie Dove, George K. Arthur, William S. Hart, Estelle Taylor, Ruth Roland, Tom Mix, Leatrice Joy, Charles Chaplin, Norma Shearer, Elinor Glyn, Pauline Starke.

Chapter Notes

Preface

1. *Motion Picture*, October, 1932, p. 77.
2. *Picture Play Magazine*, April, 1932, p. 78.
3. Jane Ardmore Papers, box 13, file 13, AMPAS.
4. *Photoplay*, September, 1932, p. 37.
5. *Motion Picture*, October, 1932, p. 51.
6. *Ibid.*, September, 1932, p. 51.

Chapter 1

1. Also referred to as Wandsback, Hamburg-Wandsbeck, Wannsbeck or any one of a number of other variations.
2. Retrieved January 9, 2007, from http://www.answers.com/topic/wandsbek.
3. Strasse is the designation for boulevard, e.g., Lubeckerstrasse or Lubecker Boulevard translated.
4. Wandsbek City Directory, Adressbuch Wandsbek, 1877.
5. "Rennbahn" loosely translates to racetrack. Neither home still stands; in July, 1943, much of Wandsbek was destroyed during Operation Gomorrah, a series of air raids conducted by over 1,500 Royal Air Force and United States Army Air Forces bombers that immolated most of Hamburg during the heaviest assault in the history of aerial warfare. The "Hiroshima of Germany" resulted in a firestorm; a tornado of fire that erupted into a huge outdoor blast furnace with 150 mile per hour winds and temperatures approaching 1,500°F. As asphalt burst into flame, people were literally cooked inside air raid shelters and sucked off the sidewalks as almost ten square miles of Hamburg and most of Wandsbek was incinerated. Almost 45,000 people were killed in a single night.
6. Friederike Levy didn't appear in any records until later U.S. Census records in the 1900s. The 1920 census listed Henriette as living with William and Friederike Marcus and listed as William's mother-in-law, Friederike's mother. Friederike and William Marcus were married in Wandsbek in 1894 and a son, Siegbert, was born on July 9, 1895. That family sailed for New York in 1896.
7. Betsy Bern, interview with EJF, December, 2007.
8. Retrieved January 9, 2007, from http://www.jewishvirtuallibrary.org.
9. Hamburg Amerikanische Packetfahrt Actien Gesellschaft (HAPAG), Hamburg-Amerika Line, archives of Liste der Reisenden, October 7, 1909.
10. Hamburg-Amerika Linie, Liste der Reisenden, October 7, 1909.
11. Special Documents Collection, Gjenvick-Gjønvik Archives, document #654-276-9987.
12. Emigration Port Hamburg, retrieved January 11, 2007, from http://fhh1.hamburg.de/fhh/internetausstellungen/emigration/englisch/A/6.htm.
13. Steiner, Edward A., *On the Trail of the Immigrant*, p. 30.
14. *Ibid.*, p. 33.
15. *Ibid.*, p. 36.
16. Susan Swiggum, www.theshipslist.com, correspondence with EJF.
17. On March 8, 1910, the *Pennsylvania* rammed and sank the schooner *Gertrud* in the mouth of the River Elbe and had to be rebuilt. She was rebuilt to 13,333 tons with accommodation for 404 2nd and 2,200 3rd class passengers and on July 18, 1914 commenced her last Hamburg to New York crossing. At the outbreak of World War I the ship took refuge in New York and in April, 1917 was seized by the United States. Renamed the S.S. *Nansemond*, she was used as a Navy transport until 1919. She was scrapped in the Hudson River in 1924. Don Hazeldine, www.shiphistory.co.uk, correspondence with EJF.
18. Brochure, Anchor Line, from the

Gjenvick-Gjønvik Maritime Collection SDC 314252353. These shipboard mess tins often became the only utensils in the homes of new arrivals to the United States.

19. Staatsarchiv Hamburg, *Hamburger Passagierlisten, 1850–1934 (Hamburg Passenger Lists, 1850–1934)*, Bestand: 373–7 I, VIII (Auswanderungsamt I). Mikrofilmrollen K 1701-K 2008, S 17363-S 17383, 13116-13183.

20. Gjenvick-Gjønvik Archives' Maritime Collection SDC 741055056.

21. Staatsarchiv Hamburg, *Hamburger Passagierlisten, 1850–1934 (Hamburg Passenger Lists, 1850–1934)*, Bestand: 373–7 I, VIII (Auswanderungsamt I). Mikrofilmrollen K 1701-K 2008, S 17363-S 17383, 13116-13183.

22. Retrieved January 10, 2007 from http://fhhl.hamburg.de/fhh/internetausstellungen/emigration/englisch/F/48.htm.

23. Today the neighborhood is known as East Harlem or El Barrio (Spanish Harlem) and stretches from First to Fifth Avenue and from East 96th to 125th Street.

24. New York City Housing Authority. The massive project stretches from Lenox Avenue to 1st, is three blocks wide and includes three other groups of buildings named for Dr. Martin Luther King, civil rights leader James Weldon Johnson, and Thomas Jefferson. Almost 50 buildings hold 5,600 apartments and 12,500 people.

25. 1900 U.S. Federal Census, New York, New York, Manhattan, District 836, Sheet 6.

26. Central Park history from *The Park and the People: A History of Central Park*, retrieved January 25, 2007, from www.centralparkhistory.com.

27. Versus the enrollment; attendance represents the average number of students served by schools on a given day while enrollment is the number of students registered by the Board of Education. From 1887 to 1907, the number of registered students varied greatly from the number that attended classes on a daily basis. Statistics from the City of New York. *Annual Financial and Statistical Report: 1906-07-08*, Special Collections, Teacher's College, Columbia University.

28. From "The Largest Public School in the World," *The New York Times*, November 25, 1900.

29. *9th Annual Report of the City Superintendent of Schools to the Board of Education of the City of New York (1907)*, Special Collections, Teachers College, Columbia University.

30. Covello, Leonard, *The Heart Is the Teacher*, p. 23.

31. *Ibid.*, p. 25.

32. Background regarding ALS (Lou Gehrig's Disease) from National Institute of Neurological Disorders and Stroke. In addition to Gehrig, other well-known people killed by the disease include boxer Ezzard Charles, baseball player Jim "Catfish" Hunter, famed blues guitarist Leadbelly, and actor David Niven. Astronomer and writer Stephen Hawking continues to bring attention to the disease.

33. Rockefeller Archive Center, Rockefeller Family Archives, 1819-(1879–1898), John D. Rockefeller's Charity Index Cards, Social Welfare and Moral Reform Organizations & Institutions, Montefiore Home, 1896–1898.

34. Among the 200,000 people buried at Mt. Zion are lyricist and songwriter Lorenz Hart (of the team of Rodgers and Hart), *Day of the Locust* writer Nathanael West, and Theresa Moers (Weinstein), who was murdered in Los Angeles by boxer Norman "Kid" McCoy in 1924.

35. 1910 U.S. Federal Census, State of New York, New York, Bronx, District 1606, Sheet 23A. The census form appears to say "3281" but Paul's American Academy of Dramatic Arts application and audition report clearly lists "3781."

36. U.S. Draft Registration, Henry J. Levy, June 5, 1917.

37. *The New York Times*, August 28, 1884.

38. Henry C. de Mille wrote several plays and movie screenplays made after his 1893 death, including the screenplay for Lionel Barrymore's *Men and Women* (1914). His wife Beatrice Samuel wrote about a dozen screenplays in 1916–1917 including Wallace Reid's *The Devil Stone* (1917). She died in 1923. William used the family surname de Mille during his entire life while his brother Cecil B. used DeMille once he arrived in Hollywood. When Cecil left for Hollywood in 1911 William refused to go along, assuming his foray into the movies would fail. Cecil vowed at the time that his elder brother would someday be known as "C.B.'s brother."

39. Dozens of other famous names have attended the AADA over the years, including Pat O'Brien and Spencer Tracy (1923), Agnes Moorehead (1929), Jennifer Jones (1939), Kirk Douglas (1941), Grace Kelly (1949), Robert Redford (1959), and Danny DeVito (1966).

40. It has been noted in some sources that Paul auditioned in 1910 but the AADA records confirm 1909. All information pertaining to Paul's audition from American Academy of Dramatic Arts, Audition Report, Paul Levy, September 13, 1909.

41. Chapin, Robert Colt, *The Standard of Living Among Workingmen's Families in New York City*, p. 5.

42. Retrieved February 14, 2007, from http://mysite.verizon.net/vze85s68/training.

43. The Empire Theater continued to host the greatest names in theater into the 1940s, in-

cluding John Gielgud, Lillian Gish, Dame Judith Anderson, Burgess Meredith, Julie Harris, and dozens of others. In 1948 and in disrepair it was purchased by the Astor estate but instead of being restored, it was demolished in 1953. Frohman himself was at the height of his career when he died in 1915. He controlled over 200 theaters in London and the U.S. and had produced over 700 plays when he sailed to London aboard the RMS *Lusitania*, which was torpedoed and sunk by German submarines. Handing his life preserver to actress Rita Jolivet, he quoted Peter Pan, saying, "Why fear death. It's the most beautiful adventure in life." Interestingly, at the moment of the sinking, John Ryland, his office manager in New York, walked into Frohman's office and allegedly saw him sitting at his desk! Thinking he had left on the ship, Ryland asked the figure if he could help, and was told, "No, you can't help me, John. Just leave me alone for a few minutes. Thanks, and goodbye." When Ryland returned with Frohman's son and another man a few minutes later, the office was empty, of course. At the time of the bizarre conversation, the group was not aware of the ship's sinking.

44. Cast members included Rachel Ridgley, Philip Barrison, Grant Ervin, Edward Lindsley, Eleanor Taylor, Jean Marcet, and Margaret Greene.

45. In 1912 Greene appeared in the play *Ready Money*, which was produced by Harry H. Frazee. Frazee is notorious among Boston Red Sox fans: When he owned the team, he sold Babe Ruth to the Yankees in 1919 for $125,000 to finance the play *No, No, Nanette*. Greene later appeared in a 1919 play *A Regular Feller* with an unknown young actor (playing a chauffeur) named George Cukor, who became one of the most distinguished directors in the movies. In the 1917 film *One Law for Both*, Greene's co-star was Rita Jolivet, who had been traveling with Charles Frohman aboard the RMS *Lusitania* and was saved when Frohman gave her his life jacket.

46. 1910 U.S. Federal Census, New York, New York, Manhattan, District 562, sheet 11A.

47. Stenn, David, *Bombshell: The Life and Death of Jean Harlow*, p. 90.

48. Bernays became a business icon by applying psychology to marketing, first writing publicity for Broadway plays and WWI propaganda. His most stunning success was for the 1920 National Association for the Advancement of Colored People (NAACP) convention in Atlanta. Bernays and his wife and partner crafted a subtle campaign directed toward less tolerant southerners reinforcing the importance of black people to the southern economy. For the first time southern whites were quoted supporting the black movement, a stunning achievement.

He managed products for Ivory Soap, General Motors, and cigarettes (although in the 1960s he renounced his work after learning of the dangers). "The Father of Public Relations" died in 1995.

49. *The New York Times*, January 27, 1911.

50. *Continental Interlude I: The Futurist Moment (1909–1914)*, p. 38, downloaded February 14, 2007, from http://www.blackwellpublishing.com.

51. *New York Dramatic Mirror*, January 27, 1911.

52. *New York Daily News*, February 12, 1911.

53. *Dramatic News*, February 10, 1911.

54. Material regarding graduation exercises from *The New York Times*, March 14, 1911.

55. Miller (1859–1926) appeared in over 100 plays dating to the 1880s and produced another dozen like *The Great Divide* (1917) and *Grounds for Divorce* (1925). The Henry Miller's Theater at 124 West 3rd Street hosted some of the most famous actors and plays in U.S. theater and, interestingly a good number of Miller's performers earned even higher acclaim in the movies — stars like Alla Nazimova, Ruth Chatterton, Billie Burke, Ina Claire, Laura Hope Crews, Henry B. Walthall, James Kirkwood, and Fred Esmelton.

56. Betty Lawson, American Academy of Dramatic Arts, correspondence with EJF. The Class of 1910: Alfred Miller Botsford, Quincy, Ill.; Abner Cassidy, St. Louis; Roy Clemens, Wellesley Hills, Mass.; Joseph Culligan, New York City; Herman George Joslin, Rockford, Ill.; Donald MacDonald, Lima, Ohio; Kalman Edwin Matthews, Brooklyn; James Wheaton Mott, Salem, Ore.; Carl Nagel, Berlin, Germany; Myron Z. Paulson, Homestead, Pa.; Sidney Powell, Omaha, Neb.; Tom Powers, Louisville, Ky.; Gerald Quina, Pensacola, Fla.; Ernst John Rowan, Milwaukee; George Handy Shelton, Grand Rapids; William Starling, Hopkinsville, Ky.; Mary Alden, New Orleans; Lucille Leanette Arnold, New York City; Beatrice Bentley, New York City; Lucia Bronder, Brooklyn; Laurett Browne, New York City; Margaret Alma Stevens Foster, Toronto; Pauline Langdon, Jacksonville, Fla.; Alice Lindahl, San Francisco; Aline McDermott, Jersey City; Alice Newell, Philadelphia; Ernestine Peabody, Dayton, Wash.; Florence Phelps, New York City; Ann Pittwood, Ore.; and Kathryn Vincent, Montclair, N.J.

57. Mary Alden died in 1946 at the Motion Picture Country Home in Woodland Hills.

58. Tom Powers died in 1955 in Hollywood.

59. *New York American*, September 8, 1932.

60. Marx, Samuel, and Joyce Vanderveen,

Deadly Illusions: Jean Harlow and the Murder of Paul Bern, p. 93.

61. *Ibid.*, p. 182.

62. Birth records from 1880 to 1886 contained no Roddy references at all. Death records from 1883 to 1899 contained no death records for either William Roddy or Lillian Johnston Roddy, nor did Probate or Estate records. It is virtually certain that young Dorothy did not live near Columbus, Ohio.

63. 1900 U.S. Federal Census, Indiana, Madison County, Greene Township, District 100, Sheet 4.

64. The Whitmer farm was located near present-day Ingalls, Indiana.

65. In her Audition Report, Dorothy was described as "heavy" and her proportions as "stout" though it was noted that she was in "good" physical condition.

66. *Canton Daily News*, September 1, 1926.

67. Application for Marriage License-Male, Lowell Mellett, June 22, 1907, Application for Marriage License-Female, Dorothy Roddy, June 22, 1907, Marion County.

68. Lowell Mellett spent World War I in Europe reporting front-line stories for the UP, after which he worked for several newspapers, eventually becoming editor-in-chief of the *Washington Daily News*. On December 18, 1941, Roosevelt appointed Mellett head of the Office of Government Reports, which in 1942 became the Bureau of Motion Pictures in the powerful Office of War Information (OWI). The OWI served as a liaison between the government and the motion picture industry, in effect directing the government's propaganda efforts by controlling the content and theme of wartime films through Mellett's Bureau of Motion Pictures (BMP). The group was known in the press as "Mellett's Madhouse." He also has the distinction of participating in the first private presidential conversation ever recorded on an Oval Office taping system, a 1940 chat with President Roosevelt about his re-election campaign. Mellett left government in 1946 and wrote for several newspapers including the *Washington Star*. A strident and vocal critic of the McCarthy Committee activities, Mellett continued writing until his 1960 death in Washington, D.C.

69. All material concerning Dorothy Millette audition from American Academy of Dramatic Arts, Audition Report, May 8, 1911, p. 130, Mrs. L. Melette (Dorothy Roddy Mellett).

70. Arliss starred on the English stage and came to America in 1902 and top-lined the most popular plays of the early 20th century like *The Eyes of the Heart* (1905) and *Disraeli* (1911). He once told a court that he was the best actor in the world, explaining, "You see, I'm under an oath." He moved to movies in 1921, reprising his stage roles in both *The Devil* and *Disraeli*. He earned an Academy Award for Best Actor for his second film version of *Disraeli* in 1929, and is credited with discovering and supporting a young Bette Davis. He died in London in 1946. Davey was known around the world simply as "Mrs. Fiske." She appeared in, wrote, or produced hundreds of plays during a sixty-year career that began in 1871.

71. Betty Lawson, American Academy of Dramatic Arts, correspondence with EJF.

72. Wearing, J. P. *The London Stage, 1890–1899: A Calendar of Plays and Players. Vol. 1*, p. 665.

73. *Indianapolis Star*, November 14, 1915.

74. *Ibid.*, May 28, 1916.

75. *The New York Times*, November 15, 1908.

76. Among the few mentions of American players among Ben Greet rolls was Lawrence Eyre in 1913.

77. Retrieved February 23, 2007, from http://www.rollins.edu/theatre/annierussellthe atre.shtml.

78. *The Toronto Daily Star*, May 2, 1913.

79. Russell retired in 1918 and moved to Winter Park, Florida. From 1923 until her death in 1932 she was Artistic Director and taught theater at Rollins (Florida) College. The beautiful Annie Russell Theater, known as "The Annie," survives at the school.

80. *The New York Times*, June 22, 1913.

81. In 1926 the theater was torn down and replaced by a 20-story office building.

82. *The New York Times*, October 21, 1912. Coincidentally, the same column also noted the formation of the Screen Club, a private club exclusive to motion pictures, at 103 West 45th. Officers were King Baggott (president), John Bunny (vice-president), C.A. Willat (treasurer), and George M. ("Bronco Billy") Anderson, Maurice Costello and Arthur Johnson. The Screen Club was the precursor to the Actor's Equity group founded the next year and the later Screen Actors Guild.

83. *The New York Times*, November 12, 1912.

84. Loney, Glenn. *Twentieth-Century Theatre*, *Vol. 1*, p. 64. Supporting cast: Westley (Claudio), Giddens (Dogberry), Percy Lyndal (Don Pedro), W. Mayne Lynton (Don Juan), Rose Bender (Hero), Permain (Leonato), Power, Hudson, Devereaux, Harold Meitzer, Thomas Fallon, Ed Longman, and Henrietta Goodwin.

85. Supporting cast: Westley, Giddens, Lyndal, W. Mayne Lynton, Power, Ffoillett Paget, Goodwin and May Murillo.

86. *The New York Times*, March 25, 1913.

87. *The Toronto Daily Star*, May 1, 1913.

88. *Ibid.*, March 15, 1914.

89. According to *The New York Times,* the idea of limiting childbirth was first suggested by "Dr. Moses, a representative of the German Socialist Party," but he was absolutely opposed by "saner" members of his party and the German public.

90. *The New York Times,* September 29, 1913.

91. *Ibid.,* September 29, 1913.

92. *Ibid.,* October 14, 1913.

93. *Ibid.,* October 30, 1913.

94. *Ibid.,* November 1, 1913.

95. In 1916, *The Guilty Man* ran for about 50 performances at the Astor Theater; future movie actors Lowell Sherman, Irene Fenwick and Stuart Robson were in the cast.

96. *The New York Times,* February 26, 1914. The rest of the company included Virginia Erwin, Charles and Bessie Fischer, Phillip Hillman, Eva Condon, John Cromwell, Edward McWade, George Williams, Ralph Howard and Ford Wilson.

97. Internet Broadway Database.

98. *The New York Times,* January 27, 1914.

99. *Too Many Cooks* notes here from *The New York Times,* February 26, 1914.

100. *The New York Times,* May 29, 1914.

101. *Toronto World,* September 13, 1914.

102. *The Toronto Daily Star,* September 15, 1914.

103. Calculating the relative value of $100 in 1925 to today's worth is a relative process, depending on the variable or combination of variables used. For example, using the Consumer Price Index it's worth $1,150 (11 times value, or $1,100), using nominal Gross Domestic Product model (a combination of product costs) the value is $5,627 (56 times value, or $5,600), and using the unskilled wage cost it's worth $3,954.95 (40 times value or $4,000). Although it dilutes the pure scientific validity, for a reasonable average we use 25 times value, or $100 in 1920 is assumed to be worth $2,500 today.

104. *The Toronto Star,* August 29, 1914.

105. After Craven's travels with *Too Many Cooks* he appeared in *Under Fire* with two young actors named Edward G. Robinson and Frank Morgan. His 1924 play *New Brooms (1925)* was made into a movie which led him to Hollywood and writing films like Laurel & Hardy's classic *Sons of the Desert* (1933) and *State Fair* (1933). In 1932 he began acting and appeared in almost 40 films like *That's Gratitude* (1934), *Our Town* (1940, which he adapted for film), and *My Best Gal* (1944). He returned regularly to Broadway and died in Hollywood on September 1, 1945, at 70.

106. Mintz, S. (2003), *The Movies as a Cultural Battleground, Digital History,* retrieved March 15, 2005, from http://www.digitalhistory.uh.edu.

107. Botnick, Vicki, American Film Institute, *The First Fifty Years of American Film,* Fathom Archives, Columbia University.

108. *The Sneeze* was apparently filmed on January 7, 1894, although some film historians date the film to 1893.

109. *The New York Times,* April 21, 1896.

110. Pratt, George, *Spellbound in Darkness,* p. 27.

111. Wanamaker, Mark, *The First Studios,* retrieved March 15, 2005, from http://www.free-culture.org.

112. Cook, Pam (editor), *The Cinema Book,* p. 4.

113. Sniper story from Ramsaye, Terry, *A Million and One Nights: A History of the Motion Picture,* p. 575. Dwan story from Bogdanovich, Peter, *Allan Dwan: The Last Pioneer,* p. 17.

114. Wanamaker, Mark, *The First Studios,* retrieved June 24, 2007 from http://www.free-culture.cc/notes/12.

115. MacDonald, Cathy, "Treasure Hunt: Gordon Parsons' Celluloid Search," *Halifax Sunday Daily News,* February 5, 1989, p. 21. Porter was Edison's primary cameraman.

116. "Eastern Eye: A Nova Scotia Filmography/1899–1973," Retrieved May 28, 2007, from http://www.gov.ns.ca/nsarm/databases/easterneye

117. Mack information from *The Moving Picture World,* February 13, 1915, Vol. 24, p. 994, B.C. Feature information from *The Moving Picture World,* March 6, 1915, Vol. 23, p. 1475.

118. *The Moving Picture World,* February 20, 1915., Vol. 24, p. 1170.

119. *The Toronto Star,* August 29, 1914.

120. The address does not match present-day addresses; Adelaide Street has been re-numbered.

121. *The Toronto Star,* June 14, 1914.

122. Morris, Peter, *Embattled Shadows: A History of Canadian Cinema,* p. 52.

123. *The Moving Picture World,* February 13, 1915, Vol. 24, p. 994.

124. The rest of the company included Marie Cummings, Reina Carruthers, May Anderson, Margaret Jackson, Frank Crane, Eugene Frazier, Frank Preistland, and H. Webb Chamberlain.

Chapter 2

1. *The Toronto Star,* October 30, 1914.

2. *Toronto City Directory, 1915.* The 1915 Directory listed addresses and information as of the end of 1914.

3. Retrieved May 26, 2007, from www.wikepedia.org/Parkdale.

4. Retrieved June 14, 2007, from http://www.toronto.ca/culture/history.

5. Hiebert, Daniel, *Jewish Immigrants and the Garment Industry of Toronto, 1901–1931: A Study of Ethnic and Class Relations*, p. 243.

6. Harney, Robert F., *Chiaroscuro: Italians in Toronto, 1815–1915, Polypony*, Vol. 6, 1984, p. 45.

7. *The Moving Picture World*, December 15, 1914, Vol. 22, p. 1563.

8. *The Moving Picture World*, April 10, 1915, Vol. 25, p. 257, and Gutteridge, Robert W., *Magic Moments: First 20 Years of Moving Pictures in Toronto (1894–1914)*, p. 197.

9. *The Moving Picture World*, November 14, 1914, Vol. 22, p. 1257.

10. *The Moving Picture World*, February 13, 1915, Vol. 24, p. 994. The first feature film produced in Canada was probably Canadian Bioscope's *Evangeline*, released in 1913.

11. *The Moving Picture World*, January 2, 1915, Vol. 24, p. 108.

12. *The Toronto Star*, March 17, 1915, *The Moving Picture World*, April 17, 1915, Vol. 25, p. 426, and *The Moving Picture World*, January 2, 1915, Vol. 24, p. 108.

13. Over two dozen of the *Broncho Billy* westerns starring Gilbert M. "Broncho Billy" Anderson were denied distribution for everything from "too much gunplay" to being "immoral and criminal." Records from Quebec Film Commission, Censorship List, 1913–1916.

14. *The Moving Picture World*, January 23, 1915, Vol. 24, p. 550.

15. *Jack Canuck*, January, 1915.

16. *The Moving Picture World*, January 23, 1915, Vol. 24, p. 550.

17. Morris, p. 53.

18. Beury's first film was the 1915 prize fight between Jess Willard and Jack Johnson in Havana, Cuba.

19. *The Hartford Courant*, September 14, 1924.

20. *New York City Directory*, 1916.

21. Dimmick, Ruth Crosby, *Our Theaters and Yesterday: A Study of Manhattan Island's Theaters from 1732 to 1913*.

22. *The New York Times*, March 1, 1914.

23. *Ibid.*, Letters to the Editor, Bodnar, Theodore A., February 23, 2007.

24. Leeds, Mark, *The Encyclopedia of New York City*, p. 111. The fire, believed to have been caused by a match accidentally tossed into a pile of straw, turned tragic due to a combination of corroded hoses which burst when water flowed, new paint which accelerated the fire, rotted cork in the 2,500 life jackets which acted as lead weights when they mixed with water, and the captain's decision to try to race to 148th Street instead of beaching the ship. Virtually all of the passengers were women and children, and hundreds of widowers committed suicide in the aftermath of the disaster. After the accident, most of the people living in Little Germany migrated northward to the Yorkville neighborhood. Additional *Slocum* information from Kathy Jolowicz, referring to Rust, Claude, *The Burning of the General Slocum* and O'Donnell, Ed, *Ship Ablaze*.

25. *The New York Times*, April 24, 1916. Rachmann renamed the Yorkville the Yorkville Deutsches Theater and catered even more directly to the German patrons, but with the U.S.'s entrance into World War I, "Deutsches" was dropped from the name and it was renamed the Yorkville Theatre. The theater building still stands, but the interior was renovated to accommodate the office building that stands still today. Most of the original façade remains.

26. Frank Lea Short and Frank McGinn directed and the complex sets were designed by Ernest Albert.

27. *The New York Times*, January 4, 1906. Chapin was featured as Lincoln, Francis McGinn as Secretary Edwin M. Stanton, David R. Young and Malcolm Duncan as the soldiers, George Clarke as Tad Lincoln, W.H. Pascoe as Gen. Joseph Hooker, Maude Granger as Mary Todd Lincoln, Francis McGinn as White House attendant Old Edward, and Daisy Lovering as Kate Morris. Also appearing were Julius Barton and J.H. Lewis.

28. Dixon, Thomas, *The Leopard's Spots: A Romance of the White Man's Burden 1865–1900, The Clansman: An Historical Romance of the Ku Klux Klan, The Traitor*. D.W. Griffith later recreated a version of Dixon's racist views in his classic *The Birth of a Nation*, which was titled *The Clansman* when it premiered. Dixon said he would "allow none but the son of a Confederate soldier to direct the film version of *The Clansman*." Griffith was the son of a Confederate general.

29. *The New York Times*, April 1, 1906.

30. Chapin is sometimes listed as the producer of Thomas Ince's 101-Bison film *In Love and War* (1913) which starred Wallace Reid and Marshall Neilan and was filmed in April and released on June 17. It would be surprising if Chapin were indeed involved in that film; he was on the East Coast and all of Reid's films during the first half of 1913 were filmed in Santa Barbara, California, when he worked with American Film Company and Allan Dwan.

31. World War I Draft Registration, Paul Bern, no. 31-9-125-A, June 5, 1917.

32. "Events in his life" from *The Hartford Courant*, February 18, 1918. Series notes from

American Film Institute, Catalog of Films, no. 14746.

33. *The New York Times,* June 22, 1917.

34. Supporting cast: George Periolat, Allan Forrest, Henry A. Barrows, Ashton Dearholt, and Spottiswoode Aitken. Minter's mother Margaret Shelby also had a small role in the Lloyd Ingraham–directed film.

35. *The New York Times,* March 21, 1917.

36. Individual advertisements for the films from *The New York Times,* July 24, 1917, and March 9, 1918, and *The Hartford Courant,* March 25, 1918.

37. *The New York Times,* June 3, 1918.

38. *Who's Who in Victorian Cinema,* retrieved June 24, 2007, from http://www.victorian-cinema.net/pathe.

39. *The New York Times,* May 8, 1918.

40. *Ibid.,* May 18, 1919.

41. Supporting cast: Bert Apling, Joseph Swickard, Virginia Eames, Charles Rogers, and George Fields.

42. Also referred to as *The Light of the Western Stars, The New York Times,* January 4, 1919.

43. *The New York Times,* June 15, 1919.

44. *Ibid.,* September 19, 1919.

45. American Film Institute, Catalog of Films, no. 15426.

46. Brownlow, Kevin, *The Parade's Gone By...,* p. 22. The DeMille brothers insisted on spelling their individual names differently. William not only convinced Lasky to script his own movies but to closely script the filming, a radical idea. It was a coup to obtain the services of Turnbull and MacAlarney, who were at the time the dramatic critic and city editor, respectively, of the *New York Herald Tribune.*

47. *The New York Times,* April 18, 1920.

48. 1920 U.S. Federal Census, New York, New York, Manhattan, District 774, Sheet 2.

49. *Los Angeles Record,* September 9, 1932.

50. 1920 U.S. Federal Census, New York, New York, Manhattan, District 375, Sheet 34-B.

51. Henriette Levy travel records from Ellis Island archives, Passenger Manifest, *Amerika,* April 23, 1910, line 0012. Marcus employment from U.S. Draft Registration, Siegbert Marcus, June 5, 1917. Residence information from 1920 U.S. Federal Census, New York, Bronx, District 412, Sheet 8-A.

52. American Film Institute, Catalog of Films, no. 16183, and Garza, Janiss, *All Movie Guide,* retrieved June 28, 2007, from http://movies2.nytimes.com.

53. Little information remains concerning *Greater Than Love* beyond a meager cast list and the March 15, 1920, copyright date. Those dates typically coincided with the beginning of actual production.

54. American Film Institute, Catalog of Films, no. 16232.

55. Eugene Zukor, from Gabler, Neal, *An Empire of Their Own,* p. 37.

56. Aberdeen, J.A., *Hollywood's Lone Wolf,* from the Society of Independent Motion Picture Producers archive and database.

57. Berg, A. Scott, *Goldwyn: A Biography,* p. 69.

58. Cowl's *The Spreading Dawn* was delayed when a supporting actor died after most of the film was completed, forcing Goldwyn to reproduce the backgrounds for fifteen scenes that had been completed.

59. Will Rogers story from Berg, p. 69. Landscaping from Fussell, Betty Harper, *Mabel: Hollywood's First I-Don't-Care-Girl,* p.118.

60. *The New York Times,* March 14, 1920.

61. Berg, p. 89.

62. A small amount of shooting was done in Pittsburgh, Pennsylvania.

63. American Film Institute, Catalog of Films, no. 2337.

64. *The New York Times,* October 18, 1920.

65. *Ibid.,* August 15, 1920.

66. *The New York American,* September 9, 1932.

67. *Rochester Times-Union,* September 10, 1932.

68. *The New York American,* September 12, 1932.

69. Retrieved June 30, 2007, from http://www.gpnotebook.co.uk.

70. Blythewood became internationally known after chief psychiatrist and medical director Dr. Harry Tiebout suggested that patient Marty Mann read *Alcoholics Anonymous* in the spring of 1939 as part of her treatment for alcoholism. When she earned a reputation as the first woman to stay sober in the U.S., the book, moment and the location became part of A.A. lore. On March 30, 1943, Clara Frauenthal, one of the First Class passengers who survived the sinking of the *Titanic,* died after 16 years at Blythewood. She was committed when she suffered a breakdown after the 1927 suicide of her husband, who jumped off of a New York hospital and killed himself. The couple had been on their honeymoon cruise aboard the ill-fated ship.

71. *Rochester Times-Union,* September 10, 1932.

72. *Los Angeles Examiner,* September 8, 1932.

73. *Ibid.,* September 10, 1932.

74. *The Sheboygan Press,* September 15, 1932.

75. *New York American,* September 10, 1932.

76. *The New York Times,* September 9, 1932.

77. *Ibid.*, November 7, 1920.
78. Rue de St. Felix was renamed Beach 14th Street in the 1930s.
79. Retrieved January 26, 2007 from www.arrts-arrchives.com/rock.html.
80. The popular park remained open until 1985.
81. Davis, Lisa Selin, *Crowded Houses*, retrieved January 26, 2007, from www.national trust.org.
82. Bay Avenue was renamed Seagirt Avenue in the 1930s. It is the main street running next to the beach through that part of Rockaway Beach. Today there is a wide beach at the end of what used to be Rue de St. Felix (Beach 14th Street) but in 1920 there was just a short stretch of grassy dunes and a steep embankment above the water.
83. *Queens Daily Sun*, October 5, 1920.
84. State of New York, Department of Health of the City of New York, Certificate of Death, Henrietta [*sic*] Levy, September 15, 1920.
85. *Rochester Times-Union*, September 12, 1932.
86. *The New York Times*, October 31, 1920.
87. Quoted from Paris, Barry, *Garbo*, p. 7.
88. Coincidently, Parker lived at the Algonquin during the time that Dorothy did. She was a member of the famed Algonquin Round Table of writers and intellectuals.
88. *San Francisco Chronicle*, June 22, 1936.
89. Henderson, Robert, *D. W. Griffith: The Years at Biograph*, p. 22.
90. Cronyn, Thoreau, "The Truth About Hollywood," *New York Herald*, March 12, 1922.
91. Lambert, Gavin, *Norma Shearer*, p. 102.
92. St. Johns, Adela Rogers, *The Life of Wallace Reid: The Tragedy of an American Idol, Liberty Magazine*, June 30, 1928, p. 44.
93. Lasky, Jesse L., *I Blow My Own Horn*, p. 95.
94. Even as late as 1930, the population was barely 5,600. Source: U.S. Census Bureau.
95. Zollo, Paul, *Hollywood Remembered: An Oral History of Its Golden Age*, p. 22.
96. Starr, Kevin, *Material Dreams: Southern California Through the 1920s*, p. 13.

Chapter 3

1. 1921 Los Angeles City Directory. Georgia Street was sometimes called South Georgia Street simply because it was among other "South" streets. The block is just northeast of the Staples Center and the intersection of the Hollywood (101) and Santa Monica (10) Freeways.
2. Sanford Map Company, Los Angeles, 1923, Map 75.

3. Details concerning the Crawford from 1930 U.S. Federal Census, Los Angeles County, Los Angeles, District 350, Sheet 11-A, and Sanford Map Company, Los Angeles, 1923, Map 75.
4. 1920 U.S. Federal Census, California, Los Angeles County, Los Angeles, District 457, Sheet 2-B.
5. Los Angeles City Directory, 1921, p. 520.
6. Fussell, Betty Harper, *Mabel: Hollywood's First I Don't Care Girl*, p. 7.
7. Berg, p. 76.
8. *Stevens Point Daily Journal*, May 29, 1922.
9. Fussell, p. 119.
10. Beauchamp, Cari, *Without Lying Down: Frances Marion and the Powerful Women of Early Hollywood*, p. 297.
11. Marx, Samuel, *Mayer and Thalberg: The Make-Believe Saints*, p. 47.
12. Fussell, p. 118.
13. Fox, Charles D., and Milton L. Silver, *Who's Who on the Silver Screen* (reprint of 1920 edition), p. 335. Schertzinger was the son of a concert violinist, a prodigy at the Academy of Music at Nine, schooled at the University of Pennsylvania and the University of Brussels. He was he first to compose a musical score for a movie, 1916's *Civilization*. When sound arrived in 1927, Schertzinger returned to music and composed songs for dozens of hit films, many of which premiered after his untimely 1941 death. His songs were featured in films like *The Fleet's In* (1942), *Double Indemnity* (1944), *Gilda* (1946), and *Plaza Suite* (1971).
14. *The Davenport Democrat and Leader*, June 11, 1922.
15. American Film Institute, Catalog of Films, no. 1503.
16. The eventual release of the film, in April, 1922, was probably driven more by Normand's involvement in scandals surrounding William Desmond Taylor and herself than Goldwyn's interest in releasing the obviously substandard film.
17. Fussell, p. 127.
18. The *Edgar* films were *Edgar and the Teacher's Pet, Edgar's Hamlet, Get-Rich-Quick Edgar, Edgar's Sunday Courtship, Edgar's Jonah Day, Edgar Takes the Cake, Edgar Camps Out, Edgar, the Explorer, Edgar's Little Saw* (all 1920 releases) and *Edgar's Country Cousin, Edgar's Feast Day*, and *Edgar, the Detective* (1921 releases).
19. The cast varied only slightly during the series; Arthur H. Little, Katherine Bates, William Ellingford, Edouard Trebaol, Henry Van Sickle, and Ellison Manners each appeared in two or three of the chapters.
20. *The New York Times*, May 5, 1921.
21. *The Indianapolis Star*, January 12, 1921.

22. *Stars of Photoplay*, 1924 edition.
23. *Oakland Sunday Tribune*, December 26, 1920.
24. *The New York Times*, November 21, 1920.
25. Edmonds, Andy, *Frame-Up!: The Untold Story of Roscoe "Fatty" Arbuckle*, p. 143.
26. Director Eddie Sutherland identified "The Count" as Keystone worker Hughie Faye.
27. Vogel, Michelle, *Olive Thomas: The Life and Death of a Silent Film Beauty*, p. 75.
28. Eyman, Scott, *Mary Pickford: America's Sweetheart*, p. 98. The pathetic Pickford lived off of Thomas' $500,000 life insurance policy for three years before he died of a drug overdose in 1926.
29. *The New York Times*, November 23, 1920.
30. Beauchamp, p. 102.
31. Carey Wilson (1889–1962) wrote 75+ screenplays from 1920 to 1946 like the classic *Ben-Hur: A Tale of Christ* (1925) and several 1940s *Andy Hardy* films. He was also alleged to have produced all of the *Andy Hardy* films, although sources disagree whether is was Wilson or J.J. Cohn. His voice was well-known (he narrated dozens of MGM newsreels and films during the 1930s and 1940s) and he was one of the 36 founders of the Academy of Motion Pictures Arts and Sciences. He was married to his second wife, actress Carmelita Geraghty, for 30 years until his death on February 1, 1962, in Hollywood, following a stroke.
32. Fountain, p. 81.
33. Gilbert's two long-time houseboys worked for him from until his death; he made bequests to both in his will.
34. Most records note the John Gilbert-Leatrice Joy wedding as taking place in 1923 but their daughter Leatrice Fountain alleged that the couple was secretly married in 1921. Dated events — when Gilbert moved into Kings Road, production dates of the films Joy worked on at times of separations and reconciliations, etc.— lend significant weight to Joy's earlier date.
35. Fountain, p. 81; "near-fatal accident" from Golden, Eve, *Platinum Girl: The Life and Legend of Jean Harlow*, p. 95.
36. Zollo, p. 222.
37. Both letters from Marx and Vanderveen, p. 96.
38. Ben Deeley (1878–1924) was a vaudevillian who appeared in his first film, *The Patchwork Girl of Oz*, in 1914. He appeared in several dozen films during the next ten years before dying in Hollywood in 1924. His death was attributed to pneumonia, but was likely brought on by a severe drug problem. He and La Marr were married in 1918 and divorced in the summer of 1921.

39. It was reported that she was orphaned and adopted as a month-old infant but that can't be confirmed. Her family maintained she was born in North Yakima but she usually claimed Virginia as her birthplace. None of her stories could be confirmed through available records; making it more difficult, no birth records exist for Reatha Watson in either state.
40. She was just 18. The La Marr legend grew over the years and her age exaggerated to as young as 14 when the case was heard but period newspaper stories confirm she was 18 at the time of her arrest.
41. Social worker comments from *Oakland Tribune*, January 25, 1914. Juvenile judge's comments from *Los Angeles Herald Tribune*, January 24, 1914. BEAUTY TOO DANGEROUS from *Los Angeles Herald Tribune*, January 25, 1914.
42. St. Johns, Adela Rogers, *Love, Laughter and Tears: My Hollywood Story*, p. 147.
43. *The Mountain Democrat*, June 13, 1914.
44. *Oakland Tribune*, July 5, 1914.
45. The name was a wry comment on her two-month elopement-marriage to Arizona to a man named Brad Lytell, who allegedly died just after they wed.
46. *Oakland Tribune*, June 1, 1917. Separately, on May 1, 1923, Ainsworth was sentenced to a San Quentin prison term for passing bad checks allegedly so he could purchase gifts for La Marr, with whom he was still apparently smitten.
47. Mann, William J., *Wisecracker: The Life and Time of William Haines, Hollywood's First Openly Gay Star*, p. 64.
48. 1920 U.S. Federal Census, California, Los Angeles County, Los Angeles, District 374, Sheet 1B.
49. *Oakland Tribune*, April 4, 1926.
50. Zollo, p. 358.
51. St. Johns,, p. 150.
52. *Los Angeles Examiner*, September 8, 1932.
53. Betsy Bern, interview with EJF, December, 2007.
54. *Washington Post*, July 5, 1914.
55. Berg, p. 102.
56. *Ibid.*, p. 102.
57. *The New York Times*, June 26, 1921.
58. *Oakland Tribune*, July 17, 1921, and *The Indianapolis Star*, August 14, 1921.
59. *The Indianapolis Star*, August 14, 1921.
60. *The New York Times*, August 14, 1921.
61. *Ibid.*, May 8, 1921. Duer Miller spent several weeks at Goldwyn writing *The Man With Two Mothers*, and is not to be confused with another Goldwyn writer, Alice D.C. Miller, who joined the writing department in April of 1922.
62. *The New York Times*, June 5, 1921. Other supporting actors: Sydney Ainsworth,

Edythe Chapman, James Neill, Richard Tucker, M.B. Flynn, Kate Lester, and popular child actors Johnny Jones, Lucille Ricksen, and Buddy Messinger.

63. *Lima News*, July 29, 1921.

64. *The Indianapolis Star*, August 28, 1921.

65. American Film Institute, Catalog of Films, no. 1574.

66. *Washington Post*, July 31, 1921.

67. *Los Angeles Herald Examiner*, September 23, 1921.

68. *The Chillicothe Constitution*, May 16, 1922.

69. *Moving Picture World*, January 14, 1922, p. 204.

70. American Film Institute, Catalog of Films, no. 12507.

71. *Photojournalist*, August, 1921.

72. PB quotes this section from *The New York Times*, September 3, 1921.

73. PB comments this section from *Nebraska State Journal*, October 16, 1921.

74. *The New York Times*, September 15, 1922.

75. *Wichita Daily Times*, January 3, 1922.

76. The case against Lasky's studio was resolved six years later in favor of the government.

77. *The New York Times*, September 18, 1921.

78. Lasky, p. 154.

79. Arbuckle's agent and manager Lou Anger.

80. Unless otherwise noted, all quotes this section from Guild, Leo, *The Fatty Arbuckle Case*, pgs. 48–68.

81. Fussell, p. 139.

82. Giroux, Robert, *A Deed of Death: The Story Behind the Unsolved Murder of Hollywood Director William Desmond Taylor*, p. 37.

83. Stories about Rappe's amorality can be found in the writings of Mack Sennett, Adela Rogers St. Johns, and dozens of other contemporaries of Rappe.

84. *Atlanta Constitution*, September 19, 1921.

85. Fussell, p. 138 and p. 39.

86. Even today, outrageous stories are passed on as true. In the Fathom Archives at Columbia University is an otherwise well-written article, "American Film Institute: The First Fifty Years of American Film," containing, "In one of his infamous days-long parties, teeming with chorus girls and bootleg whiskey, a minor actress named Virginia Rappe died in a hotel room of peritonitis. Her ripped clothing and other circumstantial evidence suggested rape and murder, and pointed to Arbuckle as a possible suspect... He was indicted for manslaughter and the public convicted him at once, especially after newspapers revealed that the Massachusetts dis-

trict attorney had received a suspiciously generous $100,000 donation after one of Arbuckle's earlier parties in that state." In addition to the ridiculous Rappe comments, Arbuckle was not involved in the Massachusetts incident; it was a gathering of studio executives at a local brothel and he had nothing to do with the bribe paid by a Boston distributor.

87. Betsy Bern, interview with EJF, December, 2007.

88. *Los Angeles Evening Herald Express*, February 3, 1922.

89. Fussell, p. 145.

90. Lasky, p. 154.

91. Much of the information in the Taylor section was found in: Fitzpatrick, Sydney, *A Deed of Death* and the flagship website devoted to the murder, Bruce Long's amazing www.taylorology.com.

92. Police alerted Lasky to the problem; he dispatched Eyton to the scene.

93. Kirkpatrick, Sidney, *A Cast of Killers*, p. 170.

94. *L.A. Examiner*, March 27, 1926.

95. Giroux, p. 13. Many writers, this one included, reported a statement attributed to MacLean describing the person as a woman "walking like a man" (first mentioned by Minter in a 1927 interview). But recently uncovered witness statement transcripts and records including MEMORANDUM RE. JAMES KIRKWOOD AND MARY MILES MINTER indicate McLean actually told police the person she saw "could not have been a woman dressing in man's clothing." See www.pikabruce.googlepages.com/srk.

96. *Chicago News*, March 24, 1926, and *Chicago Herald Examiner*, March 25, 1926. Interestingly, a copy of "EXCERPTS OF STATEMENTS OF WITNESSES In Re WILLIAM DESMOND TAYLOR MURDER 1922–1936" and "STATEMENT OF MISS MARY MILES MINTER, in the Office of the District Attorney February 7, 1922" recently surfaced that have answered some of the myriad questions surrounding the case. As in every good scandal, though, more questions arose.

97. Giroux, p. 254.

98. *Oakland Tribune*, September 24, 1932.

99. *Los Angeles Evening Herald Express*, February 6, 1922.

100. *Chicago American*, February 14, 1922, from *Taylorology*, Issue 19, July 1994. The "affair with one of the star producers" referred to Mabel's relationship with Mack Sennett.

101. *Photoplay Magazine*, May, 1921, p. 54.

102. Smith, Wallace, *The Chicago American*, February 9, 1922.

103. *Boston Advertiser*, February 22, 1922.

104. *Ibid.*, February 20, 1922.

105. Lambert, p. 48.

106. Flamini, p. 85.

107. *Reno Evening Gazette*, September 23, 1922.

108. *The Chillicothe Constitution*, May 16, 1922.

109. *Wisconsin Rapids Daily Tribune*, August 10, 1922.

110. *The New York Times*, January 15, 1922.

111. *The Daily Courier* (Connellsville, Pennsylvania), September 15, 1922.

112. *The Los Angeles Herald Express*, September 20, 1922.

113. *The New York Times*, June 18, 1922.

114. The production company was affiliated with First National Pictures. Norma Talmadge was married to Joe Schenck and Constance was his sister-in-law.

115. *The New York Times*, May 4, 1919.

116. *Photoplay*, November, 1925, p. 106.

117. PB was not referring to class here; he was describing experience with society—the masses—in general.

118. *Davenport Democrat and Leader*, August 20, 1922.

119. PB comments this section from *The New York Times*, "Mental Action in Movies" (interview with PB), May 15, 1922.

120. *The London Post*, June 1, 1922, summarized in *The New York Times*, June 11, 1922.

121. *The New York Times*, September 3, 1922.

122. *The Lincoln Star*, June 30, 1930. Smith died in Pasadena on April 13, 1974.

123. American Film Institute, Catalog of Films, no. 1518.

124. Holubar appeared in almost 40 films between 1913 and 1917 and wrote another 25 but in 1917 concentrated on directing. His 35 films include *Sirens of the Sea* (1917) with Carmel Myers and a number of films starring his wife Dorothy Phillips. The Goldwyn favorite died after gallstone surgery in early 1923, at which time his wife left the screen, not to reappear until 1960.

125. American Film Institute, Catalog of Films, no. 3077.

126. Fountain, p. 81.

127. *Ibid.*, p. 82. Carey Wilson divorced Hope in 1924 or 1925 and wed Carmelita Geraghty, to whom he was married until his death in 1962.

128. Hall, Caine, London, 1897.

129. American Film Institute, Catalog of Films, no. 3304.

130. *Indianapolis Star*, April 9, 1923.

131. *The New York Times*, January 15, 1922.

132. *Mon Cine*, March 13, 1924.

133. *Hollywood Citizen News*, June 16, 1932.

134. De Vinna filmed some 120+ films from 1916 to 1952, including his Academy Award–winning *White Shadows of the South Seas* (1928), several 1930s Johnny Weissmuller *Tarzan* films, and several early television series like *The Roy Rogers Show*. He died in Los Angeles in 1953.

135. American Film Institute, Catalog of Films, no. 10372.

136. Langman, Larry, *American Film Cycles: The Silent Era*, p. xxi.

137. *Ibid.*, p. xx.

138. German Film Institute, archives of Berlin censorship board, no. 23.02.1924 & 01.03.1924.

139. Haines was openly disdainful of star House Peters, referring to him as "Outhouse" Peters.

140. Mann, p. 58.

Chapter 4

1. *The New York Times*, January 28, 1923.

2. Flamini, p. 25.

3. Halliwell, Leslie, *The Filmgoer's Book of Quotes*, p. 84.

4. Flamini, p. 25.

5. *The New York Times*, April 1, 1923.

6. *Indianapolis Star*, January 7, 1923.

7. Beery was an alcoholic with a terrible temper who had raped his first wife Gloria Swanson during their honeymoon and later was involved in the beating death of comedian Ted Healy.

8. The process would be repeated in the 1930's when Loretta Young became pregnant with Clark Gable's child. MGM arranged for the child to be given to a Catholic orphanage and a year later for Young to adopt her own offspring.

9. Mann, p. 65.

10. Don Gallery comments here from *Los Angeles Times*, October 11, 2007, and correspondence with EJF, October-December, 2007. When Barbara La Marr lay dying, she gave her son to her best friend, actress ZaSu Pitts, and Pitts' husband Tom Gallery.

11. *Oakland Tribune*, April 17, 1923.

12. Rin Tin Tin was found among a litter of puppies in a bombed-out kennel and brought to America by Air Force flyer Tim Duncan. Darryl Zanuck saw the dog at an L.A. dog show and recruited him for films, the success of which would eventually save Warners from financial ruin. When the animal was near death in August, 1932, Jean Harlow visited him and cradled the dog's head in her lap as he died.

13. *Los Angeles Times*, March 23, 1923.

14. Dougherty-La Marr wedding details from *Los Angeles Times*, April 7, 1923.

15. September, 1926, Mildred Gray Maryatt vs. Oscar Maryatt.

16. After leaving United Picture Theaters, Stahl later worked for Chaplin-Meyers and Anita Stewart Productions at Metro. Mayer formed a John M. Stahl Productions unit in 1922.

17. American Film Institute, Catalog of Films, no. 13076.

18. *The New York Times*, June 7, 1923.

19. Caine, Hall, New York & Philadelphia, 1921.

20. Paul is not listed in the credits but is mentioned in newspaper articles and reviews as one of the film editors.

21. American Film Institute, Catalog of Films, no. 10919.

22. *The Hartford Courant*, January 24, 1924.

23. *Los Angeles Herald Express*, January 27, 1924.

24. *The New York Times*, September 3, 1923.

25. American Film Institute, Catalog of Films, no. 10652. Lubitsch directed another adaptation of Schmidt's play for Paramount in 1932: The musical *One Hour with You* starred Maurice Chevalier and Jeanette MacDonald.

26. Eyman, Scott, *Ernst Lubitsch: Laughter in Paradise*, p. 106.

27. *The Hartford Courant*, April 6, 1924.

28. *Photoplay*, April 1, 1924, p. 61.

29. Eyman, *Lubitsch*, p. 108.

30. *Los Angeles Evening Herald Express*, June 30, 1930.

31. *Oakland Tribune*, April 17, 1924.

32. *Ibid.*, September 23, 1932.

33. American Film Institute, Catalog of Films, no. 10919.

34. *The Hartford Courant*, June 1, 1924.

35. *The New York Times*, June 1, 1924.

36. *Ibid.*, March 28, 1924.

37. *The Hartford Courant*, May 5, 1924.

38. American Film Institute, Catalog of Films, no. 10288.

39. *The New York Times*, July 25, 1924.

40. *Exhibitors Trade Review*, December 6, 1924, p. 51.

41. *The New York Times*, August 31, 1924.

42. American Film Institute, Catalog of Films, no. 13005.

43. Neill comments from *The Hartford Courant*, October 8, 1924. Paul comment from *Indianapolis Star*, November 24, 1924.

44. *The New York Times*, September 21, 1924.

45. Fountain, p. 100.

46. "[S]ensational graduate" from *The Hartford Courant*, September 16, 1924; "successor to Cecil B. DeMille" from *The New York Times*, April 3, 1925.

47. *The New York Times*, September 28, 1924.

48. Locklear was born in Hopkins County, Texas, on October 28, 1891, did jumps on a two-cylinder Indian motorcycle with the Panther City Motorcycle Club as a teenager, and in 1917 enlisted in the Air Service at Fort Sam Houston and flew in the Army Air Corps. On November 8, 1918, he was the first man to transfer from one plane to another in mid-air. His most famous stunt — the "Dance of Death" — has never been replicated. He piloted one plane, almost touching wings with a second, and on a signal the two pilots changed places, passing each other as they scampered across the wings! Locklear became wealthy and came to the attention of Hollywood in 1920 when discovered by Sydney Chaplin. On July 26, 1919, he became the first man to successfully transfer from a car to an airplane shooting a sequence for Universal's *The Great Air Robbery*. When he reportedly became engaged to his very public girlfriend Dana, he still had a wife — Ruby — back in Texas. It was Locklear's choice to film the fatal stunt at night rather than using filters to darken daylight filming.

49. *Indianapolis Star*, August 10, 1924.

50. *Motion Picture Magazine*, December, 1924.

51. American Film Institute, Catalog of Films, no. 11167.

52. "[N]ewcomer" comments from *Movie Weekly*, October 11, 1924; "froth sort of affair" from *The Hartford Courant*, September 9, 1924.

53. *The New York Times*, September 23, 1924. The later European release was entitled *One Parisian Night*.

54. *Mansfield News*, August 17, 1924.

55. Eyman, *Lubitsch*, p. 128.

56. American Film Institute, Catalog of Films, no. 13484.

57. *The Hartford Courant*, November 3, 1924.

58. *Saturday Evening Post*, March, 1924.

59. American Film Institute, Catalog of Films, no. 12759, and *The New York Times*, January 7, 1925.

60. *The Hartford Courant*, January 19, 1925.

61. *Davenport Democrat and Leader*, February 2, 1925.

62. *Chillicothe Constitution*, December 26, 1924.

63. *The New York Times*, November 9, 1924.

64. *L.A. City Directory*, 1925–1929.

65. Ince was married to actress Eleanor Kershaw, known as Nell.

66. Nell Ince reportedly lost everything in the Depression and in later years drove a cab in Hollywood.

67. *Los Angeles Herald Express*, April 12, 1925.

68. Harris was Charlie Chaplin's first child bride, as young as 14 when she became pregnant and they married in 1918. After giving birth to a boy that almost immediately died, she and Chaplin divorced and she parlayed her married name into a film career spanning 135+ films and 40 years. She died in 1944 in Hollywood.

69. American Film Institute, Catalog of Films, no. 3849.

70. "[D]azzling beauty" from *The Hartford Courant*, March 22, 1925; "comedy and pathos" from *The New York Times*, March 18, 1925; "reason was apparent" from *Appleton Post Crescent*, May 20, 1925.

71. "[F]ound spots" from *Photoplay*, November, 1925, p. 106; Olive Borden story from *Picture Play*, "Tell It to Bern," p. 49.

72. Thomas, Bob, *Joan Crawford*, p. 48.

73. Mann, p. 86 and p. 40.

74. McLellan, Diana, *The Girls: Sappho Goes to Hollywood*, p. 152.

75. Rapf comments here from Maurice Rapf, interview with EJF, August, 2002. Biographers are divided as to the existence of the film but there is circumstantial and anecdotal evidence that supports its existence. Mannix told friends he arranged the purchase and Fairbanks told friends that during his Paris honeymoon with Crawford they tried to find copies. Her FBI file includes a confirmation that "a film of Crawford in compromising positions was circulated ... to be used at smokers," according to Fred Lawrence Guiles, *Joan Crawford: The Last Word*, p. 40.

76. Thomas, *Joan Crawford*, p. 59. Given Crawford's proclivity for trading sex for career opportunity it is more likely that she kept such a gift, if in fact Paul sent it.

77. Hall, Gladys, THE LITTLE FATHER CONFESSOR OF HOLLYWOOD, July 13, 1932, Gladys Hall Papers, Box 2, Folder 55, Bern, Paul—article manuscript, AMPAS.

78. The El Tovar was featured in the 1983 film *National Lampoon's Vacation*.

79. *The Sheboygan Press*, March 29, 1925.

80. *The Los Angeles Times*, April 4, 1925.

81. American Film Institute, Catalog of Films, no. 9522.

82. *The New York Times*, June 29, 1925.

83. *Appleton Post Courant*, July 21, 1925.

84. *The Hartford Courant*, June 5, 1925.

85. *Indianapolis Star*, July 19, 1924.

86. American Film Institute, Catalog of Films, no. 10902.

87. American Film Institute, Catalog of Films, no. 1461.

88. *The New York Times*, October 25, 1925.

89. *Oshkosh Daily Northwestern*, March 6, 1926.

90. *Lima News*, October 20, 1925.

91. *Davenport Democrat and Leader*, February 22, 1925.

92. *Appleton Post Crescent*, May 13, 1925.

93. *Los Angeles Herald Express*, August 2, 1925.

94. *Reno Evening Gazette*, October 11, 1925.

Chapter 5

1. Marx, *Mayer and Thalberg*, p. 45.

2. Altman, Diana, *Hollywood East: Louis B. Mayer and the Origins of the Studio System*, p. 95.

3. Flamini, p. 51.

4. *Ibid.*, p. 52.

5. Hay, Peter, *MGM*, p. 15.

6. Berg, p. 76.

7. Thalberg biographer Roland Flamini noted that Paul and Thalberg first met after the 1924 merger that created MGM but 1923 newspaper stories confirm the earlier 1923 meeting and the original Universal connection.

8. Lewin background from Lambert, p. 78; "source of intellectual advice" from Flamini, p. 75; "best apple pie" from Carey, Gary, *All the Stars in Heaven*, p. 77; "terrific idea" from Marx, *Mayer and Thalberg*, p. 134.

9. Carey, p. 77.

10. *Oakland Tribune*, September 22, 1932.

11. *Photoplay*, November, 1925, p. 106.

12. Jane Ardmore Papers, Box 13, file 13, AMPAS.

13. *The New York Times*, November 1, 1925.

14. *Los Angeles Evening Herald Express*, August 3, 1925.

15. Flamini, p. 76.

16. *Heart of a Siren*, which co-starred Conway Tearle and Harry Morey (and a young Clifton Webb in his second movie role), was filmed in November and December, 1924, and released the following March.

17. Neighborhood description from Sanborn Map Company, Altadena, January, 1926, p. 23. Health note from *Baltimore News*, September 6, 1932.

18. Upon her death, La Marr's estate was worth less than $10,000, most of that clothes and some jewelry.

19. *Modern Screen*, September, 1932, p. 36.

20. Writing credit and La Marr casting from Marx, *Mayer and Thalberg*, p. 80. Paul is not credited with this script but Marx's note is confirmed by period newspaper accounts. *Spanish Sunlight*, New York, 1925.

21. American Film Institute, Catalog of Films, no. 9347.
22. *The Hartford Courant*, February 23, 1926.
23. *Mansfield News*, October 11, 1925.
24. *Los Angeles Herald Express*, November 15, 1925.
25. *Paris*, p. 101.
26. Notes this section from *Photoplay*, November, 1925, pp. 78.
27. *Motion Picture*, October, 1932, p. 76.
28. *Ibid.*, p. 76, and Hall, Gladys, *THE LITTLE FATHER CONFESSOR OF HOLLYWOOD*, July 13, 1932, from Gladys Hall Collection, Folder 55, Paul Bern, AMPAS.
29. *Lincoln Star*, November 18, 1925.
30. *Movie Classic*, November, 1932, p. 78.
31. *Motion Picture*, September, 1932, p. 76.
32. *Modern Screen*, September, 1932, p. 87.
33. *Nevada State Journal*, February 1, 1926.
34. *Ibid.*, February 6, 1926.
35. Louis B. Mayer thought La Marr the most beautiful woman he had ever seen, and later paid homage to her by renaming beautiful Austrian actress Hedwig Eva Maria Kiesler "Hedy Lamarr."
36. *Zanesville Signal*, February 9, 1926.
37. *Hollywood Citizen News*, date unknown, from News Bureau photo snipe text.
38. The construction scenes were filmed using the Hoover Dam construction as a backdrop.
39. Davies was paid $10,000 a week, more than any other MGM actor despite the fact that her films were only marginally successful, and owned a 14-room bungalow moved to the MGM lot with her. She and Hearst remained together — basically living as man and wife because Millicent Hearst refused to divorce her husband — until his death in 1951. She was beloved in Hollywood as much for her personality as for her connections to Hearst's publishing empire. When she left MGM for Warners, her bungalow was taken apart and moved there.
40. Paul's writing credit for *The Wilderness Woman* was mentioned in hundreds of newspapers including *The New York Times* and *The Hartford Courant*, May 8, 1926.
41. American Film Institute, Catalog of Films, no. 13347.
42. *The Hartford Courant*, April 18, 1926. Over 2,000 soldiers were recruited for military scenes and much disliked having to wear German uniforms.
43. American Film Institute, Catalog of Films, no. 9482.
44. *The Hartford Courant*, June 20, 1926.
45. *The New York Times*, August 9, 1926.
46. *Los Angeles Times*, September 8, 1932, interview with Jim Tully, a close friend of Paul.

47. London, 1927.
48. American Film Institute, Catalog of Films, no. 11452.
49. *The New York Times*, December 27, 1926.
50. *The Hartford Courant*, January 9, 1927.
51. *Motion Picture*, October, 1932, p. 76.
52. *Hollywood Citizen News*, September 6, 1932. De Putti died at Harbor Sanitarium in New York in 1941 at the age of 32 after she developed pneumonia brought on by an operation to remove a chicken bone from her esophagus.
53. Shulman, Irving, *Harlow: An Intimate Biography*, p. 16.
54. Talmadge and Roland engaged in a long and heated affair that infuriated her husband, studio executive Joe Schenck, who had to be convinced by Eddie Mannix *not* to have Roland killed or castrated. The affair lasted for years.
55. *Boston Herald*, November 22, 1926.
56. Kobler, John, *Damned in Paradise: The Life of John Barrymore*, p. 224.
57. Passenger manifest, S.S. *City of Los Angeles*, August 4, 1932.
58. Peters, Margot, *The House of Barrymore*, p. 290.
59. Plot notes for *Beloved Rogue* from American Film Institute, Catalog of Films, no. 2806, and information retrieved February 7, 2007, from http://www.silentsaregolden.com/featurefolder4/brcommentary.html.
60. *The New York Times*, March 14, 1926.
61. *The Hartford Courant*, April 15, 1926.
62. Commentary from writer James Card, published source unknown.
63. Kobler, p. 226.
64. Paris, p. 113.
65. Ibid., p. 117.
66. Higham, Charles, *Merchant of Dreams: Louis B. Mayer, MGM and the Secret Hollywood*, p.112.
67. *The New York Times*, August 30, 1926.
68. Fussell, p. 214.
69. Ibid., p. 213.
70. The couple were divorced on May 2, 1933. Pitts and John Woodall wed in early 1933 and the couple was married until her death in 1963.
71. *Mansfield News*, November 18, 1926.
72. New York, 1940.
73. American Film Institute, Catalog of Films, no. 12661.
74. *The New York Times*, March 8, 1927.
75. *The Davenport Democrat and Leader*, April 17, 1927.
76. *The Hartford Courant*, May 9, 1927.
77. *The New York Times*, January 9, 1927.
78. Eyman, Scott, *The Speed of Sound:*

Hollywood and the Talkie Revolution, 1926–1930, p. 92.

79. *Ibid.,* p. 93.

80. Eames, John Douglas, *MGM: The Complete Story,* p. 36.

81. All comments this section from *The New York Times,* January 9, 1927.

82. Eyman, *Speed of Sound,* p. 147.

83. Fussell, p. 218.

84. *Sheboygan Press,* September 13, 1935.

85. *Modern Screen,* September, 1932, p. 87.

86. *The New York Times,* January 8, 1927.

87. American Film Institute, Catalog of Films, no. 1438.

88. *Sheboygan Press,* March 28, 1927.

89. *The Hartford Courant,* January 11, 1928.

90. Paris, p. 122.

91. American Film Institute, Catalog of Films, no. 13390.

92. *Variety,* December 7, 1927.

93. Details this section from Guiles, Fred Lawrence, *Marion Davies: A Biography,* p. 220–25.

94. The entrance today is just five miles directly below the hilltop.

95. Hearst never confronted drunken guests. Those guilty would simply find their bags packed and stacked outside Casa Grande's entrance.

96. The Hearst estate was donated to the state of California in 1957 and is now one of the most spectacular state parks in the United States. Herds of zebras and other exotic animals, remnants of the original zoo, still roam the grounds.

97. U.S. Passport, Bern, Paul, no. 2201, issued Washington, D.C., August 27, 1927.

98. *The New York Times,* September 15, 1927.

99. Selznick, Irene Mayer, *A Private View,* p. 79.

100. Flamini, p. 103.

101. *The New York Times,* November 13, 1927.

Chapter 6

1. The movie was directed by Alan Crosland, who directed Barrymore's *The Beloved Rogue.*

2. Thomas, Bob, *The Clown Prince of Hollywood,* p. 61.

3. Eyman, *Speed of Sound,* p. 160.

4. Flamini, p. 110.

5. McLellan, p. 94.

6. As it was, it would take over two years to fit the first 10,000 theaters.

7. Eyman, *Speed of Sound,* p. 160.

8. Flamini, p. 112.

9. *Ibid.,* p. 111.

10. Stenn, David, *Clara Bow: Runnin' Wild,* p. 151.

11. Dane's body went unclaimed, so Buster Keaton appealed to Eddie Mannix and MGM paid for his funeral.

12. Hay, p. 62. The assignment launched Douglas Shearer on a 40-year career in sound that included 14 Academy Awards and a reputation as an innovator in the industry.

13. *The Hartford Courant,* October 7, 1928.

14. *Syracuse Herald,* November 15, 1928.

15. American Film Institute, Catalog of Films, no. 2763.

16. *Los Angeles Times,* November 5, 1928.

17. *Syracuse Herald,* June 17, 1928.

18. Marx, p. 111.

19. *Los Angeles Evening Herald Express,* August 10, 1928.

20. There are some newspaper stories describing the silent version and an initial release on August 28, 1928.

21. Adrian was the most prolific and perhaps most talented costume designer in Hollywood history. Born Adrian Adolph Greenberg in Naugatuck, Connecticut, he was brought to Hollywood by Natasha Rambova to work on Valentino costumes and created wardrobes for 250 films including *The Hooded Falcon* (1924), all of Garbo's MGM films, *Letty Lynton* (1932), *Naughty Marietta* (1935), and *The Wizard of Oz* (1939). After a thirty-year career he died in Hollywood in 1959.

22. American Film Institute, Catalog of Films, no. 9405, and *The New York Times,* April 1, 1929.

23. *The New York Times,* April 1, 1929.

24. Marx and Vanderveen, p. 171. Marx, who changed his stories regularly, had earlier written that Paul "turned red and ran out the door."

25. Marx, p. 81.

26. After the failure of his MGM films, DeMille, believing he was washed up in Hollywood, fled to Europe and considered staying there. He would return to produce some of the greatest films ever made during a career lasting into the 1950s.

27. *Los Angeles Times,* February 1, 1929.

28. American Film Institute, Catalog of Films, no. 9318. Notices were published in *Helena Independent,* January 30, 1929, *Los Angeles Times,* January 29, 1929, and *The New York Times,* December 15, 1928.

29. American Film Institute, Catalog of Films, no. 11013.

30. Supporting cast: Montague Shaw,

Johnny Morris, Kewpie Morgan, Clarence
Geldert, Erich von Stroheim, Jr., and Chuck
Reisner, Jr.
    31. American Film Institute, Catalog of
Films, no. 12379.
    32. *The Hartford Courant*, August 15,
1929, and *Circleville Telegram*, April 16, 1929.
    33. *Los Angeles Times*, February 16, 1929.
    34. Eyman, *Speed of Sound*, p. 229.
    35. *Los Angeles Evening Herald Express*,
December 26, 1928.
    36. Contract, Hal Roach Studios, Inc.,
and Harlean McGrew II, dated December 26,
1928, with addendum dated December 27, 1928.
    37. *Los Angeles Times*, February 6, 1929.
    38. American Film Institute, Catalog of
Films, no. 12447. The film has no relation to
the 1940 Clark Gable-Joan Crawford film of the
same title.
    39. *Los Angeles Times*, February 26, 1929.
    40. Director reassignment from *Los Ange-
les Times*, February 10, 1929, and February 6,
1929. Conselman demand from *Los Angeles
Times*, December 12, 1928. Darling song contract problem from *Los Angeles Times*, January 8,
1929. Darling wrote the song with George Green
and George Warroner and then contracted with
Watterson, Berlin and Snyder, one of the largest
music publishers in the country, to sell his song,
"Listen, Baby." Production problems review
from *Los Angeles Times*, March 10, 1929. Paul's
other assignments from *Syracuse Herald*, March
30, 1929.
    41. *Los Angeles Times*, "Speaking of My-
self," by Jean Harlow, November 27, 1934.
Confirmed by Patsy Bern, interview with EJF,
December, 2007.
    42. *Ibid.*, March 3, 1929.
    43. The University of Southern Califor-
nia: Under the Direction of Dean Rockwell
Hunt, Class Description, May 3, 1930.
    44. Comments here from *Los Angeles
Times*, March 7, 1929. Thalberg and love story
from Loos, Anita, *Kiss Hollywood Good-By*, p. 36.
    45. Lambert, p. 137.
    46. *Los Angeles Times*, March 24, 1929.
    47. *Coshocton Tribune*, April 17, 1929.
    48. American Film Institute, Catalog of
Films, no. 9124, and *The Hartford Courant*, August 2, 1929.
    49. *Film Daily*, August 25, 1929.
    50. *The Hartford Courant*, February 3,
1930.
    51. American Film Institute, Catalog of
Films, no. 8794.
    52. *The Hartford Courant*, January 26,
1930.
    53. Higham, *Merchant of Dreams*, p. 145.
    54. *Los Angeles Examiner*, June 17, 1927.
Their film was edited by D.W. Griffith.

    55. *Los Angeles Times*, May 14, 1929.
    56. American Film Institute, Catalog of
Films, no. 9985.
    57. Selznick, p. 176.
    58. *Ibid.*, p. 177.
    59. *Screenland Magazine*, July, 1932.
    60. Lincoln Quarberg Papers, Folder 82,
Box 3, Jean Harlow clippings, AMPAS.
    61. Stenn, *Bombshell*, p. 10.
    62. Lincoln Quarberg Papers, Folder 62,
Box 2, Caddo Company biographies-publicity,
The Inside Story of Jean Harlow, AMPAS.
    63. Wayne, Jane Ellen, *Gable's Women*, p.
90. According to Wayne, Bello "dabbled inces-
tuously with [her]."
    64. Marx and Vanderveen, p. 99, and Lin-
coln Quarberg Papers, Folder 62, Box 2, Caddo
Company biographies-publicity, *The Inside Story
of Jean Harlow*, AMPAS.
    65. *Los Angeles Evening Herald Express*, July
21, 1930.
    66. Other stories in the Jean Harlow files
at AMPAS identify her friend as Lucille Lee.
Jean herself identified the Fox casting person as
"Mr. Ryan" in later interviews.
    67. Lincoln Quarberg Papers, Folder 82,
Box 3, Jean Harlow clippings, AMPAS.
    68. Carpenter, *Jean Harlow, Our Life Story
by Jean Harlow's Mother*, portions published in
Modern Romance, November 20, 1937, Gladys
Hall Papers, Box 2, Folder 55, Bern, Paul—article manuscript, AMPAS.
    69. Stenn, *Bombshell*, p. 20.
    70. Stenn, *Clara Bow*, p. 179.
    71. Stenn, *Bombshell*, p. 170.
    72. Coffee, Lenore, *Storyline: Recollections
of a Hollywood Screenwriter*, p. 100, quoted from
Beauchamp, p. 214.
    73. *Los Angeles Evening Herald Express*, July
10, 1930.
    74. Lincoln Quarberg Papers, Folder 82,
Box 3, Jean Harlow clippings, AMPAS.
    75. Selznick, p. 177.
    76. Vertical File Collection, Box 3, Folder
35, I. Shulman notes regarding Jean Harlow,
AMPAS. It's hard to believe Landau represented
Paul; his long-time agent, Paul Kohner, was also
from Hamburg and worked with Paul for years.
Also, there is evidence that Landau and Bern
deeply disliked each other.
    77. When he began the film, Hughes took
flying lessons so the pilots would respect his direction, and went on to become the most successful aviator in the world, holder of every major
speed and distance record. He is remembered as
much for his aviation prowess as his film work.
    78. Vertical File Collection, Box 3, Folder
35, I. Shulman notes regarding Jean Harlow,
AMPAS.
    79. Screen tests reference Lincoln Quar-

berg Papers, Folder 62, Box 2, Caddo Company biographies-publicity, *The Inside Story of Jean Harlow*, p. 21, AMPAS. Hughes quote re: Jean's voice from Hack, Richard, *Hughes: The Private Diaries, Memos and Letters*, p. 75.

80. Lincoln Quarberg Papers, Folder 62, Box 2, Caddo Company biographies-publicity, *The Inside Story of Jean Harlow*, p.22, AMPAS, and Hack, Richard, *Hughes: The Private Diaries, Memos and Letters*, p. 76.

81. $500 story from Vertical Files, Box 3, Folder 34, Irving Shulman correspondence regarding Jean Harlow, Arthur Landau to Irving Shulman, undated, AMPAS; "three months overdue" from Vertical Files, Box 3, Folder 34, Irving Shulman correspondence regarding Jean Harlow, Arthur Landau to Irving Shulman, July 24 11, 1962, AMPAS; "Big Jean" story from Correspondence, Jean Harlow Bello to Gladys Hall, Gladys Hall Papers, Box 6, Folder 231, Harlow, Jean — correspondence, AMPAS. "Mama Jean" from Box 1, File 7, Shulman/Jean Harlow (correspondence), Arthur Landau Correspondence Files, AMPAS.

82. *Los Angeles Times*, August 4, 1932.

83. *Hollywood Daily Citizen*, "Society in Filmland," October 2, 1929.

84. Duncan's next film was *Five and Ten* (1931), during which she became fast friends with Marion Davies, who introduced her to Stephen "Laddie" Sanford, heir to the Bigelow-Sanford Carpet fortune. She made a few more films before marrying Sanford in 1933 and retiring from films to live in Palm Beach, Florida. She was the grande dame of Palm Beach during her later life, active in charitable work and Palm Beach society. Her neighbor and close friend Rose Kennedy joined her entertaining the likes of the Duke and Duchess of Windsor and the King and Queen of Jordan. She died in her Palm Beach mansion on May 9, 1993.

85. *Los Angeles Times*, October 20, 1929. Kapurhala, once home to Indian royalty, was located in the Punjab region of India.

86. New York, 1928.

87. American Film Institute, Catalog of Films, no. 13442.

88. *The Hartford Courant*, April 14, 1930.

89. Comments this section from *The Hartford Courant*, February 2, 1930.

90. *Los Angeles Times*, November 30, 1930.

91. American Film Institute, Catalog of Films, no. 11752.

92. *The Hartford Courant*, May 18, 1930.

Chapter 7

1. Beauchamp, p. 250. Biographers claimed Garbo only did the film because her

Beverly Hills bank failed and she lost her fortune, but that bank failure didn't occur until June 7, 1932.

2. American Film Institute, Catalog of Films, no. 648.

3. *Los Angeles Times*, February 23, 1930.

4. *The New York Times*, May 6, 1930.

5. *Ibid.*, March 30, 1930.

6. American Film Institute, Catalog of Films, no. 3776.

7. *Los Angeles Times*, January 26, 1930.

8. *Hollywood Daily Citizen*, "Society in Filmland," November 6, 1929.

9. Embassy Club event details from *Los Angeles Times*, November 29, 1929. "Jean Harlow was on his arm" from *Los Angeles Evening Herald Express*, September 7, 1932. "He glowed" from Moffitt, J.C., "The Tragedy of Paul Bern: A Man Always in Love," *Los Angeles Examiner*, September 19, 1932.

10. *Los Angeles Times*, December 31, 1929.

11. *Ibid.*, January 19, 1930.

12. *Ibid.*, January 1, 1930 and Los Angeles Evening Herald, January 4, 1930.

13. McLellan, p. 117.

14. *Los Angeles Record*, March 3, 1930.

15. American Film Institute, Catalog of Films, no. 11755.

16. Garbo note from *Los Angeles Evening Herald*, January 15, 1930. *Rogue Song* premiere notes from *Los Angeles Times*, January 19, 1930.

17. *Los Angeles Times*, February 18, 1930.

18. *Ibid.*, February 21, 1930.

19. *Ibid.*, November 15, 1929.

20. Fussell, p. 228.

21. Hall, Gladys, THE LITTLE FATHER CONFESSOR OF HOLLYWOOD, July 13, 1932, Gladys Hall Papers, Box 2, Folder 55, Bern, Paul — article manuscript, AMPAS.

22. *Los Angeles Evening Herald Express*, February 24, 1930.

23. *The Bee* (Danville, Virginia), March 1, 1930.

24. *Los Angeles Times*, February 7, 1929.

25. Deed of Trust 1209365, Escrow 8296-D, First National Bank of Beverly Hills, September 27, 1930.

26. Selznick, p. 176.

27. Marx and Vanderveen, p. 106.

28. *Movie Classic Magazine*, November, 1932, p. 66.

29. Goudal turns to decorating from *Los Angeles Times*, August 31, 1931. Notes on Grieve-Goudal romance from Hall, Gladys, THE LITTLE FATHER CONFESSOR OF HOLLYWOOD, July 13, 1932, Gladys Hall Papers, Box 2, Folder 55, Bern, Paul — article manuscript, AMPAS.

30. Ron Hale to EJF, June, 2007.

31. *Los Angeles Times*, September 6, 1932.

32. *Los Angeles Record*, March 19, 1930 and Hollywood Daily Citizen, March 19, 1930.

33. *Los Angeles Times*, March 16, 1930.

34. *Hollywood Citizen News*, April 2, 1930.

35. *The Los Angeles Evening Herald Express*, April 6, 1930.

36. Marx and Vanderveen, p. 102.

37. *Hollywood Daily Citizen*, April 23, 1930.

38. *Los Angeles Times*, April 22, 1930.

39. *Hollywood Daily Citizen*, "Society in Filmland," April 22, 1930.

40. Crane Gartz's company manufactured auto parts; he founded Cragar Company in 1930 to produce specialty wheels and the company became one of the most successful specialty wheel companies in the world, still in business today.

41. Still standing today, just up the road from the lavish Thalberg house, the Mayer house is best-known as the site of several trysts between President John F. Kennedy and Marilyn Monroe. During the 1960s, Peter Lawford, Kennedy's brother-in-law, owned the house and arranged the meetings.

42. *Los Angeles Times*, April 30, 1930.

43. Selznick, p. 176.

44. *Los Angeles Times*, May 22, 1930.

45. *Ibid.*, May 28, 1930.

46. Higham, Charles, *Howard Hughes: The Secret Life*, p. 49.

47. *Los Angeles Times*, May 28, 1930.

48. *True Story*, March, 1935, p. 85.

49. Marx and Vanderveen, p. 102.

50. Stenn, *Bombshell*, p. 47.

51. *Variety*, June 4, 1930.

52. Flamini, p. 144.

53. Marx and Vanderveen, p. 18.

54. *Modern Screen Magazine*, October, 1930, from Lincoln Quarberg Papers, Folder 62, Box 3, Caddo Company biographies, AMPAS.

55. Lincoln Quarberg Papers, Folder 62, Box 2, Caddo Company biographies-publicity, *The Inside Story of Jean Harlow*, AMPAS.

56. Vertical Files, Box 3, Folder 34, Irving Shulman correspondence regarding Jean Harlow, Arthur Landau to Irving Shulman, undated, AMPAS.

57. *Modern Screen*, October, 1930.

58. *Ibid.*, June 16, 1930.

59. Vertical File Collection, Box 3, Folder 35, I. Shulman notes regarding Jean Harlow, AMPAS.

60. American Film Institute, Catalog of Films, no. 10502.

61. *The Hartford Courant*, August 24, 1930.

62. *Hollywood Daily Citizen*, "Society in Filmland," July 9, 1930.

63. *Los Angeles Times*, July 13, 1930.

64. *Los Angeles Evening Express*, July 23, 1930.

65. New York, September 19, 1928.

66. American Film Institute, Catalog of Films, no. 7840.

67. *The Boston Globe*, October 22, 1930.

68. *The Hartford Courant*, October 18, 1930.

69. Lambert, p. 170.

70. Tiomkim-Rasch party notes from *Los Angeles Times*, August 3, 1930. *Holiday* premiere notes from *Illustrated Daily News*, August 3, 1930.

71. New York, September 11, 1912.

72. *Photoplay*, December, 1930.

73. *Los Angeles Evening Herald Express*, August 28, 1930.

74. 1930 U.S. Federal Census, California, Los Angeles County, Los Angeles, District 97, Sheet 12-A.

75. Russian Eagle Café story from *Los Angeles Evening Herald Express*, December 17, 1930; "favorite meals" from Lincoln Quarberg Papers, Folder 82, Box 3, Jean Harlow clippings, AMPAS.

76. Selznick, p. 176.

77. *Los Angeles Times*, September 12, 1930.

78. *Hollywood Daily Citizen*, "Society in Filmland," September 17, 1930.

79. American Film Institute, Catalog of Films, no. 5893.

80. *Film Daily*, June 21, 1931.

81. *Hollywood Reporter*, March 7, 1931.

82. Comments here from *Los Angeles Times*, November 30, 1930.

83. *Los Angeles Evening Herald*, April 4, 1931.

84. Paris, 1884.

85. Garbo received Academy Award nominations in 1930 for both *Anna Christie* (her first talkie) and *Romance*, but Norma Shearer won for her work in *The Divorcee*.

86. *Hollywood Daily Citizen*, "Society in Filmland," October 15, 1930. Also attending the Lowe-Tashman party: Malcolm St. Clair, Dorothy Jordan, Marjorie Beebe, A.L. Christie, Maurice Revnes, Charles Christie, Carl Laemmle, Jr., and Sol Lesser. Also attending the MGM wedding: James Newcomb, Joseph Rapf, William Thalberg and Larry Weingarten, Charlotte Wood, Madelaine Ruthven, Thalberg secretary Vivian Newcomb, Mae Gelber and Edith Farrell, Pete Smith, Cliff Edwards and Jack Cummings.

87. *Los Angeles Times*, December 12, 1930.

88. *Hollywood Daily Citizen*, "Society in Filmland," November 12, 1930, and *Los Angeles Times*, November 16, 1930.

89. *The Atlanta Constitution*, September 10, 1932.

90. *Los Angeles Times*, November 16, 1930.
91. *Ibid.*, November 23, 1930.
92. *Los Angeles Evening Herald Express*, November 29, 1930.
93. *Los Angeles Evening Express*, December 16, 1930.
94. *Los Angeles Times*, December 22, 1930.
95. Hughes notes from Higham, *Howard Hughes*, p. 14. *Hollywood Daily Citizen*, December 31, 1930. Also attending: Betty Jolley, Ella Wickersham, Marcella Zwebella, Ruth Shields, Gano Lightfoot, Neal Iredell, Charles Persoll, Ramsen Roland and Paul Reynolds.
96. *Los Angeles Evening Herald*, January 3, 1931.
97. *Los Angeles Times*, January 3, 1931.

Chapter 8

1. *Los Angeles Times*, December 19, 1930.
2. *Hollywood Daily Citizen*, January 14, 1931. Also attending; Joseph Mars, Edgar Selwyn, Edwin Justus Mayer, Harlan Thompson, and Ernie Mankiewicz.
3. *Los Angeles Times*, February 1, 1931.
4. Day, Beth, *This Was Hollywood*, p. 84, quoted from Beauchamp, p. 271.
5. *Los Angeles Times*, May 10, 1931.
6. American Film Institute, Catalog of Films, no. 7379. Marion's original finale was much more powerful: Scorpio engages Newton in a life-or-death fight back at the stockyards from which he began his improbable rise to power and kills Newton but is stomped to death by stampeding animals. Censors decreed that justice should be done in "an orderly fashion" so Marion changed the ending.
7. "Neither of us knew much..." from *Hollywood Magazine*, "What I Think About Jean Harlow, by Clark Gable," August, 1935, quoted from Stenn, *Bombshell*, p. 52. "I know I'm the worst..." from *Kansas City Times*, June 9, 1937, quoted from Stenn. "You're not the kind of girl..." from Jane Ardmore Papers, Box 13, file 13, AMPAS.
8. Beery was a contemptible drunk who would later join his mobster friends Pat DiCicco and Cubby Broccoli, beating comedian Ted Healy to death outside the Trocadero. MGM covered up his involvement; DiCicco fled L.A. forever and Broccoli was given a director position that he parlayed into a successful career. He became rich producing James Bond movies.
9. Golden, p. 101.
10. *Los Angeles Times*, February 1, 1931.
11. Tornabene, Lyn, *Long Live the King*, p. 142.
12. *Chicago Daily Tribune*, July 12, 1931.
13. Phillips was murdered in 1911, just be-

fore *Susan Lenox* was published, by a crazed reader who believed he had maligned his sister in an earlier book.
14. *Photoplay*, October, 1931.
15. *Hollywood Reporter*, August 11, 1931.
16. American Film Institute, Catalog of Films, no. 1139.
17. Marx, *Mayer and Thalberg*, p. 188.
18. Party notes *Los Angeles Evening Herald Express*, March 6, 1931; "squired about" reference *Chicago Daily Tribune*, March 22, 1931; "Ernest Torgler" reference Stenn, *Bombshell*, p. 64.
19. *Los Angeles Times*, April 4, 1931.
20. *San Francisco Chronicle*, September 7, 1932.
21. *Hollywood Daily Citizen*, "Society in Filmland," April 7, 1931. Also attending: Lloyd Wright, Arthur Hornblow, Laura Hope Crews, Elsie Janis, and Walter Huston. It was the same 933 Rexford Drive mansion that Benjamin "Bugsy" Siegel commandeered in a scene recreated in the 1991 film *Bugsy*.
22. *Ibid.*, April 8, 1931. Also attending: Sol Wurtzel, B.P. Schulberg, Laura Hope Crews, Mary Duncan, Ina Claire, Aileen Pringle, Winfield Sheehan, and Herman Mankiewicz.
23. Thalberg party notes from *Evening Herald Express*, April 20, 1931. Ocean House details from Wallace, David, *Lost Hollywood*, p. 86–91.
24. *Shanghai Gesture* notes from *Hollywood Daily Citizen*, "Society in Filmland," April 22, 1931. Blum and Myers party notes from *Hollywood Daily Citizen*, April 29, 1931.
25. Contract Memorandum, Fox Film Corporation Studio and The Caddo Co., Inc., April 6, 1931.
26. *Chicago Daily Tribune*, May 3, 1931.
27. Oriental Theater notes from *Chicago Daily Tribune*, May 17, 1931. Bello a "zero" from Stenn, *Bombshell*, p. 60.
28. Federal Bureau of Investigation, Abner Zwillman files, File no. 62-36085, Sec. 1, Serial 44, memo: June 7, 1950.
29. Parsons, Harriett, "Keyhole Portraits," *Los Angeles Times*, June 25, 1932.
30. Higham, *Howard Hughes*, p. 58–59. In Marx and Vanderveen, p. 121, Marx notes that Zwillman gave friends lockets with Jean's pubic hair. It was also said that he wore one himself but it's difficult to imagine the mobster wearing a locket.
31. Paul's letter ran in every L.A. newspaper and many out-of-town; this from *Los Angeles Record*, June 9, 1931.
32. Donations from *Los Angeles Times*, July 5, 1931. Results from *Los Angeles Times*, July 24, 1931.

33. *Los Angeles Evening Express*, June 12, 1931. Also in the Gaynor-Peck group were John Monk Saunders and Fay Wray, Monte Blue, and William Howard.

34. *Los Angeles Times*, June 21, 1931. Richard Schayer wrote almost 125 scenarios from 1916 into the 1950s including *Flame of the Desert* (1919), *Tell It to the Marines* (1926), *The Cameraman* (1928), *Dance, Fools, Dance* (1931), *Trader Horn* (1931), and *The Mummy* (1932). He died in Hollywood in 1956.

35. *The Man in Possession* story from *Los Angeles Evening Express*, June 19, 1931. Jackson party from *Los Angeles Times*, June 21, 1931.

36. Don Gallery, correspondence with EJF, August-November, 2007. Imported to the island for early movies, buffalo, deer, and elk thrived and survive to this day.

37. Lambert, p. 146, and Flamini, p. 149.

38. Fountain, p. 219.

39. American Film Institute, Catalog of Films, no. 5879.

40. *Variety*, November 21, 1931.

41. *Los Angeles Record*, November 23, 1931.

42. Fountain, p. 219.

43. Marx and Vanderveen, p. 189.

44. Fire Department notes from *Los Angeles Evening Herald*, July 25, 1931. Vacation plans from *Los Angeles Evening Herald*, July 16, 1931. The trip would be shortened to one month because of production responsibilities.

45. *Los Angeles Times*, July 10, 1931.

46. *Photoplay*, February, 1936, p. 15.

47. Guest list from *Los Angeles Times*, August 9, 1931. Dempsey story from *Los Angeles Times*, August 4, 1931. When the divorce was finally settled in July 1933, the astute Taylor left with $40,000 (perhaps $1,500,000 today) in cash, three cars and their $150,000 estate at 5254 Los Feliz Boulevard. When a fan asked for an autograph on paper which had Dempsey's name on top she wrote, "This is the last time that son-of-a-bitch will be on top of me."

48. *Los Angeles Evening Express*, August 5, 1931.

49. *Los Angeles Evening Herald Express*, August 6, 1931.

50. Luncheon story from *Los Angeles Times*, August 5, 1931. Claire party story from *Los Angeles Times*, July 26, 1931.

51. *Los Angeles Evening Herald Express*, September 24, 1931.

52. Capra, Frank, *The Name Above the Title*, p. 134.

53. Stenn, *Bombshell*, p. 65.

54. *Chicago Daily Tribune*, June 11, 1937.

55. Lincoln Quarberg Papers, Folder 82, Box 3, Jean Harlow clippings, AMPAS.

56. Film reviews from *The New York Times*, October 31, 1931, and *The Hartford*

Courant, November 6, 1931. Robert Williams death notes from *Los Angeles Times*, November 4, 1931.

57. *Chicago Daily Tribune*, August 13, 1931.

58. *The New York Times*, September 27, 1931.

59. Paul tried to cast John Gilbert from *Los Angeles Evening Herald Express*, July 7, 1931. The other films shared by the Barrymores were *Grand Hotel* (1932), *Dinner at Eight* and *Rasputin and the Empress* (both 1933).

60. American Film Institute, Catalog of Films, no. 7717.

61. *Los Angeles Times*, March 6, 1932.

62. Casting notes from *Chicago Daily Tribune*, November 15, 1931. "Freelancers" note from *Chicago Daily Tribune*, February 7, 1932.

63. *Los Angeles Times*, September 19, 1931.

64. *Ibid.*, August 31, 1931.

65. *San Francisco Chronicle*, October 12, 1931.

66. *Hollywood Citizen News*, November 10, 1931.

67. *Los Angeles Evening Herald*, November 13, 1931 and November 16, 1931, *The New York Times*, November 19, 1931.

68. *Los Angeles Times*, November 20, 1931.

69. "[P]lay up the search" from Loos, p. 39; "outlived more bad roles" from *The Hartford Courant*, May 14, 1932.

70. Parsons, Louella O., *Los Angeles Times*, January 1, 1932.

71. *Hollywood Citizen News*, September 10, 1932.

72. Lambert, p. 151.

73. Flamini, p. 139.

74. Browning's film appalled viewers and it wasn't shown for over 40 years, but in the 1980s, interest in his groundbreaking horror films led to a resurgence. *Freaks* is known as one of the most interesting horror films ever made.

75. Wedding details from *Los Angeles Times*, November 28, 1931. "Enthusiastic bachelors" story from *Los Angeles Times*, December 6, 1931.

76. *Hollywood Daily Citizen*, December 7, 1931.

77. *Los Angeles Times*, December 27, 1931.

78. Granlund, Nils Thor, with Sid Feder and Ralph Hancock, *Blondes, Brunettes and Bullets*, letter from Granlund to Sam Bischoff, May 15, 1954, quoted from Stenn, *Bombshell*, p. 67.

79. *Screen Play Magazine*, March, 1932, p. 17 & 65.

80. Higham, *Merchant of Dreams*, p. 174.

81. *Hollywood Citizen News*, December 30, 1931.

82. Marx and Vanderveen, p. 196.

83. *Los Angeles Times*, December 27, 1931.

84. Higham cites "confidential sources" for

the Morris-Harlow anecdote, which may or may not have been accurate.

85. Schatz, p. 120.

86. When Crawford approached Thalberg and requested the role and he told her there was only one woman at MGM to play it, a disgusted Crawford told him, "Let me guess. Marie Dressler?" and stomped out of his office. Paul's American Academy classmate Mary Alden also appeared in *Strange Interlude.*

87. *Hollywood Citizen News*, August 5, 1932.

88. *Los Angeles Times*, December 27, 1931.

89. Hall, Gladys, THE LITTLE FATHER CONFESSOR OF HOLLYWOOD, July 13, 1932, Gladys Hall Papers, Box 2, Folder 55, Bern, Paul—article manuscript, AMPAS.

90. Parsons, Louella, *Jean Harlow's Life Story by Louella Parsons*, p. 18.

91. *Hollywood Citizen News*, January 20, 1932.

92. Paris, p. 271.

93. Schatz, Thomas, *The Genius of the System*, p. 119.

94. *Los Angeles Times*, February 29, 1932.

95. Carey, p. 153. Caddo Company, Assignment of Contract to Metro-Goldwyn-Mayer, March 19, 1932.

96. *Modern Romance*, "Our Life Story by Jean Harlow's Mother," November 20, 1937.

97. *Screenland Magazine*, July, 1932.

98. Marx and Vanderveen, p. 160.

99. Selznick, p. 178.

100. Thomas, Bob, *Thalberg: Life and Legend*, quoted from Stenn, *Bombshell*, p. 76.

101. Flamini, p. 144, and *The Hartford Courant*, May 7, 1932.

102. "[S]exquisite" reference from Jane Ardmore Papers, Box 13, file 13, AMPAS; "alabaster outlaw" from *Screenplay*, October, 1932.

103. *Screen Book Magazine*, October, 1932, p. 19.

104. *True Story*, March, 1935, p. 89.

105. *Ibid.*, p. 85.

106. *Modern Screen Magazine*, from Lincoln Quarberg Papers, Folder 62, Box 3, Caddo Company biographies, AMPAS.

107. Chester Morris from *Kansas City Journal-Post*, September 29, 1932. "If men were stupid" from Loos, p. 41.

108. Lincoln Quarberg Papers, Folder 62, Box 2, Caddo Company biographies-publicity, The Inside Story of Jean Harlow, AMPAS.

109. Lincoln Quarberg Papers, Folder 62, Box 2, Caddo Company biographies-publicity, "The Inside Story of Jean Harlow," AMPAS.

110. Gebhart, Myrtle, "The Most Beautiful Women in the World," *Los Angeles Times*, December 6, 1931.

111. *Chicago Daily Tribune*, May 10, 1931.

112. Stenn, *Bombshell*, p. 81.

113. Loos, p. 42.

114. "Random Notes from Jean Harlow's Mother," Vertical File Collection, Box 3, Folder 35, I. Shulman notes regarding Jean Harlow, AMPAS.

115. Parsons, Harriett, "Keyhole Portraits," *Los Angeles Times*, June 25, 1932.

116. Hall, Gladys, unpublished manuscript, "Never Goodbye," Gladys Hall Papers, Box 6, Folder 230, article manuscripts, AMPAS.

117. *Screen Play Magazine*, September, 1931, p. 22.

118. Arthur Landau to Irving Shulman, July 13, 1962, I. Shulman correspondence files, AMPAS.

119. Golden, p. 248.

120. Hall, Gladys, unpublished manuscript, "Never Goodbye," Gladys Hall Papers, Box 6, Folder 230, article manuscripts, AMPAS.

121. Jane Ardmore Papers, Box 13, file 13, AMPAS.

122. *New Movie Magazine*, December, 1933, quoted from Stenn.

Chapter 9

1. Correspondence, Irene Harrison to Dorothy Millette, May 13, 1932.

2. *Real-life Crimes and How They Were Solved*, Vol. 5, Part 70, p. 1530.

3. *Los Angeles Times*, September 10, 1932.

4. Correspondence, Paul Bern to Dorothy Millette, March 29, 1932.

5. *Picture Play*, April, 1932, p. 49.

6. Flamini, p. 141.

7. *Grand Hotel* was the most profitable movie of MGM's most profitable year. When most studios lost money in 1932, MGM earned over $8,000,000 (almost $200,000,000 today).

8. Not long after, Irving Thalberg ended Fitzgerald's Hollywood experiment by firing the writer. Thalberg was angry that Fitzgerald got drunk at one of the Thalbergs' Sunday afternoon gatherings at the beach. Fitzgerald wrote his story "Crazy Sunday" describing the ill-fated party.

9. Carey, p. 154.

10. *Hollywood Reporter*, June 18, 1932.

11. Flamini, p. 145, and Loos, p. 43.

12. *New York American*, September 9, 1932.

13. *The New York Times*, September 10, 1932, and *San Francisco Chronicle*, September 10, 1932.

14. *Startling Detective Adventures*, "Jean Harlow's Fatal Love and the Secret of Paul Bern," December, 1932, p. 35.

15. *Hollywood Citizen News*, May 11, 1932.
16. Itinerary from *Hollywood Citizen News*, May 16, 1932. Parsons column, *Los Angeles Times*, May 16, 1932. Starr column, *Los Angeles Evening Herald Express*, June 16, 1932.
17. *Los Angeles Times*, "Speaking of Myself," by Jean Harlow, November 28, 1934.
18. *Ibid.*, June 26, 1932.
19. *Ibid.*, June 25, 1932.
20. *Hollywood Reporter*, June 18, 1932.
21. *The Hartford Courant*, July 9, 1932.
22. *Moving Picture World*, July, 1932.
23. "[S]it at his feet" from Mary and Vanderveen, p. 172; "loneliest girl in Hollywood" from Lincoln Quarberg Papers, Folder 82, Box 3, Jean Harlow clippings, AMPAS; "bombshell and egghead" from Golden, p. 89; "little gentleman of MGM" from Jane Ardmore Papers, Box 13, file 13, AMPAS; "he doesn't talk" from Stenn, *Bombshell*, p. 86.
24. *Screen Play Magazine*, September, 1931, p. 22.
25. Selznick, p. 178.
26. *Movies*, November, 1932, p. 12.
27. Shulman, *Harlow*, p. 12.
28. Mama Jean quote from *Modern Romance*, "Our Life Story by Jean Harlow's Mother," November 20, 1937. Marcella Rabwin story from Stenn, *Bombshell*, p. 86.
29. Vertical Files, Box 3, Folder 34, Irving Shulman correspondence regarding Jean Harlow, Arthur Landau to Irving Shulman, undated, AMPAS.
30. *Los Angeles Record*, June 6, 1932.
31. *Hollywood Citizen News*, June 21, 1932.
32. "[O]ther night" from *Screen Book Magazine*, "Jean Harlow's Whirlwind Romance," October, 1932, p. 63; "second attempt" from *Modern Screen*, September, 1932, p. 87.
33. *Hollywood Citizen News*, June 21, 1932.
34. Gladys Hall notes here from Hall, Gladys, THE LITTLE FATHER CONFESSOR OF HOLLYWOOD, July 13, 1932, from Gladys Hall Collection, Folder 55, Paul Bern, AMPAS.
35. Fairbanks, Douglas, Jr., *Salad Days*, quoted from Stenn, *Bombshell*, p. 84.
36. Lincoln Quarberg Papers, Folder 62, Box 2, Caddo Company biographies-publicity, The Inside Story of Jean Harlow, AMPAS.
37. Marx, *Mayer and Thalberg*, p. 186.
38. Jane Ardmore Papers, Box 13, file 13, AMPAS.
39. *True Story*, March, 1933, p. 90.
40. *Screen Weekly*, July 16, 1932.
41. *True Story*, March, 1933, p. 90.
42. *Screen Book Magazine*, "The Inside Story of Jean Harlow's Whirlwind Romance," October, 1932, p. 19 and 63.

43. *Hollywood Citizen News*, June 25, 1932.
44. Paul comments from *True Story*, March, 1933, p. 90; "plans are in her hands" from *Screen Weekly*, July 16, 1932, p. 21; bridesmaid story from Shulman, *Harlow*, p. 17.
45. *True Story*, March, 1933, p. 90.
46. *Los Angeles Times*, June 26, 1932.
47. Gladys Hall notes here from Hall, Gladys, THE LITTLE FATHER CONFESSOR OF HOLLYWOOD, July 13, 1932, from Gladys Hall Collection, Folder 55, Paul Bern, AMPAS.
48. Several magazine sources, and Hall, Gladys, THE LITTLE FATHER CONFESSOR OF HOLLYWOOD, July 13, 1932, from Gladys Hall Collection, Folder 55, Paul Bern, AMPAS.
49. *Hollywood Citizen News*, June 24, 1932.
50. Jetta Belle Chadsey was actually Mama Jean's aunt, but was probably Jean's closest relative. Jean confided in Jetta about everything, and adored her favorite "Aunt Jetty."
51. *Los Angeles Times*, July 10, 1932.
52. The name is often spelled "Ingatieff"; "Alexander Ignatieff, painter, 932 N Ardmore" appears in the 1936 L.A. City Directory and "Alexander D Ignatieff, painter, 1065 N Kingsley Dr" in the 1939 Directory. But the correct spelling appears to be "Ignatiev" and "Alexander Ingatiev, artist, 1123? N Ardmore" is the mural's creator. He had a 50-year career as a painter and animator working for Walt Disney on films like *Snow White & the Seven Dwarfs* (1937) and later for cartoon creators Chuck Jones and Hanna-Barbera before dying in Laguna Beach, California, in 1995. The Easton mural was done with a paint-mixing method that was lost at the turn of the century; when the mural resurfaced 65 years later, it retained the same vivid colors as the day it was hung above Paul's living room.
53. According to Harold Grieve's Creditor's Claim against Paul's estate, work had begun (and Paul had been making partial payments on his account) as far back as April, 1932. From Creditor's Claim, H.H. Grieve, November 29, 1932, Estate of Paul Bern Probate record no. 130814.
54. Details of Grieve's work from Creditor's Claim, H.H. Grieve, November 29, 1932, Estate of Paul Bern Probate record no. 130814.
55. Ron Hale to EJF, June, 2007.
56. *Motion Picture*, December, 1932, p. 36.
57. *Los Angeles Times*, September 6, 1932.
58. *Tacoma Daily Ledger*, September 7, 1932.
59. *Los Angeles Times*, June 22, 1932, *Hollywood Citizen News*, June 23, 1932, from Lincoln Quarberg Papers, Folder 82, Box 3, Jean Harlow clippings, AMPAS.
60. *Los Angles Times*, July 3, 1932.

61. *Hollywood Citizen News*, June 27, 1932.

62. The magnificent Tudor mansion and estate still stands; from 2003 to 2005, Jennifer Aniston and Brad Pitt owned the home before putting it on the market for almost $40,000,000.

63. Selznick, p. 179.

64. *Screen Book Magazine*, "Jean Harlow's Whirlwind Romance," October, 1932, p. 20, and *Photoplay*, September, 1932, p. 36.

65. Note-card description from *Selznick*, p. 179, Landau letter from Box 1, File 7, Shulman–Jean Harlow (correspondence), Arthur Landau Correspondence Files, AMPAS.

66. Gift records from *Los Angeles Record*, Morin, Relman, "The Life Story of Jean Harlow," July 4, 1932. "Paul's parents" from Betsy Bern, interview with EJF, December, 2007.

67. Other people reported to have attended were Louis B. Mayer and his wife, Mayer's secretary Ida Koverman, Howard Hughes, Barbara Brown's parents, and Howard Strickling. None were included in fairly detailed press accounts of the weekend nor were they in any of the dozens of photos taken the day of the wedding.

68. Wedding stories from various sources, including *Los Angeles Record*, July 4, 1932, *Los Angeles Times*, July 4, 1932, *Hollywood Citizen News*, July 3, 1932.

69. Shulman. *Harlow*, p. 25.

70. Invitation from the collection of Darrell Rooney.

71. *Los Angeles Times*, July 5, 1932.

72. *Los Angeles Evening Herald Express*, July 6, 1932.

73. Marx and Vanderveen, p. 172.

74. Shulman, *Harlow*, p. 124.

75. "[M]y daughter's career" from Marx, *Mayer and Thalberg*, p. 189; "guests came and went" from Vertical Files, Box 3, Folder 34, Irving Shulman correspondence regarding Jean Harlow, Arthur Landau to Irving Shulman, April 11, 1962, AMPAS; "champagne and caviar" from Shulman, *Harlow*, p. 126.

76. *Photoplay*, September, 1932, p. 88.

77. *Los Angeles Times*, July 6, 1932.

78. *Photoplay*, September, 1932, p. 36.

79. *Screen Play Magazine*, September, 1932.

80. Golden, p. 62.

81. *Los Angeles Times*, August 13, 1932.

82. *Hollywood Citizen News*, July 30, 1932.

83. Schatz, p. 120.

84. *Hollywood Citizen News*, "Society in Filmland," July 27, 1932.

85. Creditor's Claim, The May Department Store Company, October 7, 1932, Estate of Paul Bern, Probate record no. 130814.

86. Vertical File Collection, Box 3, Folder 35, I. Shulman notes regarding Jean Harlow, AMPAS. Amadeo Peter Giannini founded Citizens Trust in L.A. and later merged with Bank of America of California. He was the president of the new Bank of America.

87. *New York American*, September 7, 1932.

88. *Hollywood Citizen News*, August 1, 1932.

89. *Selznick*, p. 175.

90. Creditor's Claim, May Department Store Company, October 7, 1933, Estate of Paul Bern, Probate record no. 130814.

91. Creditor's Claim, Cherry Ticket Agency, January 224, 1933, Estate of Paul Bern, Probate record no. 130814.

92. *Los Angeles Times*, May 6, 1932.

93. *Ibid.*, August 13, 1932.

94. *Ibid.*, July 28, 1932. Lily Damita was married to director Michael Curtiz from 1925–1926 and Errol Flynn from 1935–1942.

95. Stenn, *Bombshell*, p. 96.

96. Golden, p. 102.

97. *Los Angeles Times*, September 7, 1932.

98. Rin Tin Tin background retrieved August 1, 2007, from http://www.rintintin.com/story.htm.

99. *Los Angeles Times*, August 11, 1932.

100. *Los Angeles Record*, August 13, 1932.

101. Schatz, p. 103. As early as February, 1930, *Photoplay* asked "Is John Gilbert Through?" By late 1932 he was. After finally leaving MGM in 1933, Gilbert made one low-budget feature for Columbia and retired in a liquor-fueled haze to his Tower Road mansion, where he finally succumbed to the effects of alcoholism on January 9, 1936. He was 38 years old.

102. Production notes, *Red Dust*, and Paris, p. 205.

103. *Los Angeles Evening Herald Express*, July 16, 1932.

104. Marx and Vanderveen, p. 223.

105. Vertical Files, Box 3, Folder 34, Irving Shulman correspondence regarding Jean Harlow, Arthur Landau to Irving Shulman, December 18, 1962, AMPAS.

106. Creditor's Claim, Metro-Goldwyn-Mayer, March 24, 1933, Estate of Paul Bern, Probate record no. 130814, telephone calls from MGM to Mark Hopkins Hotel.

107. Vertical Files, Box 3, Folder 34, Irving Shulman correspondence regarding Jean Harlow, Arthur Landau to Irving Shulman, April 11, 1962, AMPAS.

108. On August 15, the *Los Angeles Record* mentioned that the script was "not yet ready."

109. *Los Angeles Record*, August 14, 1932.

110. Creditor's Claim, Metro-Goldwyn-Mayer, March 24, 1933, Estate of Paul Bern,

Probate record no. 130814, charge: limousine to pick Paul up in Glendale.

111. Creditor's Claim, Sada's Flowers, November 22, 1932, Estate of Paul Bern, Probate record no. 130814.

112. Moffitt, J.C., "The Tragedy of Paul Bern: A Man Always in Love," *Los Angeles Examiner*, September 19, 1932. In 1928, March printed 750 copies of his poem-story, which was promptly banned in Boston. It was re-discovered in the 1960s and adapted for Broadway in 2000.

113. Stenn, *Bombshell*, p. 98.

114. August purchase history from Creditor's Claims, Estate of Paul Bern, Probate record no. 130814.

115. Marx and Vanderveen, p. 8.

116. *The New York Times*, September 11, 1932.

117. *The Baltimore News*, September 6, 1932.

Chapter 10

1. Fredric March phone call from Creditor's Claim, Metro-Goldwyn-Mayer, March 24, 1933, Estate of Paul Bern, Probate record no. 130814, telephone call from MGM to March, Beverly Hills, Sept. 2. Notes re: *China Seas* script revision from Schatz, p. 121.

2. Marx and Vanderveen, p. 238.

3. Creditor's Claim, Ambassador Hotel, November 15, 1932, Estate of Paul Bern, Probate record no. 130814.

4. Moffitt, J.C., "The Tragedy of Paul Bern: A Man Always in Love," *Los Angeles Examiner*, September 19, 1932.

5. *Los Angeles Times*, September 7, 1932.

6. Testimony of Clifton Earl Davis and John Herman Carmichael, September 8, 1932.

7. Marx and Vanderveen, p. 216.

8. *Los Angeles Record*, September 6, 1932.

9. Carmichael testimony, September 8, 1932.

10. Davis would later embellish his story, claiming to have discovered a bloody, broken glass he carried into the house to try and fix, finding Paul's body. But he failed to mention John Carmichael also on the floor, and the broken glass was still at the pool later in the day.

11. Marx and Vanderveen, p. 3.

12. Selznick, p. 179.

13. Stenn, *Bombshell*, p. 107.

14. Marx and Vanderveen, p. 4.

15. Vorkapich and his wife gave a detailed description of the limousine's flight to a *Los Angeles Herald* reporter; the story ran Tuesday, September 6, 1932.

16. *Los Angeles Record*, September 6, 1932.

17. Marx and Vanderveen, p. 256.

18. *Los Angeles Herald*, September 6, 1932, and Marx and Vanderveen, p. 257.

19. Higham, *Merchant of Dreams*, 184.

20. Body position from Higham, *Merchant of Dreams*, p. 183. Moving the guestbook from Marx, *Mayer and Thalberg*, p. 191.

21. Marx, *Mayer and Thalberg*, p. 152.

22. Lambert, p. 179.

23. "[Q]uietly as possible" from Irving Thalberg testimony, September 8, 1932. Details of first police contact and response from Coroner's Register, no. 12573, Name of Deceased: Paul Bern. Early reports also listed Detective Lt. Frank Condaffer among the officers responding. Sketchley was chief of detectives. "Extra editions" from Stenn, *Bombshell*, p. 108.

24. *Los Angeles Record*, September 6, 1932.

25. Harlow biographer David Stenn was told that Bello and Gable were deep-sea fishing that day, but it would seem difficult for Strickling to get Gable off of a fishing boat and through a marina. That Monday, every marina was filled with thousands of Labor Day boaters. Nowhere was it reported that Gable was seen that day. Sam Marx's account of a bird-hunting trip to the desert makes more sense, but either could be true.

26. Jones telegram from Higham, *Merchant of Dreams*, p. 186, *Los Angeles Herald Examiner*, September 8, 1932, and *Los Angeles Record*, September 8, 1932; "lack of marital relations" from *Los Angeles Examiner*, September 8, 1932.

27. *Hollywood Citizen News*, September 7, 1932.

28. *The New York Times*, September 7, 1932.

29. Crawford role note from Eve Golden, interview with Lisa Burks, retrieved from www.lisaburks.com. Also *Hollywood Citizen News*, September 6, 1932.

30. "ROCKED HOLLYWOOD" from *Los Angeles Record*, September 6, 1932. Photo with "X" from *Los Angeles Times*, September 7, 1932.

31. "[S]trikes deep into the heart" from *Los Angeles Times*, September 6, 1932; "student of suicide" from *The Baltimore Sun*, September 6, 1932; "sixth member" from *San Francisco Examiner*, September 6, 1932; "unhappy viewpoint" from *Los Angeles Examiner*, September 6, 1932.

32. *Los Angeles Examiner*, September 7, 1932.

33. "SUICIDAL MANIA" from *San Francisco Chronicle*, September 7, 1932; "suicides at all in Paul's family" from *Hollywood Citizen News*, September 7, 1932.

34. *Los Angeles Record*, September 6, 1932.

35. *New York American*, September 7, 1932.

36. Los Angeles County Department of Public Health, Standard Certificate of Death, no. 10179, Paul Bern.

37. "[P]revent a happy marriage" from *Los Angeles Record*, September 8, 1932; "physical stripling" from *Los Angeles Record*, September 9, 1932.

38. *Los Angeles Record*, September 6, 1932.

39. Silberberg and Blum were MGM lawyers but were presented to the press as representing Jean (Silberberg) and Henry Bern (Blum). Paul's 1932 lawyer was Oscar Cummins.

40. John Carmichael quotes this section from *Los Angeles Record*, September 6, 1932.

41. *Los Angeles Times*, September 7, 1932.

42. Marx and Vanderveen, p. 212.

43. Vorkapich interview from *Los Angeles Record*, September 6, 1932. "ADDS TO MYSTERY" from The Baltimore News, September 6, 1932.

44. Dorothy shopping from Marx and Vanderveen, p. 221. Dorothy drops off luggage from *The New York Times*, September 10, 1932.

45. *San Francisco Chronicle*, September 10, 1932.

46. Retrieved November 1, 2007 from http://www.deltaking.com.

47. *Startling Detective Adventures*, "Jean Harlow's Fatal Love and the Secret of Paul Bern," December, 1932, p. 35.

48. *Kansas City Journal-Post*, September 7, 1932.

49. "I don't know" from *Montana Standard*, September 8, 1932. "I have no idea" from *Los Angeles Examiner*, September 8, 1932.

50. *Sheboygan Press*, September 8, 1932, *The New York Times*, September 7, 1932, summarized in *Mayer and Thalberg*, p. 192.

51. *Los Angeles Times*, September 6, 1932.

52. Henry Bern's comments in Kansas City were quoted in dozens of papers on September 8 and 9, 1932, including *The New York Times*, *The Los Angeles Examiner*, *The Los Angeles Times*, and *The Kansas City Star*.

53. *Los Angeles Times*, September 10, 1932.

54. *Ibid.*, September 10, 1932, and *The Atlanta Constitution*, September 10, 1932.

55. *Nevada State Journal*, September 15, 1932.

56. *San Francisco Chronicle*, September 10, 1932.

57. Atthog was also referred to as "Atthome" in some accounts.

58. "[R]ecluse…" from *Hollywood Citizen News*, September 7, 1932; "due to overwork" from *Montana Standard*, September 8, 1932; "physiological characteristics" and "threatened his bride" from *Los Angeles Times*, September 9, 1932; "would you shoot yourself" from *Tacoma Daily Ledger*, September 8, 1932.

59. Higham, *Merchant of Dreams*, p. 187.

60. *Los Angeles Examiner*, September 8, 1932.

61. "[S]niff out the candle" from *Los Angeles Examiner*, September 7, 1932; "student of suicide" from *The New York Times*, September 7, 1932; "outlived his usefulness" from Flamini, p. 161; Mendes quote from *The New York Times*, September 7, 1932.

62. Marx and Vanderveen, p. 93.

63. *The New York Times*, September 8, 1932.

64. "[D]on't quote me" from *Los Angeles Record*, September 8, 1932.

65. St. Johns, p. 150.

66. "WILL TRAGEDY" from *Los Angeles Record*, September 6, 1932, "JEAN HARLOW FILM CAREER" from *The New York Times*, September 8, 1932 and *The Los Angeles Times*, September 8, 1932, "SUICIDE OF HUSBAND" from *Reno Evening Sun*, September 8, 1932. "Where does Jean go" from *Hollywood Citizen News*, September 8, 1932.

67. "PROBE FILM TRAGEDY FLAWS" from *Tacoma Daily Ledger*, September 7, 1932; "POLICE HUNT SECOND NOTE" from *Washington Post*, September 7, 1932.

68. "[K]new who was" from *Hollywood Citizen News*, September 7, 1932; "2? hours later" from *Los Angeles Evening Herald Express*, September 7, 1932; "when Bern was shot" from *The Los Angeles Times*, September 7, 1932.

69. *Los Angeles Times*, September 8, 1932.

70. *Ibid.*, September 8, 1932.

71. *Tacoma Daily Ledger*, September 7, 1932.

72. Uttal notes from *The New York Times*, September 8, 1932, and *Los Angeles Record*, September 8, 1932.

73. *The New York Times*, September 9, 1932, and September 11, 1932.

74. Coincidentally, where Howard Hughes flew out of and built his record-breaking racing aircraft.

75. *Los Angeles Times*, September 8, 1932.

76. *Ibid.*, September 9, 1932.

77. *Los Angeles Examiner*, September 10, 1932.

78. *The Daily Independent* (Monhassen, Pennsylvania), September 9, 1932.

79. *New York American*, September 8, 1932.

80. *Wisconsin Rapids Daily Tribune*, September 8, 1932.

81. "FIRST WIFE NAMED" from *The New York Times*, September 9, 1932; "BERN ROMANCE WITH MYSTERY" from *Los Angeles Examiner*, September 8, 1932; "BERN MARRIED" from *New York American*, September 8, 1932; "gorgeous red-headed creature"

from *Los Angeles Examiner*, September 8, 1932; "morally her husband" from *The Los Angeles Examiner*, September 8, 1932; "other woman" from *The Sheboygan Press*, September 8, 1932.

82. "[U]nhappy man of 41" from *Rochester Times-Union*, September 8, 1932; "Violence" note from *San Francisco Chronicle*, September 8, 1932, and *New York American*, September 8, 1932.

83. *New York Times*, September 8, 1932.

84. *Rochester Times Union*, September 8, 1932.

85. Notes this section from Coroner's Register, Los Angeles County, p. 285, File No. 42753.

86. *Los Angeles Times*, September 10, 1932.

87. Testimony of Bello, Carmichael, Thalberg, Greenwood, and Garrison from In the Matter of the Inquisition Upon the Body of Paul Bern-Deceased, September 8, 1932.

88. Coroner's Register, no. 42573.

89. *Los Angeles Record*, September 8, 1932, *San Francisco Chronicle*, September 8, 1932.

90. *New York American*, September 9, 1932.

91. Among dozens of others, the fight story appeared in *Los Angeles Examiner*, September 9, 1932, *New York American*, September 9, 1932, and the *Rochester Times-Union*, September 9, 1932.

92. "Other Women's" from *The New York Times*, September 9, 1932; "PHANTOM BEAUTY" from *Los Angeles Record*, September 9, 1932; "MORE THAN ONE WIFE" from *Statesville Daily Record*, September 9, 1932.

93. *Los Angeles Examiner*, September 10, 1932.

94. Funeral notes from *Los Angeles Times*, September 10, 1932. Other accounts numbered those outside at 300, 500, 1,500, and (in *Time* magazine) 2,000.

95. Stenn, *Bombshell*, p. 120.

96. Lambert, p. 181.

97. *Los Angeles Times*, September 10, 1932.

98. *The New York Times*, September 10, 1932.

99. Wayne, Jane Ellen, p. 91, and Flamini, p. 163.

100. Stenn, *Bombshell*, p. 121.

101. Marx and Vanderveen, p. 112.

102. *The New York Times*, September 10, 1932.

103. *Los Angeles Times*, September 10, 1932.

104. "SEARCH FOR BODY" from *Los Angeles Examiner*, *Stevens Point Daily Journal*, and *San Francisco Chronicle*, all September 10, 1932. "BERN FOUGHT" from *Rochester Times-Union*, September 10, 1932. "JEAN HARLOW FLED" from *Rocky Mountain News*, September 10, 1932.

105. *Rocky Mountain News*, September 10, 1932.

106. "Miss Millette had nothing to do with it" from *Rocky Mountain News*, September 10, 1932; "many affairs" from *The Atlanta Constitution*, September 10, 1932.

107. Marx and Vanderveen, p. 223. The "JUSTIFICATION" letter was also reported by police and in newspapers, including the *Los Angeles Examiner*, on September 12, 1932. Several sources indicated the word "justification" was written at the bottom of a letter, but a more likely scenario is the use of a blotter.

108. *Nevada State Journal*, September 11, 1932.

109. Paul's sister Friederike was interred with Paul after her death, and Sig Marcus is interred in a wall vault below. Sanctuary of Faith, Section F-96, Niche D.

110. *Los Angeles Evening Herald Express*, September 12, 1932.

111. *Los Angeles Times*, September 12, 1932, and Stenn, *Bombshell*, p. 122.

112. Golden, p. 110.

113. Lincoln Quarberg Papers, Folder 82, Box 3, Jean Harlow clippings, AMPAS.

114. *Los Angeles Examiner*, September 12, 1932.

115. Department of Public Health, Sacramento County, Death Certificate, Dorothy Millette, no. 32-049225, September 17, 1932.

116. *The Atlanta Constitution*, September 10, 1932.

117. Coroner's Register, no. 42573.

118. *Ironwood Daily Globe*, September 17, 1932, and Marx and Vanderveen, p. 246.

119. *Los Angeles Evening Herald Express*, September 15, 1932.

120. *Nevada State Journal*, September 18, 1932.

121. County of Sacramento, In the Matter of the Inquisition Upon the Remains of Dorothy Millette-Deceased, September 21, 1932.

122. Vertical Files, Box 3, Folder 34, Irving Shulman correspondence regarding Jean Harlow, Arthur Landau to Irving Shulman, April 11, 1962, AMPAS.

123. Richard Lewis, interview with EJF, July, 2007. According to the artist's widow and daughter, Ignateiv was extremely proud of his creation and had planned to remove the piece for Harlow, but before he could do so was wounded in a shooting. When he recovered, the mural was gone.

124. "[F]illed to capacity" from *Los Angeles Evening Herald Express*, October 19, 1932.

Final discharge note from Estate of Paul Bern, Final Discharge of Executrix, February 20, 1937. Unless otherwise noted, estate notes this section from Estate of Paul Bern, Probate record no. 130814. For comparable valuations, calculating the relative value of $100 in 1925 to today's worth is a relative process, depending on the variable or combination of variables used. For example, using the Consumer Price Index it's worth $1,150 (11 times value, or $1,100), using nominal Gross Domestic Product model (a combination of product costs) the value is $5,627 (56 times value, or $5,600), and using the unskilled wage cost it's worth $3,954.95 (40 times value or $4,000). Although it dilutes the pure scientific validity, for a reasonable average we us 25 times value, or $100 in 1920 is assumed to be worth $2,500 today.

125. *Los Angeles Evening Herald Express*, January 26, 1934.

126. Creditor's Claim, Boulevard Super Service, November 15, 1932, Estate of Paul Bern, Probate record no. 130814.

Chapter 11

1. *Motion Picture*, September, 1932, pgs. 64, 81. *Modern Screen*, September, 1932, p. 36. *Screen Book Magazine*, September, 1932, p. 18. *Time*, September 19, 1932, p. 20.

2. "[B]y his bedside" quote from Shulman, *Harlow*, p. 18; "best liked and respected" quote from *Los Angeles Times*, September 7, 1932.

3. Carmichael's comments were printed in hundreds of newspapers, including *Hollywood Citizen News*, *The New York Times*, *Los Angeles Times*, and *Kansas City Journal-Post*, all September 6, 1932. Bello comment from *Kansas City Journal-Post*, September 6, 1932.

4. Mayer's call to Thalberg was reported in dozens of papers like *Film Daily*, *Los Angeles Examiner*, and *Hollywood Citizen News*, September 6, 1932. Subsequent calls were noted in several books like Stenn's *Bombshell*, Marx and Vanderveen's *Deadly Illusions*, Thomas' *Thalberg*, and Higham's *Merchant of Dreams*. "Mayers awakened" from Higham, *Merchant of Dreams*, p. 183.

5. Marx and Vanderveen, p. 214.

6. Strickling comment from Higham, *Merchant of Dreams*, p. 184. Landau comment from Vertical Files, Box 3, Folder 34, Irving Shulman correspondence regarding Jean Harlow, Arthur Landau to Irving Shulman, undated, AMPAS

7. From Clifton Davis' grand jury testimony, February 28, 1933, quoted from Marx and Vanderveen, p. 214.

8. Maurice Rapf, interview with EJF, August, 2002.

9. *Los Angeles Record,* September 6, 1932.

10. Marx dinner notes from Marx and Vanderveen, p. 8. Physician comments from *The New York Times*, September 11, 1932. Miramar Hotel story from *The Baltimore News*, September 6, 1932. Carey Wilson story from Moffitt, J.C., "The Tragedy of Paul Bern: A Man Always in Love," *Los Angeles Examiner*, September 19, 1932.

11. Jackson drowned off Laguna Beach on May 27, 1932, while swimming with friends Robert Armstrong and writer Arthur Caeser. Jackson swam out past the breakwater at the base of Thalia Avenue in Laguna, tired, and drowned before Armstrong and Caeser could reach him. His wife and a group of friends watched helplessly from the beach, but Paul was on his vacation to Central America and Mexico from May 16 to June 15. Even so, writer Charles Higham wrote that Paul was depressed because he was swimming with Jackson when he died. (He also mistakenly wrote that Jackson drowned in Malibu.)

12. "[A]ny wolf in Hollywood" from Paris, Barry, *Louise Brooks*, p. 363. Sally Rand story from Higham, *Merchant of Dreams*, p. 191.

13. Carey Wilson story from *Los Angeles Times*, September 21, 1932. Family history from Betsy Bern, interview with EJF, December, 2007.

14. From Farber, Stephen, and Marc Green, *Hollywood on the Couch: A Candid Look at the Overheated Love Affair Between Psychiatrists and Movie Makers*, quoted from *The New York Times*, December 26, 1993.

15. Discussed in Higham, *Merchant of Dreams*, p. 191. Book information from Creditor's Claim, Dora Ingram Book Shop, November 22, 1932, Estate of Paul Bern Probate record no. 130814.

16. Unless otherwise noted, quotes and details this section from Shulman, *Harlow*, pgs. 27–42.

17. Vertical Files, Box 3, Folder 34, Irving Shulman correspondence regarding Jean Harlow, Arthur Landau to Irving Shulman, December 18, 1962, AMPAS.

18. Vertical Files, Box 3, Folder 35, Irving Shulman notes regarding Jean Harlow, AMPAS.

19. Vertical Files, Box 3, Folder 34, Irving Shulman correspondence regarding Jean Harlow, Arthur Landau to Irving Shulman, December 18, 1962, AMPAS.

20. *Time*, July 3, 1964.

21. Dale Eunson letter to Hedda Hopper, June 30, 1964, Hedda Hopper Papers, AMPAS.

22. Loos, p. 161.

23. Selznick story from Selznick, p. 77.

Fairbanks claim from Fairbanks, Douglas, *Salad Days*, p. 193.

24. Moore, Colleen, *Silent Star*, p. 60.

25. *Modern Romance,* OUR LIFE STORY by JEAN HARLOW'S MOTHER, November 20, 1937.

26. *Los Angeles Times*, September 7, 1932.

27. Vertical Files, Box 3, Folder 34, Irving Shulman correspondence regarding Jean Harlow, Arthur Landau to Irving Shulman, December 18, 1962, AMPAS.

28. "[O]rdering her back" from Vertical File Collection, Box 3, Folder 35, Irving Shulman notes regarding Jean Harlow, AMPAS; "blackmail Bern" from Vertical Files, Box 3, Folder 34, Irving Shulman correspondence regarding Jean Harlow, Arthur Landau to Irving Shulman, December 18, 1962, AMPAS; "won't allow them to be seen" from Vertical File Collection, Box 3, Folder 35, Irving Shulman notes regarding Jean Harlow, AMPAS; "hurt Harlow" from Vertical Files, Box 3, Folder 34, Irving Shulman correspondence regarding Jean Harlow, Arthur Landau to Irving Shulman, April 11, 1962, AMPAS.

29. Winifred Carmichael comments here from her grand jury testimony, February 28, 1933, quoted from Marx and Vanderveen, p. 216.

30. Marx and Vanderveen, pgs. 243–44.

31. "[H]onorable man" quoted from Henry Bern, from Betsy Bern, interview with EJF, December, 2007.

2. "[S]uicide whitewash" from *The Hartford Courant*, October 29, 1960; "couldn't hold a husband" from *The Hartford Courant*, October 25, 1960.

3. McKesson quote from *The Los Angeles Times*, October 24, 1960; "unconfirmed rumor" from *The Los Angeles Times*, October 28, 1960.

4. *Time*, July 23, 1965.

5. Retrieved August 4, 2008 from http://www.tvguide.com/movies/harlow/review.

6. Sally Forrest, correspondence with EJF.

7. *Los Angeles Times*, September 27, 1935, from Lincoln Quarberg Collections, Folder 82, Jean Harlow clippings, AMPAS.

8. Federal Bureau of Investigation, Abner Zwillman files, File no. 62-36085, Sec. 1, Serial 44, memo: November 9 & 10, 1938.

9. *Los Angeles Times*, September 20, 1932.

10. Flamini, p. 162.

11. *Hollywood Citizen News*, June 8, 1937.

12. Bailey-Goldschmidt, Janice, Mary C. Kalfatovic and Martin R. Kalfatovic, *The Journal of Popular Culture*, "'I Remember It Well': Paul Bern, Jean Harlow, and the Negotiation of Information," p. 225.

13. Steen, *Bombshell*, p. 237.

14. Mannix quote from Shulman, *Harlow*, p. 392. Mama Jean rejects Christian Science from Kay Mulvey Williams letter to Hedda Hopper, June 25, 1964, Hedda Hopper Papers, AMPAS.

Epilogue

1. Weinstock, Matt, "Hecht Revives Harlow Story," *Los Angeles Times*, October 27, 1960.

Bibliography

Newspaper Archives

Adams County News, Gettysburg, Pennsylvania

Appleton Post Crescent, Appleton, Wisconsin

Atlanta Constitution, Atlanta, Georgia

Baltimore Herald, Baltimore, Maryland

Baltimore News, Baltimore, Maryland

Bedford Gazette, Bedford, Pennsylvania

Bee, Danville, Virginia

Bismarck Daily Tribune, Bismarck, North Dakota

Boston Herald, Boston, Massachusetts

Boston Post, Boston, Massachusetts

Bridgeport Telegram, Bridgeport, Connecticut

California Eagle, Los Angeles, California

Charleroi Mail, Charleroi, Pennsylvania

Chicago American, Chicago, Illinois

Chicago Daily Tribune, Chicago, Illinois

Chicago Sunday Tribune, Chicago, Illinois

Chicago Tribune, Chicago, Illinois

Chillicothe Constitution Tribune, Chillicothe, Missouri

Chronicle Telegram, Elyria, Ohio

Circleville Herald, Circleville, Ohio

Clearfield Daily Progress, Clearfield, Pennsylvania

Cleveland Herald, Cleveland, Ohio

Colorado Springs Gazette, Colorado Springs, Colorado

Columbus Citizen, Columbus, Ohio

Coshocton Tribune, Coshocton, Ohio

Daily Kennebec Journal, Kennebec, Maine

Daily Nevada State Journal, Reno, Nevada

Daily News, Los Angeles, California

Davenport Democrat and Leader, Davenport, Iowa

Decatur Daily Dispatch, Decatur, Illinois

Decatur Herald, Decatur, Illinois

Denton Journal, Denton, Maryland

Des Moines News, Des Moines, Iowa

Dothan Eagle, Dothan, Alabama

Edwardsville Intelligencer, Edwardsville, Illinois

Fort Wayne Journal Gazette, Fort Wayne, Indiana

Freeborn County Standard, Albert Lea, Minnesota

Gazette Bulletin, Williamsport, Pennsylvania

Gettysburg Times, Gettysburg, Pennsylvania

Halifax Sunday Daily News, Halifax, Nova Scotia, Canada

Havre Daily News Promoter, Havre, Montana

Helena Independent, Helena, Montana

Herald, Arlington Heights, Illinois

Hollywood Citizen News, Hollywood, California

Hollywood Daily Citizen, Hollywood, California

Hollywood Evening News, Los Angeles, California

Hollywood Reporter, Hollywood, California

Indiana Evening Gazette, Indiana, Pennsylvania

Indianapolis Star, Indianapolis, Indiana

Indianapolis Sunday Star, Indianapolis, Indiana

Iowa City Press Citizen, Iowa City, Iowa

Kansas City Star, Kansas City, Missouri

Lancaster Daily Gazette, Lancaster, Ohio

Lima News, Lima, Ohio

Los Angeles City News, Los Angeles, California

Los Angeles Downtown News, Los Angeles, California
Los Angeles Evening Herald, Los Angeles, California
Los Angeles Evening Herald Express, Los Angeles, California
Los Angeles Examiner, Los Angeles, California
Los Angeles Herald, Los Angeles, California
Los Angeles Herald Examiner, Los Angeles, California
Los Angeles Herald Express, Los Angeles, California
Los Angeles Illustrated Daily News, Los Angeles, California
Los Angeles Mirror, Los Angeles, California
Los Angeles Post-Record, Los Angeles, California
Los Angeles Record, Los Angeles, California
Los Angeles Sentinel, Los Angeles, California
Los Angeles Times, Los Angeles, California
Los Angeles Tribune, Los Angeles, California
Los Angeles Weekly, Los Angeles, California
Manitoba Free Press, Winnipeg, Manitoba, Canada
Mansfield News, Mansfield, Ohio
Marion Star, Marion, Ohio
Middlesboro Daily News, Middlesboro, Kentucky
Minneapolis Journal, Minneapolis, Minnesota
Modesto Evening News, Modesto, California
Nashua Telegraph, Nashua, New Hampshire
Naugatuck Daily News, Naugatuck, Connecticut
Nevada State Journal, Reno, Nevada
Los Angeles Herald, Los Angeles, California
New York Herald Tribune, New York, New York
New York Times, New York, New York
Newark Daily Advocate, Newark, Ohio
The News, Frederick, Maryland
Port Arthur News, Port Arthur, Texas
Port Washington Standard, Port Washington, Wisconsin
Redlands Daily Review, Redlands, California
Reno Evening Gazette, Reno, Nevada
Reno Gazette, Reno, Nevada
Reno Weekly Gazette, Reno, Nevada
Rochester Times Union, Rochester, New York
Rocky Mountain News, The Denver, Colorado
San Francisco Chronicle, San Francisco, California

Sheboygan Press, Sheboygan, Wisconsin
Statesville Daily Record, Statesville, North Carolina
Statesville Landmark, Statesville, North Carolina
Stevens Point Daily Journal, Stevens Point, Wisconsin
Topeka Journal, Topeka, Kansas
Toronto World, Toronto, Ontario, Canada
Trenton Evening Times, Trenton New Jersey
Van Nuys News, Van Nuys, California
Washington Herald, Washington, D.C.
Washington Post, Washington, D.C.
Washington Times-Herald, Washington, D.C.
Waukesha Freeman, Waukesha, Wisconsin
Weekly Evening Gazette, Reno, Nevada
Weekly Gazette Stockman, Reno, Nevada
Wichita Beacon, Wichita, Kansas
Wichita Daily Times, Wichita, Texas
Wisconsin Rapids Daily Tribune, Wisconsin Rapids, Wisconsin
Witchita Daily Times, Witchita Falls, Texas
Wyoming State Tribune, Cheyenne, Wyoming

Books and Articles

Abel, Richard. *The Red Rooster Scare: Making American Cinema, 1900–1910*. Berkeley: University of California, 1999.
Acker, Ally. *Reel Women: Pioneers of the Cinema, 1896 to the Present*. New York: Continuum, 1991.
Alleman, Richard. *The Movie Lover's Guide to Hollywood*. New York: Harper Colophon Books, 1985.
Alpert, Hollis. *The Barrymores*. New York: Dial Press, 1964.
Altman, Diana. *Hollywood East: Louis B. Mayer and the Origins of the Studio System*. New York: Birch Lane Press, Carol Publishing Group, 1992.
Anger, Kenneth. *Hollywood Babylon*. New York: Dell, 1981.
_____. *Hollywood Babylon II*. New York: Dutton, 1984.
Astor, Mary. *A Life on Film*. New York: Delacourte, 1967.
Auburn, Mark S. "The Pleasures of Sheridan's *The Rivals*: A Critical Study in the Light of Stage History." *Modern Philology*, Vol. 72, No. 3 (Feb., 1975), pp. 256–71.

Austin, John. *Hollywood's Unsolved Mysteries.* New York: Shapolsky Publishers, 1990.

Backhouse, Charles. *Canadian Government Motion Picture Bureau, 1917–1941.* Ottawa: Canadian Film Institute, 1974.

Bacon, James. *Hollywood is a Four-Letter Word.* New York: Avon Books, 1977.

_____. *Made in Hollywood.* Chicago: Contemporary Books, 1977.

Bailey-Goldschmidt, Janice, Mary C. Kalfatovic, and Martin R. Kalfatovic. "'I Remember It Well': Paul Bern, Jean Harlow, and the Negotiation of Information." In *The Journal of Popular Culture.* Vol. 30, Issue 3, "I Remember It Well': Paul Bern, Jean Harlow, and the Negotiation of Information." Winter, 1996.

Baxter, John. *Hollywood in the 30s.* New York: A.S. Barnes, 1968.

Beattie, Eleanor. *The Handbook of Canadian Film.* 2nd ed. Toronto: Peter Martin Associates, 1977.

Beauchamp, Cari. *Without Lying Down: Frances Marion and the Powerful Women of Early Hollywood.* New York: Scribner, 1997.

Beaver, Frank. *One Hundred Years of American Film.* New York: Macmillan Library Reference USA, 2000.

Behlmer, Rudy. *Inside Warner Bros. (1935–1951).* New York: Viking Penguin, 1985.

Berg, A. Scott. *Goldwyn: A Biography.* New York: Knopf, 1989.

Berton, Pierre. *Hollywood's Canada: The Americanization of Our National Image.* Toronto: Pierre Berton Enterprises, 1975.

Blum, Daniel, and enlarged by John Willis. *A Pictorial History of the American Theatre, 1860–1985.* New York: Crown Publishers, 1986.

Brooks, Louise. *Lulu in Hollywood.* New York: Alfred A. Knopf, 1982.

Brown, T. Allston. *History of the American Stage: Containing Biographical Sketches of Nearly Every Member of the Profession That Has Appeared on the American Stage, From 1733 to 1870.* New York: Dick and Fitzgerald, 1870.

Brownlow, Kevin. *Behind the Mask of Innocence: Sex, Violence, Prejudice, Crime: Films of Social Conscience in the Silent Era.* Berkeley: University of California Press, 1990.

_____. *Hollywood: The Pioneers.* New York: Knopf, 1980.

_____. *The Parade's Gone By.* New York: Knopf, 1968.

Bryan, George. compiler, *Stage Lives: A Bibliography and Index to Theatrical Biographies in English.* Westport, CT: Greenwood Press, 1985.

Burroughs, Marie. *Art Portfolio of Stage Celebrities.* Chicago: Marquis, 1894.

Butler, Ivan. *Silent Magic: Rediscovering the Silent Film Era.* New York: Ungar, 1988.

Cahn, William. *The Laugh Makers: A Pictorial History of American Comedians.* New York: Bramhall House, 1957.

Carey, Gary. *All the Stars in Heaven.* New York: E.P. Dutton, 1981.

_____. *Anita Loos: A Biography.* New York: Alfred A. Knopf, 1988.

Chapin, Robert Colt. *The Standard of Living Among Workingmen's Families in New York City.* Beloit College, 1909.

Cini, Zelda, and Bob Crane, with Peter H. Brown. *Hollywood: Land and Legend.* Westport, CT: Arlington House, 1980.

Cooper, Miriam, and Bonnie Herndon. *Dark Lady of the Silents: My Life in Early Hollywood.* New York: Bobbs-Merrill, 1973.

Covello, Leonard, and Guido D'Agostino. *The Heart Is the Teacher.* New York: McGraw-Hill, 1958.

Crivello, Kirk. *Fallen Angels: The Lives and Untimely Deaths of 14 Hollywood Beauties.* Secaucus: Citadel Press, 1988.

Crowther, Bosley. *Hollywood Rajah: The Life and Times of Louis B. Mayer.* New York: Henry Holt, 1960.

_____. *The Lion's Share: The Story of an Entertainment Empire.* New York: Dutton, 1957.

Davis, Dentner. *Jean Harlow, Hollywood Comet.* London: Contable House, 1975.

Day, Beth. *This Was Hollywood.* New York: Doubleday, 1960.

DeMille, Cecil B. *The Autobiography of Cecil B. DeMille.* Englewood Cliffs, New Jersey: Prentice-Hall, 1959.

Dressler, Marie. *My Own Story.* Boston: Little, Brown, 1934.

Eames, John Douglas. *The MGM Story.* New York: Crown, 1971.

Edmonds, Andy. *Frame-Up!: The Untold Story of Roscoe "Fatty" Arbuckle.* New York: William Morrow, 1991.

Edwards, Anne. *The DeMilles: An American Family.* New York: Harry N. Abrams, 1988.

Eells, George. *Hedda and Louella*. New York: G.P. Putnam, 1972.

Everson, William K. *American Silent Film*. New York: Da Capo Press, 1998.

_____. *The Films of Hal Roach*. New York: Museum of Modern Art, 1971.

_____. *The Films of Laurel and Hardy*. New York: Museum of Modern Art, 1967.

Eyman, Scott. *Ernst Lubitsch: Laughter in Paradise*. New York: Simon and Schuster, 1993.

_____. *Mary Pickford: America's Sweetheart*. New York. Donald I. Fine, 1990.

Fairbanks, Douglas, Jr. *The Salad Days*. New York: Doubleday, 1988.

Fairbanks, Letita and Ralph Hancock. *Douglas Fairbanks: The Fourth Musketeer*. New York: Henry Holt, 1953.

Farber, Stephen and Marc Green. *Hollywood Dynasties*. New York: Delilah Communications, 1984.

Finler, Joel W. *The Hollywood Story*. New York: Crown, 1988.

Flamini, Roland. *Thalberg: The Last Tycoon and the World of MGM*. New York: Crown, 1994.

Forkner, John L. *History of Madison County, Indiana, Vol. I & Vol. II*. Chicago: Lewis Publishing, 1914.

Foster, Charles. *Stardust and Shadows*. Toronto: Dundurn, 2000.

Fountain, Leatrice Joy Gilbert. *Dark Star: The Untold Story of the Meteoric Rise and Fall of the Legendary John Gilbert*. New York: St. Martin's Press, 1985.

Fowler, Gene. *Father Goose: The Biography of Mack Sennett*. New York: Crown, 1934.

_____. *Good Night Sweet Prince: The Life and Times of John Barrymore*. New York: Buccaneer Books, 1943.

Freedland, Michael. *The Warner Brothers*. New York: St. Martin's Press, 1983.

Gabler, Neal. *An Empire of Their Own: How the Jews Invented Hollywood*. New York: Crown, 1988.

Gardiner, Gerald. *The Censorship Papers: Movie Censorship Letters From the Hays Office: 1934–1968*. New York: Dodd, 1987.

Gilbert, John. "*Jack Gilbert Writes His Own Story.*" *Photoplay*, June–September, 1928.

Golden, Eve. *Platinum Girl—The Life and Legend of Jean Harlow*. New York: Abbeville Press, 1991.

Gould, Leo. *The Fatty Arbuckle Case*. New York: Patrick Library, 1962.

Griffith, Richard, and Arthur Mayer. *Movies: The Sixty-Year History of the World of Hollywood*. New York: Bonanza Books, 1957.

Gutteridge, Robert W. *Magic Moments: First 20 Years of Moving Pictures in Toronto (1894–1914)*. Gutteridge-Pratley Publications, 2000.

Hamburg-Amerika Linie. Liste der Reisenden, October 7, 1909.

Harney, Robert F. *Chiaroscuro: Italians in Toronto, 1815–1915. Polypony*, Vol, 6, 1984, Multicultural History Society of Ontario.

Helm, T.B. (editor), *History of Madison County, Indiana*, Chicago: Kingman Brothers, 1880.

Henderson, Robert M. *D.W. Griffith: His Life and Work*. New York: Ferrar, Straus & Giroux, 1972.

Herzog, Peter, and Roman Tozzi. *Living Life and Not Fearing Death: The Life of Lya de Putti*. New York: Corvin, 1993.

Hiebert, Daniel. *Jewish Immigrants and the Garment Industry of Toronto, 1901–1931: A Study of Ethnic and Class Relations, Annals of the Association of American Geographers*. Vol. 83, No. 2 (June, 1993).

Higham, Charles. *Cecil B. DeMille*. New York: Scribner's, 1973.

_____. *Hollywood at Sunset*. New York: Saturday Review Press, 1972.

_____. *Howard Hughes: The Secret Life*. New York: G.P. Putnam's Sons, 1993.

_____. *Merchant of Dreams: Louis B. Mayer and the Secret Hollywood*. New York: Donald I. Fine, 1993.

_____. *Warner's Brothers*. New York: Scribner's, 1975.

Hutton, Laurence. *Curiosities of the American Stage*. New York, 1891.

Kanin, Garson. *Hollywood*. New York: Viking Press, 1967.

Katz, Ephraim. *The Film Encyclopedia*. New York: Thomas Y. Crowell, 1979.

Keylin, Arlene, and Suri Fleischer (editors). *Hollywood Album: Lives and Deaths of Hollywood Stars from the Pages of* The New York Times. New York: Arno Press, 1979.

_____, (editors). *Hollywood Album 2: Lives and Deaths of Hollywood Stars from the Pages of* The New York Times. New York: Arno Press, 1979.

Kobler, John. *Damned in Paradise: The Life of John Barrymore*. New York: Atheneum, 1977.

Kotsilibas-Davis, James and Myrna Loy. *Being and Becoming.* New York: Alfred A. Knopf, 1987.

Kovan, Florice Whyte. *Rediscovering Ben Hecht: Selling the Celluloid Serpent.* Washington, D.C., Snickersnee Press, 1999.

Lambert, Gavin. *Nazimova.* New York: Knopf, 1997.

_____. *Norma Shearer.* New York: Knopf, 1990.

Lamparski, Richard. *Lamparski's Hidden Hollywood: Where the Stars Lived, Loved and Died.* New York: Fireside Books, 1981.

_____. *Whatever Happened to...*, various volumes. New York: Crown Publishers, various publication dates.

Langman, Larry. *American Film Cycles: The Silent Era.* Westport, CT: Greenwood Press, 1998.

Lasky, Jesse L. *I Blow My Own Horn.* Garden City, NJ: Doubleday, 1957.

_____. *Whatever Happened to Hollywood?* New York: Funk & Wagnall, 1975.

Leeds, Mark. *Encyclopedia of New York City.* New York: Passport Books, 1999.

Leider, Emily W. *Dark Lover: The Life and Death of Rudolph Valentino.* New York: Faber and Faber, 2003.

Lewtin, Lucy. *Nazimova: My Aunt.* Ventura: Minuteman Press, 1978.

Lockwood, Charles. *Dream Palaces: Hollywood at Home.* New York: Viking Press, 1981.

_____. *The Guide to Hollywood and Beverly Hills: The Best.* New York: Crown, 1984.

Loney, Glenn. *Twentieth-Century Theatre.* 2 vols. New York: Facts on File, 1983.

Loos, Anita. *Cast of Thousands.* New York: Viking, 1977.

_____. *A Girl Like I.* New York: Viking, 1966.

_____. *Kiss Hollywood Good-bye.* New York: Grosset and Dunlap, 1975.

_____. *The Talmadge Girls.* New York: Viking, 1978.

Madsen, Alex. *The Sewing Circle: Female Stars Who Loved Other Women.* New York: Birch Lane Press/Carol Publishing Group, 1995.

Mander, Raymond, and Joe Mitchenson. *Hamlet Through the Ages.* London: Rockliff, 1952.

Mann, William J. *Wisecracker: The Life and Times of William Haines, Hollywood's First Openly Gay Star.* New York: Viking, 1998.

Marx, Samuel. *Mayer and Thalberg: The Make-Believe Saints.* New York: Random House, 1975.

_____, and Joyce Venderveen. *Deadly Illusions: Jean Harlow and the Murder of Paul Bern.* New York: Random House, 1990.

McClellan, Diana. *Cut to the Chase: A Biography of Buster Keaton.* New York: Harper-Collins, 1995.

_____. *The Girls: Sappho Goes to Hollywood.* New York: St. Martin's Griffin, 2000.

McLean, Adrienne L., and David A. Cook (editors). *Headline Hollywood: A Century of Film Scandal.* Rutgers University Press, 2000.

Moore, Colleen. *Silent Star.* New York: Doubleday, 1968.

Mordden, Ethan. *Movie Star: A Look at the Women Who Made Hollywood.* New York: St. Martin's Press, 1983.

Morris, Michael. *Madam Valentino: The Many Lives of Natacha Rambova.* New York: Abbeville Press, 1991.

Morris, Peter. *Embattled Shadows: A History of Canadian Cinema.* Montreal: McGill-Queen's University Press, 1978.

Odell, George Clinton Densmore. *Annals of the New York Stage, 15 Vols.* New York: Columbia University Press, 1927–1949.

Paris, Barry. *Garbo.* New York: Alfred A. Knopf, 1995.

_____. *Louise Brooks.* New York: Alfred A. Knopf, 1989.

Parish, James Robert, with Ronald L. Bowers. *The MGM Stock Company: The Golden Era.* New Rochelle, NY: Arlington House, 1973.

Parsons, Louella. *The Gay Illiterate.* New York: Doubleday, 1944.

_____. *Jean Harlow's Life Story by Louella Parsons.* Dunellen, NJ: Dell Publishing, 1937.

_____. *Tell It to Louella.* New York: Putnam, 1961.

Pascal, John. *The Jean Harlow Story.* New York: Popular Library, 1965.

Quirk, Lawrence J. *Norma: The Story of Norma Shearer.* New York: St. Martin's Press, 1988.

Ramsaye, Terry, editor. *A Million and One Nights: A History of the Motion Picture.* New York: Simon and Schuster, 1926.

_____. *1936–37 International Motion Picture Almanac.* New York: Quigley, 1936.

Rigdon, Walter. *Biographical Encyclopedia and Who's Who of the American Theatre.* New York: Heinemann, 1966

Roberts, Edward. *The Sins of Hollywood: An Expose of Movie Vice: A Group of Stories of Actual Happenings Reported and Written by a Hollywood Newspaper Man.* Los Angeles: Hollywood Publishing, 1922.

Robinson, David. *From Peep Show to Palace: The Birth of American Film.* New York: Columbia, 1996.

_____. *Hollywood in the Twenties.* London– New York: Zwemmer/Barnes, 1968.

Rosenzweig, Roy, and Elizabeth Blackmar. *The Park and the People: A History of Central Park.* New York: Cornell University Press, 1998.

St. Johns, Adela Rogers. *The Honeycomb.* Garden City, New York: Doubleday, 1969.

_____. *Love, Laughter and Tears: My Hollywood Story.* New York: Doubleday, 1978.

Sarniske, Dennis. *Crossroad of the Stars.* Victoria, British Columbia, Canada: Trafford Publishing, 2005.

Schickel, Richard. *D.W. Griffith: An American Life.* New York: Simon and Schuster, 1984.

Schulberg, Budd. *Moving Pictures: Memoirs of a Hollywood Prince.* Briarcliff Manor, New York: Stein & Day, 1981.

Schultz, J.H. *Salmonsens Konversationsleksikon,* 2nd ed., vol. XXIV, entry: "Wandsbeck," 1928.

Screen Stars' Love Life Album. New York: Dell Publishing, 1932.

Seiler, Robert M., and Nathanson, Zukor. *Famous Players: Movie Exhibition in Canada, 1920–1941. American Review of Canadian Studies.* March 22, 2006.

Sennett, Mack, and Cameron Shipp. *King of Comedy.* Garden City, New York: Doubleday, 1954.

Sennett, Robert S. *Hollywood Hoopla: Creating Stars and Selling Movies in the Golden Age of Hollywood.* New York: Billboard Books, 1988.

Shipman, David. *The Great Movie Stars.* New York: Da Capo Books, 1982.

Shulman, Irving. *Harlow: An Intimate Biography.* New York: Bernard Geis Associates, 1964.

_____. *Valentino.* New York: Trident Press, 1967.

Skal, David J., and Elias Savada. *Dark Car-*
nival: The Secret World of Tod Browning, Hollywood's Master of the Macabre.* New York: Anchor Books, 1995.

Slade, Becka. "Feminism in Hollywood: The Acceptance of the Woman Director." Thesis outline. Western Connecticut State University.

Starr, Kevin. *Material Dreams: Southern California Through the 1920s.* New York: Oxford University Press, 1991.

Steiner, Edward A. *On the Trail of the Immigrant.* 5th ed. New York: Fleming H. Revell, 1906.

Stenn, David. *Bombshell: The Life and Death of Jean Harlow.* New York: Doubleday, 1993.

_____. *Clara Bow: Runnin' Wild.* Doubleday, 1991.

Strang, Lewis C. *Players and Plays of the Last Quarter Century.* Boston: L. C. Page, 1902.

Thomas, Bob. *King Cohn: The Life and Times of Harry Cohn.* New York: G.P. Putnam, 1967.

Timberlake, Craig. *The Bishop of Broadway: The Life and Work of David Belasco.* Library Publishers, 1954.

Tornabene, Lynn. *Long Live the King: A Biography of Clark Gable.* New York: Putnam's, 1976.

Torrence, Bruce T. *Hollywood: The First 100 Years.* New York: Zoetrope, 1982.

Truitt, Evelyn Mack. *Who Was Who on Screen—First Edition.* New York: R.R. Bowker, 1974.

_____. *Who Was Who on Screen—Second Edition.* New York: R.R. Bowker, 1977.

_____. *Who Was Who on Screen—Third Edition.* New York: R.R. Bowker, 1983.

_____. *Who Was Who on Screen.* New York: R.R. Bowker, 1984.

Vidor, King. *A Tree Is a Tree.* New York–Hollywood, Samuel French, 1989.

Vinson, James (editor). *The International Dictionary of Films and Filmmakers—First Edition, Volume 3: Actors and Actresses.* Chicago: St. James Press, 1986.

Vogel, Michelle. *Olive Thomas: The Life and Death of a Silent Film Beauty.* Jefferson, NC: McFarland, 2007.

Wakeman, John (editor). *World Film Directors, Volume One, 1890–1945.* New York: H.W. Wilson, 1987.

Walker, Alexander. *Rudolph Valentino.* New York: Stein & Day, 1970.

_____. *Sex in the Movies.* Middlesex, U.K.: Penguin Books/Harmondsworth, 1968.

_____. *Shattered Silents: How the Talkies Came to Stay.* New York: Morrow, 1979.

Wallace, David. *Lost Hollywood.* New York: LA Weekly, St. Martin's Press, 2001.

Wearing, J.P. *American and British Theatrical Biography: A Directory.* Metuchen, NJ: Scarecrow Press, 1979.

_____. *The London Stage, 1890–1899: A Calendar of Plays and Players.* 2 vols., Metuchen, NJ: Scarecrow Press, 1976.

Webb, Michael, editor. *Hollywood: Legend and Reality.* Boston: Little, Brown, 1986.

Weiss, Ken. *To the Rescue: How Immigrants Saved the American Film Industry, 1896–1912.* San Francisco: Austin & Winfield, 1997.

Who Was Who in the Theatre, 1912–1976: A Biographical Dictionary of Actors, Actresses, Directors, Playwrights, and Producers of the English-Speaking Theatre Compiled From Who's Who in the Theatre, Volumes 1–15 (1912–1972). Detroit: Gale Research, 1978.

Windeler, Robert. *Sweetheart: The Story of Mary Pickford.* New York: Praeger Publishers, 1974.

Zierold, Norman. *The Moguls.* New York: Coward-McCann, 1969.

Zollo, Paul. *Hollywood Remembered: An Oral History of Its Golden Age.* New York: Cooper Square Press, 2002.

Zukor, Adolph. *The Public is Never Wrong.* New York: Putnam's, 1953.

Periodicals

Exhibitor's Herald-World, August 17, 1929

Exhibitor's Trade Review, August 10, 1918, August 17, 1918, October 19, 1918, October 26, 1918, November 2, 1918, November 16, 1918, January 25, 1919, February 15, 1919, March 15, 1919, June 28, 1919, August 23, 1919, October 18, 1919, March 20, 1920, April 3, 1920, October 30, 1920, April 29, 1922, June 17, 1922, December 9, 1922

Film Daily, February 10, 1924, September 21, 1924, October 17, 1926, January 16, 1927, December 7, 1927, January 8, 1928, January 22, 1928, August 8, 1928, January 23, 1929, April 7, 1929, June 9, 1929, August 4, 1929, August 25, 1929, November 17, 1929, February 9, 1930, August 24, 1930,

February 8, 1931, May 3, 1931, June 28, 1931, July 19, 1931, July 25, 1931, September 20, 1931, October 18, 1931, November 18, 1931, January 3, 1932, January 6, 1932, February 28, 1932, April 17, 1932, March 4, 1932, May 12, 1932, May 25, 1932, May 26, 1932, June 5, 1932, July 1, 1932, July 15, 1932, September 6, 1932, November 2, 1932, November 5, 1932, December 3, 1933

Film Weekly, September 16, 1932, September 23, 1932, October 6, 1932, October 27, 1932

Hollywood Film, April 7, 1929, October 11, 1930, November 29, 1930, January 3, 1931, January 31, 1931, February 7, 1931, February 14, 1931, April 4, 1931, May 30, 1931, October 10, 1931, October 11, 1931, October 17, 1931, November 29, 1931, December 5, 1931, December 12, 1931, December 31, 1931, January 21, 1932, January 23, 1932, March 12, 1932, April 30, 1932, May 26, 1932, August 6, 1932, August 27, 1932, January 21, 1933

Hollywood Reporter, August 5, 1931, August 28, 1931, September 24, 1931, November 14, 1931, December 1, 1931, July 1, 1931, July 3, 1931, July 13, 1931, July 19, 1931, July 23, 1931, July 25, 1931, August 11, 1931, August 19, 1931, September 15, 1931, September 24, 1931, October 1, 1931, October 18, 1931, October 19, 1931, November 6, 1931, November 14, 1931, November 27, 1931, December 1, 1931, December 8, 1931, December 10, 1931, January 6, 1932, January 9, 1932, February 6, 1932, February 9, 1932, February 13, 1932, February 20, 1932, March 12, 1932, March 14, 1932, June 8, 1932, June 14, 1932, June 18, 1932, June 24, 1932, July 5, 1932, August 23, 1932, September 6, 1932, September 7, 1932, September 8, 1932, September 10, 1932, September 13, 1932, September 15, 1932, September 18, 1932, September 21, 1932, October 11, 1932

Jack Canuck Magazine, January, 1915

Liberty Magazine, December 23, 1932, December 31, 1932, December 16, 1933

Life, March 25, 1926, September 26, 1929, January 1, 1933

Mon Ciné (France), January 11, 1923, March 13, 1924

Motion Picture Herald, January 17, 1931, March 7, 1931, June 14, 1931, July 18, 1931,

October 24, 1931, October 25, 1931, January 9, 1932, April 16, 1932, April 25, 1931, January 16, 1932, April 16, 1932, May 14, 1932, June 11, 1932, June 25, 1932, October 22, 1932

Motion Picture Magazine, July, 1931, September, 1931, July, 1932, August, 1932, September, 1932, October, 1932, February, 1932

Motion Picture News, October 19, 1918, February 1, 1919, February 15, 1919, March 1, 1919, March 15, 1919, June 28, 1919, August 23, 1919, October 18, 1919, October 25, 1919, December 20, 1919, March 20, 1920, April 3, 1920, May 8, 1920, August 28, 1920, October 9, 1920, October 30, 1920

Motography, July 7, 1917

Movie Classic, September, 1932, October, 1932, December, 1932, February, 1933

Movie Mirror, July, 1931, November, 1931, June, 1932, July, 1932, August, 1932, September, 1932, October, 1932, November, 1932, December, 1932, January, 1933, March, 1933

Moving Picture World, May 29, 1914, November 14, 1914, November 21, 1914, January 2, 1915, January 23, 1915, February 13, 1915, February 20, 1915, February 27, 1915, March 6, 1915, April 10, 1915, April 17, 1915, May 8, 1915, April 14, 1917, May 19, 1917, June 2, 1917, April 13, 1918, November 2, 1918, January 25, 1919, February 1, 1919, February 15, 1919, May 2, 1919, June 28, 1919, August 23, 1919, March 20, 1920, August 21, 1920, January 14, 1922, May 6, 1922, December 9, 1920, February 16, 1924, October 23, 1926, January 15, 1927, April 2, 1927

New York Dramatic Mirror, May 5, 1917, May 26, 1917, June 2, 1917, November 28, 1920,

New Yorker, August 30, 1930

Photoplay, April, 1924, November, 1925, May, 1926, December, 1926, February, 1927, June, 1927, June, 1928, July, 1928, August, 1928, September, 1928, July, 1932, August, 1932, September, 1932, November, 1932, January, 1933, March, 1933

Screen Book, October, 1932, November, 1932, December, 1932, March, 1933

Screenplay Magazine, October, 1932

Time Magazine, September 11, 1933

True Story, March, 1935.

Variety, April 27, 1917, January 31, 1919,
March 7, 1919, June 15, 1919, June 20, 1919, April 3, 1920, June 16, 1922, December 1, 1922, February 7, 1924, September 10, 1924, February 24, 1926, October 13, 1926, January 12, 1927, March 16, 1927, December 7, 1927, January 11, 1928, January 18, 1928, August 12, 1928, January 23, 1929, April 3, 1929, June 5, 1929, July 31, 1929, August 28, 1929, November 20, 1929, March 19, 1930, June 4, 1930, August 27, 1930, February 11, 1931, May 6, 1931, June 30, 1931, September 22, 1931, October 20, 1931, January 5, 1932, March 1, 1932, April 19, 1932, June 7, 1932, July 5, 1932, November 8, 1932

Wid's Film Daily, June 7, 1917, September 15, 1918, January 19, 1919, August 17, 1919, March 14, 1920, March 28, 1920, May 30, 1920, June 4, 1922

Internet

www.afi.com (American Film Institute catalog of films)

www.america-at-war.net (general reference; World War I history)

www.archives.gov (National Archives)

www.arrts-arrchives.com/rock (general reference; rail service from Manhattan to Rockaway Beach in the early 1900s)

www.artsci.washington.edu (general reference; U.S. theaters)

www.assumption.edu/acad/ii/Academic/history (William Desmond Taylor background)

www.beneathlosangeles.com (general reference; Los Angeles death stories)

www.cah.utexas.edu/newspapers/morgues (newspaper morgue research)

www.cecilbdemille.com (Cecil B. DeMille materials)

www.centralparkhistory.com (general reference; Central Park and New York in 1900)

www.century-of-flight.net (Ormer Locklear background)

www.chilit.org (background on the play *The Dream of a Spring Morning*)

www.cinema.ucla.edu (UCLA Film & Television Archive)

www.eh.net (money conversion tables)

www.fathom.com (Fathom Archives; Columbia University; American Film Institute, The First Fifty Years of American Cinema) www.fb10.uni-bremen.de/anglistik (general reference; history of American theater)

www.fhh1.hamburg.de/fhh/internetausstel lungen/emigration/englisch/emigration_ index (general reference; history of emigration from Hamburg, Germany)

www.film.virtual-history.com/page. php?id=553 (general information, film history)

www.genealogienetz.de/reg/HAM/hamburg-e (Hamburg, Germany, genealogical records)

www.gdhamann.blogspot.com (newspaper archive materials)

www.greatwar.nl (general reference; World War I history)

www.history.sandiego.edu/gen/st (general reference; Hollywood and World War I)

www.hffi.org (general reference; history of American theater)

www.hollywood.com (general reference; City of Hollywood background)

www.hollywoodreporter.com (*Hollywood Reporter* history)

www.iath.virginia.edu (Duncan Sisters background)

www.ifa.org (International Film Institute; film history and reference)

www.images.library.uiuc.edu (historic maps)

www.imdb.com (general reference; movie history and biographical info)

www.kino.com (general reference; silent film background)

www.lapl.org (Los Angeles Public Library)

www.lcweb2.loc.gov (Library of Congress, American Memories website)

www.lib.unb.ca (Ben Greet history)

www.liveworkplayoutwest.com/yorkvillehis tory (general reference; Yorkville, New York City, history)

www.ninds.nih.gov/disorders/amyotrophic lateralsclerosis (National Institute of Neurological Diseases and Stroke, background on Amyotrophic Lateral Sclerosis)

www.oscars.org (Academy of Motion Pictures Arts & Sciences research site)

www.pages.prodigy.net/vicdru (Los Angeles cemetery materials)

www.prmuseum.com (Edward L. Bernays biography)

www.reelclassics.com (general reference; film research site)

www.rintintin.com (Rin Tin Tin background)

www.rollins.edu (Annie Russell Old English Comedy Company)

www.sdrc.lib.uiowa.edu (Ben Greet Players background)

www.silent-movies.com/Arbucklemania (miscellaneous silent movie personalities)

www.silentladies.com (general reference; silent film research site)

www.theshipslist.com/pictures/pennsylvania (SS *Pennsylvania* history)

www.theshipslist.com/ships/lines/hamburg (Hamburg-Amerika line history)

www.titansofhollywood.com (Zukor and Loew background)

www.usc.edu/isd/archives/la/scandals/taylor (USC silent movie film site)

www.utdallas.edu/library/collections/speccoll (Ormer Locklear background)

www.vaudeville.org (general reference; vaudeville history)

www.whitleyheights.com (Whitley Heights materials)

www.world-theatres.com (general reference; theater history site)

www.xroads.virginia.edu ("Shots in the Dark: Sex, Drugs, Women and the Murder of William Desmond Taylor")

Index